Feminism & Political Theory

Feminism & Political Theory

E D I T E D   B Y
Cass R. Sunstein

THE UNIVERSITY OF CHICAGO PRESS
Chicago and London

The essays in this volume originally appeared in issues of *Ethics: An International Journal of Social, Political and Legal Philosophy*. Acknowledgment of the original publication date can be found on the first page of each essay.

The University of Chicago Press, Chicago 60637
The University of Chicago Press, Ltd., London
©1982, 1983, 1984, 1986, 1987, 1989 and 1990 by The University of Chicago
All rights reserved. Published 1990
Printed in the United States of America
94 93 92 91 90   5 4 3 2 1

Grateful acknowledgment is made to Harvard University Press for permission to reprint "Sexuality, Pornography, and Method: 'Pleasure under Patriarchy'" from *Toward a Feminist Theory of the State* ©1989 by Catherine A. MacKinnon

Library of Congress Cataloging in Publication Data

Feminism and political theory / edited by Cass R. Sunstein.
    p.   cm.
  ISBN 0-226-78008-2 (alk. paper): $35.00 (est.).—ISBN
0-226-78009-0 (pbk.: alk. paper): $14.95 (est.)
    1. Feminism—Political aspects.   2. Women in politics.
3. Political science.   I. Sunstein, Cass R.
HQ1206.F447   1990
305.42—dc20   90-30656
                                                                   CIP

CONTENTS

ACKNOWLEDGMENTS

This book grows out of and expands on a symposium on the same subject published in the journal *Ethics,* and I am most grateful to the editor of that journal, Russell Hardin, for his constant encouragement and good counsel. Associate editors Richard Arneson and Robert Goodin provided invaluable help with the symposium and with this book. They participated in the lengthy process of inviting submissions and reviewing and selecting manuscripts, and their comments on the papers that appear in this collection were extraordinarily helpful. Steven Hetcher, managing editor of *Ethics,* was a constant source of guidance, and he provided indispensable aid in coordinating the various manuscripts and encouraging the project to completion.

Even more than most, this book is a collective product—above all, of the authors of the essays that follow, but also of the people I have mentioned here. I am extremely grateful for their help.

C.R.S.
December 1989
Chicago, Illinois

Introduction: Notes on Feminist Political Thought*

Cass R. Sunstein

The recent growth of feminist thought has produced a wide range of work in political theory—as it has in most areas of the social sciences and the humanities. A large amount of feminist writing deals with various aspects of the social subordination of women. Much of it also discusses the ways in which that historical fact has affected political theory and political practice; and it explores the possibilities for reformulating both by eliminating gender biases. The purpose of this book is to collect some of the most original and important work at the intersection of feminism and political theory—in an effort to present, for general readers, students, and specialists alike, a representative, wide-ranging, but relatively unified set of readings on feminist political thought.

Although one of the most striking features of feminist political theory is its diversity, the essays in this collection, and most feminist work in political theory, can be organized around a set of common themes. Some of these themes have been developed into large-scale critiques, and in some cases reconstructions, of important strains in modern political thought. The critiques tend to emphasize that important aspects of traditional political thought are based on gendered ideas; the reconstructions attempt to develop alternatives. For example, feminist work challenges traditional views of sex and the family, contending that the emphasis on community and consent have created important errors (see the contributions in this book by Marilyn Friedman, Catharine MacKinnon, Susan Moller Okin, and Laurie Shrage). At the same time, some feminist work challenges certain forms of liberalism and of social contract theory by undermining its individualistic assumptions (see the contributions by Virginia Held, Annette Baier, Okin, and Iris Marion Young). Feminist writings are often unified by attempts to enrich and alter conventional understandings of both community and individual autonomy. Both individualistic and communitarian understandings have come under sharp attack.

For purposes of this introduction, it will be useful to outline some of the themes of feminist political thought and to discuss their relationship to the essays in this book.

* I am grateful to Mary Becker, Stephen Holmes, Martha Minow, and David Strauss for helpful comments.

1

THE QUESTION OF "DIFFERENT VOICE": CARE, JUSTICE, AND RIGHTS

A good deal of feminist work is responsive to Carol Gilligan's influential challenge to Lawrence Kohlberg's theory of moral development.[1] In Gilligan's view, Kohlberg's theory, which purports to generalize across social differences, is in fact based on male norms. Gilligan's study argues that the moral development of young girls is different from that of young boys—that girls are inclined to focus on responsibility, context, and connection, whereas boys tend to favor abstractions, rights, autonomy, and separation.

Gilligan writes: "The moral imperative . . . [for] women is an injunction to care, a responsibility to discern and alleviate the 'real and recognizable trouble' of this world. For men, the moral imperative appears rather as an injunction to respect the rights of others and thus to protect from interference the rights to life and self-fulfillment. . . . The standard of moral judgment that informs [women's] assessment of self is a standard of relationship, an ethic of nurturance, responsibility, and care. . . . Morality is seen by these women as arising from the experience of connection and conceived as a problem of inclusion rather than one of balancing claims."[2]

For political theory, this account is noteworthy above all because Kohlberg's theory of the stages of moral development is closely connected with prominent approaches to questions of social justice. If Kohlberg's theory of development is based on male norms, and ignores an important alternative, the same may be true of (to take a not entirely random example) contractarian theories of politics. Thus Gilligan's "ethic of care" is opposed, in much feminist work, to the "ethic of justice" associated with social contract theory, most notably that of John Rawls. Views in this general category—many of them diverging from Gilligan—have led to feminist challenges to approaches that purport, for normative or explanatory purposes, to treat people as self-interested maximizers of private or existing desires. Such approaches, it is contended, are false to the experiences and understandings of many women; and those experiences and understandings should not be devalued.

It is important to emphasize that there is no necessary connection between Gilligan's discussion of moral development and any particular approach to politics. A rights-based system of politics might provide the necessary conditions for community; it might protect against the abuse of public and private power; it might be defensible on any number of

---

1. C. Gilligan, *In a Different Voice* (Cambridge, Mass.: Harvard University Press, 1982). L. Kohlberg, "The Development of Children's Orientation toward a Moral Order. 1: Sequence in the Development of Moral Thought," *Vita Humana*, vol. 6 (1963), "Stage and Sequence: The Cognitive Developmental Approach to Socialization," in *Handbook of Socialization and Research*, ed. D. A. Goslin (Chicago: Rand McNally, 1969).

2. Gilligan, pp. 100, 159–60.

other grounds. But the divergent moral development of men and women—if it can be established—seems especially interesting if there is a relationship between conventional approaches to politics and distinctly male ethical norms.

In "Justice, Care, and Gender," Owen Flanagan and Kathryn Jackson undertake to review recent work by Kohlberg, Gilligan, and others on the question of different voice. Pointing to what they consider to be serious ambiguities and implausibilities in Kohlberg's responses to Gilligan, they argue that there is no unitary kind of moral personality. In their view, moral psychology is "tiered," in the sense that it contains a range of virtuous and nonvirtuous dispositions; there are more than two general orientations to morality and ethics. Flanagan and Jackson also explore the question whether the two dispositions might be logically compatible, or might both be brought on any particular problem.

John Hardwig's "Should Women Believe in Rights?" argues that in close personal relationships, as distinct from cases involving strangers, it is not appropriate to think in terms of rights. In his view, the use of rights-based principles in personal relationships is unhealthy and potentially oppressive. Hardwig does not argue that current relationships between men and women reflect equality, mutuality, or freedom. But he does claim that the response to the domination that can be found in some such relationships is to eliminate the domination, not to apply "rights."

Susan Moller Okin's contribution, "Reason and Feeling in Thinking about Justice," is a response to the numerous feminist critiques of social contract theory in general and of Rawls in particular. Such critiques typically challenge the abstraction of the original position, its foundations in rational choice theory, and its asserted inattentiveness to differences between individuals and groups on the one hand and to concrete social contexts on the other.[3] Okin's response takes the form of an interpretation of social contract theory, and of Rawls's effort more specifically, so as to accommodate some of the concerns of the feminist attack on (liberal?) conceptions of justice.

The apparent foundations of Rawls's theory in rational choice theory have led to a variety of challenges. One response, often coming from rational choice theorists themselves, is that Rawls's principles—most importantly the difference principle—would not emerge from the original position as he defines it. By contrast, feminists (among others) have argued that Rawls's approach is tied to an egoistic conception of human nature and that it is excessively rationalistic and acontextual. On the other hand, the abstraction of Rawls's approach might be counted a virtue. In some circumstances, the fact that political actors must be blind to individual characteristics—of race, gender, religion, and political belief—is surely a significant advantage.

3. See, e.g., S. Benhabib, "The Generalized and the Concrete Other," in *Feminism as Critique: On the Politics of Gender*, ed. S. Benhabib and D. Cornell (Minneapolis: University of Minnesota Press, 1987).

In Okin's view, the original position need not and should not be understood either abstractly or in terms of rational choice. On the contrary, she argues that Rawls's approach can be recast in terms that immunize it from the feminist critique. Above all, Okin contends that the original position forces political actors to be empathetic. In the original position, those who are supposed to choose principles of justice are deprived of knowledge of their place in society. As a result, the original position forces the choosers to take the standpoint of (among others) the disadvantaged. For this reason, Okin argues, the choosers are not required to be or to think as if they were "disembodied nobodies" but are instead required to "think from the position of *everybody*, in the sense of *each in turn*." On this view, the original position is not at all abstraction from difference and contingency but is instead rooted in "an appreciation and concern for social and other human *differences*."

This understanding of the original position serves largely to collapse the distinction between an ethic of care and an ethic of justice and to recast in a new light the goals, central to contractarian and liberal thought, of impartiality and universalizability. Okin emphasizes as well that Rawls's theory ignores problems of gender structure and above all the question of justice within the family, which, she claims, leads to tension for his theory. In her view, the logic of the original position draws the traditional family and gender structure into severe question.

If Okin's general argument is correct, it is possible to bridge the division between the feminist critique of social contract theory and at least some forms of contractarianism: the dichotomy between an ethic of care and an ethic of justice seems to dissolve. But other pieces in this collection—notably Iris Marion Young's essay, discussed below—attempt to provide reasons for skeptisicm about this strategy.

Some feminist work attempts to analyze the consequences of practices distinctive to women—most notably, the experiences associated with reproduction—for political and social theory. For example, it is sometimes said that women's reproductive functions, and male responses to those functions, have played a large role in the creation of a split between the public and private spheres; in the devaluation of domestic roles; in certain conceptions of the distinction between reason and passion (often described along gender lines [see Okin's contribution to this collection]); and in the emphasis, most prominent in republican thought, on the creation of public spheres for the expression of male solidarity and sometimes for the achievement of a kind of immortality.

Virginia Held's contribution to this collection, "Birth and Death," belongs in this category. Held argues that the act of giving birth—unlike the act of dying—has often been described as an essentially natural process not involving elements of human choice. In her view, the decision to give birth is a self-conscious one over which women have frequently exercised control. In Held's view, the alternative devaluing and disregarding of the reproductive act and of reproductive choice has both reflected the social subordination of women and distorted political thought.

In "A Marxist Approach to Women's Nature," Nancy Holmstrom argues against biological explanations of sex role differences, contending that social factors, and especially women's labor, are of central importance to the creation of these differences. In her view, women's responsibility for child care and everyday housework are crucial determinants of "women's nature." Holmstrom supports this view by examining cross-cultural differences between the sexes. At the same time, Holmstrom argues that the cognitive and affective differences between men and women are largely a product of social and historical circumstances. She concludes by contrasting her approach with the Marxist theory of human nature, suggesting that current women's nature reflects a distinctive absence of freedom and that any sex-differentiated society would lack this freedom.

EQUALITY AND INEQUALITY IN POLITICS AND ELSEWHERE

In arguments made in the 1970s for the Equal Rights Amendment, the principal norm underlying much feminist work was one of formal equality. In this view, distinctions between men and women should (almost always) be abolished. More recently, norms of formal equality have been thrown into sharp question—and the resulting debate has produced an outpouring of work on the appropriate meaning of equality in this and other contexts. The major problems here are twofold.

First, formal equality—defined as a refusal to permit women to be treated differently from men—will sometimes undermine rather than promote the cause of equality (understood in more substantive terms) as between men and women. Consider, for example, the fact that the achievement of formal equality with respect to alimony, child custody, and divorce has in many settings aggravated the real world inequality of women. Second, some aspects of the social inequality of women are entirely unaddressed by formal equality as it is usually understood. The principal problem has to do with the application of norms of formal equality to settings of "real differences" between men and women. How, for example, ought one to think of equality and discrimination in the settings of reproductive rights, family and social welfare policy, sex-related violence, and the continuing differences in the domestic and economic responsibilities and welfare of mothers and fathers? Formal equality often considers these issues to raise no problem of inequality at all; but if that view is accepted, many arenas of sex discrimination will be unaddressed.

One consequence of questions of this sort is to draw into doubt the idea (or at least usual applications of the idea) that the function of an equality norm is to require that those similarly situated be treated similarly.[4] (Of course this idea—like the norm of formal equality itself—is highly ambiguous, and it might well be possible to reconceive both in ways responsive to the feminist critique.) Another consequence is to

---

4. See C. MacKinnon, *Sexual Harassment of Working Women: A Case of Sex Discrimination* (New Haven, Conn.: Yale University Press, 1979).

suggest that the question of equality is not whether there are "differences" between the two groups subject to comparison but is instead what sort of political and social difference the actual difference makes. In this view, the ultimate goal should be to develop an understanding of inequality as the systemic subordination of certain social groups.

Such an understanding would call for a novel conception of the nature of inequality and discrimination; and it remains for this understanding to be worked out in detail. But the contributions to this collection by Catharine MacKinnon and Iris Marion Young, both outlined in more detail below, are centrally concerned with the problem. MacKinnon examines the relationship between sexuality and inequality; Young explores the relationship of reproductive capacities to that problem.

Sometimes feminist work on equality turns into a critique of universality. This critique often takes the form of an emphasis on the importance of differences among social groups for political deliberation and political interaction. This critique is represented by Iris Young's contribution here, "Polity and Group Difference: A Critique of the Ideal of Universal Citizenship." Sometimes the critique of universality is relatively specialized, emphasizing that social and legal practices are based on partial norms that they deem universal. Here some of the challenges to formal equality, noted above, become relevant. Consider, for example, the fact that workplaces, insurance policies, and educational systems tend to be tailored to male career patterns and that changes in those systems are often considered to provide "special benefits" or "affirmative action" for women. Young argues that rights sometimes thought to be "special" from one point of view might well be necessary in order to ensure equal citizenship. In this sense, and perhaps in others, the distinction between affirmative action and nondiscrimination tends to dissolve.

In other forms, the critique of universality amounts to a challenge to contractarian approaches insofar as they suggest that unanimity or consensus might be reached by political deliberators. Sometimes the critique is an attack on political conceptions—associated with some forms of liberal, republican, and radical thought—that emphasize the duty of the citizen to the "common good." In the face of sharp differences in social experience, the idea that political actors should look to the interests of the community as a whole seems alternatively mystical, tyrannical, or perverse. For feminists in particular, the problem is that universalist claims have tended to exclude women or to make women's claims appear deviant when measured against established norms.

This attack has some resemblance to challenges to notions of the "public interest" as those challenges appear in the work of Schumpeter and in the writings of many economists and economically oriented political scientists.[5] But the goal of Young's essay is hardly to celebrate approaches

---

5. See J. Schumpeter, *Capitalism, Socialism, and Democracy* (New York: Harper & Row, 1975).

to politics that seek to find an equilibrium among the prepolitical "interests" of private actors. Her purpose is instead to develop approaches to citizenship and to structure political institutions so as to ensure that disadvantaged groups are not erased, or deemed partial and parochial in their emphasis, in politics, or private interests and private injuries. It is in this spirit that Young argues in favor of developing mechanisms to ensure group representation in political life.

A number of questions are of course raised by proposals for group representation, including the risks of political instability, the dangers of marginalizing the disadvantaged, and the potential problem of entrenching current minorities as such. There are further questions about identifying the groups to be represented, the institutionalization of group differences, the nature of political deliberation among those differently situated, and the possibility of reaching closure. On this score, as on others, there is some tension between Young's and Okin's contributions to this book.

Nancy Fraser's contribution to this collection, "Talking about Needs: Interpretive Contests as Political Conflicts in Welfare-State Societies," is a good example. Fraser's goal is to trace the social construction of needs: the ways in which needs come to be recognized as such, and are placed on the political agenda, as a result of the efforts and understandings of different social movements. In Fraser's view, needs cannot be seen as prepolitical or as independent of culture and politics. Fraser offers a number of illustrations, many of them coming from feminist work, of practices currently described as "needs" that have assumed that status only recently and as a result of a particular constellation of social forces.

Fraser's essay raises two further questions, on which she touches briefly. The first has to do with the precise mechanism by which social needs are recognized as such. The second involves the normative problem of how to decide which harms—of the multiple injuries that society does or does not recognize as "needs"—ought to receive a response from the political community. Fraser's ultimate goal is to contribute to a discussion of the processes by which that question might be answered.

In some respects, feminist critiques of contractarian approaches to justice might be thought to overlap with arguments made by modern communitarian critics of liberalism.[6] In both critiques, systems based on rights and autonomy, and seeking to provide well-defined constraints on the private and public spheres, are distinguished from systems that emphasize the possibility of making political choices through a form of political deliberation that includes empathy. But there are significant differences as well.[7] The capacity for connection and care is, in some

---

6. See, e.g., M. Sandel, *Liberalism and the Limits of Justice* (Cambridge: Cambridge University Press, 1982); A. MacIntyre, *After Virtue: A Study in Moral Theory* (Notre Dame, Ind.: University of Notre Dame Press, 1981).

7. See R. West, "Jurisprudence and Gender," *University of Chicago Law Review* 55 (1988): 1–72.

feminist accounts, treated as an ordinary part of women's personality—
at least in this culture, and perhaps partly as a result of the social subordination of women—rather than as the precious outcome of a hard-
won battle to be achieved through struggling against existing premises
and institutions. Moreover, the feminist approach tends to be quite skeptical
about the authority wielded by communities over individuals.

Marilyn Friedman's essay, "Feminism and Modern Friendship: Dis-
locating the Community," is a critical encounter with some of the communitarian critics of liberal thought. Stressing the experiences of women
in private and public collectivities, Friedman argues that there are numerous
problems with the communitarian's affirmative case. This is so particularly
in light of the exercise of oppression by private and public groups—
including religious groups and the family—that are so celebrated by
many communitarians. In these circumstances, the communitarian's enthusiastic approval of the "embedded" self has ironic albeit unintended
dimensions (on which, see also Catharine MacKinnon's contribution to
this book).

Observing that attempts to overcome atomism take the form of
reviving community, Friedman argues that such attempts must incorporate
some of the aspirations of those forms of political liberalism against which
communitarians rebel. Thus she distinguishes sharply between voluntary
and ascriptive communities, emphasizing the importance of "exit" as a
constraint on local tyranny. A norm of individual autonomy, to operate
in both public and private spheres, appears to underlie Friedman's critique
of communitarianism and her endorsement of voluntary association.
Autonomy is understood not in economic terms (as respect for given or
purely private preferences) but, instead, as a belief in individual immunity
from collective control by large and small organizations.

PUBLIC/PRIVATE; COERCION AND CONSENT; SEXUALITY

a) Many feminists have dealt with the allocation of social power in areas
that have been studied relatively infrequently. Relations between men
and women provide the foundation for an inquiry into ways of understanding such notions as coercion, power, and consent. Some of this work
can be connected with various attacks, prominent in the 1970s, on pluralist
conceptions of power.[8] Here the problem is to explore not only how one
group is able to force another to do what it wants but also how certain
issues come to be put on the political agenda and, more generally, how
preferences and beliefs are formed. See Fraser's essay for an example.

b) From a slightly different direction, a large amount of feminist
work has attempted to show the ways in which the private sphere contains
mechanisms of oppression. The family is of course the principal example
here. Frequently treated, in law and theory, as an autonomous realm
deserving protection from public intervention, the family often contains

8. See, e.g., S. Lukes, *Power: A Radical View* (New York: Macmillan, 1974).

a variety of mechanisms for subordinating women. Principal objects of study here include domestic violence and the allocation and valuation of work associated with child care and housekeeping. Here the traditional household, usually celebrated in communitarian terms, is subject to feminist critique.

Much of this work argues that modes of interaction that appear consensual in fact reflect forms of social coercion. This claim fits comfortably with recent developments in social choice theory that stress that private preferences are not exogenous and prepolitical but, instead, adpative to available opportunities.[9] The phenomenon of endogenous preferences, or of preferences that are a product of limited options, finds a good test case—and strong confirmation—in studies of gender relations. That phenomenon in turn has consequences for usual understandings of autonomy and welfare, and the possible need for public intervention to support both. If preferences are adaptive to available opportunities, collective intervention designed to shape preferences might promote both autonomy and welfare.[10] Catharine MacKinnon's contribution to this collection, to be discussed shortly, bears on this problem.

c) Some feminist work asserts that the social subordination of women and sexuality are closely intermingled. In this light, it is no puzzle that a large part of the feminist movement has concentrated on the social and legal treatment of rape, prostitution, male control of reproduction, and sexual harassment. The empirical work here has attempted to show the pervasive and systemic quality of all these practices; the theoretical work considers the implications of the fact that legal and social systems tend to treat them as infrequent or marginal. Consider in this regard the fact that sexual harassment has been recognized as a legal category only in the last decade or so and that marital rape was not treated as a crime until quite recently (and even now the law here is in a primitive state). Some of the relevant work emphasizes the analogies between rape and prostitution and forms of interaction between men and women that are taken as normal and unobjectionable. The same argument is the source of the controversy over the definition of and appropriate response to sexual harassment.

Laurie Shrage's contribution to this collection, "Should Feminists Oppose Prostitution?" deals with the question of prostitution. She argues that prostitution both reflects and perpetuates the social subordination of women. Shrage endorses and amplifies the feminist critique of the claim that prostitution is an unobjectionable exercise of contractual liberty. In Shrage's view, prostitution is a product of particular, identifiable beliefs

9. See J. Elster, *Sour Grapes: Studies in the Subversion of Rationality* (Cambridge: Cambridge University Press, 1983); J. Roemer, "Rational Choice Marxism," in *Analytical Marxism,* ed. J. Roemer (Cambridge: Cambridge University Press, 1986).

10. See C. Sunstein, "Disrupting Voluntary Transactions," in *NOMOS XX: Markets and Justice,* ed. J. Chapman and J. Pennock (1989), and "Legal Interference with Private Preferences," *University of Chicago Law Review* 53 (1986): 1129–74.

and attitudes, and the industry of prostitution is sustained and organized by principles that "underlie pernicious gender asymmetries in many domains of our social life."

In "Defending Prostitution," Carole Pateman similarly rejects the contractarian view that because of the need to respect consent, free will, and voluntariness, prostitution is morally unproblematic. For Pateman, commodification of women's bodies cannot be assimilated to ordinary purchases and sales. Prostitution, she argues, is a form of submission. It should not be treated as free consent.

Political theory has often dealt uneasily or not at all with the relationship of sexuality to political power. Freud of course attempted to explore the problem, but his discussion of gender relations is notoriously inadequate. The most prominent modern example is the work of Michel Foucault, which stresses the variability of social mechanisms for understanding, creating, and controlling sexual behavior; but Foucault's lengthy work on the subject (astonishingly) deals not at all with questions of power as between men and women. Catharine MacKinnon's contribution here, "Sexuality, Pornography, and Method: 'Pleasure under Patriarchy,'" explores the social and political meaning and consequences of sexuality for issues of gender and equality. The essay provides the theoretical underpinnings for MacKinnon's well-known efforts to regulate pornography.

MacKinnon's basic argument is that sexuality ought to be seen as socially constructed rather than as natural; that sexuality, as currently constituted and practiced, is a central though overlooked ingredient in the subordination of women; that theories that celebrate the liberation of sexual drives disguise this fact and often serve—in purpose, in effect, or both—to increase the sexual availability of women to men; and that the case of pornography cannot be treated as marginal or deviant but, instead, reveals something significant about the nature of sexuality and gender relations. MacKinnon's basic argument is that political theory must deal with questions of sexuality if the sources of inequality as between men and women are to be understood. The argument bears as well on the relationship of objectification to ethics and politics.

MacKinnon's analysis helps to explain why some feminists have found the control of pornography to be an important subject. If widespread physical abuse of women occurs in and results from pornography, and if pornography plays a role in reflecting and perpetuating conceptions of sexuality that are an ingredient in sexual inequality, then efforts to understand and regulate pornography might be thought central to feminist theory and practice.

TRUST AND RESPONSIBILITY

Some work in feminist political theory provides reasons for skepticism about social contract theory and models of social and political life that grow out of contractual ideas. Here the relevant work tends to emphasize issues of trust and responsibility, rather than duties assumed voluntarily by social actors.

In "Trust and Antitrust," Annette Baier argues that political and moral philosophers have focused far too much on contractual relations and far too little on relations of trust, prominently including the morality or immorality of those relations under conditions of inequality. Baier urges that it is sometimes immoral to expect or meet trust, for trust includes a special form of vulnerability. Both exploitation and fellowship thrive in relations of trust. At the same time Baier observes that voluntary agreement, so central to liberal morality, has not been the dominant model of social life for women (and certain other groups). The trust relationships that have structured women's lives "were not entered into by free choice, or by freely giving or receiving promises." Baier concludes with a "moral test for trust." She claims that a trust relationship is morally corrupt if its continuation depends either on the successful cover-up of breaches of trust or on threat advantages held by one or the other side.

In "The Duty to Relieve Suffering," Susan James argues against a theory of individual rights that would prohibit punishment for the refusal to diminish suffering. Discussing issues of causation, she argues that it is circular to say that people have an obligation only to relieve harms that they have themselves caused. James argues that unfamiliar moral theory has too frequently been the source of arguments about any such obligation. In her account, existing arguments, strictly applied and taken seriously, for a duty here would condemn a wide range of individual and governmental practices that are currently tolerated.

Cheshire Calhoun's essay, "Responsibility and Reproach," deals with a problem that cuts across many of the questions discussed in this collection. That problem has to do with the attribution of responsibility or blame in "abnormal" moral contexts, in which the criteria for making moral judgments are not generally available and understood. The central case here is sexist behavior engaged in by people whose wrongdoing is widespread or even pervasive, and who are responding to widely held social norms.

Calhoun contends that people who engage in such behavior are not themselves blameworthy but that their moral failings should nonetheless be reproached. She claims that a moral reproach is necessary in order to publicize the relevant standard and to convey the obligatory force of normative commands. Calhoun's essay—like the other contributions to this book—attests to the ways in which feminist work in political theory has cast light both on the social subordination of women and on the extraordinarily wide range of ethical and political issues that are implicated by efforts to promote equality on the basis of sex.

Part I

The Question of Different Voice:
Care, Justice, and Rights

Reason and Feeling in Thinking about Justice*

Susan Moller Okin

Recent feminist scholarship has challenged the corpus of Western political thought in two new ways. Some works focus first on either the absence or the assumed subordination of women in a political theory, and then go on to ask how the theory would have to change in order to include women on an equal basis with men. Some focus more immediately on how the gendered structure of the societies in which theorists have lived has shaped their central ideas and arguments and consider how these ideas and arguments are affected by the adoption of a feminist perspective.[1] In this paper, I hope to contribute something to the second project. I raise, though do not by any means fully answer, some questions about the effects that assumptions about the gendered structure of society have had on thinking about social justice. In so doing, I suggest that some recent distinctions that have been made between an ethic of justice and an ethic of care may be at least overdrawn, if not false. They may obfuscate rather than aid our attempts to achieve a moral and political theory that we can find acceptable in a world in which gender is becoming an increasingly indefensible mode of social organization.[2]

* This paper has benefited from the comments and criticisms of Sissela Bok, Joshua Cohen, George Pearson Cross, Amy Gutmann, Robert O. Keohane, Will Kymlicka, Robert L. Okin, John Rawls, Nancy Rosenblum, Cass R. Sunstein, Joan Tronto, and Iris Young. Nevertheless, I regret that I have not been able to respond adequately to all of their objections and suggestions.

1. Works falling primarily within the first category include Lorenne Clark and Lynda Lange, *The Sexism of Social and Political Thought* (Toronto: University of Toronto Press, 1979); Jean Bethke Elshtain, *Public Man, Private Woman: Women in Social and Political Thought* (Princeton, N.J.: Princeton University Press, 1981); and Susan Moller Okin, *Women in Western Political Thought* (Princeton, N.J.: Princeton University Press, 1979). Works within the second include Mary O'Brien, *The Politics of Reproduction* (London: Routledge & Kegan Paul, 1981); and Judith H. Stiehm, ed., *Women's Views of the Political World of Men* (Dobbs Ferry, N.Y.: Transnational Publishers, 1984). The essays in Carole Pateman and Elizabeth Gross, eds., *Feminist Challenges: Social and Political Theory* (Boston: Northeastern University Press, 1987) span both categories.

2. For example, see Carol Gilligan, *In a Different Voice* (Cambridge, Mass.: Harvard University Press, 1982); and Nel Noddings, *Caring: A Feminine Approach to Ethics and Moral Education* (Berkeley and Los Angeles: University of California Press, 1984). See Owen Flanagan and Kathryn Jackson, "Justice, Care and Gender: The Kohlberg-Gilligan Debate

This essay originally appeared in *Ethics* 99, January 1989.

I shall focus on two major philosophers—primarily Rawls, and Kant as a major influence on him—and consider how their assumptions about the division of labor between the sexes, with women taking care of the realm of human nurturance, have a fundamental effect upon their accounts of moral subjects and the development of moral thinking. This is exemplified in their tendencies to separate reason from feelings and to require that moral subjects be abstracted, in their deliberations, from the contextuality and contingencies of actual human life.

John Rawls's *A Theory of Justice* has been the inspiration, in one way or another, for much of contemporary moral and political theory.[3] I am not going to focus primarily here on what it says—or, as it happens, mostly does not say—about women and gender. I am going to focus on the effects of assumptions about gender on central aspects of the theory. I shall first outline Kant's and Rawls's contrasting accounts of how one learns to be a moral person. I shall then argue that, despite this important area of contrast, the strong influence of Kant leads to Rawls's expressing his major ideas primarily in the language of rational choice. This leaves them unnecessarily open to two criticisms: that they involve unacceptably egoistic assumptions about human nature and that they are of little relevance to actual people thinking about justice.[4] Whereas Rawls's theory is sometimes viewed as excessively rationalistic, individualistic, and abstracted from real human beings, I will argue that, at its center (though frequently obscured by Rawls himself) is a voice of responsibility, care, and concern for others. This paper is, in part, an attempt to develop a feminist approach to social justice, which centers on a reinterpretation of Rawls's central concept, the original position.

In another sense, however, the paper is a feminist *critique* of Rawls. For he, unlike Kant but in line with a long tradition of political and moral philosophers including Rousseau, Hegel, and Tocqueville, regards the

Revisited," *Ethics* 97 (1987): 622–37, for a valuable alternative approach to this issue, which focuses on recent moral development theory, especially the Kohlberg-Gilligan debate, and provides an excellent selective list of references to what has rapidly become a vast literature. See also Gertrud Nunner-Winkler, "Two Moralities? A Critical Discussion of an Ethic of Care and Responsibility versus an Ethic of Rights and Justice," in *Morality, Moral Behavior, and Moral Development*, ed. W. Kurtines and J. Gewirtz (New York: Wiley, 1984), pp. 348–61; Joan Tronto, " 'Women's Morality': Beyond Gender Difference to a Theory of Care," *Signs: Journal of Women in Culture and Society* 12 (1987): 644–63; and Lawrence Blum, "Gilligan and Kohlberg: Implications for Moral Theory," *Ethics* 98 (1988): 472–91.

3. John Rawls, *A Theory of Justice* (Cambridge, Mass.: Harvard University Press, 1971). Subsequent references to this book (*TOJ*) will be given parenthetically in the text.

4. Thomas Nagel, "Rawls on Justice," in *Reading Rawls*, ed. Norman Daniels (New York: Basic, 1974), pp. 1–16 (reprinted from *Philosophical Review*, vol. 72 [1973]), makes the former argument; Michael J. Sandel, *Liberalism and the Limits of Justice* (Cambridge: Cambridge University Press, 1982) makes both arguments; the latter argument is made by both Alasdair MacIntyre, *After Virtue* (Notre Dame, Ind.: Notre Dame University Press, 1981); and Michael Walzer, *Spheres of Justice* (New York: Basic, 1983), and *Interpretation and Social Criticism* (Cambridge, Mass.: Harvard University Press, 1987).

family as a school of morality, a primary socializer of just citizens. At the same time, along with others in the tradition, he neglects the issue of the justice or injustice of the gendered family itself. The result is a central tension within the theory, which can be resolved only by opening up the question of justice within the family.

THE KANTIAN HERITAGE

Why did Rawls cast his theory, or much of it, in the language of rational choice? Why did he present it this way rather than as a theory that requires empathy even on the part of those artificial moral agents who inhabit the original position, and that requires not only empathy but far-reaching benevolence on the part of ordinary human beings who are prepared to abide by the principles of justice? Only the Kantian heritage can explain these things. The way Rawls presents his theory of justice reflects both Kant's stress on autonomy and rationality as the defining characteristics of moral subjects and his rigid separation of reason from feeling and refusal to allow feeling any place in the formulation of moral principles. Rawls says of Kant, "He begins with the idea that moral principles are the object of rational choice. . . . Moral philosophy becomes the study of the conception and outcome of a suitably defined rational decision" (*TOJ*, p. 251).[5] He frequently and explicitly acknowledges the connections between his theory and Kant's. The concept of the veil of ignorance, he says, is implicit in Kant's works, and the concept of the original position is an attempt to interpret Kant's conception of moral principles as formulated under "conditions that characterize men as free and equal rational beings" (*TOJ*, p. 252).

The Kantian connection, I suggest, made it extremely difficult for Rawls to acknowledge any role for empathy or benevolence in the formulation of his principles of justice and, instead, impelled him in the direction of rational choice. Kant is abundantly clear that feelings are to have no place in the foundations of morality. "No moral principle is based," he says, "as people sometimes suppose, on any *feeling* whatsoever. . . . For feeling, no matter by what it is aroused, always belongs to the order of *nature*."[6] He does not say so here, but he clearly means "nature, as contrasted with freedom." Kant so rejects the idea that feelings have anything to do with moral motivation that he considers that an act that is in accordance with duty, but is performed out of love or sympathetic inclination, has "no genuinely moral worth." It is only when such actions are performed from duty—because the moral law requires them—that they have moral content.[7]

5. See also John Rawls, "Kantian Constructivism in Moral Theory," *Journal of Philosophy* 77 (1980): 515–72.

6. Immanuel Kant, *The Doctrine of Virtue, pt. 2: Metaphysic of Morals,* trans. Mary J. Gregor (New York: Harper & Row, 1964), p. 33.

7. Immanuel Kant, *Groundwork of the Metaphysic of Morals,* trans. H. Paton (1948; reprint, New York: Harper & Row, 1964), pp. 66–67.

Kant is able to conclude that feeling and love have no part in the foundations of morality only because he neglects a very important type of human love. In *The Doctrine of Virtue,* he classifies love into two types. One he calls "practical love" or benevolence; this, he says, sometimes *results* from the performance of the duty to help others. Kant discusses the saying "you *ought* to *love* your neighbour as yourself." He says it "does not mean: you should immediately (first) love him and (afterwards) through the medium of this love do good to him. It means, rather: *do good* to your fellow-man, and this will give rise to love of man in you."[8] Such moral feelings, far from leading to principles of morality, can only follow from principles established independently of them. Kant does not, however, regard them as morally insignificant, since the moral feeling that follows from the thought of the law can be a significant factor in making us conscious of our obligations.[9] The other type of feeling Kant recognizes is called "pathological feeling" or attraction. "Pathological," as used here, does not mean that there is anything *wrong* with it, as it would signify in modern usage, but simply that it is "affective." As contrasted with moral feeling, which "can only follow from the thought of the law," pathological feeling "precedes the thought of the law." Being contingent and subject to change, belonging to the order of nature rather than to the order of autonomy or reason, however, this type of feeling can play no part in the formulation of the moral law.

Kant's brief account of moral education, as presented near the end of *The Doctrine of Virtue,* reflects this account of the relation (or, rather, comparative lack of it) between feelings and moral thinking. The moral catechism Kant presents in the form of a dialogue between teacher and pupil is, as he says, "developed from ordinary human reason." The teacher questions the pupil, and then "the answer which he methodically draws from the pupil's reason must be written down and preserved in precise terms which cannot easily be altered, and so be committed to the pupil's *memory."* These memorized pieces of reasoning are then supplemented by *"good example"* on the teacher's part, as well as his pointing out the *"cautionary* example" of others.[10] Subsequent to formulating principles on the basis of reason, the pupil becomes conditioned, by imitation, into virtuous inclination and action.

This arid presentation of moral education is closely related to Kant's incomplete account of the varieties of human love, which in turn is made possible by the fact that women play only a peripheral role in his philosophy. His reduction of love to two types, the moral feeling of benevolence that follows from the recognition of duty, and the affective love that he calls "mere inclination," leaves out at least one very important kind of love. This is the love that is typified by parent/child relations, under favorable

8. Kant, *The Doctrine of Virtue,* pp. 62–63.
9. Ibid., p. 59.
10. Ibid., pp. 151–52; emphasis in the original.

circumstances at any rate. It is usually made up of elements of affective love and of benevolence, but it also involves far more. The benevolence in it does not spring from the recognition of duty, and the affection in it is usually far from being "mere inclination," with the fickleness suggested by those terms. It is a kind of love that develops over time and that has its origins in attachment so close that, for the young infant, it constitutes complete psychological identification. It is fed by attachment, continued intimacy, and interdependence. On the other hand, it is a kind of love that has disastrous consequences if there is no willingness on the part of the parent to recognize and to appreciate differences between the child and her- or himself. This kind of love is fundamental to human life and relationship since it is the first kind of love we experience (if our circumstances are fortunate) regardless of our sex, and it has, of course, constituted throughout history a much larger part of women's than of men's experience.

Kant seems to have been unable to perceive either the moral relevance or the moral potential of this kind of love. This is probably due to the fact that, accepting without question the gendered division of labor that prevailed around him, he defined a moral world that excluded women. That may seem too extreme a statement. Let me point out, however, that while in most of his central works of moral philosophy Kant defines the moral subjects of whom he speaks as not only human beings but also "all rational beings as such," in less noticed works from the earliest to the last, he makes it clear that women are not sufficiently rational and autonomous to be moral subjects. In an early essay, entitled *Observations on the Feeling of the Beautiful and Sublime,* he says of women that their "philosophy is not to reason, but to sense."[11] Their virtue, unlike men's, is to be inspired by the desire to please; for them, he asserts, there is to be "nothing of duty, nothing of compulsion, nothing of obligation!"[12] In one of his very last works, the *Anthropology from a Pragmatic Point of View,* although, most uncharacteristically, he says that male and female are both rational beings, he takes back any thought of moral autonomy in the case of a married woman, by pointing out that she is necessarily subject to her husband and a legal minor. "To make oneself behave like a minor," he says, "degrading as it may be, is, nevertheless, very comfortable."[13] It is not difficult to tell, from such remarks, where women stand (perhaps it is more appropriate to say "where women *sit*") on Kant's moral scale.

11. Immanuel Kant, *Observations on the Feeling of the Beautiful and Sublime,* trans. John T. Goldthwait (Berkeley: University of California Press, 1960), p. 79. Kant's word is *empfinden.* It is sometimes, with equal appropriateness, translated as "to feel." I am grateful to Suzanne Altenberger for advice on this matter.

12. Ibid., sec. 3, p. 81.

13. Immanuel Kant, *Anthropology from a Pragmatic Point of View,* trans. Victor Lyle Dowdell (Carbondale: Southern Illinois University Press, 1978), pp. 216, 105.

Thus the moral division of labor between the sexes is very clear in Kant's writings. The virtues he assigns to women, as appropriate for their role in the gendered social structure, and particularly within the family, are virtues ranked far lower than the virtues assigned to men. As Lawrence Blum says about the moral rationalist, in a discussion of Kant and Hegel: "It is the male qualities whose highest expression he naturally takes as his model. In the same way it is natural for him to ignore or underplay the female qualities as they are found in his society—sympathy, compassion, emotional responsiveness. He fails to give these qualities adequate expression within his moral philosophy. The moral rationalist philosopher thus both reflects the sexual value hierarchy of his society and indirectly gives it a philosophic grounding and legitimation."[14]

Thus, Kant neglected the moral significance of an extremely important kind of human love, and of the moral qualities that can arise from it, because of his devaluing of women and exclusion of them from the realm of moral subjects. While endorsing what Blum says above, Jean Grimshaw has recently argued, in her excellent book *Philosophy and Feminist Thinking*, that, although Kant implicitly excludes women from his philosophical ideals, he "could, without inconsistency, have retained his view about 'moral worth', but changed his view of women."[15] I do not think he could, for though women are so peripheral as to be virtually absent from his moral world, the role they are assumed to play behind the scenes would appear to be necessary for its continuance. Women as Kant perceived them, inspired by feeling and by the desire to please, provide both the essential nurturance required for human development, and a realm of existence without which the moral order he prescribes for the world outside the family seems intolerable in its demands.[16] Kant's exclusion of women is of significance not only for women; it has a distorting effect on his moral philosophy as a whole.

To the extent that it derives from Kant in some of its basic assumptions about what it means to be a moral subject, Rawls's theory of justice suffers to some extent from this same distortion. As I will argue, Rawls is unwilling to call explicitly on the human qualities of empathy and benevolence in the working out of his principles of justice and in his lengthy description of the process of deliberation that leads to them. However, his original

14. Lawrence Blum, "Kant's and Hegel's Moral Rationalism: A Feminist Perspective," *Canadian Journal of Philosophy* 12 (1982): 296–97.

15. Jean Grimshaw, *Philosophy and Feminist Thinking* (Minneapolis: University of Minnesota Press, 1986), p. 49.

16. A possible response to this might be to suggest that a twentieth-century Kantian, not regarding the remaining social subordination of women as natural, would view both men and women as equally moral subjects with the same moral worth. But unless the conceptions of a moral subject and moral worth were to be relevantly adapted, this would result in family life's being governed by principles as strictly rationalist as the moral world outside rather than as providing a haven from this world, as Kant seems to have envisaged.

position consists of a combination of assumptions—mutual disinterest and the veil of ignorance—that, as he says, "achieves the same purpose as benevolence" (*TOJ*, p. 148). Before going on to discuss this, however, let us look at Rawls's account of how people develop a sense of justice. For despite his Kantian assumptions about rationality and autonomy, and the related rational choice language of much of his theory, Rawls's account of moral development is very different from Kant's and indicates clearly that rationality is not a sufficient basis on which to found or sustain his theory of justice.

RAWLS AND THE SENSE OF JUSTICE: THE SIGNIFICANCE OF GENDER

There is little indication, throughout most of *A Theory of Justice*, that the modern liberal society to which the principles of justice are to be applied is deeply and pervasively gender structured. As I shall argue, this neglect of gender has major implications for the practical feasibility of Rawls's principles of justice. In particular, there is very little mention of the family, the linchpin of the gender structure. Although Rawls, for good reason, mentions the "monogamous family" in his initial list of major institutions that constitute the "basic structure" to which the principles of justice are to apply, he never applies the two principles of justice to it. In fact, his assumption that those in the original position are "heads of families" prevents him from doing this (*TOJ*, p. 128). A central tenet of the theory, after all, is that justice characterizes institutions whose members could hypothetically have agreed to their structure and rules from a position in which they did not know which place in the structure they were to occupy. But since those in the original position are all heads of families, they are not in a position to settle questions of justice *within* families. In fact, if we discard the "heads of families" assumption, take seriously the notion that those in the original position are ignorant of their sex as well as their other individual characteristics, and apply the principles of justice to the gender structure and the family arrangements of our society, considerable changes are clearly called for.[17]

Instead, apart from being briefly mentioned as the link between generations necessary for Rawls's "savings principle," and as an obstacle to fair equality of opportunity, the family appears in Rawls's theory in only one context (albeit one of considerable importance): as the earliest school of moral development. Rawls argues, in a much neglected section of part 3 of *A Theory of Justice*, that a just, well-ordered society will be stable only if its members continue to develop a sense of justice—"a strong and normally effective desire to act as the principles of justice require" (*TOJ*, p. 454). He specifically turns his attention to the question

17. Susan Moller Okin, "Justice and Gender," *Philosophy and Public Affairs* 16 (1987): 42–72.

of childhood moral development, aiming to indicate the major steps by which a sense of justice is acquired.

In this context, Rawls *assumes* that families are just, though he has provided no reasons for us to accept this assumption (*TOJ*, p. 490). Moreover, these supposedly just families play a fundamental role in moral development. The love of parents for their children, coming to be reciprocated in turn by the child, is important in his account of the development of a sense of self-worth. By loving the child and being "worthy objects of his admiration, . . . they arouse in him a sense of his own value and the desire to become the sort of person that they are" (*TOJ*, p. 465). Healthy moral development in early life, Rawls argues, depends upon love, trust, affection, example, and guidance (*TOJ*, p. 466).

Later in moral development, at the stage he calls "the morality of association," Rawls perceives the family, which he describes in gendered terms, as a "small association, normally characterized by a definite hierarchy, in which each member has certain rights and duties" (*TOJ*, p. 467). It is the first of many associations in which, by moving through a sequence of roles and positions, our moral understanding increases. The crucial aspect of the sense of fairness that is learned during this stage is the capacity to take up the different points of view of others and to see things from their perspectives. We learn to perceive, from what they say and do, what other people's ends, plans, and motives are. Without this experience, Rawls says, "we cannot put ourselves into another's place and find out what we would do in his position," which we need to be able to do in order "to regulate our own conduct in the appropriate way by reference to it" (*TOJ*, p. 469). Participation in different roles in the various associations of society leads to the development of a person's "capacity for fellow feeling" and to "ties of friendship and mutual trust" (*TOJ*, p. 470). Rawls says that, just as in the first stage certain natural attitudes develop toward the parents, "so here ties of friendship and confidence grow up among associates. In each case certain natural attitudes underlie the corresponding moral feelings: a lack of these feelings would manifest the absence of these attitudes" (*TOJ*, p. 471).

This whole account of moral development is strikingly unlike that of Kant, for whom any feelings that did not follow from independently established moral principles were morally suspect. Unlike Kant, with his arid, intellectualized account of moral learning, Rawls clearly acknowledges the importance of feelings in the development of the capacity for moral thinking. In accounting for his third and final stage of moral development, where persons are supposed to become attached to the principles of justice themselves, Rawls says that "the sense of justice is continuous with the love of mankind" (*TOJ*, p. 476). At the same time, he allows for the fact that we have particularly strong feelings about those to whom we are closely attached and says that this is rightly reflected in our moral judgments: even though "our moral sentiments display an independence from the accidental circumstances of our world, . . . our natural attachments to particular persons and groups still have an appropriate place" (*TOJ*, p. 475). His differences from Kant's views are clear from his indications that empathy, or imagining oneself into the place of others, plays a major role in moral development. It is not surprising that he turns away from Kant, to moral philosophers such as Adam Smith, Elizabeth Anscombe, Philippa Foot, and Bernard Williams, in developing his ideas about the moral emotions or sentiments (*TOJ*, pp. 479 ff.).

In Rawls's summary of his three psychological laws of moral development (*TOJ*, pp. 490–91), the fundamental importance of loving parenting for the development of a sense of justice is manifest. The three laws, Rawls says, are "not merely principles of association or of reinforcement . . . [but] assert that the active sentiments of love and friendship, and even the sense of justice, arise from the manifest intention of other persons to act for our good. Because we recognize that they wish us well, we care for their well-being in return" (*TOJ*, p. 494). Each of the laws of moral development, as set out by Rawls, depends upon the one before it, and the first assumption of the first law is: "given that family institutions are just. . . ." Unlike Kant, with his nameless, but no doubt male, tutor, Rawls frankly admits that the whole of moral development rests upon the loving ministrations of those who raise small children from the earliest stages, and on the moral character of the environment in which this takes place. At the foundation of the development of the sense of justice, then, are an activity and a sphere of life that—though by no means necessarily so—have throughout history been predominantly the activity and the sphere of women.

Rawls does not explain the basis of his assumption that family institutions are just. If gendered family institutions are *not* just but are, rather, a relic of caste or feudal societies in which roles, responsibilities, and resources are distributed, not in accordance with the two principles of justice but in accordance with innate differences that are imbued with enormous social significance, then Rawls's whole structure of moral development seems to be built on uncertain ground. Unless the households in which children are first nurtured, and see their first examples of human interaction, are based on equality and reciprocity rather than on dependence and domination, as is too often in fact the case, how can whatever love they receive from their parents make up for the injustice they see before their eyes in the relationship between these same parents? Unless they are parented equally by adults of both sexes, how will children of both sexes come to develop a sufficiently similar and well-rounded moral psychology as to enable them to engage in the kind of deliberation about justice that is exemplified in the original position? And finally, unless the household is connected by a continuum of associations to the larger communities within which people are supposed to develop fellow feelings for each other, how will they grow up with the capacity for enlarged sympathies such as are clearly required for the practice of justice?

On the one hand, Rawls's neglect of justice within the family is clearly in tension with his own theory of moral development, which *requires* that families be just. On the other hand, his conviction that the development of a sense of justice depends on attachments to and feelings for other persons, originating in the family, is in tension with the "rational choice" language that he frequently employs in laying out his theory of justice. I shall now look at this prevailing mode of interpreting Rawls and then go on to suggest an alternative account of the original position, which is both consistent with much that he says about it and much more compatible with his own account of moral development. It is this alternative account of what goes on in the original position that leads me to suggest that one is not forced to choose between an ethic of justice and an ethic of sympathy or care, nor between an ethic that emphasizes universality and one that takes account of differences.

THE ORIGINAL POSITION

The original position is at the heart of Rawls's theory of justice. It is both his most important contribution to moral and political theory and the focus of most of the controversy and disputes that the theory still attracts more than fifteen years after its publication. How the original position is understood and interpreted is extremely important for both the internal coherence and the persuasiveness of the theory. First I shall lay out briefly the set of conditions that Rawls calls the original position. Then I shall look at the way that Rawls presents it, at least some of the time, a presentation that I think has led to some of the criticisms that have been made of it. Then I will explain my alternative reading, which I think is faithful to Rawls's essential meaning. This alternative reading suggests that Rawls is far from being a moral rationalist and that feelings such as empathy and benevolence are at the very foundation of his principles of justice. The alternative reading, I suggest, leaves the original position, and indeed the whole theory, less susceptible to criticism.

In sum, Rawls's specifications for the original position are as follows: the parties are rational and mutually disinterested, and while no limits are placed on the *general* information available to them, they deliberate behind a "veil of ignorance" that conceals from them all knowledge of their individual characteristics: "No one knows his place in society, his class position or social status, nor does anyone know his fortune in the distribution of natural assets and abilities, his intelligence, strength, and the like. [Nor do the parties know] their conceptions of the good or their special psychological propensities" (*TOJ*, p. 12). The critical force of the original position can be appreciated from the fact that some interesting critiques of Rawls's theory have resulted from others' interpreting the original position more radically or broadly than its creator did. Beitz has argued, for example, that there is no justification for not extending its application to the population of the entire planet, which would lead to challenging virtually everything that is currently assumed in the dominant "statist" conception of international relations.[18] Some of us, feminist critics, have suggested that if we do away with the "heads of families" assumption, and take seriously the fact that those behind the veil of ignorance cannot know their *sex,* we must engage in a radical questioning of the gender structure, which Rawls himself leaves virtually unmentioned.[19]

In *A Theory of Justice* itself, Rawls foresees that problems will arise if readers focus separately on each of the assumptions made about parties in the original position, rather than taking the device as a whole. He warns that the theory may be interpreted as based on egoism if the mutual disinterest assumption is taken in isolation from the other specifications: "the feeling that this conception of justice is egoistic is an illusion fostered by looking at but one of the elements of the original position" (*TOJ,* p. 148).[20] He also addresses in advance those who are likely to ask, having taken note of what would be decided in the original position, what relevance it may have for actual human beings who know who they are and what their social position is. He responds like this:

> The conditions embodied in the description of this situation are ones that we do in fact accept. Or if we do not, then we can be persuaded to do so by philosophical considerations of the sort occasionally introduced. Each aspect of the original position can be given a supporting explanation. Thus what we are doing is to combine into one conception the totality of conditions that we are ready upon due reflection to recognize as reasonable in our conduct with respect to one another. Once we grasp this conception, we can at any time look at the social world from the required point of view. [*TOJ,* p. 587][21]

On the other hand, in a recent response to critics, Rawls says something that does not seem easy to reconcile with this conception of the original position as an explicitly moral point of view that we can adopt in real life by thinking in the appropriate way. He first reiterates the ideas expressed in the passage I just quoted, by saying that we can enter the original position at any time, simply by reasoning for principles of justice as we would if constrained by its restrictions (on our knowledge, motivations, and so on). But then he adds to this the following: "When, in this way, we simulate being in this position, our reasoning no more commits us to a metaphysical doctrine about the nature of the self than our playing a game like Monopoly commits us to thinking that we are landlords

18. Charles Beitz, *Political Theory and International Relations* (Princeton, N.J.: Princeton University Press, 1979).

19. See Jane English, "Justice between Generations," *Philosophical Studies* 31 (1977): 91–104; Deborah Kearns, "A Theory of Justice—and Love: Rawls on the Family," *Politics* 18 (1983): 36–42; and Okin, "Justice and Gender."

20. See also Rawls, "Kantian Constructivism," p. 527.

21. See also ibid., p. 518.

engaged in a desperate rivalry, winner take all."[22] This juxtaposition of the original position as a moral point of view, a way of reasoning about principles of justice, with the original position as analogous to a game, without moral significance, identifies a tension in the way the original position is presented throughout Rawls's works. In order to see what leads to such criticisms as I have mentioned above, and to consider how they can be fully answered, it is important to look at each side of this tension, in turn.

First, I shall look at how central aspects of the Kantian heritage— especially the presentation of moral subjects as, above all, rational, au- tonomous, and freed from contingency—influence Rawls in the direction of perceiving what he is doing as a branch of rational choice theory. Given this interpretation, the Monopoly analogy is perfectly appropriate. Then I shall sketch out an alternative reading of the theory, and of the original position in particular, which explains better what it is that makes it into an appropriate "moral point of view" that we can be persuaded to accept. I shall pay particular attention to the question, What do we have to be like, in order to be prepared to take up this point of view and to formulate our principles of justice in accordance with its demands? This is the crucial issue on which I think some parts of Rawls's theory are misleading, due to his identification with Kantian ways of thinking about the foundations of principles of justice and right.

THE "RATIONAL CHOICE" INTERPRETATION AND ITS IMPLICATIONS

Rawls states early on and repeats a number of times throughout his construction of the theory of justice that it is "a part, perhaps the most important part, of the theory of rational choice" (*TOJ*, p. 16). Recently, he has said that this was a "very misleading" error and that "there is no thought of trying to derive the content of justice within a framework that uses an idea of the rational as the sole normative idea."[23] Once we look at the implications of the rational choice reading of the theory, I

22. John Rawls, "Justice as Fairness: Political, not Metaphysical," *Philosophy and Public Affairs* 14 (1985): 239.

23. Rawls, "Justice as Fairness," p. 237, n. 20. Rawls's movement in this direction is already clearly apparent in the first of the Dewey lectures (Rawls, "Kantian Constructivism"), where he pays much attention to the distinction between the rational and the reasonable. Here, the rational still denotes the advantage of the individual, as in rational choice theory, but the reasonable is defined by moral conceptions such as reciprocity and mutuality. Principles are reasonable only if they are publicly acceptable by moral persons as fair terms of cooperation among them. Rawls seems to draw a clear distinction between thinking about justice and thinking about rational choice when he says: "Familiar principles of justice are examples of reasonable principles, and familiar principles of rational choice are examples of rational principles. The way the Reasonable is presented in the original position leads to the two principles of justice" (p. 530). He also states clearly that, in his theory, "the Reasonable presupposes and subordinates the Rational" (p. 530). See especially pp. 517–22 and pp. 528–30.

suggest that we will be able to see why Rawls has reconsidered it. Purging the theory of the rational choice connection and its implications strengthens it and renders it far less vulnerable to some of its critics.[24]

Let us first look at how Rawls conceives of his theory as a branch of rational choice theory. First, he associates the rationality and mutual disinterest of the parties with rational choice theory (*TOJ*, pp. 13–14). The actors in such a theory are assumed to be egoists, and while Rawls specifies that his parties are not to be understood as egoists in the colloquial sense of being interested only in such things as wealth, prestige, and domination, they *are* to be conceived of as "not taking an interest in one another's interests" (*TOJ*, p. 13). The rationality of the parties is also specified as that standard in economic or other rational choice theory— as instrumental rationality, or "taking the most effective means to given ends" (*TOJ*, p. 14). Rawls explains a number of times that these assumptions are made about the parties in the original position in order that the theory not depend on strong assumptions. He says, for example, that "the original position is meant to incorporate widely shared and yet weak conditions. A conception of justice should not presuppose . . . extensive ties of natural sentiment. At the basis of the theory, one tries to assume as little as possible" (*TOJ*, p. 129; see also pp. 18 and 583). At this point, however, one needs to take heed of Rawls's own warning not to focus on the individual assumptions made about the parties in the original position but to look at the concept as a whole. Rawls claims that each of the assumptions "should by itself be natural and plausible; some of them may seem innocuous or even trivial" (*TOJ*, p. 18). The question is, however, how weak do the assumptions look when considered *together*? And is it possible, considering them together, still to conceive of the theory as an example of rational choice theory?

In rational choice theory, choice under certainty requires the individual to have both vast quantities of relevant knowledge about the environment and a well-organized and stable system of preferences.[25] It is on the basis of these, but especially the knowledge of his or her "independent utility

24. See n. 4 above. In addition, a number of rational choice theorists have criticized Rawls's conclusions as much too egalitarian to have emerged from a situation of rational choice (see, e.g., David Gauthier, *Morals by Agreement* [Oxford: Clarendon Press, 1986], pp. 245–67).

25. Conventional rational choice theory distinguishes three modes of deliberation and choice, correlated with three different sets of assumptions about what is known by the actors. Choice under certainty depends on the actors knowing with certainty the outcome of each choice and the utility of that outcome. Choice under risk occurs when all the possible outcomes and their utility are known, as well as the probabilities of their occurrence. Choice under uncertainty occurs when knowledge of the probabilities is absent or incomplete. These nomenclatures are not always strictly adhered to. Rather confusingly, the actor's preparedness to take risks is a more important factor in the case of the third set of assumptions (see John C. Harsanyi, *Rational Behavior and Bargaining Equilibrium in Games and Social Situations* [Cambridge: Cambridge University Press, 1977], chap. 3). I am grateful to Richard Arneson for helping me to correct some confusions in this part of the paper.

function" that individuals are presumed able to choose, from the alternatives open, the option that will permit each to reach the highest attainable point on his or her preference scale. In conditions where this knowledge about individual preferences is presumed not available, reasoning in accordance with abstract probabilities comes into play. We must compare the specifications of Rawls's original position with these assumptions.

In Rawls's account of the original position, mutual disinterest and instrumental rationality feature only in conjunction with the veil of ignorance. On the one hand, the parties try to maximize what rational choice theory calls their "utility functions." They realize that, as individuals *having* distinct ends and interests (even though these are not revealed to them) they all have an equal stake in promoting and protecting what Rawls calls the "primary goods"—those basic liberties and goods that are prerequisite for the pursuit of distinct ends and interests. In this respect, then, as Rawls acknowledges, there might as well be just one person behind the veil of ignorance since the deliberations of all are identical. On the other hand, the parties do not have any knowledge of their separate, distinct, individual interests. Rawls says of them that "in choosing between principles each tries as best he can to advance *his interests,*" and that he will rank the options "according to how well they further *his purposes,*" and so on (*TOJ,* pp. 142, 143; emphasis added). But what sense does it make to talk of mutually disinterested individuals pursuing their interests when, to the extent that their interests are distinct and differentiated, they have no knowledge of them? Clearly, choice under certainty, which requires both the knowledge of outcomes and of the utility of these outcomes, is ruled out. The branches of rational choice theory that remain potentially applicable are choice under risk and choice under uncertainty.

Choice under risk, however, involves taking into account the probability of the occurrence of different outcomes. Rawls does not allow this to happen, by specifying that the veil of ignorance "excludes all but the vaguest knowledge of likelihoods. The parties have no basis for determining the probable nature of their society, or their place in it" (*TOJ,* p. 155). As he points out, this stipulation means that the parties "have strong reasons for being wary of probability calculations if any other course is open to them" (*TOJ,* p. 155). Thus choice under risk is ruled out. Rawls says, indeed, that "the veil of ignorance leads directly to the problem of choice under uncertainty" (*TOJ,* p. 172). There is, however, no generally accepted theory of rational choice under uncertainty, and we must still ask: How *do* the parties deliberate, in coming to their conclusions?

Rawls further reduces the applicability of rational choice theory by specifying that the parties are to have no knowledge of their aversion from or propensity for taking risks. By prohibiting the parties from having any knowledge of *either* the probabilities themselves *or* their own attitudes toward taking chances, Rawls decisively rules out the modes of deliberation that rational choice theory typically turns to under such conditions as otherwise defined. When he specifies the situation as one of choice under uncertainty, he suggests another possible mode of reasoning: "Of course, it is possible to regard the parties as perfect altruists and to assume that they reason as if they are certain to be in the position of each person. This interpretation of the initial situation removes the element of risk and uncertainty" (*TOJ*, p. 172). Rawls does not consider himself to be taking this route, believing as he does that it leads to classic utilitarianism rather than to the two principles of justice.[26] But, as I shall argue, because he reduces the knowledge of those in the original position to the point where they cannot employ probabilistic reasoning and cannot be assumed to take risks, Rawls *does* have to rely on empathy, benevolence, and equal concern for others as for the self, in order to have the parties come up with the principles they choose, especially the difference principle. This takes him far from anything in rational choice theory.

Rawls compares the assumptions he makes about those in the original position with other assumptions that include benevolence. He considers whether his own theory requires that the parties be moved by benevolence or by an interest in one another's interests. And he states clearly that "the combination of mutual disinterest and the veil of ignorance *achieves the same purpose as benevolence. For this combination of conditions forces each person in the original position to take the good of others into account*" (*TOJ*, p. 148; emphasis added). It is important to pause and think about this statement. For what it means is that it is only because those in the original

26. In sec. 30 of *A Theory of Justice* Rawls discusses the ethical position that would be adopted by a perfect altruist (a person "whose desires conform to the approvals of . . . a rational and impartial sympathetic spectator"). Imagining himself in the place of each person in turn, the perfect altruist is supposed to arrive at classical utilitarian conclusions since "sympathetically imagined pains cancel out sympathetically imagined pleasures, and the final intensity of approval corresponds to the net sum of positive feeling" (p. 187). It is not clear to me why the imagining of the altruist should involve the conflation of all persons into one that results in adoption of the classical principle of utility. I agree with Nagel (Thomas Nagel, *The Possibility of Altruism* [Princeton, N.J.: Princeton University Press, 1978], p. 138), who concludes that "this situation is unimaginable, and in so far as it is not, it completely distorts the nature of the competing claims." Rawls then imagines the benevolent person in another way—as one who "is to imagine that he is to divide into a plurality of persons whose life and experience will be distinct in the usual way . . . [with] no conflation of desires and memories into those of one person." Under *these* conditions, Rawls thinks that "the two principles of justice . . . seem a relatively more plausible choice than the classical principle of utility" (p. 191). It seems completely reasonable that a benevolent spectator who imagined experiencing the distinct lives of all those concerned separately (the only way that makes any sense to me) would be more likely to adopt the two principles than the classical principle of utility. It is implausible to expect that the pains experienced in one life would be balanced off by the pleasures experienced in another—even if lived by the same person (see Nagel, *The Possibility of Altruism*, pp. 140–42). Rawls argues that a party in the original position, who knows that he will live *one* of the lives, but does not know *which* one, will be even less likely to favor aggregative solutions, or to trade off the pains of some against the pleasures of others. But he resists the idea that such a party needs benevolence since he considers that the veil of ignorance and mutual disinterestedness serve as its functional equivalents.

position are assumed to be behind the veil of ignorance that they can be presented as the "rational, mutually disinterested" agents characteristic of rational choice theory. They can be perceived as thinking only for themselves, *only* because they do not know *which self* they will turn out to be and, therefore, must consider the interests of all possible selves equally.

Having stated that his assumptions achieve the same purpose as that of benevolence, Rawls goes on to argue that his assumption of mutual disinterest and the veil of ignorance has enormous advantages over the assumption of benevolence plus knowledge since the "latter is so complex that no definite theory at all can be worked out." Too much information is required, and unanswered questions remain about the "relative strength of benevolent desires." His assumptions, by contrast, he says, have the "merits of simplicity and clarity," as well as the advantage of being "weak stipulations" (*TOJ*, pp. 148–49). The illusion that the stipulations are weak is not hard to dispel; it is only if they are considered in isolation from each other (just what Rawls warns us against) that they can be seen as weak. In fact, the veil of ignorance is *such* a demanding stipulation that it converts what would, without it, be self-interest into benevolence or the equal concern for others. As for the advantage of simplicity and clarity, when we look at the original position in the only way in which it is intelligible (which is far distant from any rational choice theory), we find that it cannot escape most of the complexities of benevolence plus knowledge. To be sure, the issue of "the relative strength of benevolent desires" is not a problem for those behind the veil of ignorance: since one does not know which person one will turn out to be, one's rational self-interest presumably directs one to being equally concerned for each. But in order to think reasonably in the original position, one must presumably have knowledge of the essential aspects of the lives of persons of all different imaginable types and in all different imaginable social positions. In the absence of knowledge about their own particular characteristics, those in the original position cannot think from the position of *nobody* (as Rawls's desire for simplicity might suggest); they must think from the position of *everybody*, in the sense of *each in turn*. This is far from a simple demand.[27]

In fact, when we consider the reasoning engaged in by the parties in the original position, we can see that this *is* what they do. For example,

27. In a later discussion, Rawls again suggests significant differences between the reasoning of the parties and the self-interest characteristic of conventional rational choice theory. He says: "In the original position we may describe the parties either as the representatives (or trustees) of persons with certain interests or as themselves moved by these interests. It makes no difference either way, although the latter is simpler and I shall usually speak in this vein" (Rawls, "Kantian Constructivism," pp. 524–25). As I have suggested, the latter description is not simpler. For in a situation in which the identity and particular characteristics of the self are unknown there is no difference between self-interest and the representation of the interests of others. Whichever description Rawls chooses, the complexities are the same, and neither can be equated with the situation in rational choice theory.

in formulating the principle that protects equal liberty of conscience, Rawls makes it clear that the parties, who of course do not know what their moral or religious convictions are, "must choose principles that secure the integrity of their religious and moral freedom" (*TOJ*, p. 206). But in the absence of knowledge about the self, including the absence of probabilities, the only way to do this is to imagine oneself in the position of those whose religious practices and beliefs or lack thereof will require most tolerance on the part of others—the religiously "least advantaged," one might call them. It is not easy for an essentially nonreligious person, trying to imagine her- or himself into the original position, to adopt the standpoint of a fundamentalist believer; nor is it easy for a devoutly religious person to imagine the situation of a nonbeliever in a highly religious society. To do either requires, at the very least, both strong empathy and a preparedness to listen carefully to the very different points of view of others.

This method of thinking in the original position is most obviously required in the formulation of the difference principle. There, the maximin rule "directs our attention to the worst that can happen under any proposed course of action, and to decide in the light of that" (*TOJ*, p. 154). In considering permissible inequalities, "one looks at the system from the standpoint of the least advantaged representative man" (*TOJ*, p. 151). And, of course, once we challenge Rawls's traditional belief that questions about justice can be resolved by "heads of families," the "least advantaged representative woman," who is likely to be considerably *worse* off, has to be considered equally. Especially for those accustomed by class position, race, and sex to privilege, wealth, and power, a real appreciation of the point of view of the worst-off is likely to require considerable empathy and capacity to listen to others.[28]

On this interpretation, the original position is *not* an abstraction from all contingencies of human life, as some of Rawls's critics, and even Rawls himself at his most Kantian, present it. It is, rather, as Rawls's own theory of moral development strongly indicates, much closer to an appreciation and concern for social and other human *differences*. Neither does it seem that the theory requires us to regard ourselves as "independent in the sense that our identity is never tied to our aims and attachments," as Sandel says that it does.[29] For there is nothing implausible or inconsistent about requiring us to distance ourselves from our particular aims and

28. For a very interesting discussion of the problems of considering "the other" in moral and social theory, see Joan Tronto, "Rationalizing Racism, Sexism, and Other Forms of Prejudice: Otherness in Moral and Feminist Theory" (Hunter College of the City University of New York, Department of Political Science, New York, 1987, typescript). Compare Kenneth Arrow, *Collected Papers: Social Choice and Justice* (Cambridge, Mass.: Harvard University Press, Belknap Press, 1983), pp. 98, 113–14, for doubts about whether different people with different life experiences can ever have the same information, and can therefore achieve the criterion of universalizability that is required by a theory of justice.

29. Sandel, p. 179.

attachments for the purpose of arriving at principles of justice, while acknowledging that we may to some extent identify with them as we go about living our lives. The original position requires that, as moral subjects, we consider the identities, aims, and attachments of every other person, however different they may be from ourselves, as of equal concern with our own. If we, who *do* know who we are, are to think *as if* we were in the original position, we must develop considerable capacities for empathy and powers of communicating with others about what different human lives are like. But these alone are not enough to maintain in us a sense of justice. Since we know who we are, and what are our particular interests and conceptions of the good, we need as well a great commitment to benevolence; to *caring* about each and every other as much as about ourselves.

Rawls states clearly in several passages that abiding by the principles of justice that would be chosen in the original position requires motivations on the part of real human beings—especially the powerful and privileged—that are far from being self-interested: "To be sure, any principle chosen in the original position may require a large sacrifice for some. The beneficiaries of clearly unjust institutions (those founded on principles that have no claim to acceptance) may find it hard to reconcile themselves to the changes that will have to be made" (*TOJ,* p. 176). But he also speaks of a sense in which abiding by the principles of justice is in the self-interest of all—in the sense of *moral* self-interest. In the well-ordered, just society, "everyone's acting to uphold just institutions is for the good of each. . . . When all strive to comply with these principles and each succeeds, then individually and collectively their nature as moral persons is most fully realized, and with it their individual and collective good" (*TOJ,* p. 528).

All this takes us very far from the language of rational choice, which may explain Rawls's subsequent rejection of his own initial characterization of his theory. In such language, there is no room for a distinction between self-interest and moral self-interest. As I have suggested, Rawls's theory is much better interpreted as a theory founded upon the notion of equal concern for others than as a theory in which "mutual disinterest" has any significance, except as but *one* of several assumptions in a construction that serves not simply as a "device of representation" (as he has called the original position) but also as a device of empathy and benevolence. Indeed, such an interpretation is supported by much of Rawls's own text, and especially by his theory of moral development. On the other hand, it requires that the theory be purged of all suggestions that it is a part of rational choice theory.

It will perhaps be useful to place my reinterpretation of Rawls in the context of the contrasting arguments of several other feminist theorists. For it challenges the views of some who have found such theories of justice to be either incomplete or unacceptable from a feminist point of view. Gilligan, for example, in her critique of the moral development theory of the Kohlberg school (which owes much to Rawls's work on justice), contrasts the morality of care, contextuality, and concern for others with the morality of justice, rights, and rules. She associates the former voice primarily with women and the latter with men.[30] As I have argued elsewhere, many of the respondents whom Gilligan identifies as speaking in the "different voice" use it to express as fully universalizable a morality of social concern as respondents who express themselves in the language of justice and rights.[31] Thus the implication frequently drawn from her work, that women's morality tends to be more particularistic and contextual, appears to be unfounded. Here, by arguing that Rawls's theory of justice is itself centrally dependent upon the capacity of moral persons to be concerned about and to demonstrate care for others, especially others who are most different from themselves, I have presented another piece of argument that questions the wisdom of distinguishing between an ethic of care and an ethic of justice.

In Noddings's view, justice has been much overrated as the fundamental virtue, and principles have been overvalued as a tool for thinking about ethical problems.[32] These mistaken emphases are attributed to an overly individualistic and abstract male bias in moral philosophy. Justice itself, according to this view, should be at least supplemented, if not supplanted, by an ethic of caring, in which one's responsibility to care for those close to one takes priority over or entirely replaces what have generally been regarded as obligations to a broader range of people, or even humanity at large. While the feminist interpretation of Rawls that I have presented above argues that feelings such as caring and concern for others are essential to the formulation of principles of justice, it does not suggest that such principles can be replaced by contextual caring thinking. The problem, I suggest, is not principles or rules per se but the ways in which they have often been arrived at. If the principles of justice are founded, as I have suggested that Rawls's are, not on mutual disinterest and detachment from others but on empathy and concern for others—including concern for the ways in which others are different from ourselves—they will not be likely to lead to destructive rules that have tragic consequences when applied to those we love.[33]

The argument presented above also contrasts with recent work on theories of justice by Young and Benhabib. Young argues that the ideal of impartiality and universality in moral reasoning is misguided and works in opposition to feminist and other emancipatory politics because it attempts to eliminate otherness and difference and creates a false dichotomy between reason and feeling.[34] She thus finds Rawls's theory

30. Gilligan.

31. Susan Moller Okin, "Thinking Like a Woman," in *Theoretical Perspectives on Sexual Difference*, ed. Deborah Rhode (New Haven, Conn.: Yale University Press, in press).

32. Noddings.

33. Compare ibid., p. 44.

34. Iris Marion Young, "Toward a Critical Theory of Justice," *Social Theory and Practice* 7 (1981): 279–301, and "Impartiality and the Civic Public," in *Feminism as Critique*, ed. Seyla Benhabib and Drucilla Cornell (Minneapolis: University of Minnesota Press, 1987).

to be as rationalist, monological, and abstracted from particularity as Kant's. Benhabib makes the closely related claim that, in universalistic moral theories, such as Kohlberg's and Rawls's, "ignoring the standpoint of the concrete other leads to epistemic incoherence." In Rawls's original position, she claims, "The *other as different from the self*, disappears. . . . Differences are not denied; they become irrelevant." With only a "generalized other," Benhabib remarks, "what we are left with is an empty mask that is everyone and no one."[35]

I have attempted here to respond to such feminist critiques of Rawlsian thinking about justice by disputing the dichotomies they draw between justice and care, in the works of Gilligan and Noddings, and, in the works of Benhabib and Young, between impartiality and universalizability on the one hand, and the recognition of otherness and difference on the other. I have argued that Rawls's theory of justice is most coherently interpreted as a moral structure founded on the equal concern of persons for each other as for themselves, a theory in which empathy with and care for others, as well as awareness of their differences, are crucial components. It is, certainly, the case that Rawls's construction of the original position is designed so as to eliminate from the formulation of the principles of justice biases that might result from particular attachments to others, as well as from particular facts about the self. Surely impartiality in this sense is a reasonable requirement to make of a theory of justice.[36] But nevertheless, as I have argued here, the only coherent way in which a party in the original position can think about justice is through empathy with persons of all kinds in all the different positions in society, but especially with the least well-off in various respects. To think as a person in the original position is not to be a disembodied nobody. This, as critics have rightly pointed out, would be impossible. Rather, it is to think from the point of view of everybody, of every "concrete other" whom one might turn out to be.

For real people, who of course *know* who they are, to think *as if* in the original position requires that they have well-developed capacities for empathy, care, and concern for others—certainly not self-interest and instrumental rationality. In order to develop the sense of justice that is required of people if a well-ordered society is to have any hope of

35. Seyla Benhabib, "The Generalized and the Concrete Other," in Benhabib and Cornell, eds., p. 89 and passim.

36. The pitfalls of rejecting the goals of impartiality and/or universalizability, and of associating women or feminist theory with such a position, seem to me to be underestimated in the arguments made by Benhabib, Noddings, and Young, as well as in the implications drawn by Gilligan from her data. As I have argued elsewhere, to the extent that findings about women's moral development are interpreted to mean that women are more attached than men to particular others and less able to be impartial or to universalize in their moral thinking, they seem not only to misread the data but to reinforce the negative stereotyping of women that has been employed to exclude them from political rights and positions of public authority (Susan Moller Okin, "Thinking Like a Woman").

being achieved or, once achieved, preserved, human beings must be nurtured and socialized in an environment that best develops these capacities in them. By acknowledging the importance of such feelings for the development of a sense of justice, Rawls breaks away from the rationalist Kantian mode of thinking that casts a strong influence over much of his theory. To the extent that these aspects of the theory are emphasized, and it is thereby freed from some of its most Kantian language and assumptions, it is less open to some of the criticisms that have been made of it—and especially of its central concept, the original position. But such an emphasis at the same time draws attention to the fact that the theory as it stands contains an internal paradox. Because of Rawls's assumptions about the gendered family, he has not applied the principles of justice to the realm of human nurturance, which is so crucial for the achievement and the maintenance of justice.

Justice, Care, and Gender: The Kohlberg-Gilligan Debate Revisited

Owen Flanagan and Kathryn Jackson

I

In 1958, G. E. M. Anscombe wrote, "It is not profitable for us at present to do moral philosophy; that should be laid aside at any rate until we have an adequate philosophy of psychology, in which we are conspicuously lacking" (p. 186). Anscombe hinted (and she and many others pursued the hint) that the Aristotelian tradition was the best place to look for a richer and less shadowy conception of moral agency than either utilitarianism or Kantianism had provided.

In the same year Anscombe published "Modern Moral Philosophy," Lawrence Kohlberg completed his dissertation at the University of Chicago, a dissertation that laid the foundations for what has been the dominant program in moral psychology for the last twenty-odd years. The contrast between the sort of Aristotelian philosophical psychology Anscombe envisaged and Kohlberg's program could not have been starker. Anscombe recommended that the concepts of "*moral* obligation and *moral* duty . . . and of what is *morally* right and wrong, and of the *moral* sense of 'ought,' ought to be jettisoned . . . because they are survivors . . . from an earlier conception of ethics which no longer survives, and are only harmful without it" (p. 186). Kohlberg meanwhile claimed that people at the highest stage of moral development "answer [moral dilemmas] in moral words such as *duty* or *morally right* and use them in a way implying universality, ideals and impersonality" (1981, p. 22). And while Anscombe pointed to Aristotle as the possibility proof that ethics could be done with a more robust and realistic conception of moral agency than the will-o'-the-wisp Enlightenment conception which Iris Murdoch describes as "thin as a needle" (1970, p. 53) and Alasdair MacIntyre depicts as "ghostlike" (1982), Kohlberg derided Aristotelianism, calling it the "bag of virtues" model; and he explicitly rejected the view that personality is divided up "into cognitive abilities, passions or motives, and traits of

This essay originally appeared in *Ethics* 97, April 1987.

character." Instead, he proposed that virtue is one and "the name of this ideal form is justice" (1981, pp. 30–31). For Kohlberg the morally good person is simply one who reasons with, and acts on the basis of, principles of justice as fairness.

Despite the fact that Kohlberg's theory has come to dominate the thinking of moral psychologists (but hardly the thinking of moral philosophers who think about moral psychology), critics abound. One of the more widely known challenges to Kohlberg's theory comes from his colleague and former collaborator, Carol Gilligan. Over the past fifteen years, Gilligan has been listening to women and men talk about morality. Her book, *In a Different Voice* (1982), is both a challenge to the comprehensiveness of Kohlberg's theory and a revealing look at the way liberal society distributes various psychological competencies between the sexes. Gilligan describes a moral universe in which men, more often than women, conceive of morality as substantively constituted by obligations and rights and as procedurally constituted by the demands of fairness and impartiality, while women, more often than men, see moral requirements as emerging from the particular needs of others in the context of particular relationships. Gilligan has dubbed this latter orientation the "ethic of care," and she insists that the exclusive focus on justice reasoning has obscured both its psychological reality and its normative significance.

Whereas justice as fairness involves seeing others thinly, as worthy of respect purely by virtue of common humanity, morally good caring requires seeing others thickly, as constituted by their particular human face, their particular psychological and social self. It also involves taking seriously, or at least being moved by, one's particular connection to the other (see Flanagan and Adler 1983). Gilligan's claim is that once the dispositions that underlie such caring are acknowledged, the dominant conception of moral maturity among moral psychologists and moral philosophers will need to be reconceived (Gilligan 1983; also see Blum 1980).

The purpose of this essay is to gain some perspective on the philosophical stakes in the moral psychology debate by surveying and critically evaluating Gilligan's writings subsequent to her book—writings in which she attempts to extend, clarify, and defend her views—as well as recent work of Kohlberg's in which he responds to Gilligan's challenge. Some recent philosophical literature is also discussed.

II

One issue in need of clarification is the precise nature of the ethic of care and its relation within moral personality to the ethic of justice. In her most recent writings, Gilligan characterizes the two ethics as "different ways of viewing the world" that "organize both thinking and feeling" (1986, in press *a*, in press *c*), and she returns continually to the imagery of a gestalt shift (e.g., the vase-face illusion) to make it clear that she thinks that the two ethics involve seeing things in different and competing ways. The justice orientation organizes moral perception by highlighting issues of fairness, right, and obligation. Indeed, a person entirely in the grip of the justice orientation may be able to see a problem as a moral problem only if such issues can be construed in it. The care orientation meanwhile focuses on other saliencies: on the interconnections among the parties involved, on their particular personalities, and on their weal and woe.

The claim is that typically one orientation dominates moral thinking and that the direction of dominance is gender linked. Recent research shows that while most people introduce both care and justice considerations when discussing moral problems, over two-thirds present three-quarters or more considerations in one mode or the other. Furthermore, men and women distribute themselves bimodally on the justice and care ends of the scale (Lyons 1983; Gilligan and Wiggans 1986).

It is significant that there are such differences in the way men and women conceive of the moral domain and in the way they choose to talk about the moral issues they confront in real life. But two things must be kept in mind. First, although one way of conceiving of moral problems dominates, most individuals use both orientations some of the time. Therefore the differences between two individuals with contrasting dominant orientations will be more like the differences between two people—one of whom tends to see physical objects in functional terms and only secondarily in aesthetic terms, and another person with reversed dominance—than like the difference between occupants of totally alien universes. Second, the data on how people in fact conceive of morality have no simple and direct implications on the issues of how the domain of morality is best conceived, what virtues and reasoning skills are required by morality, and how best a particular moral issue is construed.

One need not be committed to any implausible version of moral realism to maintain that the most defensible specification of the moral domain will include issues of both right and good, that moral life requires a multiplicity of virtues, and that the description under which a particular problem is best understood is at least partly constrained by the kind of problem it is. The first two points seem fairly obvious, so let's focus on the third.

In several places, Gilligan suggests that every problem that can be construed morally can be construed from either the justice or care orientation (Gilligan 1986; Gilligan and Wiggans 1986). Suppose this is right. Imagine someone who sees the problem of repaying or forgiving foreign loans as an issue of *love* between nations; or a mother who construes all positive interactions with her children as something they are *owed*. There may still be good reasons for preferring one construal over another. Generally speaking, there are two sorts of grounds that might recommend one construal over another and thus that might recommend educating moral agents to be disposed to make one interpretation rather than another. First, there might be normative reasons. Although a particular type of issue, say, parent-child relations, can be construed theoretically from the perspective of either of Gilligan's two orientations, the different construals lead to different kinds of worlds, one of which is more desirable than the other, all things considered. Second, there might be reasons having to do with our basic psychological makeup for making use of different dispositions and reasoning strategies for dealing with different kinds of problems. For example, if one accepts Hume's insight about the difficulty of widening fellow feeling indefinitely, then it makes sense to inculcate beliefs and principles which produce moral sensitivities in situations where no positive feelings exist among the parties.

The data Gilligan and her co-workers have gathered point to the existence of something like such a psychological division of labor with different kinds of moral problems drawing out different kinds of moral response. Recall that most people use both orientations some of the time and that the choice of orientation depends at least in part on the type of problem posed. Indeed, standard Kohlbergian dilemmas, such as the Heinz dilemma (should Heinz steal the drug which could help his dying wife from the avaricious pharmacist who will not sell it at a fair price?), generate the highest number of justice responses in both sexes; and hypothetical stories that highlight inequality or attachment result in higher rates of justice and care responses, respectively, for both men and women (Gilligan and Wiggans 1986). This is true despite continuous findings of gender differences in responses to open-ended questions about the nature of morality and one's own real-life dilemmas, as well as in the ratio of justice versus care responses to hypothetical moral dilemmas.

Such findings regarding the domain specificity of moral response, especially in light of the point about better and worse construals, indicate that although Gilligan's gestalt-shift metaphor is illuminating in three ways, it is unhelpful and misleading in two others. First, it is helpful in drawing attention to the fact that just as some people have trouble ever seeing one or the other available images in a gestalt illusion, so too there are some people who have trouble understanding talk of rights or alternatively talk of love; they just can't see what you are talking about. Second, the metaphor highlights the findings that for most individuals one way of seeing moral problems dominates the other way of seeing to some degree, and that the direction of dominance is correlated with gender. Finally, the metaphor draws attention to the fact that there are some moral problems—abortion, for example—the proper construal of which is deemed by all parties to be a matter of the greatest importance, but for which the proper construal is an issue of deeply incompatible perception.

There are undoubtedly also problems of less monumental importance for which there are no clear grounds for preferring one construal over the other. In one study by a member of Gilligan's group, teenagers of both sexes were good at switching from their preferred orientation when asked if there was another way to think about a certain problem, but all subjects believed that their preferred mode gave rise to the most defensible solution. Barring radical discrepancies from a normative point of view as to what action is prescribed or how things turn out, there may well be nothing definitive to say about the preferability of one construal over the other in many specific cases (although there might well be objections to general dominance of one orientation), since personal style, even if socially constructed and gender linked, has certain saving graces on the side of cognitive economy once it is in place. Or to put the point more contentiously: in some cases the preferred mode of moral construal may be the most defensible simply because it is preferred.

Nevertheless, what is misleading about the gestalt metaphor is that, just as not all visual stimuli are ambiguous in the way gestalt illusions are, so too not all moral issues are so open to alternative construals. To be sure, the psychological apparatus involved in moral appraisal involves learning and underdetermination in a way visual perception does not, and thus moral construal is more tradition sensitive than visual perception. But again there may be both normative reasons and reasons of cognitive economy for teaching moral agents to be sensitive to certain saliencies (e.g., anonymity among parties, prior explicit contracts) in such a way that these saliencies are more or less sufficient to generate one construal (e.g., a justice construal) rather than some other. As we have seen, some of Gilligan's own data indicate that something like this happens for at least some problems for both men and women.

The second and more important way the gestalt metaphor is misleading has to do with the fact that there is a deep and important difference between visual perception and moral construal which the metaphor obscures. Whereas it is impossible to see both the duck and the rabbit at the same time in the duck-rabbit illusion, it is not impossible to see both the justice and care saliencies in a moral problem and to integrate them in moral deliberation. This is because moral consideration, unlike visual perception, takes place over time and can involve the assimilation and accommodation of as much, and as messy, information as we like. It is wrong, therefore, to suggest, as Gilligan does in one place, that the two perspectives are "fundamentally incompatible" (Gilligan, in press *b;* also see Lyons 1983).

The point is that there is no logical reason why both care and justice considerations cannot be introduced, where relevant, into one and the same reasoning episode. *Heinz,* after all, should steal the drug because it is *his* wife; and his wife should get the drug because *any* human life is more important than any avaricious pharmacist's desire to make some extra money.

This is not to deny that in some cases construing a particular problem from both perspectives will block moral clarity about what should be done (see Flanagan and Adler 1983), nor is it to deny that for the sake of normative elegance and psychological stability it will be important to have some, even imperfect, decision procedure to resolve such conflicts. But, as we have suggested, one possibility is that the saliencies construable in a particular situation will make different sorts of considerations differentially relevant to that situation and, in that way, will keep intractability (but, possibly, not a sense of moral costs) to a minimum. The important point is that there is no impossibility in imagining persons who are both very fair and very caring and who, in addition, have finely honed sensitivities for perceiving moral saliencies and seeing particular problems as problems of certain multifarious kinds.

Thinking of moral psychology as variegated, as composed of a wide array of attitudes, dispositions, rules of thumb, and principles that are designed for multifarious sorts of situations, suggests a move in a more virtue-theoretical direction and, thus, a return to the sort of conceptual model that has been out of favor in the cognitive-developmental tradition since Piaget's *The Moral Judgment of the Child* (1932).[1] Indeed, the more plausibility one assigns to an Aristotelian conception of moral psychology, the more credible will be the suspicion that Gilligan's expansion of Kohlberg's model to include two general orientations is still insufficently fine grained to be adequate from either a psychological or normative point of view. There are three reasons for this. First, we still lack a clear (and remotely complete) taxonomy of the various dispositions—the cognitive and affective attitudes—that constitute the care orientation, and the same goes for the justice orientation. This failure to provide a more fine-grained analysis is more understandable for Kohlberg than for Gilligan. After all, Kohlberg believes that morality is decidedly not a matter of special-purpose virtues, dispositions, and reasoning strategies but, rather, consists of the application of a unified general-purpose style of thinking. But there is every reason to think that Gilligan's program would benefit from moving in a more virtue-theoretical direction insofar as the conception of moral agency she describes is potentially so much thicker than Kohlberg's, embedded as it is in self-conception and social context.

In the second place, we lack a careful analysis of the differences between good and morally problematic or even corrupt kinds of care. Care can be corrupt either because of qualitative features of the caring relationship (e.g., it is based on insincerity or coercion) or because of the relationship's content (e.g., the parties have bad aspirations for each other or give sensitive attention to meeting each other's corrupt needs and desires). (See Baier [1986]; Gilligan does some of this in her own attempt to emulate stage theory [1982, p. 105].)

Third, even if we accept the plausible view that moral psychology is neither totally modular (as in vulgar Aristotelianism) nor totally unified and general purpose (as in vulgar Kantianism) but, rather, is tiered, containing both virtuous and vicious dispositions to think and react in certain ways as well as a general higher-level moral orientation (which may or may not have power over the lower levels), there is good reason

---

1. The rest of cognitive psychology, of course, has gone increasingly homuncular.

to think that there are more than two such general orientations.[2] For example, Charles Taylor (1982) has described moral outlooks guided by the commitments to personal integrity, to perfection, and to liberation which cannot be assimilated under either of Gilligan's two rubrics, let alone under Kohlberg's one (see Miller [1985] for descriptions of some even more alien moral orientations); and it is hard to see how virtues like courage or moderation fall under either orientation.

The issues of the scope of morality and the range of realizable moral conceptions are of the utmost importance. What moral psychologists conceive of as possible determines how they understand and classify moral personalities. But if the possibility range is too narrowly conceived or too culture bound or too gripped by a contentious normative conception, actual psychological realities may be missed.

In addition to these issues, there is still the important question of precisely what sort of adjustment Gilligan thinks work such as hers warrants in our conception of moral maturity. She was not clear on this matter in her book, and her recent work still shifts between the ideas that the two ethics are incompatible alternatives to each other but are both adequate from a normative point of view; that they are complements of one another involved in some sort of tense interplay; and that each is deficient without the other and thus ought to be integrated.

One might think that our claim that there is no logical incompatibility between the two ethics and thus no logical problem with bringing both kinds of considerations to any problem (which is not to imply that the two sets of concepts can be applied without conflict in every place) means that there is nothing to block the tactic of pursuing the integrationist strategy less hesitantly. But here Gilligan has some interesting things to say about the psychological origins of the two orientations. Although there may be no logical incompatibility between the concepts of justice and care (and their suites), Gilligan suggests in many places that there is a deep-seated psychological tension between the two perspectives, a tension rooted in the fact that the two ethics are built out of etiologically distinct underlying competencies which make different and competing psychological demands on moral agents. It is the differences in origin and underlying cognitive and motivational structure which make integration of the two orientations in particular moral agents hard to realize and which, at the same time, explain the data on gender differences.

2. Both Gilligan and Kohlberg take narrative data to be a fairly accurate index of the more general orientation. This is problematic. The relationship between first-person speech acts and underlying psychology is a widely discussed issue in contemporary philosophy of mind and cognitive psychology, and there is reason to think that our deficiencies in giving accurate self-assessments run very deep. Confabulation is an especially salient worry when the speech acts are being offered in response to issues which connect so obviously as do moral problems with issues of self-worth and with how one is perceived by others. Gilligan and Kohlberg are strangely silent on such matters.

Gilligan accepts a roughly neo-Freudian account of early childhood. This account turns on two main variables: (1) the psychological situation of the child as both dependent and attached and (2) the typical differences between maternal and paternal relations with the child. The basic story goes like this: The child has continuous experiences of both her relative powerlessness vis-à-vis her parents and her powerful attachment to them. The experiences of powerlessness and inequality give rise to the search for independence and equality and thereby provide fertile ground for the notions of fairness and autonomy (and their opposites) to take root. Meanwhile, the experiences of deep attachment and connection, of moving and being moved by others, provide the ground for the dispositions that will guide later attachments—for compassion, love, and altruism. Together, "the different dynamics of early childhood inequality and attachment lay the groundwork for two moral visions—of justice and of care" (Gilligan and Wiggans 1986).

Even if one accepts that it is the alleged tension between the two kinds of early experiences that grounds the tension between the two ethics (one might be skeptical on grounds that there is a high degree of overlap between the two kinds of experiences), this tension does not explain the data on gender differences. Here Gilligan follows Nancy Chodorow's (1978) influential analysis of gender differentiation. Initially for children of both sexes, the relationship with the primary caretaker, typically the mother, is one of powerful attachment and identification. However, as the child gets older and begins the project of carving out a self-concept, she starts to identify strongly with her same-sex parent, and parents reinforce this identification. In the typical family where the mother has a greater nurturing role than the father, boys will have to shift their initial identification with the mother to the father. Girls, meanwhile, do not need to reorient their initial identification but only to intensify the one that already exists. This means that the project of separation is more salient and more pressing for boys than for girls. Furthermore, because of the mutual feelings of identification between mother and daughter, girls will have richer experience than boys with attachment and con-nectedness. According to Chodorow, "Boys . . . have to curtail their primary love and sense of empathic tie with their mother. A boy has been required to engage in more emphatic individuation and a more defensive firming of experienced ego boundaries . . . . Girls emerge from this period with a basis for 'empathy' built into their primary definition of self in a way that boys do not" (1978, pp. 166–67).

Assuming this story is true, it should be obvious, first, that there is nothing necessary (although there may be biological and social pressures in certain directions) about the way we arrange nurturance nor about the particular ways parents treat their male and female children, and thus the story is not required to turn out exactly the way it now does. If there were greater sharing in nurturance by both parents, the process of acquiring a self-concept would not make such different demands and rest on such different experiences for boys and girls. Resultant attitudes about autonomy, attachment, and so on might not be as different as they now are. But, second, the latter analysis does indicate why, given current practices (with their long cultural histories), we cannot be sanguine about the possibilities for inculcating moral sensibilities which support both a rich sense of justice and care and a well developed sense of autonomy and connection in one and the same agent.

Full-fledged integration aside, it is important to consider what role, if any, the experiences and dispositions which underlie each ethic have in contributing to morally good forms of the other. Again, it is important not to lose sight of the fact that the early experiences of powerlessness and attachment overlap.

Annette Baier has made some interesting suggestions in this regard. Her basic insight is similar to Hume's about the problem with Hobbes's state-of-nature hypothesis, namely, it ignores the fact that for any human interaction to take place, including even "a war of each against each," there must first be family and nurturance. Otherwise the helpless infant will not survive its first nights.

Baier argues first that theories of justice, including Rawls's, need to assume that there will be loving parents in order to ensure the stability of a just society and the development of a sense of justice in new members. "Rawls's theory like so many other theories of obligation, in the end must take out a loan not only on the natural duty of parents to care for children ... but on the natural virtue of parental love .... The virtue of being a *loving* parent must supplement the natural duties and obligations, if the just society is to last beyond the first generation" (Baier 1985, unpublished section).

Second, Baier argues that the dispositions to be fair and to keep contracts presuppose (psychologically and normally, but not logically) that the agent has been cared for and has had experiences of trust. "Promises presuppose both experience of longer on-going trust relationships *not* necessarily initiated by any voluntary act (with parents or with friends) so that the advantages of such future-involving mutual trust be already clear, and also an already established climate of trust enabling one to choose to get close enough to a stranger to exchange words or goods or handshakes with him" (Baier 1986).

Baier's argument suggests the further insight that the moral disposition to be just normally presupposes not only that the agent is attached to certain abstract concepts and ideals, but also, more fundamentally, that he is attached to and cares for his community, and that he has a sense that his own good and that of those he cares for most is associated with general adherence to these ideals. Without such cares and attachments, first to those one loves and secondarily to some wider community to which one's projects and prospects are intimately joined, the moral disposition to justice—as opposed to the purely prudential disposition to justice—has no place to take root.

There is no objection in principle to using one set of virtues and dispositions to support or strengthen another set. The point is simply, as Baier puts it, that "a decent morality will *not* depend for its stability on forces to which it gives no moral recognition" (1985, unpublished section).

III

The question arises as to what Kohlberg makes of the ethic of care and the various dispositions and experiences that constitute it. What sort of recognition does he think this ethical perspective deserves? What is its relation to the conception of morality as justice that he more than anyone else has championed?

At first, Kohlberg (1982) flirted with the strategy of simply denying that there is such an ethic and thereby denying that there is anything of *moral* psychological importance to recognize. Kohlberg admits that initially he found Gilligan's work unwelcome and preferred to read it as concerned with ego psychology but not with moral psychology (1982, p. 514). This suggestion in itself displays a very unrealistic view about the isolation of moral psychology from overall personality.

Lately Kohlberg seems to have come around to seeing that Gilligan's challenge was more apt than he first admitted. In two long coauthored essays (both with Charles Levine and Alexandra Hewer) in the second volume of his collected papers (1984), Kohlberg attempts to set forth a more complete and satisfactory response to Gilligan's work. On an initial reading, Kohlberg appears to concede many of the main points of contention. Reflecting on his original theory, he writes, "I assumed that the core of morality and moral development was deontological; that is it was a matter of rights and duties or prescriptions" (p. 225). These "starting assumptions led to the design of a research instrument measuring reasoning about dilemmas of conflicting rights or the distribution of scarce resources, that is, justice concerns. We did not use dilemmas about prosocial concerns for others that were not frameable as rights conflicts" (p. 304). "We admit, however, that the emphasis on the virtue of justice in my work does not fully reflect all that is recognized as being part of the moral domain" (p. 227).

In speaking specifically of his standard measurement tool, Kohlberg says, "We do agree that our justice dilemmas do not pull for the care and response orientation, and we do agree that our scoring manual does not lead to a full assessment of this aspect of moral thinking" (1984, p. 343; see also pp. 305–7 and 622–23). Kohlberg now recommends, therefore, understanding his theory as a "rational reconstruction of justice reasoning: emphasizing the nomenclature 'justice reasoning,' since the . . . stages have more typically been called stages of moral development [by him]" (1984, p. 224).

Despite such concessions, it is really quite difficult to put one's finger on how Kohlberg now intends his theory to be interpreted, and sometimes what is conceded with one hand seems to be withdrawn with the other. Indeed, on a closer reading, it is hard to read Kohlberg as completely sincere in the latter concessions, for he also puts forward a variety of claims that are at odds with them.

For example, although Kohlberg now acknowledges that his theory is not comprehensive, he continues to promote a restricted conception of morality which belies this concession. In particular, he continues to make two common but questionable claims about the nature of morality. First, there is the claim that all moral judgments have certain formal features such as prescriptivity (i.e., they entail obligations) and universalizability (1984, pp. 293–96). Second, there is the claim that *"moral* judgments or principles have the central function of resolving interpersonal or social conflicts, that is, conflicts of claims or rights" (p. 216).

Both points are problematic. With regard to the first point, imagine a complex judgment about how one can best help a friend who is depressed. The judgment here will involve assessment of particular features of both parties. What one can do for a friend is, after all, determined in large part by the kinds of persons both are, the characteristic patterns of interaction between the two, and so on. It is implausible to think that there is anything interestingly universalizable about such a judgment or that there is necessarily any judgment of obligation involved. Indeed, where friendship or love truly exists, thinking about what one is obligated to do can, as Bernard Williams has put it in a related context, involve "one thought too many" (1981, p. 18).

With regard to the second point, the same example serves to show that it is simply not obvious that morality has the central function of resolving "conflicts of claims or rights." To be sure, this is an important function of moral theory, and the function most visible in public debates, but to conceive of this function as central and other functions of morality as peripheral is to beg the interesting question of how best to conceive of the domain of morality. There is too much moral energy expended on self-improvement and the refinement of character, on respectful interactions with loved ones, friends, and strangers, and on supererogation for such a claim to be acceptable without considerable defense. None is given.

At one point Kohlberg stresses that his conception of "morality as justice best renders our view of morality as universal. It restricts morality to a central minimal core, striving for universal agreement in the face of more relativist conceptions of the good" (1984, p. 306). And in many places he emphasizes that there are two senses of the word "moral"— one sense is that of "the moral point of view" with the alleged formal features, the other sense refers to "personal" issues—to things like friendship, family relations, supererogation, and so on (p. 232). Kohlberg points out that how one treats the latter issues is widely acknowledged to be a relative matter (but, one must stress, not completely relative).

Still two issues must be kept distinct. It is one thing to want to study a certain kind of moral thinking because it is more stable (the function of a theory of justice is, after all, to produce such stability in interpersonal relations among individuals who may have no personal connections) or because it is easier to talk about in terms of the theoretical framework of cognitive-developmental stage theory. Kohlberg (1984, pp. 236–49) makes it clear that one reason he prefers to study justice reasoning is that he thinks that there are "hard" stages, that is, stages which satisfy standard Piagetian criteria of universality, irreversibility, and so on, of justice reasoning (see Flanagan [1984] for doubts about this) but not of reasoning about personal issues. But such theoretical attractions are irrelevant to the issues of psychological realism, normative adequacy, and the domain of the moral.

Once Kohlberg's proprietary attempt to restrict our conception of the domain of the moral is seen for what it is, his "total disagreement" (1984, p. 342) with Gilligan regarding gender differences is of little moment. Kohlberg clings to the fact that such differences are minimal or nonexistent in studies using his standard justice dilemmas as the test instrument (see Walker [1984] for a review; but see Baumrind [in press] for a criticism of Walker). The fact remains that there are, as Kohlberg acknowledges (p. 350), gender differences in preferred orientation, in response ratios, and so on, even if there are none for one restricted type of moral problem. Such findings point to differences in moral psychology unless one implausibly restricts the domain of inquiry.

In several places Kohlberg tries a more interesting tactic than the one of restricting the conception of morality to what he studies. This tactic starts by accepting that "personal morality" is part of the domain of the moral (1984, pp. 234–35) but then moves to claim that justice lies in some subsuming relation to this morality. In speaking specifically of Gilligan's work, he says, "The two senses of the word *moral* do not represent two different moral orientations existing at the same level of generality and validity" (p. 232).

The overall strategy is to make an argument for the "primacy of justice," either by arguing that considerations of justice trump considerations of care when the two conflict or by arguing that justice is in some sense necessary for care but not the other way around (see Kohlberg 1981, p. xiii; Kohlberg 1984, p. 305).

The first idea, that the demands of justice must be met before all others, is a familiar one within the context of liberal political theory. However, it is important to emphasize that, even within the liberal tradition, the claim that justice is trump applies in the first instance to the arrangement of basic social institutions. Many liberal philosophers are hesitant about any simple and straightforward extension of the deontological constraints governing political practices to individual behavior.

Furthermore, even if one holds that considerations of justice are overriding at the individual level, nothing follows about how often considerations of justice are germane. If, as seems the case for most of us, the larger part of moral life takes place in situations and contexts in which considerations of justice are not especially relevant, then the "primacy of justice" must be an important principle to have, and sensitivities to issues of justice will need to be well honed; but the virtue of justice will not be doing most of the work in the actual moral lives of most persons.

The second idea—that justice is necessary for care—comes in two forms. First, there is the claim that conditions of social justice must obtain for the personal virtues associated with both justice and care to thrive. "It seems to us . . . that morally valid forms of caring and community presuppose prior conditions and judgments of justice" (Kohlberg 1984, p. 305). Second, there is the claim that the personal virtue of justice is necessary for the personal virtue of care. "In our view special obligations of care presuppose, but go beyond, the general duties of justice, which are necessary, but not sufficient for them" (p. 229). "More than justice is required for resolving many complex moral dilemmas, but justice is a necessary element of any morally adequate resolution of these conflicts" (p. 370).

The first point is important. There is something obviously right about the view that morality is not a purely individual project and that personal virtue takes root best in a just society. But once we push things back to the basic social conditions necessary for morality, we come again upon the point that all societies, just or unjust, stable or unstable, egalitarian or nonegalitarian, presuppose prior relations of care between new members and those members involved in child rearing. There is in the end something misleading in the widely held view that justice is the first virtue of society. Indeed, although it is wise to resist lexically ordering the basic virtues required for an ongoing morally good society or for a morally good personality, there is no incoherence in putting care first when it comes to creating the possibility conditions for family, wider community, and individual character in the first place.

The second claim that personal justice has some essential connection to the other virtues comes in several versions. The strongest and most implausible claim is that personal justice is sufficient for moral goodness overall. With the possible exception of Plato, no one has held this view. The reason is that it is easy to imagine someone who espouses and abides by some defensible conception of justice but who is morally deficient in other ways.

Kohlberg intends something weaker than the implausible sufficiency claim. His proposal, however, is ambiguous between two different claims: (1) that experiences of fairness and the development of the disposition to be just are necessary for the causal formation of whatever psychological competencies turn out to be associated with Gilligan's ethic of care, but not vice versa; and (2) that the display of any other virtue necessarily presupposes possession of the virtue of justice, but not vice versa. Showing either claim 1 or 2 would help support the claim that the two ethics do not "exist at the same level of generality and validity."

With regard to claim 1, we have already expressed the opinion that experiences of care and caring have an important role in laying the foundations for any ethical sense whatsoever (see Noddings [1984] for someone who makes too much of this point). Hence we already have grounds for doubting the claim that justice has some unique foundational status with regard to the formation of other virtues or to overall moral psychology.

When one focuses less on the basic experiences necessary for developing a moral sense and looks more closely at the sort of explicit moral instruction that takes place between parents and children (something neither Gilligan nor Kohlberg does), the claim that the acquisition of the personal virtue of justice has unique foundational status also seems implausible. To be sure, parents often say things like "Kate, look how sad David is; he deserves a turn too." But it is most plausible to read such statements as presupposing that some of the competencies, dispositions, and beliefs required by justice and care are required by morally good forms of either. It is hard to see how we could teach children about kindness without teaching them certain things about fairness, but it is equally hard to see how we could teach them about fairness without teaching them certain things about kindness and sensitivity to the aims and interests of others. The situation is one of mutual support rather than a necessary condition in only one direction.

The fact that normally both justice and care are built out of some of the same underlying competencies does not imply, however, that a mature sense of justice is necessary for the display of the other virtues or for responding to every particular moral problem (claim 2 above). First, there are some persons who we think of as virtuous in certain ways and in certain domains, but who we do not think are very fair or just; and the same holds true in the other direction. Second, it is possible to imagine individuals in whom beneficence is so sensitively and globally developed that the virtue of justice, as normally conceived, is not only unnecessary for the display of the other virtues, but is even unnecessary in situations in which ordinary persons with less saintly personalities would need to call upon it. Third, and setting such moral exotica aside, there are many moral problems which have nothing to do with justice. It is implausible, therefore, to think the personal virtue of justice is necessarily implicated in our dealings with such problems.

To question the truth of the necessary condition claim as a psychological thesis is not to deny what is normatively important about it. A morally good life overall requires fairness because the possession of the virtues associated with care might well, if not tempered by justice, result in immorality, for example, chauvinism, in certain circumstances. But the same holds true in the other direction.

In several places, Kohlberg tries to make the normative point but links it with the implausible psychological one. He says, "In our philosophic end point of moral reasoning, the hypothetical sixth stage, there occurs, we believe, an integration of justice and care that forms a single moral principle" (1984, p. 344). And elsewhere he claims that the two orientations converge at the highest stage because the "principle of persons as ends is common to both" (p. 356).

This way of talking is misleading in two respects. First, Kohlberg now acknowledges (1982, p. 523; 1984, p. 215) that his highest stage of moral development is purely hypothetical; that in over twenty-five years of research, he and his colleagues have been unable to confirm the existence of stage 6. This means that the claim that justice and care converge at the highest stage to "form a single moral principle" is a claim for which there is no empirical evidence. Second, it is extremely doubtful for reasons Gilligan and others (Blum 1980) have expressed, that a normatively adequate moral psychology is best thought of in terms of the possession of a single unified faculty and, even less plausibly, in terms of the possession of a "single moral principle."

Still, Gilligan's own view that morality consists of "two voices" needs further refinement, development, and defense before its full psychological and normative importance is clear. We need to know more about many things, including the precise nature and extent of the gender differences, the social causes of these differences, content effects, the fine-grained features of the ethic of care, the role of the competencies it makes use of in justice reasoning, and the plausibility of carving morality into only two voices.

IV

The view that there is one ideal type of moral personality—a unique way moral psychology is best ordered and moral reasoning conducted—is the psychological side of the coin whose other face contains the image of morality as a unitary domain with a determinate and timeless nature. Much recent work in moral philosophy has questioned this view of morality as a clearly carved domain for which a unified theory can be produced. Such work suggests that our attitudes and expectations about underlying moral psychology may also need to be revised. Rejection of the doctrine of the "unity of the moral" (Taylor 1982) may also require rejection of its close relative—the doctrine that there is one ideal type of moral personality.

A reasonable hypothesis is that moral personality occurs at a level too open to both social and self-determination for us to expect there to be any unique and determinate set of dispositions, capacities, attitudes, and types of reasoning which ideally underwrite all moral responsiveness. This means that we will have to learn to tolerate, and perhaps applaud, a rich diversity of good moral personalities. The fact that this will be hard for those still in the grip of the doctrine of the "unity of the moral" in no way belies the possibility that this is the right road to go.

REFERENCES

Anscombe, G. E. M. 1958. Modern Moral Philosophy. *Philosophy* 33:1–19. Reprinted in *Ethics*, ed. Judith J. Thomson and Gerald Dworkin, pp. 186–210. New York: Harper & Row, 1968.

Baier, Annette C. 1985. What Do Women Want in a Moral Theory? *Nous* 19:53–65, including a section omitted from published article that was provided by courtesy of the author.

Baier, Annette C. 1986. Trust and Antitrust. *Ethics* 96:231–60.

Baumrind, Diana. In press. Sex Differences in Moral Reasoning: Response to Walker's Conclusion That There Are None. *Child Development.*

Blum, Lawrence. 1980. *Friendship, Altruism, and Morality.* London: Routledge & Kegan Paul.

Chodorow, Nancy. 1978. *The Reproduction of Mothering.* Berkeley: University of California Press.

Flanagan, Owen. 1984. *The Science of the Mind.* Bradford Books Series. Cambridge, Mass.: MIT Press.

Flanagan, Owen, and Adler, Jonathan. 1983. Impartiality and Particularity. *Social Research* 50:576–96.

Gilligan, Carol. 1982. *In a Different Voice.* Cambridge, Mass.: Harvard University Press.

Gilligan, Carol. 1983. Do the Social Sciences Have an Adequate Theory of Moral Development? In *Social Sciences as Moral Inquiry,* ed. N. Hann, R. Bellah, P. Rabinow, and W. Sullivan, pp. 33–51. New York: Columbia University Press.

Gilligan, Carol. 1986. Reply to "On *In a Different Voice:* An Interdisciplinary Forum." *Signs* 11:324–33.

Gilligan, Carol. In press *a.* Remapping Development: The Power of Divergent Data. In *Value Presuppositions in Theories of Human Development,* ed. L. Cirillo and S. Wapner. Hillsdale, N.J.: Lawrence Erlbaum Associates.

Gilligan, Carol. In press *b.* Remapping the Moral Domain: New Images of the Self in Relationship. In *Reconstructing Individualism: Autonomy, Individuality and the Self in Western Thought,* ed. T. C. Heller, M. Sosna, and D. Wellbery. Stanford, Calif.: Stanford University Press.

Gilligan, Carol. In press *c.* Moral Orientation and Moral Development. In *Women and Moral Theory,* ed. Eva Feder Kittay and Diana T. Meyers. Totowa, N.J.: Rowman & Littlefield.

Gilligan, Carol, and Wiggans, Grant. 1986. The Origins of Morality in Early Childhood Relationships. Harvard University, typescript.

Kohlberg, Lawrence. 1981. *Essays on Moral Development.* Vol. 1, *The Philosophy of Moral Development.* New York: Harper & Row.

Kohlberg, Lawrence. 1982. A Reply to Owen Flanagan and Some Comments on the Puka-Goodpaster Exchange. *Ethics* 92:513–28.

Kohlberg, Lawrence, with Levine, Charles, and Hewer, Alexandra. 1984. Moral Stages: A Current Statement. Response to Critics. Appendix A. In *Essays on Moral Development.* Vol. 2, *The Psychology of Moral Development,* by Lawrence Kohlberg, pp. 207–386, 621–39. New York: Harper & Row.

Lyons, Nona Plessner. 1983. Two Perspectives: On Self, Relationships, and Morality. *Harvard Educational Review* 53:125–45.

MacIntyre, Alasdair. 1982. How Moral Agents Become Ghosts. *Synthese* 53:292–312.

Miller, Richard. 1985. Ways of Moral Learning. *Philosophical Review* 94:507–56.

Murdoch, Iris. 1970. *The Sovereignty of the Good.* Boston: Routledge & Kegan Paul.

Noddings, Nel. 1984. *Caring: A Feminine Approach to Ethics.* Berkeley and Los Angeles: University of California Press.

Piaget, Jean. 1932. *The Moral Judgment of the Child.* New York: Free Press.

Taylor, Charles. 1982. The Diversity of Goods. In *Utilitarianism and Beyond,* ed. Amartya Sen and Bernard Williams. Cambridge, Mass.: Harvard University Press.

Walker, Lawrence J. 1984. Sex Differences in the Development of Moral Reasoning: A Critical Review. *Child Development* 55:677–91.

Williams, Bernard. 1981. Persons, Character, and Morality. In *Moral Luck,* by Bernard Williams. Cambridge: Cambridge University Press.

Should Women Think in Terms of Rights?*

John Hardwig

Women's liberation, it is often said, strikes closer to home than other forms of human liberation. Although basic shifts in attitudes are required for the liberation of, for example, workers or blacks and other ethnic minorities, these types of liberation could be accomplished without fundamental changes in what we call our "private" lives or our personal relationships. The liberation of blacks or workers is largely an affair of public roles and institutions, a matter of social justice, and it is thus carried out relatively impersonally and anonymously in the marketplace and workplace, the university and governmental institutions. Granted, if the liberation of blacks and workers is to be complete, I might have to be willing to have some in my club and my suburb. Some of my best friends might then be blacks or workers, and I might even have to be willing to have my daughter marry one. Nonetheless, it might well be true that my club and neighborhood, my friendships, and my relationship to my daughter could go on pretty much as before, once "they" had been admitted.

Women's liberation encompasses these sorts of public issues; it certainly does include matters of social justice impersonally administered by impersonal institutions. And these issues are important. But women's liberation goes further and invades my personal and private life. If women are to be liberated, I must learn new ways of loving and leaving, and I must develop new modes of caring, different styles of friendship, and a new kind of sexuality. Because women's liberation strikes closer to home in this way, gut-level issues and responses are raised. One might expect me and other members of the dominant class—males, in this case—to be more threatened by women's liberation than by other forms of human liberation. Women, as well, may be more threatened and frightened by

* I have benefited from comments on earlier versions of this paper by Amelie Rorty and members of her 1980 NEH seminar—Mary Wiseman, Marcia Aufauser, Lynn Konrad, Dan DiNicola—and by Martha Lee Osborne and many of her students, Mary Read English, Jim Read, Eva Hill, Ileana Grams, B. C. Postow, and George Graham. Those who are familiar with the thought of these philosophers will easily recognize that many of them think that I did not learn nearly enough from their comments.

This essay originally appeared in *Ethics* 94, April 1984.

the prospect of their liberation than are other oppressed classes. But if the liberation of women is also the liberation of men, the rewards of this kind of liberation should also be greater, for it promises to transform our personal and private lives, not just to reorganize our public institutions.

It is clear that women have been oppressed. And they have been oppressed not only in the context of large-scale, impersonal social institutions but in the context of intimate, personal relationships as well. Thus it has seemed to many feminists that we could move toward healthier personal relationships if we would think more about the rights of persons in intimate relationships. In order to combat the tendency for men and women to fall into roles which relegate women and their interests to a position of inferiority, personal relationships—marriage, love, friendship—should be seen on the model of a contract between independent, ideally equal parties, both of whom stand to benefit from a trade between them. Perhaps the contract should even be made explicit, thus defining the expectations, obligations, and rights of all parties. If an explicit contract could be formulated, perhaps it could be made legally enforceable, thus putting teeth in the often toothless bite of moral reason. But putting the question of legal contracts and rights aside, it seems clear to many that we need to define the moral rights of persons, especially women, in personal relationships.

However, it is not at all clear to me that the ethical categories that serve us well in contexts of relatively impersonal relationships serve us equally well in the context of personal relationships. I want, then, to make a rough distinction between personal and impersonal relationships.[1] I admit, for present purposes, that we need the category of rights to generate an ethics of impersonal relationships and that, consequently, women should think in terms of rights when raising public issues about the kind of social justice that is impersonally legislated and administered by impersonal institutions. But the question I want to raise is this, What kind of descriptive and ethical categories are appropriate in the context of close personal relationships?

I want to avoid, if possible, the question of how we are to define "close personal relationships" because the problems of definition would require another essay. I hope it will suffice to say that I want to talk about relationships characterized by intimacy, genuine care, love, and emotional involvement and that friendship, love, marriage, and family relationships, when they are healthy at least, provide the main examples of what I am calling a personal relationship. (Although the parent-child relationship is usually a close personal relationship, I will restrict my analysis to close personal relationships among adults because I am not clear enough about how to think about children and the parent-child relationship.)

---

1. The reader will easily be able to discover examples from a range of cases that fall between what I am calling personal and impersonal relationships. Definition and exploration of these kinds of intermediate cases would become interesting and important if the thesis of this essay is correct.

I will argue that thinking in terms of rights is not the way to understand what is going on in close personal relationships, that the category of rights is not an appropriate ethical category for healthy personal relationships, and that it is not the basis for an appropriate ideal for personal relationships. Let us begin by examining four different but related reasons for my view that thinking in terms of rights is not the way to think about close personal relationships.

I

1. The motivation for doing good things for those who are close to us or for not harming them must be different from the motivation involved in respecting rights. A right in you imposes an obligation on me, and I appropriately respect your rights out of an awareness of that obligation. But we do good things for those we love because we want to do them. And this motivation is important to those who are close to us; in fact it may be more important than the things that result from it. Consequently, the good things we do are tainted and perhaps even unacceptable if they are done out of a sense of obligation or because the other has a right to them. ("I don't want you to take me out, I want you to want to go out with me. If you don't want to go, let's just forget it.")[2]

In fact, my responsibilities in personal relationships cannot be fulfilled out of a sense of obligation without seriously undermining the whole relationship or revealing thereby that it is not what we had hoped and wanted it to be. I remember a student bringing my lecture on Kant's ethics to a grinding halt by asking, "Is Kant saying that I should sleep with my boyfriend out of a sense of duty?" And if a faithful husband of thirty-seven years were, on his deathbed, to turn to his wife and say, "My conscience is clear, Helen, I have always respected your rights," her whole marriage would turn to ashes. If we are close and I do not see myself as respecting your rights and you would be appalled if I did see myself in that way, then the outside ethicist ought to hesitate, at least, before he or she says, "See how he respects her rights."

2. Rights are impersonally defined, but what we want from an intimate relationship is personal affirmation. Rights are general or universal in the sense that anyone in a similar situation can claim the same rights, whereas my relationship to those I am close to is not general or universal, and it cannot be impersonally defined. Rather, my relationship to you, if we are close, is a relationship to *you*, dependent on and defined by your unique individuality and mine. If the dying husband or my dutiful

---

2. This point and many others in this essay obviously suggest that many arguments against thinking in terms of rights could also be advanced against thinking in terms of duties in the context of personal relationships. That is correct. I think I would also argue that duty is an inappropriate category in healthy personal relationships or at least that the characteristic motive in healthy personal relationships cannot be a sense of duty. However, this claim goes beyond my present scope, for although rights do imply correlative duties, a theory of duty can be developed that does not presuppose or imply a correlative theory of rights.

ethics student were to add, "And I would have done the same for anyone in your situation," that would only make matters worse.[3]

In other words, there is a difference between respecting a person and loving an individual. I respect a person, or should do so, simply because he or she is a person, but I love you because you are you, not anyone else. The category of rights is appropriate to understanding what it means to respect a person, but precisely because rights can be generally or impersonally defined, they do not elucidate what it means to affirm or care for someone. If I no longer care for you, I will still be able to respect you as a person and honor the rights you have because you are a person. But if you love me, this will not be at all what you wanted me to do.

3. My responsibilities in a personal relationship are both broader and narrower than the obligations to respect a set of rights. Rights are specifiable, in principle at least, but I doubt that there is any way to specify what my responsibilities are to my partner, lover, or friend. Also I must always be in a position to respect the rights of others, but I may be unable to fulfill my responsibilities to you as a friend, lover, or partner. Because rights are specifiable and one must always be capable of fulfilling the obligations specified by them, thinking in terms of rights encourages a kind of minimalistic ethical thinking that is inappropriate in cases of emotional involvement. If we are close, I will do many things for you that you have no right to, and I will not see my responsibilities as exhausted by respect for your rights.

Moreover, it is not the case that respect for the rights of someone who is close to me is a necessary but not sufficient condition for a healthy personal relationship. Rather, my responsibilities in a personal relationship are both broader and narrower than the obligations to respect another's rights. If you are my friend, I expect you to do more for me than respect my rights, but there are also many ways in which you do not need to respect my rights. You can invade my privacy, interrupt what I am doing, fail to respect my private property, verbally abuse or perhaps even physically assault me, and it is all right so long as I know that you are my friend. In these situations, I do not experience my rights as being violated or myself as waiving or deciding not to claim my rights. I do not conceptualize the situation in terms of rights at all. Precisely because you are my friend

---

3. The phrase "in your situation" is sometimes to be specified in ways that involve special rights, not just general rights. Although an appeal to special rights would soften the force of this point, it would not eliminate it completely. The wife in my example would not be much comforted to know that her dying husband had stuck with her because of a promise he made thirty-seven years ago and that he would have felt similarly bound to anyone to whom he had made such a promise. Nor would the reservations of my ethics student be quieted by pointing out that she is not obligated to have sex with anyone, but only with anyone with whom she has contracted this kind of relationship. For her reservations rest on the understanding that it is fundamentally unsound and inappropriate to have sex with anyone out of a sense of obligation or of his right to it.

and I know that you care for me and will keep my interests in mind, you don't have to obey the rules that govern more impersonal relationships.[4]

4. Rights have to do with the means that one employs in pursuing whatever ends one may have, but intimate relationships are supposed to be ends, not means for the pursuit of ends. The idea that you have rights which must be respected leaves me free to pursue any ends I may desire, so long as the means I employ do not violate your rights. But a personal relationship presupposes that I desire you, that you are one of my ends. For if you and your well-being are not among my ends, I cannot be said to love or care for you.

In Kantian language, the notion of respecting rights means respecting others as ends in themselves, whereas in a personal relationship, the other is to be one of my ends. Kant saw clearly that one cannot be obligated to desire a given end and that no one has the right to be the end of another. "Love," as he put it, "as an affection cannot be commanded."[5] In a healthy personal relationship, I do not respect you (in the Kantian sense) as an independent being with independent ends that have as much right to fulfillment as my ends.[6] Rather I want you, and I want your well-being, and your ends are my ends too. To have you as one of my ends is thus to see you and the realization of your goals as part of me and the realization of my goals. In healthy intimate relationships, the Kantian distinction between altruistic, moral regard for the ends of others

---

4. There is an oversimplification here which results from talking about personal relationships as if they were static and timeless. I believe that what usually happens in the history of personal relationships is this: When I am first getting to know you and find myself wanting to develop a personal relationship with you, I may scrupulously respect your rights in order to show you that I am not the kind of person who selfishly rides roughshod over others and who is thus not the kind of person you would want to be close to. In the midst of a healthy personal relationship, neither of us will, I submit, think in terms of rights. But if our relationship should disintegrate or decay, we may well begin to think in terms of rights again. And yet it is perhaps worth noting that it may not be absolutely necessary to think in terms of rights even in the worst case, when a personal relationship fails. Even in cases of divorce, which tend to be more brutal than fallings out between unmarried lovers and friends, the best endings are those that can be managed amicably without resorting to making antagonistic claims against each other. This can be done if both parties continue to care for each other and for the interests of each other even after it becomes apparent that the relationship can not or will not work. We should aspire, I believe, to learn how even to end personal relationships without resorting to thinking in terms of rights.

5. Immanuel Kant, *Fundamental Principles of the Metaphysics of Morals*, trans. T. K. Abbott (Indianapolis: Bobbs-Merrill Co., 1949), p. 17.

6. This is not, of course, to say that I do not value your independence if we are close, including your independence from me. Rather there is an important distinction between respecting you as an independent being and valuing your independence. This difference comes out when we reflect on the fact that, when we are close, your independence is and should be important to me in a way that the independence of most other people is not. Valuing your independence when we are close will also require rather different attitudes and actions of me than merely respecting someone as an independent being.

and egoistic pursuit of my own ends fails because the distinction between egoism and altruism ultimately makes no sense in this context.

II

These difficulties with thinking in terms of rights in personal relationships grow out of a more fundamental difficulty. Thinking in terms of rights rests on a picture, first sketched by Hobbes and then made more palatable by Locke, of the person as atomistic, primarily egoistic, and asocial— only accidentally and externally related to others. If we are lucky our independent interests may coincide or happily divide in a symbiotic relationship (e.g., I like to write philosophy papers, and you like to read them), but we should not expect this to be the normal state of affairs. Consequently, when we interact, our interaction is normally a trade relationship: I will give you something or do something for you, but only if you will give me something or do something comparable for me in return. A contract, implicit or explicit, may thus be necessary to lay down guidelines that will protect the interests of the party who confers the first benefit or, more generally, to insure that the flow of benefits will not become primarily or exclusively one-way. But if you and I undertake to trade, each with our own independent interests in mind, neither of us is interested primarily in fairness, and whoever is in a position of power can be expected to make trade agreements on the basis of that power, for to do otherwise would be contrary to his or her interest. Consequently, trade relationships tend to become power relationships, and we have need to talk in terms of rights, to make claims against each other, to define obligations that limit the pursuit of independent self-interest—all in the hope that, if we do so and these rights are respected, no one will get trampled in our pursuits of our independent and conflicting interests.

But I want to insist that love is never and marriage is not standardly or normatively a contract, though this may be the only way our law can define them. Friendship, love, brotherhood, and sisterhood are neither trade relationships nor the lucky confluence of interests. We do not need rights in healthy personal relationships, for rights are to protect us from others, and we do not need to be protected from those who understand and care for us. In healthy personal relationships, the model of independent self-interests simply does not apply. But it does not apply not because either party magnanimously or ignominiously sacrifices his or her interests but because the two interests are not independent, perhaps not really even two. Indeed, etymologically, the very meaning of "intimate" is tied to "innermost" and "to bring within."[7]

7. Obviously I am not claiming that in personal relationships everything is sweetness and light and harmony. I'm not that naive. There are conflicts of interests even between people who are close. But these conflicts of interest are set within the framework of the closeness and the care that each person has for the other, and, as a result, these conflicts are seen in a different light and handled differently. If we are close, then your well-being

Thinking in terms of rights then may be the right way to think in relatively impersonal contexts.[8] But in intimate contexts, this kind of thinking is both inadequate and destructive.

It is inadequate even to allow us to comprehend the kinds of oppression that can exist in personal relationships, for the root source of many forms of oppression in personal relationships is an imbalance of love, care, and concern for the interests of the other. Consider the situation in which you love and care for me but I do not love or care that much for you. In this situation, if I stay with you out of inertia, convenience, feelings of responsibility, or because I want this kind of relationship or what it brings me, the resulting relationship is in itself oppressive quite apart from any oppressive actions that may or may not follow from my lack of love for you. It is oppressive even if I carefully but uncaringly respect your rights and even promote your interests, all out of a sense of obligation. Who could endure such a relationship? (Many do of course, but at a terrible price.)

This basic oppressive ingredient in personal relationships that are asymmetrical in terms of love and concern is not a violation of anyone's rights, for no one has a right to be desired or loved by another or to be another's end. And many derivative forms of oppression—some of which can also be conceptualized as a denial of rights—are painful and injurious in large part because they testify to this asymmetry of concern, understanding, or involvement. Thus frustration will be added to the anguish of asymmetrical personal relationships if we think in terms of rights, for doing so will blind us to many varieties of oppression that can exist in personal relationships.[9]

---

and the strength and health of our relationship generally means more to me than the interest that conflicts with these things. If my interests which conflict with yours very often mean more to me than you do or our relationship does, it is probably time for us to end our relationship. Or, if we do not, it is certainly time to sit down and discuss not what claims I can legitimately make against you but what my interest means to me, what you and I mean to each other, and what this interest means to us and for us.

8. From the perspective of this paper, one of the issues that divides some conservatives, Marxists, and communitarian anarchists or socialists, on one hand, from most liberals, on the other, is, Should we strive to extend personal relationships into domains in which impersonal relationships now predominate, or are some relationships better left impersonal? Should we restructure our institutions and reeducate ourselves so that relationships in schools and universities, the legal or medical profession, the workplace and the marketplace, and even the government will be personalized? Obviously I cannot attempt to address this issue in this essay, but I would argue that no oppressed group can become completely liberated as long as we see ourselves as respecting their rights. Rather they must be accepted—seen as part of us.

9. Thus if Maggie Scarf is correct in arguing (in *Unfinished Business: Pressure Points in the Lives of Women* [New York: Doubleday & Co., 1980]) that personal relationships characteristically mean more to women than to men in our culture, this by itself would support the claim that women as a class are oppressed in personal relationships. However, on my view it would not necessarily follow that they are oppressed by the men with whom they are involved. Indeed, as Maggie Scarf (e.g., on pp. 224–28, 355–57) and many other

Moreover, thinking in terms of rights is also destructive in intimate contexts because the pictures of persons and relationships that we accept are clearly not merely descriptions or effects of the way we see things; they are causes too, governing our experience and expectations of ourselves and others. Thinking in terms of rights thus does more than reflect an egoistic, atomistic situation; it creates such a situation or reinforces our tendency to move in that direction. Thinking in terms of rights is divisive. It teaches us to think of "I" and "I versus you" instead of "we." Through accepting this picture and living in it, we become more like enemies, antagonists, or traders, at best—less like brothers, sisters, lovers, and friends.

A large part of the pain that comes from realizing that your loved one or friend has begun scrupulously respecting your rights thus comes from the awareness that he or she is treating you as a separate being, oblivious to or unconcerned with the "we" that is thereby being violated. For it is unity, a sense of community, and personal affirmation that we want in personal relationships. In a close personal relationship, I don't want you to respect my separate interests; I want to mean enough to you that you will have an interest in those interests. And if I care for you, I will want your well-being, and thus your well-being will be essential to mine too. Because thinking in terms of rights rests on an atomistic picture of us as separate, thinking in terms of rights systematically denies the unity, the togetherness, the "we" that we are trying to create. Thinking in terms of rights thus always violates the relationship, even as it strives

---

feminists point out, the problem may not be primarily a problem of present oppressors (in personal or impersonal contexts) at all. For due to their (oppressive) socialization, women sometimes find themselves too dependent and relationship oriented because they derive their total source of self and self-worth from their intimate relationships. Granted, a woman may simply need more recognition of her rights in impersonal contexts to give her viable opportunities for attaining greater independence and control of her life. But this may not be sufficient: no improvement in these opportunities will fully satisfy a woman who still derives her primary sense of self, meaning, and worth from intimate contexts. Thus it could be a mistake for a woman to believe that a fuller sense of identity would come through thinking of her rights vis-à-vis the men she is close to. Although the language of rights has sometimes been used as a tool for the needed development of an independent sense of self in intimate contexts, it is clearly not sufficient for this task, nor, as I will argue in Sec. V below, is it appropriate or necessary. Moreover, for a woman who is too dependent on intimate relationships, the language of rights will be misleading, for it too neatly "externalizes" her problem. (Obviously, however, none of this is meant to deny that women are often oppressed by the men with whom they are emotionally involved. The argument of the final section of this paper addresses this latter problem.) Of course, so long as one assumes that oppression must somehow involve the denial of rights, one must find a violated right to match any sense of oppression on pain of giving up the claim of oppression. However, if I am correct, we need instead to develop our theory of oppression so that it can comprehend the varieties of personal as well as impersonal oppression, many of which need not involve the denial of rights. (The theory of rights would also be strengthened and solidified, I suspect, if we did not feel forced to make that concept do more work than it can or should. For the attempt to make the concept of rights cover all forms of oppression has led to a situation in which all sorts of imaginative rights are claimed, and it is no longer

to protect the persons involved from violation. It thereby both testifies to and increases the separation between us, undermining the unity that is the whole point of the relationship. Atoms are ultimately alone.

III

One cannot think in terms of rights without tacitly invoking the whole conceptual structure on which such thinking rests. I have argued that thinking in terms of rights thus evokes a picture of persons as atomistic, asocial, and primarily egoistic and that this picture is not the model we want for understanding or moving toward healthy personal relationships. I now want to suggest—and I can do no more than suggest—that women should also be wary of thinking in terms of rights because this kind of thinking may be a male way of thinking.

One of the prerogatives of the dominant class is that it gets to define what is real and what is good. The prevalent pictures and models are those generated by the dominant class, generally in the perceived interest of the dominant class. Consequently, there is always a danger in any struggle for liberation that the oppressed class will accept too much of the dominant picture and thereby forfeit its soul and lose the real depth of the contribution it could make to a new society. Could thinking in terms of rights be part of a male picture of reality? I suspect that it may well be, because it involves the definition of self and the interests of self in opposition to rather than in relation to others.

I am not able to say with any precision what a female way of defining oneself and one's interests might be, and anyway, it is not up to males to say what a female style of identity is. But I do think that females in our culture define themselves more in terms of relations to others, less in terms of opposition to others.[10] What does it mean to define yourself in relation to others? Although it can easily look like a loss of identity and independence (especially from what I am now calling a male point of view), and it can easily slip into that, this need not be so. To define yourself in terms of relations to others is to see yourself and your interests as a way of being with others, not against them. It is a standing with, not apart; it is participation rather than resistance, empathy rather than antipathy, community rather than rugged individualism. To define yourself in relation to others is to accept an organic or ecological rather than an atomistic or mechanical orientation; it is to think in terms of cooperation and mutual support and aid rather than in terms of conquest, competition, domination. A relational style of identity is more dialogic, less monologic; instead of seeking to impose an order, structure, or direction, it searches

---

clear what rights can be legitimately claimed.) It goes without saying, however, that I have not here even started to construct such a theory of oppression—that would take another essay, at least.

10. I owe this point to Sarah Karasharov in an unpublished paper, "On Erwin Straus's 'The Upright Posture.'"

for an emergent, more consensual order and seeks to help it find articulation and direction.

Now, if all that is wrong with a sexist society is that women do not get equal opportunity to be and do the things that men are and do, then there is no problem with adopting a male way of thinking. But if what is wrong with a sexist society goes much deeper—if a sexist society is one-sided and one-sidedly blind to nonmasculine ways of being and thinking—then women must be careful to preserve and articulate their way of being, seeing, and thinking. The categories that I have so inadequately pointed to under the rubric of a female orientation are, I submit, much more appropriate to close personal relationships than is the category of rights. Consequently, women should not approach their personal relationships by thinking in terms of rights because to do so would be to lose touch with an essential theme in a female orientation and thereby to jeopardize the depth of the contribution women can make to a masculine culture and, more specifically, to an understanding of personal relationships.

IV

But if this is the conclusion, does it not leave us with one of the perennial problems that plague personal relationships between men and women? If it is true that the conceptual structure involved in thinking in terms of rights is an ingredient in a presently male style of identity, then we should expect that standardly men will think in terms of rights, especially their rights, even in personal relationships. And where does that leave women, especially if they are less likely to think in terms of rights— including their own rights—in personal relationships? Importing the concept of rights into the context of male-dominated personal relationships has left women thinking primarily in terms of obligations and duties, for a right in me imposes an obligation on you. And this is certainly a situation fraught with exploitation and oppression and ripe for tragedy.

All of which leads us back to the point at which we began: women are oppressed, and they are oppressed not only in the context of large-scale, impersonal social institutions but in the context of intimate, personal relationships as well. One of the tools of this oppression has been the one-sided definition of and insistence on the rights of the men in personal relationships. It goes without saying, of course, that I have not been arguing that only women should refrain from thinking in terms of rights in the context of personal relationships. The point is, rather, that neither men nor women should think in terms of rights in personal relationships, for it is the wrong kind of ethical category to apply to healthy personal relationships.

And yet women are oppressed, and the oppressed always have both more need and more justification for thinking in terms of rights than do the oppressors. (If I am an oppressor, I need not think in terms of rights because I am already getting more than I have any right to. I will thus be tempted to say and to believe that we have no need to think in terms of rights, for to do so would only upset the comfortable, informal, "friendly" relations that now exist.) It is hard, therefore, to quiet the suspicion that the argument of this paper is too idealistic and that it ignores the fact that women are often oppressed in personal relationships. The suspicion is that it might be nice if relationships were what I have suggested that healthy personal relationships are, but they usually are not, and therefore my argument just will not work, at least not in our male-dominated society.

Consequently, it might seem—even to those who are sympathetic to the main thrust of this paper—that the argument simply is not dialectical enough. Healthy personal relationships, it might be objected, must be based on mutuality, and genuine mutuality presupposes equality and freedom. But it is precisely this equality and freedom that women, as oppressed, lack, and thus before we can move into healthy mutual relationships, we must get rid of oppression, especially oppression in personal relationships. We must first develop freedom and equality. And we do that by thinking in terms of rights, which perhaps is not the ultimate ideal of a healthy personal relationship, but which is the next step we must take in moving toward healthy personal relationships.

The view that my argument needs a dialectical step can be developed on either the macrocosmic social level or the microcosmic level of the individual relationship. If the point is pressed on the macrocosmic level, one could claim that my argument is really an argument for radical feminist separatism. The feminist separatist could, I believe, accept my entire thesis: healthy personal relationships are what I have said they are and the category of rights is not appropriate in healthy personal relationships.

But, the radical feminist might continue, this only shows that women should not get emotionally involved with men. Oppression and healthy personal relationships are incompatible. Men have oppression built into their characters, if not their natures, and women have perhaps been socialized to be too passive, dependent, and relationship oriented. Moreover, it may even be impossible for a genuinely egalitarian relationship between a man and a woman to exist in a cultural context in which women are handicapped in pursuing identity and fulfillment in more impersonal contexts. Consequently, a relationship between a woman and a man in our society will inevitably fall into an oppressive pattern, even if no conscious oppressive intent is present. Of all oppressed classes, women are in the most difficult position precisely because they have a tendency to become emotionally involved with some of their oppressors, thereby undermining their attempts to become liberated. According to the radical feminist, we must thus learn to be "separate but equal" before we can have personal relationships between the sexes that are either fully satisfying or morally satisfactory: women must renounce close personal relationships with men, at least until they achieve their liberation.

I do not want to attempt here to respond to this radical feminist position. I will only say that I hope it is not true. I want to resist as hard as I can the conclusion that the only moral stance I could take toward women is to refuse to get close to any of them until after the success of the feminist revolution. For the feminist revolution comes too late and too slowly for me—by the time it has succeeded, I will be dead. I hope that love between the sexes need not be postponed until after the revolution. I might also add that men who share this hope, men who like women and value intimate relationships with them, clearly have a strong interest in making this radical feminist position untrue (a point to which I shall return).

The view that we need to move through a stage of thinking in terms of rights before we can achieve healthy personal relationships can also be pressed on the microcosmic level of the individual relationship. On this level the argument is that, although personal relationships between men and women need not be oppressive, many of them are. And when women find themselves in oppressive personal relationships and loving their oppressors in these relationships, they should think in terms of rights. If they fail to do so, it is a sign of the pathology, not the health, of the relationship. Women must learn to insist on their rights in their personal relationships in order to move out of a pathological acceptance of and even complicity with their domination by the men they are close to. On this view, this may be the only way to save the love and the relationship, for genuine and unambivalent love of the oppressor and recognition that he is your oppressor cannot coexist for long in any self-respecting person.

Although I certainly agree that women's increasing awareness of their oppression in personal as well as impersonal contexts is both healthy and beneficial, I do not believe that, in personal contexts, the appropriate response to this awareness is to think in terms of rights. My reasons for this view are three: it is a dangerous strategy to adopt; it is, in any case, insufficient; and it should be unnecessary. Let us begin with the insufficiency of this strategy.

V

It is perhaps worth emphasizing that the title of this essay is not, "Do Women Have Any Rights?" and nowhere have I argued that women have no rights in the context of personal relationships. I have assumed throughout that persons have whatever rights they have and that, although entering into or being in a personal relationship may and probably does alter one's moral rights in important ways, the existence of a personal relationship does not cancel or nullify all the rights that persons have in relation to each other. But, to repeat an earlier point, if you and I find ourselves thinking very often in terms of rights, this is evidence that our relationship has decayed or become unhealthy or never did become what we have hoped it would be.

Thinking in terms of rights, as I conceive it, is a fall-back mechanism in personal relationships which may be necessary in fundamentally unsound relationships (when genuine love and care and the concern for the well-being of the other are absent). In healthy relationships, this fall-back mechanism may perhaps be appropriately invoked, but only rarely and in unusual circumstances—when tempers flare, nerves are frayed, or the relationship is otherwise strained. If we find ourselves thinking in terms of rights, we should realize that the relationship is strained, perhaps even at a critical juncture, and that, although this fall-back mechanism may serve to protect us and some of what we want, thinking in terms of rights does not and cannot protect the core of a personal relationship. Precisely because those features of personal relationships that make them personal and worth having (love, intimacy, personal affirmation, unity) cannot be guaranteed by any system of rights, thinking in terms of rights will always be insufficient to achieve or maintain what we want in a personal relationship.

If I may use an analogy, rights are like the net underneath the tightrope act. The net keeps people and their lives from being ruined if they fall off the wire. But the act is ruined if the net actually comes into play. Maybe it would be foolish to get up on the wire if we did not know there was a net beneath us, and yet the act would be even better if we could have enough confidence in ourselves and each other to do it without thinking of the net at all.

Second, thinking in terms of rights is also a dangerous strategy to employ in personal relationships because such thinking invokes a conceptual structure which is incompatible with the structure that is normative for all personal relationships and characteristic of healthy personal relationships. That of course is part of what it means to say that thinking in terms of rights is a dialectical step on the way to a healthy personal relationship. But—and this is the danger of any dialectical step—moving to the antithetical position may make it impossible to move further, especially given the time scale within which personal relationships must succeed or fail.

Because thinking in terms of rights invokes a conceptual structure that is incompatible with healthy personal relationships, thinking in terms of rights also evokes feelings, attitudes, beliefs, and a stance toward one's partner that are incompatible with healthy personal relationships. To think in terms of rights is thus to invite me to see my interests as separable from and conflicting with your interests. It is to suggest that I should think in terms of "I" or "I versus you" instead of in terms of "we." It is to urge that I begin thinking of our relationship as a trade relationship, as is fitting for those who relate on the basis of conflicting and antagonistic interests that are not colored or modified by the meaning and concern which each has for the other. Unless one believes that progress is inevitable and that, once set afoot, it travels very rapidly, one has no guarantee that it will be possible to undo the feelings, attitudes, and beliefs about personal relationships that have been evoked by a resolute attempt to take the dialetical step to thinking in terms of rights. Having reinforced my picture of my interests as separable, independent, and antagonistically related to you and your interests, you may be unable to convince me later that this is not really so.

Now, even if thinking in terms of rights is both insufficient and dangerous, it could still be thought to be necessary. And this brings me to my final point, for I believe that thinking in terms of rights should be unnecessary, even in oppressive personal relationships, because it is stupid for me to oppress those who are close to me and whom I love and care about. Whether I realize it or not, it is not in my interest to do so because oppression is debilitating (even if the oppressed is unaware of her oppression), and it is better to share my life with someone who is not debilitated. This is the point that you must help me see if we are close and I nonetheless oppress you.

It is not as if there are no divergent and even conflicting interests in close personal relationships. There are of course. But these divergent and conflicting interests do not call for you to think in terms of rights; rather you must help me learn that I have an interest in supporting and in wanting to support your discovery and development of independent and divergent interests, because doing so will give me a more vibrant and vital person to be with, and that is better for me too. I must come to understand that it is not even in my interest to "win" in all cases of irreconcilably conflicting interests, for it is better for me to share my life with an unoppressed woman and not have everything my own way than it is to share my life with an oppressed woman, even if she satisfies my whims, because oppression is debilitating, especially at close range and in intimate contexts.

Thus the bottom line is that women need not think in terms of rights in the context of personal relationships because, so long as it is possible to appeal to the enlightened self-interest of one's partner and to mutual interests, it is not necessary to think in terms of rights. In other words, women need to educate those of their oppressors who are emotionally involved with them. Thinking in terms of rights will not be an effective educational device, for it inevitably miseducates about what healthy personal relationships are even as it instructs about the oppression that can exist in personal relationships.

Not that the lessons about the enlightened interests of the oppressors will always be easy to teach or to learn. The oppressor will always resist awareness that he is an oppressor, the knowledge that one oppresses even those he is close to is especially bitter, and it is unpleasant to discover that one has been living stupidly. But the lessons can be learned, especially since it is in the interest of the oppressor to learn them. Or if they cannot be learned, if I should prove to be completely ineducable, you should give me up as a lost cause and leave me, for you will never be able to have the kind of personal relationship you want with the likes of me.

The task of educating the oppressor may seem an unfair burden to impose on those who already bear the unfair burdens of the oppression itself. But these are the lessons we must learn if we are to understand and to have healthy personal relationships.

VI

We thus end with another of the recurrent themes of feminist thought: women's liberation is human liberation; it is good for men as well as women. In the context of large-scale or impersonal relationships, it is not always clear that this is in fact true. To give just one personal example, I believe I have a moral obligation to support affirmative action because it is implied by genuine equal opportunity and women have a right to equal opportunity. But it is not at all clear to me, while struggling to get one of those scarce jobs in philosophy, that it is really in my interest to do so, for the women who will get those jobs mean little or nothing to me. But in the context of personal relationships in which it is a question of sharing my self and my life with those few women whom I love and care about, it does seem undeniably true that I do have an interest in the liberation of these women and also in their liberation from me insofar as I oppress them. Do women really believe that their liberation is good for the men they are close to? If so, women need not think in terms of rights in the context of personal relationships. For we need not appeal to rights to get someone to do what is also best for him.

In impersonal situations, then, rights may be the correct terms in which to think. For this reason, it makes more sense for blacks or workers, patients, welfare recipients, or old people (including women in these groups) to think in terms of rights than it does for women to define their concerns about personal relationships in terms of rights. I can perhaps oppress blacks, workers, students, and old people with equanimity because these people mean so little to me. And if I grant them their rights, that may be all they want from me—precisely because we are not close. It is wrong, then, but it may not be stupid for me to oppress people who mean little or nothing to me. But though it is also wrong, more important, it is stupid for me to oppress those I care for and who are close to me. And as opposed to blacks, workers, patients, students, and welfare recipients who are not involved with me, those who are close to me will certainly not be satisfied if I grant them their rights.

A Marxist Theory of Women's Nature*

Nancy Holmstrom

Debates about women's nature are very old but far from over. In fact they have acquired a new urgency with the rise of the women's movement and with the dramatic increase in the number of women in the work force. Conservatives claim that there is a distinct women's nature that puts limits on the extent to which the traditional sexual/social roles can and should be altered. Feminists usually reject the idea, correctly pointing out that it has been used to justify women's oppression for thousands of years.

In this article I attempt to develop a Marxist approach to the question. Though such an approach is nowhere explicitly taken by Marx or Engels, it is a plausible development of their views. Marx held human nature to be determined by the social forms of human labor. I will bring out his general realist methodology and his perspective on the relation between the biological and the social. Given my interpretation of the facts about psychological differences between the sexes and the probable dependence of these differences on the sexual division of labor, this approach entails that women probably do have distinct natures. (It similarly entails that men probably have distinct natures since there is no reason to take men as the norm.) However, contrary to the usual assumption, it does not follow that sexual/social roles cannot or should not be radically altered, for men's and women's natures are socially constituted and historically evolving. Marx's approach, though novel in certain respects, accords with the methodology employed in biological classifications. I shall discuss two objections: that my account underemphasizes the biological facts and that it underemphasizes social/historical factors. On my account of women's nature, this nature can change, though it will not be easy, but nothing follows about how women ought or ought not to live. I shall conclude by considering contrasts between my Marxist approach to women's nature and Marx's approach to human nature.

I

Just as the nonhuman natural world consists of biological, chemical, and physical structures for which different sorts of explanations are appropriate,

* My thanks to Milton Fisk and Karsten Struhl for their helpful comments.

This essay originally appeared in *Ethics* 94, April 1984.

so there are many levels of explanation appropriate to human beings. The nature of a human being as a biological being would be the genotype. The philosophical question of human nature is of the nature of human beings qua social beings. According to Marx's theory, human beings have certain basic needs and capacities which are biological in origin but to some extent socially constituted:[1] "Hunger is hunger but the hunger gratified by cooked meat eaten with a knife and fork is a different hunger from that which bolts down raw meat with the aid of hand, nail and tooth."[2] Some human needs and capacities are unique to human beings, but even those that are not take uniquely human forms. As new needs and capacities are continually being created, biology remains an important determining factor, but human life progressively becomes less directly tied to its biological base.

Since human needs and capacities are expressed, shaped, and even created through the activity of satisfying needs (i.e., through labor), Marx concentrated on the form of labor characteristic of the human species. Though this species can be distinguished from others on a number of criteria, Marx says that human beings in fact begin to distinguish themselves from other species when they begin to produce their means of subsistence. Because the labor of society is institutionalized into sets of social practices and social relations, by their labor people are thereby producing their whole life. The general capacity of human beings to labor in a social and purposive way takes a variety of specific forms throughout history which in turn affect and even create other human needs and capacities.

Now obviously there are biological structures that make possible the kinds of labor that human beings do. However, the relation between biology and activity in human beings differs from that in other species in two ways: first, human biology makes possible more than just a narrow range of behavior, even within a particular historical period; and second, rather than determining the forms of human labor, human biology does no more than make possible its forms. Our large brain size, the basis of the flexibility and plasticity of human behavior and consciousness, resulted from evolution, a major determinant of which was labor. This is the basis of Engels's remark that "labor created man himself." On Marx's theory, labor is the key to an explanation of social life and social change. Since this was his concern, he emphasized the labor and not the biology.

Compare the methodology employed in biological classifications: animals are classified into the same or different species not simply on the basis of their similarities and differences but also according to the

1. As is well known, one of the most controversial areas of Marxist scholarship is whether Marx had a theory of human nature in his later work and, if so, whether it is significantly different from his earlier one. The interpretation I give below is consistent with both his early and his later work (as indicated by references). So there is some common theory of human nature, although there are also differences between his early and late ideas which are not relevant to my concerns in this paper.

2. Karl Marx, *Grundrisse* (Harmondsworth: Penguin Books, 1973), p. 92.

importance of these features within biological theory. For this reason, Chihuahuas and St. Bernards are classified as belonging to the same species, although there are greater differences between them than there are between many dogs and wolves. In analogous fashion, the differentiating characteristic of social beings should be determined by its importance in social theory. As the forms of human labor (and the resultant social practices and institutions) change, new mental and physical capacities are developed, some remain undeveloped, and others are destroyed. Hence different behavioral and psychological generalizations will be true of people who do different sorts of labor in different modes of production.

A nominalistic-empiricist approach would leave the discussion of human nature at that. However, I take Marx to have a realist approach to the philosophy of the natural and social sciences. Realists maintain that the concept of a nature—stripped of outmoded metaphysical assumptions—often plays an important explanatory role in answer to such questions as, Why do the generalizations hold? and What is the basis of the observed similarities? Biological theories, which back up some generalizations and not others, should provide some account of the mechanisms that generate the regularities. For example, realists argue that it is necessary to posit some underlying structure, common to the things defined as one species, that generates the disjunctive set of properties defining a species and causes variations in different individuals within that species.[3] (This demand is satisfied by the concept of the gene pool.) In traditional terminology, the set of properties which justify the use of the common term is called the nominal essence; the internal constitution which generates these manifest properties in accordance with laws is called the real essence.

Marx assumed the same perspective on the social world. He believed that the distinction between accidental and lawful generalizations applied to social phenomena and that certain social entities had natures, saying repeatedly that science was necessary to uncover the hidden laws of motion of capitalist society. Socioeconomic classes are not mere collections of individuals with some common economic feature—not classes simply in the logical sense. The realist methodology implies that there must be certain characteristic differences in the psychophysical structures of people who do very different sorts of labor in different modes of production to account for the observed personality and behavioral differences between them.[4] These psychophysical structures would generate and explain a wide range of human behavior within that mode of production, which

3. D. L. Hull, "Contemporary Systematic Philosophies," in *Annual Review of Ecology and Systematics,* ed. Richard Johnson (Palo Alto, Calif.: Annual Reviews, Inc., 1970), pp. 19–54, "The Metaphysics of Evolution," *British Journal of the History of Science* 3 (1966–67): 309–37, and "The Effect of Essentialism on Taxonomy: 2000 Years of Stasis, Parts 1, 2," *British Journal of the Philosophy of Science* 15 (1965): 314–26; 16 (1966): 1–18.

4. By "psychophysical" I mean to include phenomena to be explained in physical terms, psychological terms, or any mixture thereof, whatever the ultimate relation between the physical and the psychological.

the transhistorical features of human beings would not be able to do. To say in detail what these historically specific structures are and how they work would require a more adequate psychological theory than presently exists, one that integrates social and historical factors. However, an explanation of the varieties of human personality and behavior requires some such hypothesis of historically specific structures. This indicates a line of future research.[5]

Talk of "determining structures" is not inconsistent with Marx's conception of human beings as historical agents. Individually and collectively, human beings often do what they do because of their beliefs, desires, and purposes. Human beings are free in this sense. But Marx stresses that human freedom is exercised only within certain constraints—set by social, historical, and economic conditions as well as biological facts. Talk of social groups with natures is a way of bringing out those constraints. For example, we can better predict John Smith's economic behavior by knowing that he is a capitalist than by knowing his preferences, skills, personality, and character traits.

The psychophysical structures produced by the sorts of labor that people do and the resultant social relations would constitute the nature of human beings qua social beings. Although there are certain features common to these structures, they vary as a whole from one mode of production to another. Marx is denying that there is a human nature in the traditional, transhistorical sense. On his view, however, there are historically specific forms of human nature, that is, human nature specific to feudalism, to capitalism, to socialism, and so on. In traditional terminology, the (variable) psychophysical structures would be the (variable)

---

5. Some fascinating work along these lines was done by the early Soviet psychologists, Lev Vygotsky and A. R. Luria, who defined psychology to mean "the science of the socio-historical shaping of mental activity and of the structures of mental processes which depend utterly on the basic forms of social practice and the major stages in the historical development of society" (*Cognitive Development: Its Cultural and Social Foundations* [Cambridge, Mass.: Harvard University Press, 1976], p. 164). In a study of Central Asian peasants in the early 1930s, they discovered significant differences in the mode as well as the content of cognition between those living on a collective farm for two years and those engaged in traditional peasant agriculture. Specifically, the latter had difficulty with simple syllogisms while the former did not; and the latter classified objects according to what Luria called a "graphic-functional" mode as opposed to the "abstract-theoretical" mode used by the former. In attempting to give a material basis for his approach, Luria made innovative contributions to neuropsychology. Unfortunately, they did not explore the connections between social structure and noncognitive aspects of mental life. These seminal ideas have never really been developed. They were suppressed in the Soviet Union until recently and remained unknown in the West until many years later. (See also A. R. Luria, *The Working Brain: An Introduction to Neuropsychology* [New York: Basic Books, 1973], and *Higher Cortical Functions in Man* [New York: Basic Books, 1966]; Lev Vygotsky, *Thought and Language* [Cambridge, Mass.: MIT Press, 1982]). Also along these lines, Alfred Sohn-Rethel presents a convincing though speculative case for the thesis that the human capacity for abstract thinking was dependent on forms of commodity production (*Intellectual and Manual Labor: A Critique of Epistemology* [London: Macmillan Publishers, 1978]).

real essence of human beings qua social beings, and the forms of personality and behavior to which they give rise would be the nominal essence.

This acceptance of natures in the social world implies that, contrary to traditional assumptions, natures can change. Even for biological natures, however, the assumption that natures must be unchanging became less plausible after the discovery of evolution. If species can be understood as evolving sorts of things, why must natures be understood as unchanging? In Marx's view, the contrast of the social with the natural and unchanging is particularly inappropriate to human beings since they are by nature social beings with a history.

II

Let us try to apply this approach to the question of whether women (and men) can be said to have distinct natures. Distinct sex-linked natures are supposed to account for (and to justify) the distinct social roles of women and men. It is important to see first of all that the defining biological differences between men and women cannot by themselves play this explanatory role, much less the justificatory one. A woman is defined as a typical member of the female sex, which is distinguished from the male sex by its ability to conceive and bear children. Whether these biological differences cause the social differences is an empirical question that we shall discuss shortly. However, to say that men and women have distinct natures so defined would be to utter a tautology. We are looking for the nature of women and men as social groups, not as biological groups.

Do, then, men and women as social beings have distinct natures? If there are generalizations subsumable under a theory, explanatory of behavior distinctive of a given social group, this suggests that the group has a distinct nature. Indeed there are many generalizations we can make about women's behavior and roles within given cultures and many that are true cross-culturally as well. Compared to men, women spend more time taking care of children and doing other household tasks; they have less social, economic, and political power in society at large and in almost every subgroup in society; their work outside the home, if any, is usually related to the work they do inside the home; they tend to cry more easily, dress and adorn themselves distinctively, tend to have distinct recreations and pleasures, and so on.

What is the explanation? Discrimination and direct social pressure are undoubtedly part of it. But are there differences between men and women themselves that underlie the behavioral differences? Many claim that biological differences between the sexes are the most important part of the explanation.[6] However, it is highly implausible that biological differences could directly determine the social differences. If biological

6. An academic example of this point of view is Judith Bardwick, *Psychology of Women* (New York: Harper & Row, 1971); a more popular example is Steven Goldberg, "The Inevitability of Patriarchy," in *Sex Equality*, ed. Jane English (Englewood Cliffs, N.J.: Prentice-Hall, Inc., 1977).

facts are critical determinants of sexual/social roles, the connection is most likely to run through psychology; that is, biological differences cause or predispose psychological differences, which in turn cause differences in social roles. The first question, then, is whether there are psychological differences between the sexes that are relevant to their respective social roles: for example, that women are more nurturant than men and hence are more appropriate caretakers of children. If there are such differences, the next question will be about their source.

Both these questions are controversial, even among the experts. Despite this and my own serious reservations about much of the research,[7] I believe that research to show that there exist statistically significant psychological sex differences of a sort that are relevant to the different social roles men and women play.[8]

Any position regarding the source of these differences is necessarily somewhat speculative since, by and large, the researchers look only for statistically significant relationships and do not try to establish cause and effect. The prevailing hostility among academic research psychologists to any theoretical framework makes it difficult to assess the data since the significance of the data and even what needs to be explained is to some extent dependent on a theory. But the following findings strongly support the view that social factors are the primary determinants:[9] (1) Black males and white females, different biologically but with similar social handicaps, are similar in patterns of achievement scores and fear

7. These reservations are based on the following objections: First, the research is confined to artificial situations and narrow cultural contexts. Second, it concentrates on statistically significant differences and ignores the magnitude, overlap, and importance of the features. And third, it lacks a theoretical framework with which to evaluate the findings.

8. For example, women tend to have greater needs to be close to people (L. E. Tyler, *The Psychology of Human Differences* [New York: Appleton-Century-Crofts, 1965]; E. Maccoby, "Sex Differences in Intellectual Functioning," in *The Development of Sex Differences*, ed. E. Maccoby [Stanford, Calif.: Stanford University Press, 1966], pp. 25–55), to be less aggressive (E. Maccoby and L. Jacklin, *The Psychology of Sex Differences* [Stanford, Calif.: Stanford University Press, 1974]), more suggestible (Tyler; Maccoby), to be motivated more by a desire for love than by a desire for power (L. Hoffman, "Early Childhood Experiences and Women's Achievement Motives," *Journal of Social Issues* 28 [1972]: 129–55), to have greater verbal and less visual/spatial ability (Tyler; Maccoby; Maccoby and Jacklin). These differences are clearer and more significant among adolescents and adults than among young children (J. Block, "Issues, Problems and Pitfalls in Assessing Sex Differences: A Critical Review of *The Psychology of Sex Differences*," *Merrill-Palmer Quarterly* 22 [1976]: 283–308), with newborn boys and girls showing no clear psychological differences (N. Romer, *The Sex-Role Cycle* [New York: Feminist Press/McGraw-Hill Book Co., 1981], p. 7). These findings of statistically significant differences simply show that women have a trait to a higher degree than men. This is consistent with some men having it more than most women and even with a majority of women lacking it.

9. Critics of sociobiology have raised serious doubts that any specific and variable human behavioral traits are under genetic control. See in particular Stephen Jay Gould, "The Non-Science of Human Nature" and "Biological Potentiality vs. Biological Determinism," in *Ever Since Darwin* (New York: W. W. Norton & Co., 1977), pp. 237–42, 251–59; Arthur Caplan, ed., *The Sociobiology Debate* (New York: Harper & Row, 1978).

of success.[10] (2) The same physiological state can yield very different emotional states and behavior, depending on the social situation. Adrenalin produces a physiological state very much like that present in extreme fear, yet subjects injected with it became euphoric when around another person who acted euphorically and very angry when around another person who acted very angrily.[11] Thus even if sex hormonal differences between men and women affect brain functioning, as some psychologists contend, it does not follow that there necessarily will be consistent emotional and behavioral differences between men and women. (3) Different behavioral propensities, thought by many to be biologically based, disappear given certain social conditions. In one study, when both sexes were rewarded for aggressive behavior, the sex difference disappeared.[12] (4) Studies of hermaphrodites show that the crucial variable determining their gender identity is neither chromosomal sex nor hormones administered pre- or postnatally but "the consistency of being reared as feminine, especially in the early years."[13] (5) Psychological sex differences are least pronounced in early childhood and old age, when sex-role stereotypes are least powerful.[14] Furthermore, the principle of methodological simplicity supports taking environmental factors as decisive. We have at present ample evidence of environmental shaping of sex-differentiated behavior, so ample in fact that it is sufficient to account for the cognitive and personality differences we observe in children and adults. Although it is possible that future research will discover biological factors as well, there is no reason to expect this will happen.

The social roles of men and women that are related to psychological sex differences are not universal cross-culturally, but they are very prevalent.

10. Regarding achievement scores, see S. R. Tulkin, "Race, Class, Family and School Achievement," *Journal of Personality and Social Psychology* 9 (1968): 31–37; A. R. Jensen, "The Race × Class × Ability Interaction" (Ph.D. diss., University of California, Berkeley, 1970). Regarding fear of success, see P. Weston and M. Mednick, "Race, Social Class and the Motive to Avoid Success in Women," *Journal of Cross-cultural Psychology* 1 (1970): 284–91.

11. S. Schachter and J. E. Singer, "Cognitive, Social and Physiological Determinants of Emotional State," *Psychological Review* 69 (1962): 379–99. A philosopher might argue that a finer analysis would show that it was not the *same* physiological state which yielded the different results but two different states. Regardless, the study shows that the social situation is more important than the physiological factor.

12. W. Mischel, "A Social-learning View of Sex Differences in Behavior," in Maccoby, ed., pp. 56–81.

13. J. Money and M. Earhardt, *Man and Woman, Boy and Girl*, quoted in Beverly Birns, "The Emergence and Socialization of Sex Differences in the Earliest Years," *Merrill-Palmer Quarterly* 22 (1976): 250–51.

14. Romer, pp. 7, 124. Studies show that parents (as well as society) project fewer clear sex-role expectations on babies than on young children and adolescents. However, such stereotypes are projected throughout the human life: there is no time that can safely be said to be prior to socialization. Studies show that parents describe newborns in sex-stereotypic ways, even though hospital records show no objective differences, and that parents behave differently toward boy and girl babies even though they are unaware of it. Cited in ibid., pp. 139–40, nn. 3, 4, 5, 6.

Sex-differentiated socialization patterns also show little cross-cultural variation, with girls being trained for nurturance and responsibility and boys for achievement and self-reliance in both developed and under-developed societies.[15] This strongly suggests that many, though not all, of the psychological differences between men and women are very prev-alent, though not universal, cross-culturally. They are not universal to all women even within this culture. Something like the following is probably true: there is a common core of psychological traits found more among women than among men throughout the world, but women belonging to different cultures or subcultures have different subsets of this common core of traits. Though there is not enough rigorous cross-cultural psy-chological research to say for sure, this opinion accords with the an-thropological data we do have.[16]

There seem, then, to be several levels of generalizations (sociological, psychological, etc.) that are distinctive of women. By itself, however, this by no means implies that there is a distinct women's nature. As we saw in our discussion of taxonomy, the differences must be of a kind that is theoretically important. Following Marx's approach, we should expect psychological differences to be connected to differences in the sorts of labor that women do in society and to the resulting differences in social relations. Universally there is and has always been a sexual division of labor. Although there are some variations as to what labor each sex does, men generally have primary responsibility for subsistence activities; wom-en's contribution to this varies. What does not vary is that, whatever else they do, women have primary responsibility for child care and most of the everyday household work. Their contribution to subsistence depends on its compatibility with child care.[17]

Several cross-cultural studies support the Marxist assumption that it is women's distinctive labor and the different social relations resulting from it that are critical in determining these personality differences.[18]

15. H. Barry III, M. K. Bacon, and I. I. Child, "A Cross Cultural Survey of Some Sex Differences in Socialization," *Journal of Abnormal and Social Psychology* 55 (1957): 327–32.

16. Margaret Mead's ground-breaking research provides dramatic examples of societies where sex roles are very different from those familiar to us (*Sex and Temperament in Three Primitive Societies* [New York: William Morrow & Co., 1935]).

17. See Judith K. Brown, "An Anthropological Perspective on Sex Roles and Subsistence" (in *Sex Differences*, ed. Michael S. Teitelbaum [Garden City, N.Y.: Doubleday & Co., 1976], pp. 122–38), for a survey of the research on sex roles and subsistence activities. "Though men typically make a predominant contribution . . . there are numerous societies in which women make a predominant contribution" (p. 125). This variation is not random but seems to depend on two other activities which are universally sex-linked. Warfare is everywhere a predominantly male activity, and child care is everywhere a predominantly female activity. Women do more subsistence work when men are occupied by warfare and when it is compatible with child care responsibilities. Thus societies in which women predominate in subsistence activities are those which depend almost entirely on gathering or hoe cultivation.

18. See Nancy Chodorow, "Being and Doing: A Cross Cultural Guide to the Socialization of Males and Females," in *Woman in Sexist Society*, ed. V. Gornick and B. Moran (New York: Basic Books, 1971), pp. 173–97.

Striking parallels exist between cultural and sexual differences; that is, cultures differ along the same lines as those along which men and women differ in most societies. Some cultures exhibit the sort of behavior and personality usually considered masculine: everyone tends to be independent, achievement oriented, and assertive (although women still are less so than men are in the culture). In other cultures everyone tends to be compliant, obedient, and responsible—the sort of personality associated with women. Critical for us is that the differences in the "personalities" of cultures are correlated with different economies. Where animal husbandry and agriculture are the primary sources of subsistence, obedience and responsibility are essential whereas experimentation and individual initiative would be dangerous. But societies which depend largely on hunting and fishing benefit from experimentation and individual initiative and are less threatened by disobedience and irresponsibility. Women in the latter societies tend both to fish and to have their more traditional responsibilities. Though more "masculine" than men and women in other cultures, they are less "masculine" than men in their own cultures. It seems plausible to say therefore that the differences between men and women can be explained by the different sorts of labor that they do.

Within our own society, certain psychological differences between young black and young white women lend support to the hypothesis. While wealthy black adolescent girls share the traditional (white) version of femininity,[19] black adolescent girls from poor and working-class families (i.e., the majority) accept the very different values for women of strength and independence.[20] It is difficult to avoid the conclusion that the psychological differences between young black and young white women reflect the fact that black women have historically almost always been employed outside the home.

Now the Marxist view is not that there is a direct causal connection between the type of labor people do and their personality structure. Rather, the type of labor people do puts them into certain social relations, and these relations are institutionalized into sets of practices, institutions, cultural agencies, and so on. In the case of the sexual division of labor, the most important of these institutions is the family. Women are first of all raised primarily by a woman in a family. They then usually have a family of their own. Although fewer women today are full-time domestic workers than in the past, they still tend to think of their primary work and role as that of wife and mother. Their role in the family helps keep them in an inferior economic and social position. Their work outside the family, if any, is most often related to their role inside the family. Even the rare woman who both has an untraditional job and does not have a family is still shaped by the social and cultural institutions from which

19. C. B. Thoy, "Status, Race and Aspirations: A Study of the Desire of High School Students to Enter a Profession or a Technical Occupation," *Dissertation Abstracts International* 2 (1969): 10-A, abstract 3672.

20. Joyce Ladner, *Tomorrow's Tomorrow* (Garden City, N.Y.: Doubleday & Co., 1972).

she is deviating. Men who for a long time do unskilled work and are treated in a paternalistic manner at work are also psychologically affected by it, but the effect is counteracted by their dominant role in the family and by the ideology of male supremacy.

The Marxist view then is that the different generalizations true of men and women can be explained by the sexual division of labor institutionalized into sets of practices and social and cultural institutions and that this in turn can be subsumed under a theory explaining the sexual/ social division of labor. The two explanations are provided by different aspects of historical materialism. In a society where there was a significantly different sexual division of labor, different generalizations would be true of men and women. In a society where there was no sexual division of labor, there would probably be few if any generalizations that were true of men but not women, except biological ones, and there would be fewer even of these. (I shall return to this later.)

The generalizations true of women and not men describe emotions and behavior that reflect specific cognitive/affective structures more often found among women. My contention is that there is probably a common core of psychological traits found more often among women than among men throughout the world, of which women of different (sub)cultures have different subsets. The cognitive/affective structures generate the different sets of traits under different conditions. Although our knowledge at this point is too meager to say much about these structures, an adequate explanation of the differences requires that we posit such structures. What we need is a psychological theory supplemented by social and historical considerations of the kind discussed here.[21] In the traditional terminology the cognitive/affective structures would be the real essence; the disjunctive set of traits would be the nominal essence. Although the underlying structures which give rise to the different traits would more properly be called the distinct nature of women, for ordinary purposes the nature of women could be taken to be the systematically related sets of properties to which these structures give rise.

That these properties are not universal is not a reason to reject the claim that they constitute a nature. This might seem surprising, but actually it accords with the approach used in taxonomy. Contrary to Aristotelian essentialism, classifications made in biology do not require that the defining characteristics be individually necessary and jointly sufficient. The actual distribution of properties among organisms is such that most taxa names can be defined only disjunctively. Any of the disjuncts

---

21. Two recent and important books, Dorothy Dinnerstein's *The Mermaid and the Minotaur* (New York: Harper & Row, 1977) and Nancy Chodorow's *The Reproduction of Mothering* (Berkeley: University of California Press, 1978), fit this approach in that they argue that the near universal fact that women "mother" (in a psychological as well as the many physical ways) is the key to adult male and female personality structures. I disagree, however, with many of the specifics of the theories—in particular, the primary emphasis put on early childhood and on the psychological aspects of the division of labor.

is sufficient, and the few necessary properties are far from sufficient. This makes most concepts of so-called natural kinds what are called "cluster concepts." There seems no reason to apply stricter criteria in the social sphere. The account given here of women's nature makes it just such a cluster concept.

There is, then, what Marxists would call a dialectical interaction between women's labor and their nature. The sexual/social division of labor is the cause of the distinctive cognitive/affective structures that constitute women's nature, and these structures are at least a partial cause of a variety of personality traits and behavior distinctive of women, including the sorts of labor they do.

III

Let me digress for a bit to consider the objection that my arguments show that it is the biological differences between men and women and not social factors that account for these personality differences. After all, it might be argued, it is the fact that women can bear and nurse children that is the basis of the sexual/social division of labor. So, even if the latter plays some causal role as well, it is not the most basic explanation.

This point is interesting but mistaken. Not every biological difference constitutes a difference in natures. It depends on how significant causally the difference is and hence how explanatory it is. We have already seen that women are not the same at all times and in all cultures and that cultures as a whole exhibit differences similar to those between men and women in most (though not all) cultures. The biological facts—just because they are universal—cannot explain these social and historical variations. A theory which could explain them would have to be a social-historical theory. Thus, although it is obviously true that the sexual division of labor rests on the reproductive differences between the sexes, these do not constitute a difference in the natures of men and women as social beings. The significance of the biological differences depends on social-historical facts and, moreover, is maintained in every society by complicated social practices. Hence the difference in natures is primarily social and historical.

Consider this example (which I would claim to be analogous): suppose that the division of slaves into house and field workers was based entirely on the slaves' size and strength, bigger and stronger slaves becoming field workers, smaller and weaker ones becoming house workers. It is well known that there were differences in attitudes and, to some extent, personality between house and field slaves. What was the cause of these differences? Most writers point to the differences in work, working conditions, and social relations of house and field slaves. If different social conditions would have produced different psychological results, then it would be mistaken to point to the physical differences as the cause— even though they were the basis on which house and field slaves were placed in their respective social conditions.

Now some might try to extend my argument and claim not only that the differences in natures between men and women are social and historical in origin but also that the very division into men and women is social and historical in origin. After all, there is an enormous physical variety among infants and among adults. And physical similarities and differences do not by themselves determine any particular division into groups. Rather it is the significance that society gives to the physical characteristics that does this. Similar arguments regarding the classification of humanity into races are generally accepted today by informed people.

Though interesting, this argument goes wrong in its assumption as to what constitutes a biological or "natural" distinction as opposed to one that is social or historical in origin. Nothing is a "given fact of nature" in the sense presupposed in the argument. It is true that it is the significance of physical similarities and differences, rather than the physical similarities themselves, that determines a classification. Nevertheless, given that the sex difference is what allows for physical reproduction of most kinds of things, and that the distinction between things that reproduce sexually and those that reproduce by some other means is a very important one in biology, the division into two sexes has great importance for biological theory. The basis of the division into two sexes, then, is much the same as the division into species. Why should the sexual division not be called a natural distinction as well? Only if human beings were to cease to reproduce themselves sexually might the distinction between men and women cease to be of critical biological importance and hence cease to be a fundamental biological distinction. (Since they still could reproduce in the old way, however, it would still have some biological importance.) Even if that should come to pass, it would not show that until then the distinction between men and women was not a biological one. What is social and historical in origin is what is made of the distinction.

IV

It must not be forgotten that the similarities between men and women are greater than their differences. These similarities constitute their common human nature, as both biological and social beings. But within the sociohistorical category of human beings, I have argued that there are sex-differentiated natures. An individual woman will have this women's nature as a part of her human nature. She is, of course, a particular woman and more than just a woman. Aside from being human, she is, among other things, of a particular social class, race, and culture. These are categories that cut across sex lines, and some will be as important as her sex or more important. Given the methodology I am using, this means that every individual has or is constituted by several natures. There is no contradiction in this. It simply shows that there are several different sorts of facts about people and that these require different sorts of explanations, however these facts and explanations are ultimately related.

There need be no conflict between the different sorts of explanations; different areas of a woman's behavior can be explained by different aspects of her total nature. In certain conditions, however, there might be a conflict. A woman who is a wife and mother and also a wage worker will have needs and propensities based on these social relations. These will sometimes conflict, such as when she has a union meeting and responsibilities at home at the same time. Particular conditions will also make a difference: if there is a strike going on she will be more likely to go to the union meeting than at other times. We should look for theories to explain under what conditions each factor will be most important, how factors interact, and how these correlations could change given other conditions. Our theories should also explain why all this is so. Different individuals may respond somewhat differently to the same factors because of the particular conditions of their lives and their particular socialization experiences. The theories are about groups, not individuals. This is why many of the generalizations about the different social groups of which a person is a member are statistical and not universal.

It is important to make clear that the sense in which women have a distinct nature does not carry many of the usual implications of such a statement and has no implications to which feminists should object. This nature is not fixed and inevitable; natures in this sense can change. Although there is a biological element as part of its basis, the crucial determinants are not biological but social. (As we saw, even if it were entirely biological this would not make it inevitable. Not only can the biological facts be changed but also, much more important in the short run, their effects can be altered by human intervention.) That there is a distinct women's nature in my sense does not mean that every woman has this nature. The cluster of psychological traits that constitutes the nature of women as social beings need not belong to all biological females, though it would be an unusual woman to have none of the traits. Though a women's nature would explain some of women's behavior (indeed this is required for use of the concept of nature), it would not necessarily be more determinant than other aspects of her nature. Thus a woman could, over all, have more in common with a man who shared other aspects of her nature than with another woman with whom she shared this women's nature. Most importantly, a women's nature in this sense carries no moral implications about how women ought or ought not to live. Whether a type of behavior characteristic of women is morally or socially desirable is a normative issue. A further normative question is whether desirable traits should be divided up along sexual lines. Personally, I see no justification for this. In my opinion some traits more characteristic of women, such as nurturance, are desirable for everyone, while others, like passivity, are undesirable for everyone. But any opinion on this would need argumentation independent of the facts about how men and women tend to behave. The existence of socially constituted sex-differentiated natures might be relevant to the normative questions but hardly decisive.

Though talk of women's nature does not, on my account, imply that it is immutable, it does imply that it is not easily changed. The Marxist conception of a thing's nature is of something underlying and explanatory of its observable behavior. But being explanatory is not sufficient to be part of a thing's nature. Only those traits belong to a thing's nature that are systematically related, explain a variety of systematically related behavior, and are subsumable in a theoretical framework. Such features do not easily and suddenly change. A sexual division of labor with resultant psychological sex differences has been near to universal, despite variations. Today, however, things may be changing. Only a small minority of Americans (11 percent) live in the traditional nuclear family of breadwinning father, homemaker mother, and two or more children. Forty-five percent of the work force is made up of women. On the other hand, the jobs that women do for wages tend to be related to their traditional and subordinate social role: they assist, nurse, teach, serve, and clean up after others in their wage work as well as in the home. Moreover, women still do most of the parenting and housework whether or not they do wage work.[22] How much this can change within capitalism is a complicated and controversial question. And how quickly the psychological differences between the sexes would disappear if the social differences were removed remains to be seen.

In neither capitalist nor noncapitalist societies has the entry of women into paid labor been sufficient to change traditional sex roles.[23] Although one part of the traditional sexual division of labor has changed, the most important part has not. Women are oppressed by their "double duty" in both forms of society. That women working outside the home still do most of the child care and housework has to be attributed in part to psychological differences between the sexes. Even women leading fairly untraditional lives still tend to hold many of the traditional assumptions, values, expectations, and self-conceptions on a deep level. So I do not think the psychological changes will be so rapid as to refute my talk of them as "natures." On the other hand, these psychological attributes seem to be very much dependent on the objective, economic power relations between men and women. Thus, in the working class, where women's wages are a higher proportion of family income than they are in the middle class, studies show that women gain more power from employ-

22. A recent study showed that women wage workers work an average of sixty-nine hours per week (forty paid, twenty-nine unpaid), while male wage workers work an average of fifty-three hours per week (forty-four paid, nine unpaid) (cited in E. Currie, R. Dunn, and D. Fogarty, "The New Immiseration: Stagflation, Inequality and the Working Class," *Socialist Review* 10 [1980]: 7–32).

23. See Hilda Scott, *Does Socialism Liberate Women?* (Boston: Beacon Press, 1974); Maxine Molyneux, "Socialist Societies: Progress towards Women's Emancipation?" *Monthly Review* 34 (1982): 56–100.

ment.[24] And even women working in low-level traditional women's jobs have more feminist consciousness than do full-time housewives.[25] Thus there is a basis for believing that, to the extent that the sexual division of labor in society was reduced or eliminated, psychological sex differences would follow suit. As these social changes occur we are likely to see contradictions develop in the psychic structures of men and women. Using "contradiction" in the Marxist sense of structures with incompatible tendencies, the presence of contradictions in periods of change is perfectly consistent with the idea that these structures constitute natures. The difficulty of changing male and female natures does not imply that we should not try to change them. On the contrary, if they are judged to be undesirable, as I believe they are, the difficulty of change would entail that extra efforts ought to be made.

V

In the concluding section of this article I should like to explore a contrast between Marx's approach to human nature and my approach to women's nature. Although my perspective has been based on Marx's theory of human nature, there is an interesting difference on one point. The fact that human beings cannot, under capitalism, fulfill certain capacities unique to human beings is taken by many Marxists (and Marx) to be a criticism of capitalism. The fact that these aspects of their nature will be fully realized only in socialism and communism is taken to be a key reason why socialist and communist societies are in some sense better than all previous ones. Yet I have rejected any normative implications of my account of women's nature. Why is it good that human beings should fulfill their nature or aspects of their nature? And if it is good, why doesn't it follow that women should fulfill their natures too? Or is this Marxist-feminist position I have developed lacking in any consistent theoretical basis? It says that natures should be developed when I like what is part of the natures and rejects the idea when I don't like the natures.

I think there is a consistent theoretical reason for the difference on this point. It is true that of the different historical forms of human nature, such as those of feudalism, capitalism, and socialism/communism, Marx evinces a preference for the last. He often talks as if it is better that this nature should be realized and even, at times, that it is in some sense more truly human nature. What underlies this preference is not that this human nature is unique to human beings or that it differs most from the nature of other species. There is no particular reason why a group or a person should develop what is unique or special to it. Rather, Marx's preference has to do with freedom conceived as the power to act on

24. See S. J. Bahr, "Effects on Family Power and Division of Labor in the Family," in *Working Mothers*, ed. L. Hoffman and F. I. Nye (San Francisco: Jossey-Bass Inc., 1974).

25. Myra Marx Ferree, "Working Class Jobs: Housework and Paid Work as Sources of Satisfaction," *Social Problems* 23 (1976): 431–41.

one's own beliefs and desires. In Marx's theory, consciousness, and much of what is taken to be human nature, is formed by the social system in which people live. This is not to say that it is formed in every detail or that human beings are mere passive products of their society. It is to say that the broad outlines, the limits, are set by the mode of production and one's place in it. Until the institution of socialism/communism, the mode of production is not under the control of the people who live under it; social relations are exploitative and oppressive. Under socialism/communism, social relations are not exploitative because the mode of production is under conscious collective control. This means that the social determinants of human nature are under human control. Consequently there is a basis for saying that the needs, wants, and capacities that constitute the human nature of socialism and communism are acquired more freely than are those that constitute the human nature of other epochs.

There is another reason—also having to do with freedom—why Marx had a preference for the human nature of socialism and communism. As we have seen, of all the different features of a species, Marx emphasized the characteristic form of life activity as key to the nature of that species. Free, conscious activity is a transhistorical capacity of human beings that is unique to them, but it is only fully developed and realized in socialism and communism. Only when social need is the basis of production and production is under conscious collective control will there be a significant reduction of necessary labor time, beyond which, Marx says, "begins that development of human energy which is a need in itself, the true realm of freedom." He refers to this sort of labor which is only possible for most people under socialism and communism as "self-realization, objectification of the subject, hence real freedom."[26]

Thus the human nature of socialism and communism can be said to be more free than that of previous societies in two senses: first, a key aspect of this human nature is the expression of freedom, and second, the determinants of many other aspects of human nature are under people's conscious, collective control for the first time. For this reason and because it is the most developed form of what is peculiar to human beings, Marx sometimes referred to it as the most truly human nature.[27] A higher value is put on a society in which human nature takes this form because freedom is a basic value.

The women's nature discussed in this paper is disanalogous to human nature in many respects. Most important is the fact that, while there will

26. Karl Marx, *Capital* (Moscow: Progress Publishers, 1974), vol. 3, p. 820, and Marx, *Grundrisse*, p. 611.

27. Although this way of thinking about it is quite understandable, it should not be taken as negating the more relativistic analysis given earlier in the paper. See my "Free Will and a Marxist Concept of Natural Wants" (*Philosophical Forum* 6 [1975]: 423–45) for a fuller discussion of some of these issues, though with a more universalistic interpretation of Marx's theory of human nature.

always be a distinctive human nature, even in socialism/communism, it seems unlikely that there will always be a distinct women's nature. Except as a remnant of the past, there seems little reason to think that there would still be a women's nature in socialism/communism, either the present one or one specific to that society. The biological differences between men and women would remain, but this does not constitute a difference in nature for reasons discussed earlier. Moreover, the biological differences do not by themselves determine the present psychological differences between men and women. Rather, it is the sexual/social division of labor and the resulting sexually differentiated social relations and socialization that explain the differences. In Marx's theory this is determined not by biology but primarily by oppressive social, economic, and historical conditions which are not present in socialism/communism. Socialism/communism for Marx is a society of self-governing producers, the self-emancipation of the working class. Since this can come into being and survive only with the full participation of both sexes, a struggle for women's liberation is integral to the struggle for socialism. Furthermore, in a socialist society in Marx's sense there is no economic basis for women's oppression as there is in capitalism. While there might be some lingering material and psychological basis in the advantages to men, the nature both of a successful struggle for socialism and of a genuinely socialist society would substantially reduce the strength, efficacy, and longevity of such tendencies.

Now it is not impossible that the biological differences between men and women would still produce psychological differences under socialism/communism. Free, conscious activity will not take the same concrete form for everyone, and it is possible that these forms will differ along sexual lines. However, since there does not appear to be a direct biological-psychological link now, why should there be then? One could say that there would always have to be some differences in men's and women's experience of themselves as physical beings, but exactly what this means or how one would determine it is somewhat obscure. In any case, unless they were expressed in social practices and institutions, such differences, if they existed, would not have the kind of importance that would warrant speaking of them as distinct men's and women's natures. The sexual and reproductive choices women make would not have the kind of profound social consequences for women as opposed to men that they do now. So women's needs and interests, in this central and currently sex-differentiated realm, would differ very little from men's.

As we saw, the reason Marx gave a preference to the human nature of socialism and communism is that it is more freely acquired than previous forms of human nature, and freedom is a key constituent of human nature. Neither of these considerations applies to the present (and past) sex-related natures. Freedom is not a constituent of (present and past) sex-related natures, and there is no basis for saying that they were freely acquired. There is little reason to think that what is truly unique to women, bearing children, is what they would freely choose to do more than anything else. The biological differences are the basis, along with economic, social, and historical conditions, for the sexual/social division of labor and the resulting social relations—none of which are under their control. Thus the psychological sex differences that result and that constitute sex-differentiated natures are not under their control. Furthermore, ignoring the legal restrictions that exist or that have been lifted only recently, women's traditional social role and the nature associated with it involves less freedom than men's. Being a wife and mother is supposed to be women's primary aim and self-definition, and the traits desirable for women are those that make them better able to fulfill this role— being attractive to men and able to satisfy a family's needs. Leaving aside for the moment the question of whether this life is inherently less challenging and empowering than most men's lives (hence less free in Marx's sense), the point is that this is only one choice. In developed countries, at least, men have many more choices. And though, obviously, as many men are fathers as women are mothers, men are first and foremost doctors, lawyers, tailors, and sailors. Unless this is what women would be inclined to do anyway, this implies that there are greater social pressures on women than on men. When women do take on other jobs, they are still constrained by the traditional values and expectations. Standing in the way of women's wholehearted pursuit of other options are not only the objective constraints of sex discrimination and family responsibilities but, in addition, their own conflicting feelings of obligation, conflicting desires, and even habits (for example, spending a lot of time on their personal appearance). Women's lives are less free than men's are both because they are dependent on men and because they have children dependent on them. Traditional sexual values constrain women more than they do men. And women, being as a rule more passive and oriented to other people's wishes than men are, are less able to act to realize their own desires. In all these ways the present women's nature lacks the freedom involved in the human nature of socialism/communism as envisioned by Marx.

But any women's nature or indeed any sex-differentiated nature would lack this freedom. Indeed there is a contradiction in the very idea of a society in which the human nature distinctive of socialism/communism and this distinctive women's nature are both fully realized. Women (and men) are human beings. They could not simultaneously realize a limited nature determined by limiting social conditions and a nature whose essence is freedom. By definition, any sex-differentiated nature would be more limited than one not so differentiated. And while there is nothing that absolutely precludes sex-differentiated natures from being freely acquired, there seem very good empirical grounds for rejecting the idea that they could be.

Birth and Death*

Virginia Held

> Birth was not, and will not become, a worthy subject for male philosophy. It is neglected so that man may make himself. . . . Feminist philosophy will be a philosophy of birth and regeneration. [MARY O'BRIEN, *The Politics of Reproduction*][1]

I try in this paper to think anew about human birth, about the creation of human life, and about the experience of those who create human life. I argue that giving birth to human beings should not be thought to be any more "essentially natural," however that is conceptualized, than is human death. I suggest that human birth, like human death, should be understood to be central to whatever is thought to be distinctively human and that the tradition of describing birth as a natural event has served the normative purpose of discounting the value of women's experiences and activities. My discussion is often about images and associations, the preconceptual stuff philosophy should not ignore. I try to show how preconceptions shape our conceptions of birth and death, and how the standard conceptions are awry.

MAN AND NATURE

In recent years a number of feminists have successfully challenged the division that is characteristic of male thought, as so far developed—the division between "man" and "nature."[2] They have criticized the preoccupations of science and male scientists with the domination and control of nature, which has usually been conceptualized as female, and they have speculated that the thinking of women may be more apt to seek

* For extensive and helpful comments on this paper I am very grateful to Alison Jaggar, Eva Kittay, Patricia Mann, Cass Sunstein, and two anonymous editors of *Ethics*. I also thank all who commented when the paper was presented at New York University on February 29, 1988, in the Philosophy Department's Feminist Theory Lecture Series directed by Terry Winant, and those who discussed it when it was given as the Ann Palmeri Memorial Lecture at Hobart and William Smith Colleges.

1. Mary O'Brien, *The Politics of Reproduction* (London: Routledge & Kegan Paul, 1983), pp. 156 and 200.

2. See, e.g., Carolyn Merchant, *The Death of Nature: Women, Ecology, and the Scientific Revolution* (New York: Harper & Row, 1982); and Susan Griffin, *Woman and Nature* (New York: Harper & Row, 1978).

This essay originally appeared in *Ethics* 99, January 1989.

harmony between humans and their environments. Feminist theories of human progress in actual conditions should, it has been suggested, overcome the dualisms of mind and body, human and natural.

Without falling back on distinctions between "man" and "nature" as they have been formulated in the traditions of male theory, I shall nevertheless assume that we can recognize some aspects of our experience as distinctively human. Perhaps what is distinctively human should be thought of in terms of the capacities for choice, for conscious awareness, and for imaginative representation. In any case, I shall in this paper take some such characteristics for the distinctively human as given, and contrast the ways in which death and birth have been standardly interpreted. It is the contrast between death and birth on which I wish to concentrate, not the question of what, if anything, is distinctively human. I shall try to indicate the way sharp contrasts have been drawn in the traditions of male thought between the degrees of humanness thought to be involved in the events of death and birth. I shall try to suggest the extent to which the contrasts are misleading and to suggest what more satisfactory conceptions of death and birth might look like. In doing so, I shall try to show the ways in which a human being giving birth should be seen as engaged in as distinctively human an event as a human being dying. And to the extent that we continue to acknowledge a realm such as that of the "natural," human birth should not be thought to belong to it any more than does human death.[3]

There are ways in which both birth and death have been thought of as divine rather than as either human or natural events: God giveth and God taketh away. But the distinction with which I shall examine views of birth and death will be that between the human and the natural once it has been acknowledged that there is more (or less) to both the human and the natural than the hand of God.[4]

When it has been thought of as other than a manifestation of the will of God, human birth has almost always been represented as a natural, biological event, rather than as a distinctively human one. When we reflect on it with an open mind, however, we can recognize, I shall argue, that it is no more primarily a natural, biological event than is death. Philosophers and the creators of male culture throughout the ages have presented human death as distinctively human. We should, I shall try to show, recognize giving birth as no less so.

The contrast between the humanness ascribed to death and denied to birth has had vast implications for conceptions of political life and

3. For a historical account of attitudes toward death and of cultural practices surrounding dying, see Philippe Aries, *The Hour of Our Death*, trans. Helen Weaver (New York: Knopf, 1981). For a helpful discussion of views of death in the works of Goethe, Conrad, Melville, and Camus, see Konstantin Kolenda, "Facing Death: Four Literary Accounts," *Philosophic Exchange*, nos. 15–16 (1984–85), pp. 29–43.

4. I shall thus not try to cover views of childbirth, or of death, that can be thought of as primarily religious.

society. In the male realm of the polis, it is thought, men risk death for the sake of human progress; in the female realm of the household, on the other hand, it is thought that the species is merely reproduced. Clearly, in overcoming patriarchy, it will not be enough for women to be permitted to enter the "public" arena where men are willing to cause death for their beliefs. Birth and the "private" world of mothering will have to be reconceptualized and accorded the evaluations they deserve.

THE ASPECT OF CHOICE

Let us begin with the recognition that the capacity to choose (however this is further construed) is an important part of what it is to be distinctively human. And let us contrast how this capacity to choose has been emphasized with respect to death, and denied with respect to birth. Human beings, we have often been reminded, can choose what to die for. They can overcome their fears and die courageously. They can die for noble causes and die heroically. They can die out of loyalty, out of duty, out of commitment. They can die for a better future, for themselves, for their children, for humankind. They can die to give birth to nations, or democracy, to put an end to tyranny, or war. They can die for God, for civilization, for justice, for freedom. Nonhuman animals can die for none of these; that human beings can do so is an important part of and perhaps essential to what it is to be human.

Contrast all this, now, with what has been said about human birth. Birth is spoken of as a natural, biological process. That women give birth is said to make them "essentially" close to nature, resembling other mammals in this important and possibly dominant aspect of their lives. Human mothering is seen as a kind of extension of the "natural," biological event of childbirth. It is thought that women engage in the activity of mothering because they have given birth and that mothering should be incorporated into the framework of the "natural."

Until recently, childbirth has been something that has for the most part happened to women, rather than being something chosen by women. Adrienne Rich writes: "For most women actual childbirth has involved no choice whatever, and very little consciousness. Since prehistoric times, the anticipation of labor has been associated with fear, physical anguish or death, a stream of superstitions, misinformation, theological and medical theories—in short, all we have been taught we should feel, from willing victimization to ecstatic fulfillment."[5]

For most women most of the time, then, giving birth has represented most starkly women's lack of choice, their vulnerability to the forces of nature and male domination. With little chance to avoid pregnancy and few chances for abortion, women have experienced childbirth as something almost entirely outside their control.

5. Adrienne Rich, *Of Woman Born: Motherhood as Experience and Institution* (New York: Norton, 1976), p. 149.

But even in the most extreme situations, giving birth is not wholly outside the control of women. A human female can decide not to create another human being, even if to avoid doing so requires great risk. Women throughout history have attempted to end their pregnancies, often endangering their health and lives. A woman ultimately has the capacity to refuse to yield to the forces of nature and the demands of men, for these cannot take from her the possibility of attempting abortion, or of killing herself if no other means of ending her pregnancy are successful.[6] Thus any woman, unlike any animal, can intentionally avoid creating another human being. And in recent years women have increasingly been able to gain control over their capacity to give birth. Through contraception and more recently legal abortion, most women in the West now have a large measure of choice over whether or not to give birth.

If a woman chooses to try to become pregnant, or to continue with a pregnancy, she makes a choice that only a conscious human being can make, and the resulting birth is radically unlike the natural event of nonhuman birth. To construe human birth as primarily biological is as misleading as to construe human life and human death as primarily biological. Of course they are all also biological, but this is only their primary attribute in certain restricted contexts, such as a medical context, or from only one among many points of view, such as that of biology. To the extent that we recognize that there is more to human life and more to human death than can be comprehended through a biological framework, so should we recognize that there is more to human birth. If anything, giving birth is more human, because we *can* choose to avoid it, whereas death, eventually, is inevitable.

No one can possibly justify being born and no one should ever be asked to. The questions "what right do you have to have come into existence?" or "why should you have been born?" make no sense applied to the child. Any argument that a child should not have been born can only be addressed to the child's parents or to those in a position, through, for instance, social policies of various kinds, to have increased or decreased the likelihood of this birth. But the questions "why should you have a child?" or "why should you refrain from having a child?" make excellent

6. Alison Jaggar, in a private communication (January 21, 1988), has helpfully pointed out a possible paradox in the argument here, if it is supposed that what makes a human birth essentially human is that one can choose to die rather than give birth, so that once again it is the willingness to die that defines the essentially human. I do not mean to suggest that it is the woman's willingness to die that makes giving birth essentially human but, rather, that the conscious choice women can make of whether to give birth or to try not to is one of the characteristics of human birth that distinguishes it from animal birth. When less dangerous methods of avoiding or ending a pregnancy are available, there is nothing especially human about risking death to do so. Among the factors that make human birth essentially human are: that women can decide whether or not to try to end their pregnancies, that they can be conscious of the process in which they are involved, and that they can represent the surrounding decisions and events in symbolic and humanly imaginative ways.

sense addressed to potential mothers. The rarity with which these questions are seen to make human birth an other than biological event indicates yet again how unaccustomed we are to viewing the world from the point of view of women.

Men often imagine themselves to have come into existence full-blown, as rationally self-interested entities in a "state of nature."[7] Sometimes they remember that they were once children and can think back to their own childhoods or even imagine their own births. They can recognize the inappropriateness of being asked to justify their own existence. But they rarely imagine the women who gave them existence being in a position to determine whether to give them existence or not, and to do so for reasons of which women can be conscious. To understand childbirth from the point of view of women requires a shift of perspective that seems highly unusual. And yet, we can hardly hope to gain an adequate conception of human experience without exploring human life from the point of view of those in a position to create it or not create it.

Questions of what to give birth for, like questions of what to die for, or questions of what to live for, can be asked even when women have no more control over childbirth than the possibility of refusing to give birth through extreme risk to themselves.

When women have more control over whether or not to give birth, and when they have, as many now do, almost full control, the appropriateness of the questions is even more pronounced. Any woman can ask herself: Why should I give birth? What should I create a child for? To what end should I give birth? In giving birth, to what shall I be giving human expression? The compendium of reasons for which men (and women) have wondered what to die or live for can be matched by a new and even richer compendium of reasons for which women can give birth. Men (and women) can die out of loyalty, out of duty, out of commitment, and they can die for a better future. Women can give birth, or refuse to give birth, from all these motives and others. They can give birth so that a new human being can experience joy, so that humankind can continue to exist, so that the family of which they are a member can maintain itself, so that the social movement which gives them hope may have another potential adherent, so that the love they share with another may be shared with yet another. They can give birth to express their conceptions of themselves, of humanity, and of life. And so on endlessly. That women can give birth for reasons should make clear how very *unlike* a natural, biological event a human birth is.[8]

7. For a discussion of how Hobbes's conceptualizations reflect a specifically masculine point of view and a denial of mothers and mothering, see Christine Di Stefano, "Masculinity as Ideology in Political Theory: Hobbesian Man Considered," *Women's Studies International Forum* (Special Issue: *Hypatia*), vol. 6, no. 6 (1983): 633–44.

8. In patriarchal society, when reasons to give birth have been noticed, they have usually been men's reasons more than women's: the birth rate should be increased to provide new recruits for war, etc. But even bad reasons to give birth are distinctively human.

One should note that most women may not ask themselves why they should give birth, or what they should give birth for. But neither do most men (or women) ask themselves what they should die for, or even what they should live for. Most deaths are not the result of such deliberations; neither are the conducts of most lives. Most deaths happen to people, and most people live their lives with little reflection about the ends to which they can devote themselves. Nevertheless, that a human being can choose what to die for, and what to live for, characterizes our concepts of being human, and our concepts of dying a human death and living a human life. What we should open our eyes to is that women can choose what to give birth for, or what to refuse to give birth for, and that this characterizes human birth.

If it is inappropriate to ask what to give birth for, perhaps it is also inappropriate to ask what to die for. If we ought to give birth "as nature intends," to the extent that sense can be made of such a notion, and if birth should indeed be seen as "natural," then so perhaps should men live their lives and die "as nature intends," whatever that may mean. But if we recognize the appropriateness of asking for reasons to live or die one way or another, we ought to recognize reasons for giving birth. And the possibilities of deciding what to give birth for, and of choosing how to interpret what we are doing when we give birth, should characterize our concepts of woman and birth. Our concepts of woman and birth should in turn be as much at the heart of our concept of being human as are our concepts of death and of living a distinctively human life. Perhaps they should be even more central.

THE ASPECT OF AWARENESS

Consider now the aspect of human experience captured by the term 'conscious awareness.' To whatever extent other animal species may have a similar awareness, it pales beside the full human awareness of our own prospective deaths and of the meanings that can be attached to our deaths, an awareness heightened now by centuries of religious, literary, and philosophical attention. We are aware that we will die and that, in a very real sense, we die alone. We are aware that in death the selves we are as we contemplate our deaths will end. Compare this now with what is thought about birth. When birth is thought about at all in traditional male systems of thought it is usually seen in terms of "getting born," that is, of the event of the starting of a man's life. From this point of view, the point of view of a person's own birth as an infant, it must be associated with an absence of conscious awareness, not only at the event but for some time afterward. Since none of us can have been aware of our own births,[9] or can remember being born, thinking about our births, in contrast to thinking about our deaths, is thinking about a time before our own conscious awareness, the awareness with which we can think about our deaths, could have made sense to us. From the point of view

9. Not, at least, in the sense in which I am using the notion of conscious awareness.

of a man thinking about his birth and his death, there is a disanalogy.[10] Although we lose conscious awareness with death, and might lose it gradually, or before the death of our bodies, we can now be aware of what we will lose. In contrast, we could not have been aware at our births of what we would gain eventually in becoming aware. Death is seen as the ending of an awareness that is distinctively human and that has already existed. Hence a man contemplating his death will have no doubts that his death will be a human death. He can, however, and often does, see his birth as a kind of natural event subsequent to which he developed the awareness that is essential to his humanity. Or, if his religious images have led him to construe his humanity as commencing at conception, still, the event of his birth is probably construed as an event of the same type as the birth of other living creatures, part of God's plan perhaps, but not associated with a distinctively human consciousness.

Birth, then, from the point of view of the infants we once were, or of the observer of infants, is associated with the lack rather than the presence of consciousness. Death, in contrast, is what we are each approaching every day, and can be conscious of approaching throughout our lives. Sometimes persons are conscious that they are dying; we can ask of another person "does he know he's dying?" But even when death is sudden and unexpected, it is associated with the consciousness that it would come sooner or later.

If we think about birth from the point of view of the mother or potential mother, however, rather than from the point of view of a man observing an infant or thinking about the infant he once was, our conceptions of birth may be transformed. A potential mother can be consciously aware at any time that she may be the creator of a new human being, or that she may consciously seek to avoid becoming an actual mother. A pregnant woman is fully conscious for many months that she will give birth to another human being if she does not abort. She can be conscious that she can prevent this birth, although perhaps at extreme cost to herself. And upon giving birth a woman will be conscious that she has brought into existence another human being. In Eva Kittay's words, there can be for women giving birth a "wonderful consciousness of one's connection with all of nature."[11] These events of giving birth can be associated with conscious awareness as fully as any contemplation of death. And in terms of overcoming one's own limitations and death, they may far exceed anything available to men.

Consider, next, the "internal point of view" of which Thomas Nagel writes. "In acting," he observes, "we occupy the internal perspective. . . .

10. Thomas Nagel notes the very different attitudes we have toward our nonexistence prior to our births, which causes us little concern, and our nonexistence after our deaths, about which many people feel great anxiety. This illustrates in a very familiar way the disanalogy between our views of our own births and deaths (Thomas Nagel, *Mortal Questions* [London: Cambridge University Press, 1979], p. 8).

11. Eva Kittay, conversation with author, January 20, 1988.

From the inside, when we act, alternative possibilities seem to lie open before us. . . . From an external perspective . . . the agent and everything about him seems to be swallowed up by the circumstances of action; nothing of him is left to intervene in those circumstances. . . . We may elaborate this external picture by reference to biological, psychological, and social factors in the formation of ourselves and other agents. But the picture doesn't have to be complete in order to be threatening."[12] We cannot, Nagel suggests, fully accept the picture that is provided from the external perspective because "the sense that we are the authors of our own actions is not just a feeling but a belief, and we can't come to regard it as a pure appearance without giving it up altogether."[13]

Nagel thinks the problem of free will is at present insoluble, that neither the internal nor the external point of view concerning human action as so far understood is at all satisfactory. I agree. However, while almost everyone recognizes that others as well as they themselves have an internal point of view, and that the internal point of view cannot be given up without a problem for one's sense of conscious self, the concept of woman as mother has virtually omitted the internal point of view, as human mothers have been swallowed up into biological explanations and social descriptions.[14] A woman giving birth is seldom thought of from an internal point of view. A person contemplating his death from his own inner perspective understands that it cannot be adequately described only from the perspective of an external observer. That birth cannot adequately be understood from an external point of view only is an unfamiliar cultural notion. Yet it is certainly true.

THE ASPECT OF IMAGINATIVE REPRESENTATION

Consider now how the capacity for imaginative representation has been developed with respect to death and stunted with respect to birth and mothering. Tales of battle and scenes of adventure make the risking of death central to the human imagination. That human beings can consciously choose death over surrender is at the heart of the image of "man." That human beings can "transcend" their deaths by the discoveries or achievements they leave behind is part of the awareness of human beings generally.

Images of birth, on the other hand, are standardly images of natural events, if not of divine ones. Births are shrouded events, but they are

12. Thomas Nagel, *The View from Nowhere* (New York: Oxford University Press, 1986), pp. 113–14.

13. Ibid.

14. In a perceptive attempt to deal with the phenomenology of pregnancy from the subjective point of view of the mother, Iris Marion Young notes how pregnancy has been viewed: "Pregnancy does not belong to the woman herself. It either is a state of the developing foetus, for which the woman is a container; or it is an objective, observable process coming under scientific scrutiny; or it becomes objectified by the woman herself, as a 'condition.' . . . Pregnancy omits subjectivity" (Iris Marion Young, "Pregnant Embodiment: Subjectivity and Alienation," *Journal of Medicine and Philosophy* 9 [1984]: 45).

presented as things which happen, arbitrarily or inevitably, without the conscious participation of the person giving birth. Only occasionally are they imagined to be glorious events, as when they are represented as the births of the sons or prophets of a male God or the births of the heroes or adventurers who will fulfill the images familiar in representations of death.

Symbolic representations of giving birth, of creating new human persons through the distinctively human act of giving birth to a human being are rare.[15] Imaginative representations of birth from the point of view of a woman contemplating it, or of a woman experiencing a pregnancy and consciously ending or continuing it, or of a woman giving birth, are unfamiliar cultural constructions.[16] Even women who are writers and artists have rarely dealt with motherhood because it has seemed to lack value; they have often unconsciously assumed that to be serious writers and artists they must be outside rather than inside the framework of birth and mothering. The poet Adrienne Rich observed how, for many years, she did not write about her children or about mothering: "For me poetry was where I lived as no one's mother, where I existed as myself."[17]

Some feminists assert that men as a gender suffer from a preoccupation with death.[18] To the extent that dominant forms of art and culture have been largely created by men, the prevalence of death as imaginative subject would be expected. The capacity for imaginative representation of most persons is enriched in some directions and impoverished in others, depending on the cultural resources available. We can recognize how underdeveloped are the subjects of giving birth and mothering as subjects of imaginative cultural representation. This in turn means that the capacities for symbolic consideration of birth and mothering that most persons have are likely to be unnecessarily limited. Associations between death and human imaginative representations are very strong. Associations between giving birth and human imaginative representations have been very weak. But the possibilities for the imaginative consideration of giving birth, and for seeing the imaginative aspects of the activities of mothering, are of course as limitless as they are for representations of death.

15. Tillie Olsen, *Silences* (New York: Delacorte, 1979).

16. *The Birth Project*, a series of needlepoint and embroidery works designed and created under the direction of the artist Judy Chicago and shown at the R. H. Love Gallery in Chicago in 1986, and elsewhere, is remarkable in the degree to which it is innovative. Since images of birth from the point of view of those giving birth are almost nonexistent, the ones presented in this exhibition are startlingly novel.

17. Rich, p. 12.

18. See, e.g., Mary Daly, *Gyn/Ecology: The Metaethics of Radical Feminism* (Boston: Beacon, 1978). Daly, focusing especially on religious myths, believes that men as a gender display the disease of necrophilia: they desire women to be "victimized into a state of living death" (p. 59). But see especially Nancy C. M. Hartsock, "Prologue to a Feminist Critique of War and Politics," in *Women's Views of the Political World of Men,* ed. Judith Hicks Stiehm (Dobbs Ferry, N.Y.: Transnational Publishers, 1984).

Rituals surrounding human death are multiple and varied. Ritual recreations of birth, as in *couvade* (simulated birth-giving by the father), initiation rites, or the rebirth of the boy as man are common in many cultures. Restrictions on menstruating and on pregnant women are common. But rituals celebrating women's actual birth-giving are rare.[19] Thus has culture limited the imaginative representation or celebration of birth. Eva Kittay suggests that perhaps the precariousness of early human life until recently has contributed to the lack of celebration of birth itself, since if the infant may well die, one may hesitate to accord too much importance to its birth.[20] But if this were the major factor in the explanation, one would not expect *couvade* or most maternal restrictions either. With the decrease of infant mortality one could expect an increase of ritual and symbolic attention focused on birth. Without feminist awareness, however, the focus may be almost entirely on the child, as in christening rites, or on the father's role, rather than on the giving of birth by women.

In the region of experience involving the upbringing of children, the flourishing of human imagination is probably greater than in any other region of human experience. The caretakers of children, much of the time, suggest new imaginative games and encourage the flight of the child's willingness to pretend. Children fill their worlds with imagined objects, events, and experiences. These scenes and stories build on each other yet are characteristically fresh from day to day and year to year. The distinctively human symbolization involved in the development of children's speech, images, and understanding is entirely obvious. Yet representation of this experience in dominant cultural constructs often distorts the rich imaginative content of this domain, and the contributions of mothers to it, reducing child care to an aspect of the "natural." Birth and the early upbringing of children are portrayed as a kind of prehuman period in the lives of men. Little children may move about the house, like dogs and cats; they need care, like flocks and gardens. But to the extent that little children are seen as already fully human, it has in male culture been imagined to have resulted from what God rather than their mothers have given them, or to be because of the potential within them to become, as if of their own efforts, "men." And human mothering, instead of being recognized as itself composed, to a very significant extent, of imaginative representation, has been imagined to be a biological process.

19. In a 380-page book on "reproductive rituals" in some two hundred societies, the anthropologists Karen Ericksen Paige and Jeffrey M. Paige discuss *no* celebrations of actual birth. What are meant by "reproductive rituals" in the vast amount of theorizing and discussion they examine, and in their own theory to account for the rituals, are: male genital mutilation, menarcheal ceremonies, menstrual segregation practices, *couvade*, and restrictions on pregnant women (see K. E. Paige and J. M. Paige, *The Politics of Reproductive Ritual* [Berkeley and Los Angeles: University of California Press, 1981]). See also Eva Feder Kittay, "Womb Envy: An Explanatory Concept," in *Mothering: Essays in Feminist Theory*, ed. Joyce Trebilcot (Totowa, N.J.: Rowman & Allanheld, 1984), pp. 109–15.

20. Eva Kittay, conversation with author, January 20, 1988.

FEMINIST CRITIQUES

It has been said over and over in male culture that it is the natural function of women to reproduce, and then those saying this have usually gone on to say that it is also the natural function of women to care for children.[21] Since engagement in the events of giving birth, nursing, and caring for children, events seen as natural and biological, consume so much of the lives of most women, women have then been conceptualized as more immersed in nature than men.

Feminists have made the obviously valid point that men as well as women can be the caretakers of children and have shown how the concept of "natural" in the claim that women should be the ones to bring up children has been badly twisted to serve the ideological purposes of men. Men wanting to say that women ought to stay home and care for the children, or that men will make women do so if women resist, have preferred to couch these prescriptions or threats in the seemingly more neutral language of what is "natural." And feminists have successfully challenged such misuses of the term.[22]

A wide variety of feminist conceptualizations of motherhood have been proposed. Some have emphasized the relative insignificance of whether, as Plato put it, one bears or begets.[23] The fact that it is women who give birth should not be taken to imply that the whole of women's lives should be associated with motherhood, and it should not be used to justify the exclusion of women from "male" occupations. Other feminists have argued that women's reproductive biology is so fundamental a feature of the oppression of women that technological means should be developed to enable women to avoid having to give birth. Shulamith Firestone, writing early in the current wave of feminist thinking, called for birth to become something artificial, and for infants to be produced in a laboratory, so that women would no longer be defined by their biological function or be tied to its consequences.[24]

Most feminists have rejected artificial birthing as a solution to the "problem" of biology, preferring instead more natural birth processes and the social supports for childbearing and child rearing that are now

---

21. For a useful collection of what male philosophers over the centuries have said about women, see Mary Mahowald, ed., *Philosophy of Woman: Classical to Current Concepts* (Indianapolis: Hackett, 1978). See also Linda Bell, ed., *Visions of Women* (Clifton, N.J.: Humana, 1985). For discussion of such views, see especially Susan Moller Okin, *Women in Western Political Thought* (Princeton, N.J.: Princeton University Press, 1979); and Genevieve Lloyd, *The Man of Reason: "Male" and "Female" in Western Philosophy* (Minneapolis: University of Minnesota Press, 1984).

22. See, e.g., Christine Pierce, "Natural Law Language and Women," in *Woman in Sexist Society*, ed. Vivian Gornick and Barbara K. Moran (New York: Basic, 1971).

23. Plato, *Republic*, bk. 5.

24. Shulamith Firestone, *The Dialectic of Sex: The Case for Feminist Revolution* (New York: Morrow, 1970).

so inadequate.[25] In addition, recognizing the benefits for children and men as well as for women that genuinely equal participation by fathers in the care of children would bring, many feminists have sought ways to separate biological realities from the oppression of women. In doing so, the significance of the biological capacity of women to give birth has sometimes been underestimated.

Many of the feminist arguments on various sides of these issues share with nonfeminists the assumption that birth is a "natural" process. It is this assumption with which I take issue in this paper. It should, I am arguing, be rejected if a distinction is drawn anywhere, as I think it should be, between the human and the natural.

There have been a number of studies of birthing as a social rather than a natural process. Brigitte Jordan's study of birthing practices in four cultures, using a biosocial framework for its descriptions, makes clear how inadequate it is to think of human birth as primarily biological.[26] Other studies have shown how the process of giving birth was taken over and controlled by men as male obstetrics in the seventeenth and eighteenth centuries replaced the art of birthing practiced by female midwives.[27] And studies have shown us how childbirth is still an event structured by social institutions controlled by men and shaped by the ways in which men have molded the culture. That women often lose their jobs when they give birth undermines their ability to control the way giving birth will affect their lives. That the culture portrays pregnancy and childbirth as processes which should lead women to become passive recipients of the advice and treatment of a male-dominated medical profession takes from women the power to determine even that aspect of their lives which is seen as most distinctively female.[28] And the ways in which male professionals have often been able to control, through the use of what has been claimed to be "knowledge," the activities of those, almost entirely women, engaged in child care, have by now been examined.

To recognize childbirth as social, however, is not yet to acknowledge it as the fully human, as distinct from natural, event that it is. The labor of ants, for instance, can be described in social terms. Many of those who criticize the way childbirth has become a "culturally produced event" would like it to become more natural than it now is. They use the language

---

25. For an excellent account of how a recognition of women's difference from men in the area of reproduction could and should be rendered socially "costless," see Christine A. Littleton, "Reconstructing Sexual Equality," *California Law Review* 75 (1987): 201–59.

26. Brigitte Jordan, *Birth in Four Cultures: A Crosscultural Investigation of Childbirth in Yucatan, Holland, Sweden and the United States* (Montreal: Eden Press, 1980).

27. See Rich, chap. 6, "Hands of Flesh, Hands of Iron"; Barbara Ehrenreich and Deidre English, *Witches, Midwives and Nurses: A History of Women Healers* (New York: Feminist Press, 1973), and *For Her Own Good: 150 Years of Experts' Advice to Women* (New York: Doubleday, 1978).

28. See Judith Walzer Leavitt, *Brought to Bed: Childbearing in America 1750 to 1950* (New York: Oxford University Press, 1986).

of the "natural" to promote childbirth controlled by women to take the place of childbirth controlled by male institutions and male professions. But, for reasons I have tried to suggest, the language of the "natural" can be misleading.

Alison Jaggar questions whether is makes sense to speak of the biological as distinct from the social in the case of humans. "We cannot," she writes, "identify a clear, nonsocial sense of 'biology,' nor a clear, nonbiological sense of 'society.' "[29] Even something like the smaller size of women, often thought of as a biological given, can be affected by a social organization in which "the nutrition of females is inferior because of their lower social status. . . . Where human nature is concerned, there is no line between nature and culture."[30] Nevertheless, while it is clear that levels of technological development and forms of social organization deeply affect human biology, and that they certainly affect human birth and the upbringing of children, I consider it useful to maintain the possibility of distinguishing the human and the natural, and the distinctively human and the natural components of human reality. Experiences of choice, consciousness, and imaginative representation as earlier discussed are distinctively human; that calcium is a component of human bones is not.

In rejecting the division between "man" and "nature" and the consignment of women to the latter category, many feminists have recently argued that men as well as women belong to a natural universe which should be treasured rather than dominated or exploited. Adrienne Rich and others effectively protest the way childbearing has been taken over by men who control women's bodies, and child rearing by male psychiatrists and other experts who cause women to feel incompetent at even what it is supposed to be "natural" for them to do. Rich and others are critical of the way "man" sees himself as opposed to nature, and they advocate an assertion by women of their affinity with nature.

While many of us share this normative stance toward nature, we should, I think, see that it does not require a denial of significant difference between the human and the natural. Human choice, consciousness, and imagination may not adequately be reducible to natural processes. What my argument in this paper implies is that the choices, conscious experiences, and imaginative lives of women are at least as central for the concept of the distinctively human as are those of men. Instead of incorporating "man" into the domain of "nature and women," we should, I am suggesting, incorporate women into the domain of the fully human, and advocate respect by humanity even for nonhuman nature. And we should interpret giving birth as a central event in human experience.

29. Alison Jaggar, "Human Biology in Feminist Theory: Sexual Equality Reconsidered," in *Beyond Domination,* ed. Carol Gould (Totowa, N.J.: Rowman & Allanheld, 1984).

30. Ibid., pp. 37–38.

WOMEN AND REPRODUCTION

Let us look at examples of writers who, though feminist, have viewed birth as a natural, biological event, and who have thereby missed seeing its essentially human aspects. Even Simone de Beauvoir, thoroughly aware of so many of the injustices suffered by women, and coming to these views so long before most others in the recent wave of feminist thought, wrote of human birthing as a natural, animal-like process. De Beauvoir concluded that woman "is more enslaved to the species than the male, her animality is more manifest."[31]

Sherry Ortner, in an important and much cited article, agreed: "It is simply a fact that proportionately more of a woman's body space, for a greater percentage of her lifetime, and at some—sometimes great— cost to her personal health, strength, and general stability, is taken up with the natural processes surrounding the reproduction of the species."[32]

These conceptions and their implications can of course be challenged. Giving birth to a human being is no more a "natural" process than is cultivating a wheat field or taming a wild horse. It only seems so if we already, at a prior stage of the conception, deny the full humanity of the woman who gives birth. If we acknowledge her full humanity we must acknowledge the extent to which giving birth to a new human being is a human as distinct from a "natural" process as the latter term is being used. The term 'reproduction' is misleading, for it already assimilates human childbirth to the reproduction of animals. And human childbirth is radically different from the process by which animals produce repeated instances of their species.

De Beauvoir, like Hannah Arendt, sees reproduction as mere repetition.[33] "On the biological level," she writes, "a species is maintained only by creating itself anew; but this creation results only in repeating the same Life in more individuals."[34] To de Beauvoir, man, in contrast

31. Simone de Beauvoir, *The Second Sex*, trans. H. Parshley (New York: Bantam, 1953), p. 239.

32. Sherry B. Ortner, "Is Female to Male as Nature Is to Culture?" in *Woman, Culture, and Society*, ed. Michelle Zimbalist Rosaldo and Louise Lamphere (Stanford, Calif.: Stanford University Press, 1974), pp. 74–75. Though Ortner has modified her views, this essay and its formulations continue to be very influential.

33. See Hannah Arendt, *The Human Condition* (Chicago: University of Chicago Press, 1958). Arendt did not consider herself a feminist and cannot plausibly be classified as one, but from personal conversations I can record that she was beginning, late in her life, to acknowledge the validity of some feminist views.

34. De Beauvoir, pp. 58–59. For de Beauvoir, "the support of life became for man an activity and a project through the invention of the tool; but in maternity woman remained closely bound to her body, like an animal. It is because humanity calls itself in question in the matter of living—that is to say, values the reasons for living above mere life—that, confronting woman, man assumes mastery." For an excellent critical discussion of De Beauvoir on procreation, see Alison M. Jaggar and William L. McBride, " 'Reproduction' as Male Ideology," *Women's Studies International Forum* (Special Issue: *Hypatia*), vol. 8, no. 3 (1985).

with woman, much more frequently transcends, through action, the repeating of life, and "by this transcendence he creates values that deprive
pure repetition of all value."[35] De Beauvoir thinks that for women to
liberate themselves from this confinement to mere repetition, women
must be free to engage in the kind of action open to men, action which
transcends biological reproduction.

In such passages, de Beauvoir concedes what I take to be at issue:
that human childbirth is primarily a biological event. If it is not primarily
a biological event but a distinctively human event, then a woman, in
choosing to give birth to a new human being, can engage in transcendence.
No human person is a mere biological replica of any other. Every human
person is a culturally created entity as well as a biological entity. To give
birth to a new human being capable of contributing to the transformation
of human culture is to transcend what existed before. And the activity
of mothering, as it shapes a human child into a distinctive social person,
is even more clearly capable of transcendence.

De Beauvoir considers the view that "it is not in giving life but in
risking life that man is raised above the animal; that is why superiority
has been accorded in humanity not to the sex that brings forth but to
that which kills."[36] She argues eloquently against the conclusion that
women are inferior merely because they are more confined to the repetitive
biological realm than are men. But she does not dispute, as I am here
doing, the conception of childbirth as essentially biological. Similarly,
Ortner argues against the view that because they are "closer to nature,"
women should be deemed inferior, but she agrees that in fact women
are more involved with "natural functions."[37]

Ortner concludes her essay by noting that "the whole scheme is a
construct of culture rather than a fact of nature. Woman is not 'in reality'
any closer to (or further from) nature than man—both have consciousness,
both are mortal."[38] But she continues to think "there are certainly reasons
she appears that way."[39] I am trying to show why women need not even
appear to be closer to nature if we more adequately understand women
and nature. With a more satisfactory conception of human childbirth, it
can be seen that it is not the case that women are more involved than
men with merely biological processes. Ortner suggests that "ultimately,
both men and women can and must be equally involved in projects of
creativity and transcendence."[40] But she does not suggest that childbirth

35. De Beauvoir, p. 59.
36. Ibid., p. 58. For an argument that links male valuing of destruction and death
over life and birth to male envy of woman's procreative capacities, see Kittay, "Womb
Envy," p. 120.
37. Ortner, p. 76.
38. Ibid., p. 87.
39. Ibid.
40. Ibid.

can be one such project of creativity and transcendence, which is the position I am putting forward.

Elsewhere in her essay, Ortner writes of lactation and nursing as "natural."[41] But there is no reason to think of nursing as any more natural than, say, eating. What and how we eat is thoroughly cultural, and whether and how long a woman nurses is also a cultural matter. If men transcend the natural by domesticating animals, cultivating new territory, and trading foodstuffs with their neighbors, women can transcend the natural by choosing not to nurse their children when they could, or choosing to nurse when their culture tells them not to, or singing songs to their infants as they nurse, or dressing their nursing infants in the styles of their neighbors, and so forth. The culture surrounds and characterizes the activity of nursing as it does the activity of eating.

FAMILY AND POLIS

A long line of thinkers have associated the "public" sphere with the distinctively human, the "private" with the natural. They have represented the family as focused on particularistic and hence inferior concerns, often in conflict with the superior and more universal concerns of the "public" sphere.[42] In Ortner's formulation of this way in which the family has been seen, "the family (and hence women) represents lower-level, socially fragmenting, particularistic sort[s] of concerns, as opposed to interfamilial relations representing higher-level integrative, universalistic sorts of concerns."[43]

If we try to do so, it is easy enough, in questioning such an ordering of women and the family versus men and the polis, to rethink what is "lower" and what is "higher" in such a contrast. One could describe family relations as rich, subtle, and capable of emotional sensitivity, compared to legal-political relations which are rough, crude, and insensitive. One could think of family relations as "higher" in many respects, and what to conclude about the balance of both should be an open question. Though the two domains are different, and often focused on different concerns, it is clearly an unsatisfactory distortion of their reality, even as it has existed, and certainly as it could exist in the future, to think of the public sphere as distinctively human and the sphere of mothering persons and children as involved in mere reproduction.

The claim that the family is particularistic while the polis deals with what is universal is questionable even in terms of existing institutions. And if the wall between the "private" and the "public" were to be dismantled in the ways many feminists advocate, support for the claim might erode.[44]

---

41. Ibid., p. 77.
42. For example, Aristotle, Kant, Hegel, Lévi-Strauss, Arendt.
43. Ortner, p. 79.
44. See, e.g., Jaggar and McBride.

It is true that some public decisions involve large numbers of people in contrast to family decisions involving only a few. But consider a paradigm of the "public" sphere: a court of law. Here, typically, a single defendant is judged by a few individuals, and no case is quite like any other. It may be true that "universal" legal norms and requirements are being applied to this case, but in a family, so can universal norms and requirements be applied: parents may decide they ought to educate their child a certain way because they believe all parents ought to do so. Particular adolescents may seek independence from parental control; this is a "universal" of human development for which general norms can be sought. That no set of universal norms is adequate for the particular moral problems that arise in a given family can be matched by the recognition that no set of universal laws can truly do justice to all the particular aspects of a given court case. That state power is involved in a court of law can be matched by the acknowledgment that state power determines permissible family structure and greatly affects relations between family members. That individual personalities must be accommodated in family interactions can be matched by a recognition of how significantly individual personalities of lawyers, judges, jury members, defendants, and plaintiffs affect the outcomes of court decisions. And so on.

Finally, in a hierarchically organized society, the supposedly "private" decisions of powerful persons and families can affect the employment and well-being of countless others. Though we may continue to need different norms for different domains of human life,[45] we should resist the terms on which conceptual claims have been built by patriarchal society. Among the concepts most clearly in need of reconceptualization are those of "public" and "private" with their varying but characteristic associations with male and female.

The way the terms have been associated with men and women and each other has been different at different periods of history. The Greek polis was a male domain; women were confined to the household. But before the rise of liberal democracy, the family, with its clearly designated male ruler, was often seen as a model for the wider society. With the Lockean renunciation of political patriarchy, the family was relegated to a peripheral status outside and irrelevant to the political organization of "free and equal men." Since then, liberal concessions toward equality for women have usually expected women to enter a political sphere structured by concepts designed for a male polis. Recently, some feminists are reversing these expectations and are suggesting that the postpatriarchal family and its norms be considered highly relevant as a model for much more than the family.[46] Perhaps the postpatriarchal family should even be a model for much in political life.

45. See Virginia Held, *Rights and Goods: Justifying Social Action* (New York: Free Press, Macmillan, 1984).

46. See, e.g., Virginia Held, "Non-contractual Society: A Feminist View," in *Science, Morality and Feminist Theory*, ed. Marsha Hanen and Kai Nielsen, *Canadian Journal of Philosophy*,

From the time of the ancient Greeks it has been held that man "transcends" his animal, material nature while engaged in the public life of the polis, while those immersed in the daily tasks of the private household are engaged in the mere maintenance of man's material nature. We can, for reasons I have suggested, dispute this contrast. Human beings engaged in giving birth and in bringing up children are as capable of "transcending" what already exists as are those in government or the arts and sciences. Creating new human persons and new human personalities with new thoughts and attitudes is as creative an activity as humans are involved in anywhere. And the norms for this activity may be a better source of recommendations for actions in various other domains than are the norms of what has traditionally been thought to constitute "morality."[47] At least, many feminists now believe, an "ethic of care" must be taken as seriously as an "ethic of justice."

In claiming that women, in giving birth and rearing children, can indeed engage in "transcendence" and in the distinctively human and cultural activities of moving beyond mere repetition, we need of course to be on guard against misuses of such arguments. There will predictably be those who will say that since childbirth and child care are such admirable activites, women should have no complaints about being confined to them. But from recognizing that birth should be at the heart of our conceptions of life, and from celebrating the wondrousness of empowering a child to live a good human life, it absolutely does not follow that women should be confined to child rearing or encouraged to accept the leadership of men in any domain. What more plausibly is implied is that the world should be organized to be hospitable to children and conducive to the flourishing of all persons, and that men, having failed to bring about such a condition, should have their leadership replaced or supplemented by those who may, with different perspectives, methods, and abilities, do better.

Changes taking place in society in which more fathers share in parenting, and more mothers in work outside the home, are promising. There are on independent grounds excellent and obvious reasons why other forms of transcendence and cultural activity than giving birth and mothering should be fully open to women. And there may be very good reasons why child care should be fully shared by men, and reasons for men to be able in nonsexist society to participate in decisions concerning the creating of new persons. The point is that adequate conceptualizations of childbirth and child care would recognize their distinctively human features.

---

suppl. vol. 13 (Calgary: University of Calgary Press, 1987). See also Sara Ruddick, "Preservative Love and Military Destruction: Some Reflections on Mothering and Peace," in Trebilcot, ed.

47. See especially Eva Kittay and Diana Meyers, eds., *Women and Moral Theory* (Totowa, N.J.: Rowman & Littlefield, 1987). See also Carol Gilligan, *In a Different Voice: Psychological Theory and Woman's Development* (Cambridge, Mass.: Harvard University Press, 1982).

We might speculate that for the reconceptualization of childbirth and child care for which I am arguing to be successfully accepted on a wide scale in a society, men may have to engage in domestic life as fully as women, and women in the political structuring of society as fully as men. But those willing to explore feminist perspectives need not wait for such a social transformation before changing their own conceptions of birth and of family life and of their implications for political theory.

MARXIST CATEGORIES

The Marxist view of childbirth and child rearing has been essentially similar to the other views we have been examining. The traditional Marxist conception sees childbirth as an entirely biological process. And then, as Alison Jaggar notes, the implicit implication is "that women, who are primarily procreative laborers, are biologically determined to a greater extent than men are."[48] Moreover, traditional Marxists have extended the biological view of childbirth to the raising of children. "Marx and Engels," Jaggar writes, "clearly believe that the division of labor within the family is natural because it is biologically determined, 'based on a purely physiological foundation.' "[49]

Marxist analyses divide social activity into those activities connected with production, and those connected with reproduction. In industrialized society, in the view of traditional Marxists, work in the factory or on the farm belong to the sphere of production; childbirth and housework belong to the sphere of reproduction. Production transforms the human environment, making raw materials into machines and finished products; reproduction merely repeats the bringing into existence of biological human entities.[50]

---

48. Alison Jaggar, *Feminist Politics and Human Nature* (Totowa, N.J.: Rowman & Allanheld, 1983), p. 76. See also Jaggar and McBride.

49. Jaggar, *Feminist Politics and Human Nature*, p. 68.

50. In his introduction to the *Origin of the Family, Private Property and the State*, Engels wrote: "The determining factor in history is, in the final instance, the production and reproduction of immediate life. This, again, is of a twofold character; on the one side the production of the means of existence, of food, clothing and shelter and the tools necessary for that production; on the other side, the production of human beings themselves, the propagation of the species" (Frederick Engels, *The Origin of the Family, Private Property and the State*, ed. Eleanor Leacock [New York: International Publishers, 1972], p. 71). In assessing these analyses, Jaggar concludes that "the traditional Marxist categories were not designed to capture the essential features of the sexual division of labor, and it is doubtful whether they are capable of doing the job. . . . The central Marxist categories hardly apply at all to the household" (Jaggar, *Feminist Politics and Human Nature*, p. 74). Marxist theory is far more concerned with production than with reproduction. When it does examine work in the household, it considers it work outside the sphere of production, especially of capitalist production. Household work is thought of as reproducing human labor power. "Reproduction," Jaggar writes, "itself is broken down into two parts: the daily regeneration of the labor power of existing workers, through rest and food; and the production of new workers, through childbearing and childrearing." Jaggar understandably finds this way of construing the work of women to be unsatisfactory (ibid.). See also Lorenne M. G. Clark, "Consequences

Socialist feminists have objected to the faultiness of many of these conceptions. Some have pointed out that childbirth and child rearing and housework in general contribute very significantly to production. They have tried to understand the economic value and effects of the work of "servicing" existing workers through cooking, cleaning, and so forth and of "producing" new workers.[51]

Ann Ferguson and Nancy Folbre have focused on what they call "sex-affective production," or the production of that which is required for childbearing, child rearing, and "the fulfillment of human needs for affection, nurturance, and sexual expression."[52] They discuss the ways women have been oppressed by the division of labor in which "most of [the] responsibilities and requirements" of sex-affective production "are met by women."[53] The gender identity into which women are socialized "keeps them willing to give more than they receive from men in nurturance and sexual satisfaction."[54] And the division of labor by which the burdens of sex-affective production fall mainly on women "is not a neutral one, assigning 'separate but equal' roles. It is an oppressive one, based upon inequality and reinforced by social relation[s] of domination."[55]

Alison Jaggar and William McBride have noted the serious ambiguities in the categories of production and reproduction; they have concluded that the distinction distorts the reality of women's work and serves largely to obscure the way women's labor is exploited by men. They propose that "procreation and nurturing are production in the broadest Marxist sense of being necessary to human life and they are increasingly productive in the capitalist sense of falling within the market."[56] In their view, procreative and nurturing activities are "just as fully forms of human labor" as are the activities involved in agriculture or manufacturing.[57]

While these views represent highly important theoretical advances over those views which relegate childbirth and child care to a realm of biological reproduction, they do not yet seem adequate for capturing the reality of childbirth and child care. Either they subordinate relations

---

of Seizing the Reins in the Household: A Marxist-Feminist Critique of Marx and Engels," in Stiehm, ed. She shows how Marx and Engels thought the division of labor between men and women was based on "natural" physiological factors, and how they failed to see "the extent to which sexual inequality was based . . . on social conventions" (p. 181). For further discussion, see especially Jaggar and McBride.

51. See especially Maria Rosa Dalla Costa and Selma James, *The Power of Women and the Subversion of Community* (Bristol: Falling Wall, 1973); and Lydia Sargent, ed., *Women and Revolution* (Boston: South End, 1981).

52. Ann Ferguson and Nancy Folbre, "The Unhappy Marriage of Patriarchy and Capitalism," in Sargent, ed., p. 317.

53. Ibid., p. 319.

54. Ibid.

55. Ibid. See also Anne Ferguson, "On Conceiving Motherhood and Sexuality," in Trebilcot, ed.

56. Jaggar and McBride, p. 194.

57. Ibid., p. 195.

between mothering persons and children to the wider conception of economic production, or they employ concepts developed for a realm quite foreign to birth and nurturance. Since Marxist concepts of production have been developed for a context which is overwhelmingly economic, it may be almost as inappropriate to think of childbirth and child rearing as forms of "production" as it is to think of them as forms of mere "reproduction." Giving birth may be closer to artistic expression than it is to the production of material objects; both can involve very hard work but the desire to express oneself in the activity may be paramount, and certainly the activity of mothering can be more expressive than productive. Not everything that human beings do is best thought of as a form of labor. We seem to need to continue our quest for a way of conceptualizing childbirth and child care, a way that will adequately reflect and guide the experience of women.

O'BRIEN

One of the most interesting and important attempts to rethink birth has been made by Mary O'Brien. In an eloquent book, she has analyzed women's consciousness of the process of birth, showing how it must differ in significant ways from the consciousness men have of reproduction.[58] She effectively criticizes the failures of Arendt, de Beauvoir, and others to value women's reproductive labor. O'Brien emphasizes that women's reproductive labor is transformative and on a par with the transformative labor of production central to Marxist theory. She perceives the deficiencies of Marxist theories in their handling of the domain of reproduction and calls attention to the need for feminist theory concerning birth.

Her own speculations concerning the origins of patriarchy are suggestive. For men, she points out, awareness of paternity can rest only on a theory about reproduction, whereas women can directly experience genetic continuity. In her analysis, the male "alienates" his seed in the procreative process. To overcome his inability, himself, to produce a child, he acts to assure his own paternity of a given child and to establish the right to appropriate as his a child that has been produced: he bands together with other 'men to form the social framework that will keep women in a private sphere and assure his access to the means of reproductive labor.

The development of the technology by which women can control their own reproductive processes is in O'Brien's view what Hegel calls a world historical event. It can be expected to alter drastically the consciousness of women and relations between men and women. In O'Brien's view, "the freedom for women to choose parenthood is a historical development as significant as the discovery of physiological paternity. Both

---

58. See O'Brien, *The Politics of Reproduction*. See also Mary O'Brien, "Reproducing Marxist Man," in *The Sexism of Social and Political Theory*, ed. Lorenne Clark and Lynda Lange (Toronto: University of Toronto Press, 1979), p. 104.

create a transformation in human consciousness of human relations with the natural world which must, as it were, be re-negotiated."[59]

O'Brien's account is perceptive and should be examined by all who attempt to rethink the concepts of birth and motherhood. She observes that paternity is a more social than biological phenomenon: "The appropriation of the child defies the uncertainty of paternity, yet it cannot do so in biological terms. It must do so in social and ideological terms. . . . The appropriation of the child cannot be made without the cooperation of other men."[60]

Her analysis, however, seems to me too narrowly focused on the moment of birth. Giving birth can be relatively less important in a woman's life and in shaping her consciousness than the years of child rearing in which she engages. The characteristics of female consciousness may arise more from the whole process of bringing an infant into the world and then nurturing it to adulthood than from the process of reproduction seen as ending with birth.[61] And since O'Brien wishes to contrast reproduction with the production analyzed more or less adequately, in her view, by Marx, what counts as "reproduction" should include rather than exclude the upbringing of children. But then it is not true that only women can engage in reproduction, since men can share in the upbringing and daily care of children. Hence O'Brien's formulation in which "only women perform reproductive labour" is unsatisfactory.[62]

Furthermore, the concept of "reproduction" is unfortunate. It suggests repetition, copying, producing more of the same. But since each new generation of human persons is as different, in terms of the social reality each incorporates, as is each stage of the economic reality changed over the generations by the labor of production, the contrast should not be in terms of production versus reproduction. It would be more helpful to draw the distinction in terms of such notions as economic production and the creation of social persons; or in terms of shaping the environment and shaping new persons, and transforming both. As O'Brien formulates the issues, she does focus on reproduction, or the process of giving birth to infants, and the labor that is involved in this. As I try to reconceptualize birth, I look to the event of giving birth but see in it not only the fruit of a woman's labor but also of her consciousness, and in addition, the beginning of the upbringing that will be required to bring the infant to autonomous personhood. *In both giving birth and mothering the woman expresses the kind of woman she chooses to be.*

As men come to care for children, they may be able to experience much of the very genetic continuity for which O'Brien thinks they go to

59. O'Brien, *The Politics of Reproduction*, p. 22.
60. Ibid., p. 53.
61. See, e.g., Sara Ruddick, "Maternal Thinking," in Trebilcot, ed.; and Virginia Held, "Feminism and Moral Theory," in Kittay and Meyers, eds. See also Reyes Lazaro, "Feminism and Motherhood: O'Brien vs. Beauvoir," *Hypatia* 1 (1986): 87–102.
62. O'Brien, *The Politics of Reproduction*, p. 14.

such lengths to compensate. To "see oneself" in one's child, in the shape of a hand or tilt of an eyebrow, reminds one of this continuity. It may remind a father that the child is his as well as the mother's (the mother, after all, may sometimes worry also: infants are occasionally exchanged, and the one she holds in her arms may possibly not be the one to whom she has given birth . . .). This awareness on the part of men, occasioned especially in the practice of child care, can be an awareness of genetic continuity that would seem to be able, at least to some extent, to overcome the male discontinuity between copulation and birth. Even more to the point, perhaps, a shared contribution by the father in the care of the child can overshadow the "separation" in which the mother but not the father actually "creates" the infant. Fathers as well as mothers can perform the transformative labor of bringing infants to grown personhood. And adoptive parents as well as genetic parents can experience a kind of continuity.

Whether to create an infant remains the mother's and not the father's ultimate decision since after conception the potential mother has the capacity to do so and the potential father does not. From this perspective, the questions that should be asked concern what can be expected for the child and asked of the person she or he will, with care, become. Although men can participate in discussing these issues, the power to give birth remains the mother's, and the right to use or to refrain from using this power ought to be hers, at least until patriarchy has been safely overcome. And human birth should be celebrated above human death. But just as women should increasingly be recognized as having the capacities to engage in a full range of activities outside the household, the abilities of men to participate in various aspects of birth and nearly all aspects of child care should also be acknowledged.

For Mary O'Brien, the technology allowing women's control over reproduction is what can be expected to transform history.[63] The feminist revolution she believes to be occurring will, in her view, drastically alter human society by breaking down the distinction between public and private. But we might also note, I think, that a changed conception of birth and of the upbringing of children, and changed conceptions of the appropriate participation of men and women in the activities involved, could, if acted upon, have brought about many of the anticipated changes even without the technology. Since the changes could have taken place apart from the technology, arguments for such changes should depend less on the level to which science has advanced, and more on conceptions

---

63. "Reproductive process," O'Brien writes, "is not only the material base of the historical forms of the social relations of reproduction, but . . . is also a dialectical process, which changes historically" (ibid., p. 21). The first significant change in the process occurred as a change in male reproductive consciousness, with the discovery of physiological paternity. "The second and much more recent change in reproductive praxis is brought about by . . . contraceptive technology" (ibid., p. 21).

of giving birth and of mothering as central human activities rather than as merely natural, biological events.

Various feminists express worries all should share that the new technology surrounding late twentieth-century childbirth will be used to uphold patriarchy rather than to liberate women. Such techniques as in vitro fertilization and embryo transfer can deprive women of grounds they have had from which to demand consideration.[64] These are certainly concerns; they make clear that who controls technology can often be more important than technology itself. In trying to deal with conceptions of childbirth and child care, I am not suggesting that changed conceptions alone can lead to changed configurations of power in the traditional sense. I am trying only to deal with the ideas that I take to be one necessary component in a change of such power relations.

WOMEN AND PATRIARCHY

In citing the work of women, including feminist women, to illustrate the misconceptions involved in holding that women are more involved than men in the primarily biological, I do not intend to accuse such women of collaboration with patriarchy, but to substantiate the depth of the traditional distortions. If even such women as de Beauvoir and Ortner and various other feminists have been deceived by the traditional view, we can appreciate how difficult it is to break free of it.

That even so powerful an intellect as Hannah Arendt's moved so little distance beyond the mistaken view that the birthing and upbringing of children are essentially "natural" processes drenched in immanence, as distinct from the transcendence of the work performed in the polis, deepens our awareness of how subservient vast amounts of our thinking are to these faulty conceptual assumptions. That even de Beauvoir, so perceptive of the domination of women by men in so many ways, should share the mistaken construals of birth and child care as inherently "natural" reminds us of how gendered are the underlying assumptions with which we must begin and from which we can of course not break free all at once.[65] And that even the more recent thinking of many feminists retains the traditional and faulty conceptualization of human childbirth as "re-production" makes it clear that to overthrow the conceptions of patriarchy is a monumental task.

Not only has the dominant culture denigrated the giving of birth, it has also developed a venerated view of what is taken to be a form of birth-giving: intellectual and artistic creation, and it has associated this

---

64. See, e.g., Gena Corea, *The Mother Machine: Reproductive Technologies from Artificial Insemination to Artificial Wombs* (New York: Harper & Row, 1985). See also Anne Donchin, "The Future of Mothering: Reproductive Technology and Feminist Theory," *Hypatia* 1 (1986): 121–37.

65. On the ways in which the concept of "rational man" is a gendered concept, see Lloyd.

kind of creation with the male. The capacity to "give birth to" wisdom, knowledge, and art has long been set beside the mere bodily capacity to give birth to infants. Not only have such metaphors of creativity suggested that men also can give birth: they have fixed the association of "male" with the former and "higher" type of creativity, "female" with mere propagation of the species.

As Nancy Hartsock recounts the early history of such associations, "the real activity of reproduction is thus replaced by the mental activity of achieving wisdom and immortality."[66] Writing of Plato's *Symposium*, whose account of paternity can be seen also in Pythagoras and in Aristotle, she shows how the attitude has developed that "there is an opposition of creativity to fertility—the one a male capacity, the other a female property."[67] Whereas for the Homeric warrior-hero, immortality was to be achieved by dying a glorious death in battle, for Plato, "immortality can now be achieved by begetting immortal children in the forms of art, poetry, and philosophy."[68] Men, thus, are imagined to be able to give birth, by themselves, to what is truly valuable; women give birth only to flesh.

How can we possibly free ourselves from the assumptions and fundamental concepts of patriarchy?[69] To nearly all feminists, patriarchy is not inevitable. We do not know whether a tendency to wish to dominate is present or not in males, or possibly in all persons, but even if it is, this by no means suggests that society ought to be structured to reflect and to reinforce this tendency rather than to curb it. Society now curbs many "natural" tendencies: people wear eyeglasses, for instance.[70] Society counteracts innumerable tendencies toward disease and disability. Further, it establishes norms that routinely conflict with tendencies thought to be "natural." For example, it establishes what to hold concerning what belongs to whom, and it curbs tendencies to take from others what does not, according to given social rules, belong to one. That such rules concerning property have usually been highly unjust does not change the fact that they restrain various tendencies, and can be made more just. A society

66. Nancy Hartsock, *Money, Sex, and Power* (New York: Longman, 1983), p. 197. See also Kittay, "Womb Envy." For an interesting interpretation of Cartesian thought as an expression of the "*re*-birthing and re-imaging of knowledge and the world as masculine," see Susan Bordo, "The Cartesian Masculinization of Thought," *Signs: Journal of Women in Culture and Society* 11 (1986): 439–56, esp. 441. Bordo suggests that "the possibility of objectivity . . . is conceived by Descartes as a kind of *re*-birth, on one's own terms, this time" (p. 448).

67. Ibid.

68. Ibid.

69. Alison Jaggar explains, in *Feminist Politics and Human Nature*, why she avoids the use of 'patriarchy' as a general term. I share the view of others that while the forms of patriarchy have been different in different historical contexts and for different groups in them, we can usefully employ the concept to call attention to the male dominance they have in common.

70. I am grateful to Cass Sunstein for this terse example.

could well curb tendencies in men as a group to try to dominate women as a group, if such tendencies exist, and if the members of that society would choose to do so.

It is increasingly becoming clear that in trying to overcome the long history of patriarchy, we need to overthrow traditional ways of thinking as well as traditional ways of acting. Among the views that need to be turned around, as I have tried to show, are views that see human childbirth as primarily natural or biological. Also in need of transformation are views that see women as inevitably vulnerable to domination, and views that political life must always be organized around male conceptions of power.

WOMEN'S UNDERSTANDING

Some anthropologists have speculated about a time in human history that can be called prepatriarchal.[71] Mary O'Brien convincingly argues that after men discovered their role in paternity, a "generic struggle" must have occurred that was protracted and bitter.[72] Only after such a lengthy contest was the female gender subordinated. If we look ahead to images of a future in which patriarchy is finally overthrown, the images will seem less distant and less utopian if we successfully reconceptualize giving birth and creating new persons.

Goddess cults have at times been prominent, and their images may help us to free ourselves from the patriarchal images with which we have all grown up. One of the fascinations of trying to imagine prepatriarchal society, whether or not it in fact existed, is that it opens the imagination to alternative conceptions. Attention to the goddess-worship characteristic of some cultures can alter our perspective and allow us to envision a social order totally unknown to us. Adrienne Rich writes that "the images of the prepatriarchal goddess-cults did one thing; they told women that power, awesomeness, and centrality were theirs . . . the female was primary."[73] But this power was not the power to cause others to submit to one's will, the power which led men to seek hierarchical control and then contractual restraints between men of equal power. It was the power to create and to transform. Rich writes: "Not power *over others*, but transforming power, was the truly significant and essential power, and this, in prepatriarchal society, women knew for their own."[74]

Women today need to recognize as their own the extraordinary human power to transform mere genetic material into new human persons. But women would do well, I am arguing, to recognize this power, in humans, as a human rather than "natural" power, to whatever extent such a distinction is appropriate for any domain, such as that in which

71. See Rich, pp. 80–97, for discussion.
72. O'Brien, *The Politics of Reproduction*, p. 147.
73. Rich, p. 81.
74. Ibid., p. 86.

human death is distinguished from a "natural" event, and that in which human art is seen as distinctively human.

Not only would giving birth not have to be a source of oppression in a society that appropriately valued women and children, and that organized child care in supportive and considerate ways, but the capacity of women to give birth and to nurture and empower also could be the basis for new and more humanly promising conceptions than the ones that now prevail of power, empowerment, and growth. Patterns of activity to express these conceptions have begun to be imagined by various feminist writers.[75] Instead of organizing human life in terms of expected male tendencies toward aggression, competition, and efforts to overpower, and in terms of institutions to contain male aggression by balancing and equalizing the power to bend others to one's will, one might try to organize human life to nurture creativity, cooperation, and imagination, with the point of view of those who give birth and nurture taken as primary. Instead of starting with assumptions of isolated, self-seeking individuals accommodating to one another's competitive and aggressive desires, or of contending economic classes overcoming their conflicts, if one starts with the assumptions of life-giving and nurturing beings, one might be led to imagine entirely different ways of organizing society than are familiar to us.[76]

To imagine and to strive for postpatriarchal society, those who give birth and nurture need to affirm their own point of view, and to discover the outlines, the shapes, the details, and the meanings their own points of view can yield. Only when the conscious experience of mothers, potential mothers, and mothering persons are taken fully into account can we possibly develop understanding that may someday merit the description "human." And only when human birth and mothering are appreciated as the fully human achievements they are can we expect that human death will be less often pointless, debased, and unnecessarily early.

75. The best example may still be Charlotte Perkins Gilman's *Herland* (1915; reprint, New York: Pantheon, 1979). Also suggestive is Marge Piercy's *Woman on the Edge of Time* (New York: Fawcett, 1976).

76. See, e.g., Iris Marion Young, "Humanism, Gynocentrism and Feminist Politics," *Women's Studies International Forum* 8 (1985): 173–83. See also Kittay and Meyers, eds.; and Held, "Non-contractual Society: A Feminist View."

Part II

Equality and Inequality in Politics and Elsewhere

Polity and Group Difference: A Critique of the Ideal of Universal Citizenship

Iris Marion Young

An ideal of universal citizenship has driven the emancipatory momentum of modern political life. Ever since the bourgeoisie challenged aristocratic privileges by claiming equal political rights for citizens as such, women, workers, Jews, blacks, and others have pressed for inclusion in that citizenship status. Modern political theory asserted the equal moral worth of all persons, and social movements of the oppressed took this seriously as implying the inclusion of all persons in full citizenship status under the equal protection of the law.

Citizenship for everyone, and everyone the same qua citizen. Modern political thought generally assumed that the universality of citizenship in the sense of citizenship for all implies a universality of citizenship in the sense that citizenship status transcends particularity and difference. Whatever the social or group differences among citizens, whatever their inequalities of wealth, status, and power in the everyday activities of civil society, citizenship gives everyone the same status as peers in the political public. With equality conceived as sameness, the ideal of universal citizenship carries at least two meanings in addition to the extension of citizenship to everyone: (*a*) universality defined as general in opposition to particular; what citizens have in common as opposed to how they differ, and (*b*) universality in the sense of laws and rules that say the same for all and apply to all in the same way; laws and rules that are blind to individual and group differences.

During this angry, sometimes bloody, political struggle in the nineteenth and twentieth centuries, many among the excluded and disadvantaged thought that winning full citizenship status, that is, equal political and civil rights, would lead to their freedom and equality. Now in the late twentieth century, however, when citizenship rights have been formally extended to all groups in liberal capitalist societies, some groups still find themselves treated as second-class citizens. Social movements of oppressed and excluded groups have recently asked why extension of equal citizenship rights has not led to social justice and equality. Part of the answer is

This essay originally appeared in *Ethics* 99, January 1989.

straightforwardly Marxist: those social activities that most determine the status of individuals and groups are anarchic and oligarchic; economic life is not sufficiently under the control of citizens to affect the unequal status and treatment of groups. I think this is an important and correct diagnosis of why equal citizenship has not eliminated oppression, but in this article I reflect on another reason more intrinsic to the meaning of politics and citizenship as expressed in much modern thought.

The assumed link between citizenship for everyone, on the one hand, and the two other senses of citizenship—having a common life with and being treated in the same way as the other citizens—on the other, is itself a problem. Contemporary social movements of the oppressed have weakened the link. They assert a positivity and pride in group specificity against ideals of assimilation. They have also questioned whether justice always means that law and policy should enforce equal treatment for all groups. Embryonic in these challenges lies a concept of *differentiated* citizenship as the best way to realize the inclusion and participation of everyone in full citizenship.

In this article I argue that far from implying one another, the universality of citizenship, in the sense of the inclusion and participation of everyone, stands in tension with the other two meanings of universality embedded in modern political ideas: universality as generality, and universality as equal treatment. First, the ideal that the activities of citizenship express or create a general will that transcends the particular differences of group affiliation, situation, and interest has in practice excluded groups judged not capable of adopting that general point of view; the idea of citizenship as expressing a general will has tended to enforce a homogeneity of citizens. To the degree that contemporary proponents of revitalized citizenship retain that idea of a general will and common life, they implicitly support the same exclusions and homogeneity. Thus I argue that the inclusion and participation of everyone in public discussion and decision making requires mechanisms for group representation. Second, where differences in capacities, culture, values, and behavioral styles exist among groups, but some of these groups are privileged, strict adherence to a principle of equal treatment tends to perpetuate oppression or disadvantage. The inclusion and participation of everyone in social and political institutions therefore sometimes requires the articulation of special rights that attend to group differences in order to undermine oppression and disadvantage.

I. CITIZENSHIP AS GENERALITY

Many contemporary political theorists regard capitalist welfare society as depoliticized. Its interest group pluralism privatizes policy-making, consigning it to back-room deals and autonomous regulatory agencies and groups. Interest group pluralism fragments both policy and the interests of the individual, making it difficult to assess issues in relation to one another and set priorities. The fragmented and privatized nature of the political process, moreover, facilitates the dominance of the more powerful interests.[1]

In response to this privatization of the political process, many writers call for a renewed public life and a renewed commitment to the virtues of citizenship. Democracy requires that citizens of welfare corporate society awake from their privatized consumerist slumbers, challenge the experts who claim the sole right to rule, and collectively take control of their lives and institutions through processes of active discussion that aim at reaching collective decisions.[2] In participatory democratic institutions citizens develop and exercise capacities of reasoning, discussion, and socializing that otherwise lie dormant, and they move out of their private existence to address others and face them with respect and concern for justice. Many who invoke the virtues of citizenship in opposition to the privatization of politics in welfare capitalist society assume as models for contemporary public life the civic humanism of thinkers such as Machiavelli or, more often, Rousseau.[3]

With these social critics I agree that interest group pluralism, because it is privatized and fragmented, facilitates the domination of corporate, military, and other powerful interests. With them I think democratic processes require the institutionalization of genuinely public discussion. There are serious problems, however, with uncritically assuming as a model the ideals of the civic public that come to us from the tradition of modern political thought.[4] The ideal of the public realm of citizenship as expressing a general will, a point of view and interest that citizens have in common which transcends their differences, has operated in fact as a demand for homogeneity among citizens. The exclusion of groups defined as different was explicitly acknowledged before this century. In

1. Theodore Lowi's classic analysis of the privatized operations of interest group liberalism remains descriptive of American politics; see *The End of Liberalism* (New York: Norton, 1969). For more recent analyses, see Jürgen Habermas, *Legitimation Crisis* (Boston: Beacon, 1973); Claus Offe, *Contradictions of the Welfare State* (Cambridge, Mass.: MIT Press, 1984); John Keane, *Public Life in Late Capitalism* (Cambridge, Mass.: MIT Press, 1984); Benjamin Barber, *Strong Democracy* (Berkeley: University of California Press, 1984).

2. For an outstanding recent account of the virtues of and conditions for such democracy, see Philip Green, *Retrieving Democracy* (Totowa, N.J.: Rowman & Allanheld, 1985).

3. Barber and Keane both appeal to Rousseau's understanding of civic activity as a model for contemporary participatory democracy, as does Carole Pateman in her classic work, *Participation and Democratic Theory* (Cambridge: Cambridge University Press, 1970). (Pateman's position has, of course, changed.) See also James Miller, *Rousseau: Dreamer of Democracy* (New Haven, Conn.: Yale University Press, 1984).

4. Many who extol the virtues of the civic public, of course, appeal also to a model of the ancient polis. For a recent example, see Murray Bookchin, *The Rise of Urbanization and the Decline of Citizenship* (San Francisco: Sierra Club Books, 1987). In this article, however, I choose to restrict my claims to modern political thought. The idea of the ancient Greek polis often functions in both modern and contemporary discussion as a myth of lost origins, the paradise from which we have fallen and to which we desire to return; in this way, appeals to the ancient Greek polis are often contained within appeals to modern ideas of civic humanism.

our time, the excluding consequences of the universalist ideal of a public that embodies a common will are more subtle, but they still obtain.

The tradition of civic republicanism stands in critical tension with the individualist contract theory of Hobbes or Locke. Where liberal individualism regards the state as a necessary instrument to mediate conflict and regulate action so that individuals can have the freedom to pursue their private ends, the republican tradition locates freedom and autonomy in the actual public activities of citizenship. By participating in public discussion and collective decision making, citizens transcend their particular self-interested lives and the pursuit of private interests to adopt a general point of view from which they agree on the common good. Citizenship is an expression of the universality of human life; it is a realm of rationality and freedom as opposed to the heteronomous realm of particular need, interest, and desire.

Nothing in this understanding of citizenship as universal as opposed to particular, common as opposed to differentiated, implies extending full citizenship status to all groups. Indeed, at least some modern republicans thought just the contrary. While they extolled the virtues of citizenship as expressing the universality of humanity, they consciously excluded some people from citizenship on the grounds that they could not adopt the general point of view, or that their inclusion would disperse and divide the public. The ideal of a common good, a general will, a shared public life leads to pressures for a homogeneous citizenry.

Feminists in particular have analyzed how the discourse that links the civic public with fraternity is not merely metaphorical. Founded by men, the modern state and its public realm of citizenship paraded as universal values and norms which were derived from specifically masculine experience: militarist norms of honor and homoerotic camaraderie; respectful competition and bargaining among independent agents; discourse framed in unemotional tones of dispassionate reason.

Several commentators have argued that in extolling the virtues of citizenship as participation in a universal public realm, modern men expressed a flight from sexual difference, from having to recognize another kind of existence that they could not entirely understand, and from the embodiment, dependency on nature, and morality that women represent.[5] Thus the opposition between the universality of the public realm of citizenship and the particularity of private interest became conflated with oppositions between reason and passion, masculine and feminine.

The bourgeois world instituted a moral division of labor between reason and sentiment, identifying masculinity with reason and femininity

5. Hannah Pitkin performs a most detailed and sophisticated analysis of the virtues of the civic public as a flight from sexual difference through a reading of the texts of Machiavelli; see *Fortune Is a Woman* (Berkeley: University of California Press, 1984). Carole Pateman's recent writing also focuses on such analysis. See, e.g., Carole Pateman, *The Social Contract* (Stanford, Calif.: Stanford University Press, 1988). See also Nancy Hartsock, *Money, Sex and Power* (New York: Longman, 1983), chaps. 7 and 8.

with sentiment, desire, and the needs of the body. Extolling a public realm of manly virtue and citizenship as independence, generality, and dispassionate reason entailed creating the private sphere of the family as the place to which emotion, sentiment, and bodily needs must be confined.[6] The generality of the public thus depends on excluding women, who are responsible for tending to that private realm, and who lack the dispassionate rationality and independence required of good citizens.

In his social scheme, for example, Rousseau excluded women from the public realm of citizenship because they are the caretakers of affectivity, desire, and the body. If we allowed appeals to desires and bodily needs to move public debates, we would undermine public deliberation by fragmenting its unity. Even within the domestic realm, moreover, women must be dominated. Their dangerous, heterogeneous sexuality must be kept chaste and confined to marriage. Enforcing chastity on women will keep each family a separated unity, preventing the chaos and blood mingling that would be produced by illegitimate children. Chaste, enclosed women in turn oversee men's desire by tempering its potentially disruptive impulses through moral education. Men's desire for women itself threatens to shatter and disperse the universal, rational realm of the public, as well as to disrupt the neat distinction between the public and private. As guardians of the private realm of need, desire, and affectivity, women must ensure that men's impulses do not subvert the universality of reason. The moral neatness of the female-tended hearth, moreover, will temper the possessively individualistic impulses of the particularistic realm of business and commerce, since competition, like sexuality, constantly threatens to explode the unity of the polity.[7]

It is important to recall that universality of citizenship conceived as generality operated to exclude not only women, but other groups as well. European and American republicans found little contradiction in promoting a universality of citizenship that excluded some groups, because the idea that citizenship is the same for all translated in practice to the requirement that all citizens be the same. The white male bourgeoisie conceived republican virtue as rational, restrained, and chaste, not yielding

6. See Susan Okin, "Women and the Making of the Sentimental Family," *Philosophy and Public Affairs* 11 (1982): 65–88; see also Linda Nicholson, *Gender and History: The Limits of Social Theory in the Age of the Family* (New York: Columbia University Press, 1986).

7. For analyses of Rousseau's treatment of women, see Susan Okin, *Women in Western Political Thought* (Princeton, N.J.: Princeton University Press, 1978); Lynda Lange, "Rousseau: Women and the General Will," in *The Sexism of Social and Political Theory*, ed. Lorenne M. G. Clark and Lynda Lange (Toronto: University of Tornoto Press, 1979); Jean Bethke Elshtain, *Public Man, Private Woman* (Princeton, N.J.: Princeton University Press, 1981), chap. 4. Mary Dietz develops an astute critique of Elshtain's "maternalist" perspective on political theory; in so doing, however, she also seems to appeal to a universalist ideal of the civic public in which women will transcend their particular concerns and become general; see "Citizenship with a Feminist Face: The Problem with Maternal Thinking," *Political Theory* 13 (1985): 19–37. On Rousseau on women, see also Joel Schwartz, *The Sexual Politics of Jean-Jacques Rousseau* (Chicago: University of Chicago Press, 1984).

to passion or desire for luxury, and thus able to rise above desire and need to a concern for the common good. This implied excluding poor people and wage workers from citizenship on the grounds that they were too motivated by need to adopt a general perspective. The designers of the American constitution were no more egalitarian than their European brethren in this respect; they specifically intended to restrict the access of the laboring class to the public, because they feared disruption of commitment to the general interests.

These early American republicans were also quite explicit about the need for the homogeneity of citizens, fearing that group differences would tend to undermine commitment to the general interest. This meant that the presence of blacks and Indians, and later Mexicans and Chinese, in the territories of the republic posed a threat that only assimilation, extermination, or dehumanization could thwart. Various combinations of these three were used, of course, but recognition of these groups as peers in the public was never an option. Even such republican fathers as Jefferson identified the red and black people in their territories with wild nature and passion, just as they feared that women outside the domestic realm were wanton and avaricious. They defined moral, civilized republican life in opposition to this backward-looking, uncultivated desire that they identified with women and nonwhites.[8] A similar logic of exclusion operated in Europe, where Jews were particular targets.[9]

These republican exclusions were not accidental, nor were they inconsistent with the ideal of universal citizenship as understood by these theorists. They were a direct consequence of a dichotomy between public and private that defined the public as a realm of generality in which all particularities are left behind, and defined the private as the particular, the realm of affectivity, affiliation, need, and the body. As long as that dichotomy is in place, the inclusion of the formerly excluded in the definition of citizenship—women, workers, Jews, blacks, Asians, Indians, Mexicans—imposes a homogeneity that suppresses group differences in the public and in practice forces the formerly excluded groups to be measured according to norms derived from and defined by privileged groups.

Contemporary critics of interest group liberalism who call for a renewed public life certainly do not intend to exclude any adult persons or groups from citizenship. They are democrats, convinced that only the inclusion and participation of all citizens in political life will make for wise and fair decisions and a polity that enhances rather than inhibits the capacities of its citizens and their relations with one another. The

8. See Ronald Takaki, *Iron Cages: Race and Culture in 19th Century America* (New York: Knopf, 1979). Don Herzog discusses the exclusionary prejudices of some other early American republicans; see "Some Questions for Republicans," *Political Theory* 14 (1986): 473–93.

9. George Mosse, *Nationalism and Sexuality* (New York: Fertig, 1985).

emphasis by such participatory democrats on generality and commonness, however, still threatens to suppress differences among citizens.

I shall focus on the text of Benjamin Barber, who, in his book *Strong Democracy*, produces a compelling and concrete vision of participatory democratic processes. Barber recognizes the need to safeguard a democratic public from intended or inadvertent group exclusions, though he offers no proposals for safeguarding the inclusion and participation of everyone. He also argues fiercely against contemporary political theorists who construct a model of political discourse purified of affective dimensions. Thus Barber does not fear the disruption of the generality and rationality of the public by desire and the body in the way that nineteenth-century republican theorists did. He retains, however, a conception of the civic public as defined by generality, as opposed to group affinity and particular need and interest. He makes a clear distinction between the public realm of citizenship and civic activity, on the one hand, and a private realm of particular identities, roles, affiliations, and interests on the other. Citizenship by no means exhausts people's social identities, but it takes moral priority over all social activities in a strong democracy. The pursuit of particular interests, the pressing of the claims of particular groups, all must take place within a framework of community and common vision established by the public realm. Thus Barber's vision of participatory democracy continues to rely on an opposition between the public sphere of a general interest and a private sphere of particular interest and affiliation.[10]

While recognizing the need for majority rule procedures and means of safeguarding minority rights, Barber asserts that "the strong democrat regrets every division and regards the existence of majorities as a sign that mutualism has failed" (p. 207). A community of citizens, he says, "owes the character of its existence to what its constituent members have in common" (p. 232), and this entails transcending the order of individual needs and wants to recognize that "we are a moral body whose existence depends on the common ordering of individual needs and wants into a single vision of the future in which all can share" (p. 224). This common vision is not imposed on individuals from above, however, but is forged by them in talking and working together. Barber's models of such common projects, however, reveal his latent biases: "Like players on a team or soldiers at war, those who practice a common politics may come to feel ties that they never felt before they commenced their common activity. This sort of bonding, which emphasizes common procedures, common work, and a shared sense of what a community needs to succeed, rather than monolithic purposes and ends, serves strong democracy most successfully" (p. 244).

The attempt to realize an ideal of universal citizenship that finds the public embodying generality as opposed to particularity, commonness versus difference, will tend to exclude or to put at a disadvantage some

---

10. Barber, chaps. 8 and 9. Future page references in parentheses are to this book.

groups, even when they have formally equal citizenship status. The idea of the public as universal and the concomitant identification of particularity with privacy makes homogeneity a requirement of public participation. In exercising their citizenship, all citizens should assume the same impartial, general point of view transcending all particular interests, perspectives, and experiences.

But such an impartial general perspective is a myth.[11] People necessarily and properly consider public issues in terms influenced by their situated experience and perception of social relations. Different social groups have different needs, cultures, histories, experiences, and perceptions of social relations which influence their interpretation of the meaning and consequences of policy proposals and influence the form of their political reasoning. These differences in political interpretation are not merely or even primarily a result of differing or conflicting interests, for groups have differing interpretations even when they seek to promote justice and not merely their own self-regarding ends. In a society where some groups are privileged while others are oppressed, insisting that as citizens persons should leave behind their particular affiliations and experiences to adopt a general point of view serves only to reinforce that privilege; for the perspectives and interests of the privileged will tend to dominate this unified public, marginalizing or silencing those of other groups.

Barber asserts that responsible citizenship requires transcending particular affiliations, commitments, and needs, because a public cannot function if its members are concerned only with their private interests. Here he makes an important confusion between plurality and privatization. The interest group pluralism that he and others criticize indeed institutionalizes and encourages an egoistic, self-regarding view of the political process, one that sees parties entering the political competition for scarce goods and privileges only in order to maximize their own gain, and therefore they need not listen to or respond to the claims of others who have their own point of view. The processes and often the outcomes of interest group bargaining, moreover, take place largely in private; they are neither revealed nor discussed in a forum that genuinely involves all those potentially affected by decisions.

Privacy in this sense of private bargaining for the sake of private gain is quite different from plurality, in the sense of the differing group experiences, affiliations, and commitments that operate in any large society. It is possible for persons to maintain their group identity and to be influenced by their perceptions of social events derived from their group-specific experience, and at the same time to be public spirited, in the

---

11. I have developed this account more thoroughly in my paper, Iris Marion Young, "Impartiality and the Civic Public: Some Implications of Feminist Critiques of Moral and Political Theory," in *Feminism as Critique,* ed. S. Benhabib and D. Cornell (Oxford: Polity Press, 1987), pp. 56–76.

sense of being open to listening to the claims of others and not being concerned for their own gain alone. It is possible and necessary for people to take a critical distance from their own immediate desires and gut reactions in order to discuss public proposals. Doing so, however, cannot require that citizens abandon their particular affiliations, experiences, and social location. As I will discuss in the next section, having the voices of particular group perspectives other than one's own explicitly represented in public discussion best fosters the maintenance of such critical distance without the pretense of impartiality.

A repoliticization of public life should not require the creation of a unified public realm in which citizens leave behind their particular group affiliations, histories, and needs to discuss a general interest or common good. Such a desire for unity suppresses but does not eliminate differences and tends to exclude some perspectives from the public.[12] Instead of a universal citizenship in the sense of this generality, we need a group differentiated citizenship and a heterogeneous public. In a heterogeneous public, differences are publicly recognized and acknowledged as irreducible, by which I mean that persons from one perspective or history can never completely understand and adopt the point of view of those with other group-based perspectives and histories. Yet commitment to the need and desire to decide together the society's policies fosters communication across those differences.

II. DIFFERENTIATED CITIZENSHIP AS GROUP REPRESENTATION

In her study of the functioning of a New England Town Meeting government, Jane Mansbridge discusses how women, blacks, working-class people, and poor people tend to participate less and have their interests represented less than whites, middle-class professionals, and men. Even though all citizens have the right to participate in the decision-making process, the experience and perspectives of some groups tend to be silenced for many reasons. White middle-class men assume authority more than others and they are more practiced at speaking persuasively; mothers and old people often find it more difficult than others to get to meetings.[13] Amy Gutmann also discusses how participatory democratic structures tend to silence disadvantaged groups. She offers the example of community control of schools, where increased democracy led to increased segregation in many cities because the more privileged and articulate whites were able to promote their perceived interests against blacks' just demand for equal treatment in an integrated system.[14] Such cases indicate that when participatory democratic structures define citi-

12. On feminism and participatory democracy, see Pateman.

13. Jane Mansbridge, *Beyond Adversarial Democracy* (New York: Basic Books, 1980).

14. Amy Gutmann, *Liberal Equality* (Cambridge: Cambridge University Press, 1980), pp. 191–202.

zenship in universalistic and unified terms, they tend to reproduce existing group oppression.

Gutmann argues that such oppressive consequences of democratization imply that social and economic equality must be achieved before political equality can be instituted. I cannot quarrel with the value of social and economic equality, but I think its achievement depends on increasing political equality as much as the achievement of political equality depends on increasing social and economic equality. If we are not to be forced to trace a utopian circle, we need to solve now the "paradox of democracy" by which social power makes some citizens more equal than others, and equality of citizenship makes some people more powerful citizens. That solution lies at least in part in providing institutionalized means for the explicit recognition and representation of oppressed groups. Before discussing principles and practices involved in such a solution, however, it is necessary to say something about what a group is and when a group is oppressed.

The concept of a social group has become politically important because recent emancipatory and leftist social movements have mobilized around group identity rather than exclusively class or economic interests. In many cases such mobilization has consisted in embracing and positively defining a despised or devalued ethnic or racial identity. In the women's movement, gay rights movement, or elders' movements, differential social status based on age, sexuality, physical capacity, or the division of labor has been taken up as a positive group identity for political mobilization.

I shall not attempt to define a social group here, but I shall point to several marks which distinguish a social group from other collectivities of people. A social group involves first of all an affinity with other persons by which they identify with one another, and by which other people identify them. A person's particular sense of history, understanding of social relations and personal possibilities, her or his mode of reasoning, values, and expressive styles are constituted at least partly by her or his group identity. Many group definitions come from the outside, from other groups that label and stereotype certain people. In such circumstances the despised group members often find their affinity in their oppression. The concept of social group must be distinguished from two concepts with which it might be confused: aggregate and association.

An aggregate is any classification of persons according to some attribute. Persons can be aggregated according to any number of attributes, all of them equally arbitrary—eye color, the make of car we drive, the street we live on. At times the groups that have emotional and social salience in our society are interpreted as aggregates, as arbitrary classifications of persons according to attributes of skin color, genitals, or years lived. A social group, however, is not defined primarily by a set of shared attributes, but by the sense of identity that people have. What defines black Americans as a social group is not primarily their skin color; this is exemplified by the fact that some persons whose skin color is fairly light, for example, identify as black. Though sometimes objective attributes are a necessary condition for classifying oneself or others as a member of a certain social group, it is the identification of certain persons with a social status, a common history that social status produces, and a self-identification that defines the group as a group.

Political and social theorists tend more often to elide social groups with associations rather than aggregates. By an association I mean a collectivity of persons who come together voluntarily—such as a club, corporation, political party, church, college, union, lobbying organization, or interest group. An individualist contract model of society applies to associations but not to groups. Individuals constitute associations; they come together as already formed persons and set them up, establishing rules, positions, and offices.

Since one joins an association, even if membership in it fundamentally affects one's life, one does not take that association membership to define one's very identity in the way, for example, being Navajo might. Group affinity, on the other hand, has the character of what Heidegger calls "thrownness": one finds oneself as a member of a group, whose existence and relations one experiences as always already having been. For a person's identity is defined in relation to how others identify him or her, and others do so in terms of groups which always already have specific attributes, stereotypes, and norms associated with them, in reference to which a person's identity will be formed. From the thrownness of group affinity it does not follow that one cannot leave groups and enter new ones. Many women become lesbian after identifying as heterosexual, and anyone who lives long enough becomes old. These cases illustrate thrownness precisely in that such changes in group affinity are experienced as a transformation in one's identity.

A social group should not be understood as an essence or nature with a specific set of common attributes. Instead, group identity should be understood in relational terms. Social processes generate groups by creating relational differentiations, situations of clustering and affective bonding in which people feel affinity for other people. Sometimes groups define themselves by despising or excluding others whom they define as other, and whom they dominate and oppress. Although social processes of affinity and separation define groups, they do not give groups a substantive identity. There is no common nature that members of a group have.

As products of social relations, groups are fluid; they come into being and may fade away. Homosexual practices have existed in many societies and historical periods, for example, but gay male group identification exists only in the West in the twentieth century. Group identity may become salient only under specific circumstances, when in interaction with other groups. Most people in modern societies have multiple group identifications, moreover, and therefore groups themselves are not discrete unities. Every group has group differences cutting across it.

I think that group differentiation is an inevitable and desirable process in modern societies. We need not settle that question, however. I merely assume that ours is now a group differentiated society, and that it will continue to be so for some time to come. Our political problem is that some of our groups are privileged and others are oppressed.

But what is oppression? In another place I give a fuller account of the concept of oppression.[15] Briefly, a group is oppressed when one or more of the following conditions occurs to all or a large portion of its members: (1) the benefits of their work or energy go to others without those others reciprocally benefiting them (exploitation); (2) they are excluded from participation in major social activities, which in our society means primarily a workplace (marginalization); (3) they live and work under the authority of others, and have little work autonomy and authority over others themselves (powerlessness); (4) as a group they are stereotyped at the same time that their experience and situation is invisible in the society in general, and they have little opportunity and little audience for the expression of their experience and perspective on social events (cultural imperialism); (5) group members suffer random violence and harassment motivated by group hatred or fear. In the United States today at least the following groups are oppressed in one or more of these ways: women, blacks, Native Americans, Chicanos, Puerto Ricans and other Spanish-speaking Americans, Asian Americans, gay men, lesbians, working-class people, poor people, old people, and mentally and physically disabled people.

Perhaps in some utopian future there will be a society without group oppression and disadvantage. We cannot develop political principles by starting with the assumption of a completely just society, however, but must begin from within the general historical and social conditions in which we exist. This means that we must develop participatory democratic theory not on the assumption of an undifferentiated humanity, but rather on the assumption that there are group differences and that some groups are actually or potentially oppressed or disadvantaged.

I assert, then, the following principle: a democratic public, however that is constituted, should provide mechanisms for the effective representation and recognition of the distinct voices and perspectives of those of its constituent groups that are oppressed or disadvantaged within it. Such group representation implies institutional mechanisms and public resources supporting three activities: (1) self-organization of group members so that they gain a sense of collective empowerment and a reflective understanding of their collective experience and interests in the context of the society; (2) voicing a group's analysis of how social policy proposals affect them, and generating policy proposals themselves, in institutionalized contexts where decision makers are obliged to show that they have taken

15. See Iris Marion Young, "Five Faces of Oppression," *Philosophical Forum* (1988), in press.

these perspectives into consideration; (3) having veto power regarding specific policies that affect a group directly, for example, reproductive rights for women, or use of reservation lands for Native Americans.

The principles call for specific representation only for oppressed or disadvantaged groups, because privileged groups already are represented. Thus the principle would not apply in a society entirely without oppression. I do not regard the principle as merely provisional, or instrumental, however, because I believe that group difference in modern complex societies is both inevitable and desirable, and that wherever there is group difference, disadvantage or oppression always looms as a possibility. Thus a society should always be committed to representation for oppressed or disadvantaged groups and ready to implement such representation when it appears. These considerations are rather academic in our own context, however, since we live in a society with deep group oppressions the complete elimination of which is only a remote possibility.

Social and economic privilege means, among other things, that the groups which have it behave as though they have a right to speak and be heard, that others treat them as though they have that right, and that they have the material, personal, and organizational resources that enable them to speak and be heard in public. The privileged are usually not inclined to protect and further the interests of the oppressed partly because their social position prevents them from understanding those interests, and partly because to some degree their privilege depends on the continued oppression of others. So a major reason for explicit rep- resentation of oppressed groups in discussion and decision making is to undermine oppression. Such group representation also exposes in public the specificity of the assumptions and experience of the privileged. For unless confronted with different perspectives on social relations and events, different values and language, most people tend to assert their own perspective as universal.

Theorists and politicians extol the virtues of citizenship because through public participation persons are called on to transcend merely self-centered motivation and acknowledge their dependence on and re- sponsibility to others. The responsible citizen is concerned not merely with interests but with justice, with acknowledging that each other person's interest and point of view is as good as his or her own, and that the needs and interests of everyone must be voiced and be heard by the others, who must acknowledge, respect, and address those needs and interests. The problem of universality has occurred when this responsibility has been interpreted as transcendence into a general perspective.

I have argued that defining citizenship as generality avoids and obscures this requirement that all experiences, needs, and perspectives on social events have a voice and are respected. A general perspective does not exist which all persons can adopt and from which all experiences and perspectives can be understood and taken into account. The existence of social groups implies different, though not necessarily exclusive, histories, experiences, and perspectives on social life that people have, and it implies that they do not entirely understand the experience of other groups. No one can claim to speak in the general interest, because no one of the groups can speak for another, and certainly no one can speak for them all. Thus the only way to have all group experience and social perspectives voiced, heard, and taken account of is to have them specifically represented in the public.

Group representation is the best means to promote just outcomes to democratic decision-making processes. The argument for this claim relies on Habermas's conception of communicative ethics. In the absence of a Philosopher King who reads transcendent normative verities, the only ground for a claim that a policy or decision is just is that it has been arrived at by a public which has truly promoted free expression of all needs and points of view. In his formulation of a communicative ethic, Habermas retains inappropriately an appeal to a universal or impartial point of view from which claims in a public should be addressed. A communicative ethic that does not merely articulate a hypothetical public that would justify decisions, but proposes actual conditions tending to promote just outcomes of decision-making processes, should promote conditions for the expression of the concrete needs of all individuals in their particularity.[16] The concreteness of individual lives, their needs and interests, and their perception of the needs and interests of others, I have argued, are structured partly through group-based experience and identity. Thus full and free expression of concrete needs and interests under social circumstances where some groups are silenced or marginalized requires that they have a specific voice in deliberation and decision making.

The introduction of such differentiation and particularity into democratic procedures does not encourage the expression of narrow self-interest; indeed, group representation is the best antidote to self-deceiving self-interest masked as an impartial or general interest. In a democratically structured public where social inequality is mitigated through group representation, individuals or groups cannot simply assert that they want something; they must say that justice requires or allows that they have it. Group representation provides the opportunity for some to express their needs or interests who would not likely be heard without that representation. At the same time, the test of whether a claim on the public is just, or a mere expression of self-interest, is best made when persons making it must confront the opinion of others who have explicitly different, though not necessarily conflicting, experiences, priorities, and needs. As a person of social privilege, I am not likely to go outside of myself and have a regard for social justice unless I am forced to listen to the voice of those my privilege tends to silence.

16. Jürgen Habermas, *Reason and the Rationalization of Society* (Boston: Beacon, 1983), pt. 3. For criticism of Habermas as retaining too universalist a conception of communicative action, see Seyla Benhabib, *Critique, Norm and Utopia* (New York: Columbia University Press, 1986); and Young, "Impartiality and the Civic Public."

Group representation best institutionalizes fairness under circumstances of social oppression and domination. But group representation also maximizes knowledge expressed in discussion, and thus promotes practical wisdom. Group differences not only involve different needs, interests, and goals, but probably more important different social locations and experiences from which social facts and policies are understood. Members of different social groups are likely to know different things about the structure of social relations and the potential and actual effects of social policies. Because of their history, their group-specific values or modes of expression, their relationship to other groups, the kind of work they do, and so on, different groups have different ways of understanding the meaning of social events, which can contribute to the others' understanding if expressed and heard.

Emancipatory social movements in recent years have developed some political practices committed to the idea of a heterogeneous public, and they have at least partly or temporarily instituted such publics. Some political organizations, unions, and feminist groups have formal caucuses for groups (such as blacks, Latinos, women, gay men and lesbians, and disabled or old people) whose perspectives might be silenced without them. Frequently these organizations have procedures for caucus voice in organization discussion and caucus representation in decision making, and some organizations also require representation of members of specific groups in leadership bodies. Under the influence of these social movements asserting group difference, during some years even the Democratic party, at both national and state levels, has instituted delegate rules that include provisions for group representation.

Though its realization is far from assured, the ideal of a "rainbow coalition" expresses such a heterogeneous public with forms of group representation. The traditional form of coalition corresponds to the idea of a unified public that transcends particular differences of experience and concern. In traditional coalitions, diverse groups work together for ends which they agree interest or affect them all in a similar way, and they generally agree that the differences of perspective, interests, or opinion among them will not surface in the public statements and actions of the coalition. In a rainbow coalition, by contrast, each of the constituent groups affirms the presence of the others and affirms the specificity of its experience and perspective on social issues.[17] In the rainbow public, blacks do not simply tolerate the participation of gays, labor activists do

17. The Mel King for mayor campaign organization exhibited the promise of such group representation in practice, which was only partially and haltingly realized; see special double issue of *Radical America* 17, no. 6, and 18, no. 1 (1984). Sheila Collins discusses how the idea of a rainbow coalition challenges traditional American political assumptions of a "melting pot," and she shows how lack of coordination between the national level rainbow departments and the grassroots campaign committees prevented the 1984 Jackson campaign from realizing the promise of group representation; see *The Rainbow Challenge: The Jackson Campaign and the Future of U.S. Politics* (New York: Monthly Review Press, 1986).

not grudgingly work alongside peace movement veterans, and none of these paternalistically allow feminist participation. Ideally, a rainbow coalition affirms the presence and supports the claims of each of the oppressed groups or political movements constituting it, and it arrives at a political program not by voicing some "principles of unity" that hide differences but rather by allowing each constituency to analyze economic and social issues from the perspective of its experience. This implies that each group maintains autonomy in relating to its constituency, and that decision-making bodies and procedures provide for group representation.

To the degree that there are heterogeneous publics operating according to the principles of group representation in contemporary politics, they exist only in organizations and movements resisting the majority politics. Nevertheless, in principle participatory democracy entails commitment to institutions of a heterogeneous public in all spheres of democratic decision making. Until and unless group oppression or disadvantages are eliminated, political publics, including democratized workplaces and government decision-making bodies, should include the specific representation of those oppressed groups, through which those groups express their specific understanding of the issues before the public and register a group-based vote. Such structures of group representation should not replace structures of regional or party representation but should exist alongside them.

Implementing principles of group representation in national politics in the United States, or in restructured democratic publics within particular institutions such as factories, offices, universities, churches, and social service agencies, would require creative thinking and flexibility. There are no models to follow. European models of consociational democratic institutions, for example, cannot be taken outside of the contexts in which they have evolved, and even within them they do not operate in a very democratic fashion. Reports of experiments with publicly institutionalized self-organization among women, indigenous peoples, workers, peasants, and students in contemporary Nicaragua offer an example closer to the conception I am advocating.[18]

The principle of group representation calls for such structures of representation for oppressed or disadvantaged groups. But what groups deserve representation? Clear candidates for group representation in policy making in the United States are women, blacks, Native Americans, old people, poor people, disabled people, gay men and lesbians, Spanish-speaking Americans, young people, and nonprofessional workers. But it may not be necessary to ensure specific representation of all these groups in all public contexts and in all policy discussions. Representation should be designated whenever the group's history and social situation provide a particular perspective on the issues, when the interests of its

18. See Gary Ruchwarger, *People in Power: Forging a Grassroots Democracy in Nicaragua* (Hadley, Mass.: Bergin & Garvey, 1985).

members are specifically affected, and when its perceptions and interests are not likely to receive expression without that representation.

An origin problem emerges in proposing a principle such as this, which no philosophical argument can solve. To implement this principle a public must be constituted to decide which groups deserve specific representation in decision-making procedures. What are the principles guiding the composition of such a "constitutional convention"? Who should decide what groups should receive representation, and by what procedures should this decision take place? No program or set of principles can found a politics, because politics is always a process in which we are already engaged; principles can be appealed to in the course of political discussion, they can be accepted by a public as guiding their action. I propose a principle of group representation as a part of such potential discussion, but it cannot replace that discussion or determine its outcome.

What should be the mechanisms of group representation? Earlier I stated that the self-organization of the group is one of the aspects of a principle of group representation. Members of the group must meet together in democratic forums to discuss issues and formulate group positions and proposals. This principle of group representation should be understood as part of a larger program for democratized decision-making processes. Public life and decision-making processes should be transformed so that all citizens have significantly greater opportunities for participation in discussion and decision making. All citizens should have access to neighborhood or district assemblies where they participate in discussion and decision making. In such a more participatory democratic scheme, members of oppressed groups would also have group assemblies, which would delegate group representatives.

One might well ask how the idea of a heterogeneous public which encourages self-organization of groups and structures of group representation in decision making is different from the interest group pluralism criticism which I endorsed earlier in this article. First, in the heterogeneous public not any collectivity of persons that chooses to form an association counts as a candidate for group representation. Only those groups that describe the major identities and major status relationships constituting the society or particular institution, and which are oppressed or disadvantaged, deserve specific representation in a heterogeneous public. In the structures of interest group pluralism, Friends of the Whales, the National Association for the Advancement of Colored People, the National Rifle Association, and the National Freeze Campaign all have the same status, and each influences decision making to the degree that their resources and ingenuity can win out in the competition for policymakers' ears. While democratic politics must maximize freedom of the expression of opinion and interest, that is a different issue from ensuring that the perspective of all groups has a voice.

Second, in the heterogeneous public the groups represented are not defined by some particular interest or goal, or some particular political position. Social groups are comprehensive identities and ways of life. Because of their experiences their members may have some common interests that they seek to press in the public. Their social location, however, tends to give them distinctive understandings of all aspects of the society and unique perspectives on social issues. For example, many Native Americans argue that their traditional religion and relation to land gives them a unique and important understanding of environmental problems.

Finally, interest group pluralism operates precisely to forestall the emergence of public discussion and decision making. Each interest group promotes only its specific interest as thoroughly and forcefully as it can, and it need not consider the other interests competing in the political marketplace except strategically, as potential allies or adversaries in the pursuit of its own. The rules of interest group pluralism do not require justifying one's interest as right or as compatible with social justice. A heterogeneous public, however, is a *public,* where participants discuss together the issues before them and are supposed to come to a decision that they determine as best or most just.

III. UNIVERSAL RIGHTS AND SPECIAL RIGHTS

A second aspect of the universality of citizenship is today in tension with the goal of full inclusion and participation of all groups in political and social institutions: universality in the formulation of law and policies. Modern and contemporary liberalism hold as basic the principle that the rules and policies of the state, and in contemporary liberalism also the rules of private institutions, ought to be blind to race, gender, and other group differences. The public realm of the state and law properly should express its rules in general terms that abstract from the particularities of individual and group histories, needs, and situations to recognize all persons equally and treat all citizens in the same way.

As long as political ideology and practice persisted in defining some groups as unworthy of equal citizenship status because of supposedly natural differences from white male citizens, it was important for emancipatory movements to insist that all people are the same in respect of their moral worth and deserve equal citizenship. In this context, demands for equal rights that are blind to group differences were the only sensible way to combat exclusion and degradation.

Today, however, the social consensus is that all persons are of equal moral worth and deserve equal citizenship. With the near achievement of equal rights for all groups, with the important exception of gay men and lesbians, group inequalities nevertheless remain. Under these circumstances many feminists, black liberation activists, and others struggling for the full inclusion and participation of all groups in this society's institutions and positions of power, reward, and satisfaction, argue that rights and rules that are universally formulated and thus blind to differences of race, culture, gender, age, or disability, perpetuate rather than undermine oppression.

Contemporary social movements seeking full inclusion and participation of oppressed and disadvantaged groups now find themselves faced with a dilemma of difference.[19] On the one hand, they must continue to deny that there are any essential differences between men and women, whites and blacks, able-bodied and disabled people, which justify denying women, blacks, or disabled people the opportunity to do anything that others are free to do or to be included in any institution or position. On the other hand, they have found it necessary to affirm that there are often group-based differences between men and women, whites and blacks, able-bodied and disabled people that make application of a strict principle of equal treatment, especially in competition for positions, unfair because these differences put those groups at a disadvantage. For example, white middle-class men as a group are socialized into the behavioral styles of a particular kind of articulateness, coolness, and competent authoritativeness that are most rewarded in professional and managerial life. To the degree that there are group differences that disadvantage, fairness seems to call for acknowledging rather than being blind to them.

Though in many respects the law is now blind to group differences, the society is not, and some groups continue to be marked as deviant and as the other. In everyday interactions, images, and decision making, assumptions continue to be made about women, blacks, Latinos, gay men, lesbians, old people, and other marked groups, which continue to justify exclusions, avoidances, paternalism, and authoritarian treatment. Continued racist, sexist, homophobic, ageist, and ableist behaviors and institutions create particular circumstances for these groups, usually disadvantaging them in their opportunity to develop their capacities and giving them particular experiences and knowledge. Finally, in part because they have been segregated and excluded from one another, and in part because they have particular histories and traditions, there are cultural differences among social groups—differences in language, style of living, body comportment and gesture, values, and perspectives on society.

Acknowledging group difference in capacities, needs, culture, and cognitive styles poses a problem for those seeking to eliminate oppression only if difference is understood as deviance or deficiency. Such understanding presumes that some capacities, needs, culture, or cognitive styles are normal. I suggested earlier that their privilege allows dominant groups to assert their experience of and perspective on social events as impartial and objective. In a similar fashion, their privilege allows some groups to project their group-based capacities, values, and cognitive and behavioral styles as the norm to which all persons should be expected to conform. Feminists in particular have argued that most contemporary workplaces, especially the most desirable, presume a life rhythm and behavioral style typical of men, and that women are expected to accommodate to the workplace expectations that assume those norms.

19. Martha Minow, "Learning to Live with the Dilemma of Difference: Bilingual and Special Education," *Law and Contemporary Problems*, no. 48 (1985), pp. 157–211.

Where group differences in capacities, values, and behavioral or cognitive styles exist, equal treatment in the allocation of reward according to rules of merit composition will reinforce and perpetuate disadvantage. Equal treatment requires everyone to be measured according to the same norms, but in fact there are no "neutral" norms of behavior and performance. Where some groups are privileged and others oppressed, the formulation of law, policy, and the rules of private institutions tend to be biased in favor of the privileged groups, because their particular experience implicitly sets the norm. Thus where there are group differences in capacities, socialization, values, and cognitive and cultural styles, only attending to such differences can enable the inclusion and participation of all groups in political and economic institutions. This implies that instead of always formulating rights and rules in universal terms that are blind to difference, some groups sometimes deserve special rights.[20] In what follows, I shall review several contexts of contemporary policy debate where I argue such special rights for oppressed or disadvantaged groups are appropriate.

The issue of a right to pregnancy and maternity leave, and the right to special treatment for nursing mothers, is highly controversial among feminists today. I do not intend here to wind through the intricacies of what has become a conceptually challenging and interesting debate in legal theory. As Linda Krieger argues, the issue of rights for pregnant and birthing mothers in relation to the workplace has created a paradigm crisis for our understanding of sexual equality, because the application of a principle of equal treatment on this issue has yielded results whose effects on women are at best ambiguous and at worst detrimental.[21]

In my view an equal treatment approach on this issue is inadequate because it either implies that women do not receive any right to leave and job security when having babies, or it assimilates such guarantees under a supposedly gender neutral category of "disability." Such assimilation is unacceptable because pregnancy and childbirth are normal conditions of normal women, they themselves count as socially necessary work, and they have unique and variable characteristics and needs.[22]

20. I use the term "special rights" in much the same way as Elizabeth Wolgast, in *Equality and the Rights of Women* (Ithaca, N.Y.: Cornell University Press, 1980). Like Wolgast, I wish to distinguish a class of rights that all persons should have, general rights, and a class of rights that categories of persons should have by virtue of particular circumstances. That is, the distinction should refer only to different levels of generality, where "special" means only "specific." Unfortunately, "special rights" tends to carry a connotation of *exceptional*, that is, specially marked and deviating from the norm. As I assert below, however, the goal is not to compensate for deficiencies in order to help people be "normal," but to denormalize, so that in certain contexts and at certain levels of abstraction everyone has "special" rights.

21. Linda J. Krieger, "Through a Glass Darkly: Paradigms of Equality and the Search for a Women's Jurisprudence," *Hypatia: A Journal of Feminist Philosophy* 2 (1987): 45–62. Deborah Rhode provides an excellent synopsis of the dilemmas involved in this pregnancy debate in feminist legal theory in "Justice and Gender" (typescript), chap. 9.

22. See Ann Scales, "Towards a Feminist Jurisprudence," *Indiana Law Journal* 56 (1980): 375–444. Christine Littleton provides a very good analysis of the feminist debate

Assimilating pregnancy into disability gives a negative meaning to these processes as "unhealthy." It suggests, moreover, that the primary or only reason that a woman has a right to leave and job security is that she is physically unable to work at her job, or that doing so would be more difficult than when she is not pregnant and recovering from childbirth. While these are important reasons, depending on the individual woman, another reason is that she ought to have the time to establish breast-feeding and develop a relationship and routine with her child, if she chooses.

The pregnancy leave debate has been heated and extensive because both feminists and nonfeminists tend to think of biological sex difference as the most fundamental and irradicable difference. When difference slides into deviance, stigma, and disadvantage, this impression can engender the fear that sexual equality is not attainable. I think it is important to emphasize that reproduction is by no means the only context in which issues of same versus different treatment arise. It is not even the only context where it arises for issues involving bodily difference. The last twenty years have seen significant success in winning special rights for persons with physical and mental disabilities. Here is a clear case where promoting equality in participation and inclusion requires attending to the particular needs of different groups.

Another bodily difference which has not been as widely discussed in law and policy literature, but should be, is age. With increasing numbers of willing and able old people marginalized in our society, the issue of mandatory retirement has been increasingly discussed. This discussion has been muted because serious consideration of working rights for all people able and willing to work implies major restructuring of the allocation of labor in an economy with already socially volatile levels of unemployment. Forcing people out of their workplaces solely on account of their age is arbitrary and unjust. Yet I think it is also unjust to require old people to work on the same terms as younger people. Old people should have different working rights. When they reach a certain age they should be allowed to retire and receive income benefits. If they wish to continue working, they should be allowed more flexible and part-time schedules than most workers currently have.

Each of these cases of special rights in the workplace—pregnancy and birthing, physical disability, and being old—has its own purposes and structures. They all challenge, however, the same paradigm of the "normal, healthy" worker and "typical work situation." In each case the circumstance that calls for different treatment should not be understood as lodged in the differently treated workers, per se, but in their interaction

---

about equal vs. different treatment regarding pregnancy and childbirth, among other legal issues for women, in "Reconstructing Sexual Equality," *California Law Review* 25 (1987): 1279–1337. Littleton suggests, as I have stated above, that only the dominant male conception of work keeps pregnancy and birthing from being conceived of as work.

with the structure and norms of the workplace. Even in cases such as these, that is, difference does not have its source in natural, unalterable, biological attributes, but in the relationship of bodies to conventional rules and practices. In each case the political claim for special rights emerges not from a need to compensate for an inferiority, as some would interpret it, but from a positive assertion of specificity in different forms of life.[23]

Issues of difference arise for law and policy not only regarding bodily being, but just as importantly for cultural integrity and invisibility. By culture I mean group-specific phenomena of behavior, temperament, or meaning. Cultural differences include phenomena of language, speaking style or dialectic, body comportment, gesture, social practices, values, group-specific socialization, and so on. To the degree that groups are culturally different, however, equal treatment in many issues of social policy is unjust because it denies these cultural differences or makes them a liability. There are a vast number of issues where fairness involves attention to cultural differences and their effects, but I shall briefly discuss three: affirmative action, comparable worth, and bilingual, bicultural education and service.

Whether they involve quotas or not, affirmative action programs violate a principle of equal treatment because they are race or gender conscious in setting criteria for school admissions, jobs, or promotions. These policies are usually defended in one of two ways. Giving preference to race or gender is understood either as just compensation for groups that have suffered discrimination in the past, or as compensation for the present disadvantage these groups suffer because of that history of discrimination and exclusion.[24] I do not wish to quarrel with either of these justifications for the differential treatment based on race or gender implied by affirmative action policies. I want to suggest that in addition we can understand affirmative action policies as compensating for the cultural biases of standards and evaluators used by the schools or employers. These standards and evaluators reflect at least to some degree the specific life and cultural experience of dominant groups—whites, Anglos, or men. In a group-differentiated society, moreover, the development of truly neutral standards and evaluations is difficult or impossible, because female, black, or Latino cultural experience and the dominant cultures are in many respects not reducible to a common measure. Thus affirmative action policies compensate for the dominance of one set of cultural at-

23. Littleton suggests that difference should be understood not as a characteristic of particular sorts of people, but of the interaction of particular sorts of people with specific institutional structures. Minow expresses a similar point by saying that difference should be understood as a function of the relationship among groups, rather than located in attributes of a particular group.

24. For one among many discussions of such "backward looking" and "forward looking" arguments, see Bernard Boxill, *Blacks and Social Justice* (Totowa, N.J.: Rowman & Allanheld, 1984), chap. 7.

tributes. Such an interpretation of affirmative action locates the "problem" that affirmative action solves partly in the understandable biases of evaluators and their standards, rather than only in specific differences of the disadvantaged group.

Although they are not a matter of different treatment as such, comparable worth policies similarly claim to challenge cultural biases in traditional evaluation in the worth of female-dominated occupations, and in doing so require attending to differences. Schemes of equal pay for work of comparable worth require that predominantly male and predominantly female jobs have similar wage structures if they involve similar degrees of skill, difficulty, stress, and so on. The problem in implementing these policies, of course, lies in designing methods of comparing the jobs, which often are very different. Most schemes of comparison choose to minimize sex differences by using supposedly gender-neutral criteria, such as educational attainment, speed of work, whether it involves manipulation of symbols, decision making, and so on. Some writers have suggested, however, that standard classifications of job traits may be systematically biased to keep specific kinds of tasks involved in many female-dominated occupations hidden.[25] Many female-dominated occupations involve gender-specific kinds of labor—such as nurturing, smoothing over social relations, or the exhibition of sexuality—which most task observation ignores.[26] A fair assessment of the skills and complexity of many female-dominated jobs may therefore involve paying explicit attention to gender differences in kinds of jobs rather than applying gender-blind categories of comparison.

Finally, linguistic and cultural minorities ought to have the right to maintain their language and culture and at the same time be entitled to all the benefits of citizenship, as well as valuable education and career opportunities. This right implies a positive obligation on the part of governments and other public bodies to print documents and to provide services in the native language of recognized linguistic minorities, and to provide bilingual instruction in schools. Cultural assimilation should not be a condition of full social participation, because it requires a person to transform his or her sense of identity, and when it is realized on a group level it means altering or annihilating the group's identity. This principle does not apply to any persons who do not identify with majority language or culture within a society, but only to sizeable linguistic or cultural minorities living in distinct though not necessarily segregated

25. See R. W. Beatty and J. R. Beatty, "Some Problems with Contemporary Job Evaluation Systems," and Ronnie Steinberg, "A Want of Harmony: Perspectives on Wage Discrimination and Comparable Worth," both in *Comparable Worth and Wage Discrimination: Technical Possibilities and Political Realities,* ed. Helen Remick (Philadelphia: Temple University Press, 1981); D. J. Treiman and H. I. Hartmann, eds., *Women, Work and Wages* (Washington, D.C.: National Academy Press, 1981), p. 81.

26. David Alexander, "Gendered Job Traits and Women's Occupations" (Ph.D. diss., University of Massachusetts, Department of Economics, 1987).

communities. In the United States, then, special rights for cultural minorities applies at least to Spanish-speaking Americans and Native Americans.

The universalist finds a contradiction in asserting both that formerly segregated groups have a right to inclusion and that these groups have a right to different treatment. There is no contradiction here, however, if attending to difference is necessary in order to make participation and inclusion possible. Groups with different circumstances or forms of life should be able to participate together in public institutions without shedding their distinct identities or suffering disadvantage because of them. The goal is not to give special compensation to the deviant until they achieve normality, but rather to denormalize the way institutions formulate their rules by revealing the plural circumstances and needs that exist, or ought to exist, within them.

Many opponents of oppression and privilege are wary of claims for special rights because they fear a restoration of special classifications that can justify exclusion and stigmatization of the specially marked groups. Such fear has been particularly pronounced among feminists who oppose affirming sexual and gender difference in law and policy. It would be foolish for me to deny that this fear has some significant basis.

Such fear is founded, however, on accession to traditional identification of group difference with deviance, stigma, and inequality. Contemporary movements of oppressed groups, however, assert a positive meaning to group difference, by which a group claims its identity as a group and rejects the stereotypes and labeling by which others mark it as inferior or inhuman. These social movements engage the meaning of difference itself as a terrain of political struggle, rather than leave difference to be used to justify exclusion and subordination. Supporting policies and rules that attend to group difference in order to undermine oppression and disadvantage is, in my opinion, a part of that struggle.

Fear of claims to special rights points to a connection of the principle of group representation with the principle of attending to difference in policy. The primary means of defense from the use of special rights to oppress or exclude groups is the self-organization and representation of those groups. If oppressed and disadvantaged groups are able to discuss among themselves what procedures and policies they judge will best further their social and political equality, and have access to mechanisms to make their judgments known to the larger public, then policies that attend to difference are less likely to be used against them than for them. If they have the institutionalized right to veto policy proposals that directly affect them, and them primarily, moreover, such danger is further reduced.

In this article I have distinguished three meanings of universality that have usually been collapsed in discussions of the universality of citizenship and the public realm. Modern politics properly promotes the universality of citizenship in the sense of the inclusion and participation of everyone in public life and democratic processes. The realization of genuinely universal citizenship in this sense today is impeded rather than furthered by the commonly held conviction that when they exercise their citizenship, persons should adopt a universal point of view and leave behind the perceptions they derive from their particular experience and social position. The full inclusion and participation of all in law and public life is also sometimes impeded by formulating laws and rules in universal terms that apply to all citizens in the same way.

In response to these arguments, some people have suggested to me that such challenges to the ideal of universal citizenship threaten to leave no basis for rational normative appeals. Normative reason, it is suggested, entails universality in a Kantian sense: when a person claims that something is good or right he or she is claiming that everyone in principle could consistently make that claim, and that everyone should accept it. This refers to a fourth meaning of universality, more epistemological than political. There may indeed be grounds for questioning a Kantian-based theory of the universality of normative reason, but this is a different issue from the substantive political issues I have addressed here, and the arguments in this paper neither imply nor exclude such a possibility. In any case, I do not believe that challenging the ideal of a unified public or the claim that rules should always be formally universal subverts the possibility of making rational normative claims.

Feminism and Modern Friendship: Dislocating the Community*

Marilyn Friedman

A predominant theme in much recent feminist thought has been the critique of the abstract individualism which underlies some important versions of liberal political theory.[1] Abstract individualism considers individual human beings as social atoms, abstracted from their social contexts, and disregards the role of social relationships and human community in constituting the very identity and nature of individual human beings. Sometimes the individuals of abstract individualism are posited as rationally self-interested utility maximizers.[2] Sometimes, also, they are theorized to form communities based fundamentally on competition and conflict among persons vying for scarce resources, communities which represent no deeper social bond than that of instrumental relations based on calculated self-interest.[3]

Against this abstractive individualist view of the self and of human community, many feminists have asserted a conception of what might

* I am grateful to Cass Sunstein and the editors of *Ethics* for helpful comments on an earlier version of this article. This article was written with the support of a National Endowment for the Humanities Summer Stipend and a grant from the Faculty Research Committee of Bowling Green State University.

1. Compare Carole Pateman, *The Problem of Political Obligation: A Critique of Liberal Theory* (Berkeley: University of California Press, 1979); Zillah Eisenstein, *The Radical Future of Liberal Feminism* (New York: Longman, 1981); Nancy C. M. Hartsock, *Money, Sex, and Power* (Boston: Northeastern University Press, 1983); Alison M. Jaggar, *Feminist Politics and Human Nature* (Totowa, N.J.: Rowman & Allanheld, 1983); Naomi Scheman, "Individualism and the Objects of Psychology," in *Discovering Reality*, ed. Sandra Harding and Merrill B. Hintikka (Dordrecht: D. Reidel, 1983), pp. 225–44; Jane Flax, "Political Philosophy and the Patriarchal Unconscious: A Psychoanalytic Perspective on Epistemology and Metaphysics," in Harding and Hintikka, eds., pp. 245–81; and Seyla Benhabib, "The Generalized and the Concrete Other: The Kohlberg-Gilligan Controversy and Moral Theory," in *Women and Moral Theory*, ed. Eva Feder Kittay and Diana T. Meyers (Totowa, N.J.: Rowman & Littlefield, 1987), pp. 154–77.

2. Compare David Gauthier, *Morals by Agreement* (Oxford: Oxford University Press, 1986).

3. Compare George Homans, *Social Behavior: Its Elementary Forms* (New York: Harcourt, Brace & World, 1961); and Peter Blau, *Exchange and Power in Social Life* (New York: Wiley, 1974).

This essay originally appeared in *Ethics* 99, January 1989.

be called the "social self."[4] This conception fundamentally acknowledges the role of social relationships and human community in constituting both self-identity and the nature and meaning of the particulars of individual lives.[5] The modified conception of the self has carried with it an altered conception of community. Conflict and competition are no longer considered to be the basic human relationships; instead they are being replaced by alternative visions of the foundation of human society derived from nurturance, caring attachment, and mutual interestedness.[6] Some feminists, for example, recommend that the mother-child relationship be viewed as central to human society, and they project major changes in moral theory from such a revised focus.[7]

Some of these anti-individualist developments emerging from feminist thought are strikingly similar to other theoretical developments which are not specifically feminist. Thus, the "new communitarians," to borrow Amy Gutmann's term,[8] have also reacted critically to various aspects of modern liberal thought, including abstract individualism, rational egoism, and an instrumental conception of social relationships. The communitarian self, or subject, is also not a social atom but is instead a being constituted and defined by its attachments, including the particularities of its social relationships, community ties, and historical context. Its identity cannot be abstracted from community or social relationships.

With the recent feminist attention to values of care, nurturance, and relatedness—values that psychologists call "communal"[9] and which have been amply associated with women and women's moral reasoning[10]— one might anticipate that communitarian theory would offer important insights for feminist reflection. There is considerable power to the model of the self as deriving its identity and nature from its social relationships, from the way it is intersubjectively apprehended, from the norms of the community in which it is embedded.

---

4. Compare my "Autonomy in Social Context," in *Freedom, Equality, and Social Change: Problems in Social Philosophy Today*, ed. James Sterba and Creighton Peden (Lewiston, N.Y.: Edwin Mellen Press, in press).

5. Compare Drucilla Cornell, "Toward a Modern/Postmodern Reconstruction of Ethics," *University of Pennsylvania Law Review* 133 (1985): 291–380.

6. Compare Annette Baier, "Trust and Antitrust," *Ethics* 96 (1986): 231–60; and Owen Flanagan and Kathryn Jackson, "Justice, Care, and Gender: The Kohlberg-Gilligan Debate Revisited," *Ethics* 97 (1987): 622–37.

7. Compare Hartsock, pp. 41–42; and Virginia Held, "Non-contractual Society," in *Science, Morality and Feminist Theory*, ed. Marsha Hanen and Kai Nielsen, *Canadian Journal of Philosophy* 13, suppl. (1987): 111–38.

8. Amy Gutmann, "Communitarian Critics of Liberalism," *Philosophy and Public Affairs* 14 (1985): 308–22.

9. Compare Alice H. Eagly and Valerie J. Steffen, "Gender Stereotypes Stem from the Distribution of Women and Men into Social Roles," *Journal of Personality and Social Psychology* 46 (1984): 735–54.

10. Compare Carol Gilligan, *In a Different Voice* (Cambridge, Mass.: Harvard University Press, 1982).

However, communitarian philosophy as a whole is a perilous ally for feminist theory. Communitarians invoke a model of community which is focused particularly on families, neighborhoods, and nations. These sorts of communities have harbored social roles and structures which have been highly oppressive for women, as recent feminist critiques have shown. But communitarians seem oblivious to those criticisms and manifest a troubling complacency about the moral authority claimed or presupposed by these communities in regard to their members. By building on uncritical references to those sorts of communities, communitarian philosophy can lead in directions which feminists should not wish to follow.

This article is an effort to redirect communitarian thought so as to avoid some of the pitfalls which it poses, in its present form, for feminist theory and feminist practice. In the first part of the article, I develop some feminist-inspired criticisms of communitarian philosophy as it is found in writings by Michael Sandel and Alasdair MacIntyre.[11] My brief critique of communitarian thought has the aim of showing that communitarian theory, in the form in which it condones or tolerates traditional communal norms of gender subordination, is unacceptable from any standpoint enlightened by feminist analysis. This does not preclude agreeing with certain specific communitarian views, for example, the broad metaphysical conception of the individual, self, or subject as constituted by its social relationships and communal ties, or the assumption that traditional communities have some value. But the aim of the first section is critical: to focus on the communitarian disregard of gender-related problems with the norms and practices of traditional communities.

In the second part of the article, I will delve more deeply into the nature of different types of community and social relationship. I will suggest that friendships, on the one hand, and urban relationships and communities, on the other, offer an important clue toward a model of community which usefully counterbalances the family-neighborhood-nation complex favored by communitarians. With that model in view, we can begin to transform the communitarian vision of self and community into a more congenial ally for feminist theory.

THE SOCIAL SELF, IN COMMUNITARIAN PERSPECTIVE

Communitarians share with most feminist theorists a rejection of the abstractly individualist conception of self and society so prominent in modern liberal thought.[12] This self—atomistic, presocial, empty of all

11. In particular, Michael Sandel, *Liberalism and the Limits of Justice* (Cambridge: Cambridge University Press, 1982); Alasdair MacIntyre, *After Virtue* (Notre Dame, Ind.: University of Notre Dame Press, 1981).

12. Contemporary liberals do not regard the communitarians' metaphysical claims as a threat to liberal theory. The liberal concept of the self as abstracted from social relationships and historical context is now treated, not as a metaphysical presupposition but, rather, as a vehicle for evoking a pluralistic political society whose members disagree about the good for human life. With this device, liberalism seeks a theory of political process which aims

metaphysical content except abstract reason and will—is able to stand back from all the contingent moral commitments and norms of its particular historical context and assess each one of them in the light of impartial and universal criteria of reason. The self who achieves a substantial measure of such reflective reconsideration of the moral particulars of her life has achieved "autonomy," a widely esteemed liberal value.

In contrast to this vision of the self, the new communitarians pose the conception of a self whose identity and nature are defined by her contingent and particular social attachments. Communitarians extol the communities and social relationships, including family and nation, which constitute the typical social context in which the self emerges to self-consciousness. Thus, Michael Sandel speaks warmly of "those loyalties and convictions whose moral force consists partly in the fact that living by them is inseparable from understanding ourselves as the particular persons we are—as members of this family or community or nation or people, as bearers of this history, as sons and daughters of that revolution, as citizens of this republic."[13] Sandel continues, "Allegiances such as these are more than values I happen to have or aims I 'espouse at any given time.' They go beyond the obligations I voluntarily incur and the 'natural duties' I owe to human beings as such. They allow that to some I owe more than justice requires or even permits, not by reason of agreements I have made but instead in virtue of those more or less enduring attachments and commitments which taken together partly *define the person I am*" (italics mine).[14] Voicing similar sentiments, Alasdair MacIntyre writes:

> We all approach our own circumstances as bearers of a particular social identity. I am someone's son or daughter, someone else's cousin or uncle; I am a citizen of this or that city, a member of this or that guild or profession; I belong to this clan, that tribe, this nation. Hence what is good for me has to be the good for one who inhabits these roles. As such, I inherit from the past of my family, my city, my tribe, my nation, a variety of debts, inheritances, rightful expectations and obligations. These constitute the given of my life, my moral starting point. This is in part what gives my life its own moral particularity.[15]

(An aside: It is remarkable that neither writer mentions sex or gender as determining one's particular identity. Perhaps this glaring omission derives not from failing to realize the fundamental importance of gender in personal identity—could anyone really miss that?—but rather from

---

to avoid relying on any human particularities that might presuppose parochial human goods or purposes. Compare John Rawls, "Justice as Fairness: Political Not Metaphysical," *Philosophy and Public Affairs* 14 (1985): 223–51; and Joel Feinberg, "Liberalism, Community, and Tradition," drafted excerpt from *Harmless Wrongdoing*, vol. 4 of *The Moral Limits of the Criminal Law* (Oxford: Oxford University Press, 1988).

13. Sandel, p. 179.
14. Ibid.
15. MacIntyre, pp. 204–5.

the aim to emphasize what social relationships and communities contribute to identity, along with the inability to conceive that gender is a social relationship or that it constitutes communities.)

For communitarians, these social relationships and communities have a kind of morally normative legitimacy; they define the "moral starting points," to use MacIntyre's phrase, of each individual life. The traditions, practices, and conventions of our communities have at least a prima facie legitimate moral claim upon us. MacIntyre does qualify the latter point by conceding that "the fact that the self has to find its moral identity in and through its membership in communities such as those of the family, the neighborhood, the city and the tribe does not entail that the self has to accept the moral *limitations* of the particularity of those forms of community."[16] Nevertheless, according to MacIntyre, one's moral quests must begin by "moving forward from such particularity," for it "can never be simply left behind or obliterated."[17]

Despite the feminist concern with a social conception of the self and the importance of social relationships, at least three features of the communitarian version of these notions are troubling from a feminist standpoint. First, a relatively minor point: the communitarian's metaphysical conception of an inherently social self has little usefulness for normative analysis; in particular, it will not support a specifically feminist critique of individualist personality. Second, communitarian theory fails to acknowledge that many communities make illegitimate moral claims on their members, linked to hierarchies of domination and subordination. Third, the specific communities of family, neighborhood, and nation so commonly invoked by communitarians are troubling paradigms of social relationship and communal life. I will discuss each of these points in turn.

First, the communitarian's metaphysical conception of the social self will not support feminist critiques of ruggedly individualist personality or its associated attributes: the avoidance of intimacy, nonnurturance, social distancing, aggression, or violence. Feminist theorists have often been interested in developing a critique of the norm of the highly individualistic, competitive, aggressive personality type, seeing that personality type as more characteristically male than female and as an important part of the foundation for patriarchy.

Largely following the work of Nancy Chodorow, Dorothy Dinnerstein, and, more recently, Carol Gilligan,[18] many feminists have theorized that the processes of psycho-gender development, in a society in which early infant care is the primary responsibility of women but not men, result in a radical distinction between the genders in the extent to which the

16. Ibid., p. 205.

17. Ibid.

18. Dorothy Dinnerstein, *The Mermaid and the Minotaur: Sexual Arrangements and Human Malaise* (New York: Harper & Row, 1976); Nancy Chodorow, *The Reproduction of Mothering* (Berkeley: University of California Press, 1978); and Gilligan.

self is constituted by, and self-identifies with, its relational connections to others. Males are theorized to seek and value autonomy, individuation, separation, and the moral ideals of rights and justice which are thought to depend on a highly individuated conception of persons. By contrast, females are theorized to seek and value connection, sociality, inclusion, and moral ideals of care and nurturance.

From this perspective, highly individuated selves have been viewed as a problem. They are seen as incapable of human attachments based on mutuality and trust, unresponsive to human needs, approaching social relationships merely as rationally self-interested utility maximizers, thriving on separation and competition, and creating social institutions which tolerate, even legitimize, violence and aggression.

However, a metaphysical view that all human selves are constituted by their social and communal relationships does not itself entail a critique of these highly individualistic selves or yield any indication of what degree of psychological attachment to others is desirable. On metaphysical grounds alone, there would be no reason to suppose that caring, nurturant, re-lational, sociable selves were better than more autonomous, individualistic, and separate selves. All would be equivalently socially constituted at a metaphysical level. Abstract individualism's failure would be not that it has produced asocial selves, for, on the communitarian view, such beings are metaphysically impossible, but, rather, that it has simply failed the-oretically to acknowledge that selves are inherently social. And autonomy, independence, and separateness would become just a different way of being socially constituted, no worse nor better than heteronomy, depen-dence, or connectedness.

The communitarian conception of the social self, if it were simply a metaphysical view about the constitution of the self (which is what it seems to be), thus provides no basis for regarding nurturant, relational selves as morally superior to those who are highly individualistic. For that reason, it appears to be of no assistance to feminist theorists seeking a normative account of what might be wrong or excessive about competitive self-seeking behaviors or other seeming manifestations of an individualistic perspective. The communitarian "social self," as a metaphysical account of the self, is largely irrelevant to the array of normative tasks which many feminist thinkers have set for a conception of the self.

My second concern about communitarian philosophy has to do with the legitimacy of the moral influences which communities exert over their members and which are supposed to define the moral starting points of those members. As a matter of moral psychology, it is common for subjects to regard or presume as binding the moral claims made upon them by the norms of their communities. However, this point about moral psychology does not entail an endorsement of those moral claims, and it leaves open the question of whether, and to what extent, those claims might "really" be morally binding. Unfortunately, the new com-munitarians seem sometimes to go beyond the point of moral psychology to a stronger view, namely, that the moral claims of communities really are morally binding, at least as "moral starting points." MacIntyre refers to the "debts, inheritances, *rightful* expectations and obligations" which we "inherit" from family, nation and so forth.[19]

But such inheritances are enormously varied and troubling. Many communities are characterized by practices of exclusion and suppression of nongroup members, especially outsiders defined by ethnicity and sexual orientation.[20] If the new communitarians do not recognize legitimate "debts, inheritances, rightful expectations and obligations" across community lines, then their views have little relevance for our radically heterogeneous modern society. If people have "rightful expectations and obligations" across community lines, if, for example, whites have debts to blacks and Native Americans for histories of exploitation, if Germany owed reparations to non-Germans for genocidal practices, and so on, then "the" community as such, that is, the relatively bounded and local network of relationships which forms a subject's primary social setting, would not singularly determine the legitimate moral values or requirements which rightfully constitute the self's moral commitments or self-definition.

Besides excluding or suppressing outsiders, the practices and traditions of numerous communities are exploitative and oppressive toward many of their own members. This problem is of special relevance to women. Feminist theory is rooted in a recognition of the need for change in all the traditions and practices which show gender differentiation; many of these are located in just the sorts of communities invoked by communitarians, for example, family practices and national political traditions. The communitarian emphasis on communities unfortunately dovetails too well with the current popular emphasis on "the family" and seems to hark back to the repressive world of what some sociologists call communities of "place," the world of family, neighborhood, school, and church, which so intimately enclosed women in oppressive gender politics—the peculiar politics which it has been feminism's distinctive contribution to uncover. Any political theory which appears to support the hegemony of such communities and which appears to restore them to a position of unquestioned moral authority must be viewed with grave suspicion. I will come back to this issue when I turn to my third objection to communitarian philosophy.

Thus, while admitting into our notion of the self the important constitutive role played by social and communal relationships, we, from a standpoint independent of some particular subject, are not forced to accept as binding on that subject, the moral claims made by the social and communal relationships in which that subject is embedded or by which she is identified. Nor are we required to say that any particular

19. MacIntyre, p. 205; italics mine.
20. A similar point is made by Iris Young, "The Ideal of Community and the Politics of Difference," *Social Theory and Practice* 12 (1986): 12–13.

subject is herself morally obliged to accept as binding the moral claims made on her by any of the communities which constitute or define her. To evaluate the moral identities conferred by communities on their members, we need a theory of communities, of their interrelationships, of the structures of power, dominance, and oppression within and among them. Only such a theory would allow us to assess the legitimacy of the claims made by communities upon their members by way of their traditions, practices, and conventions of "debts, inheritances, . . . expectations, and obligations."

The communitarian approach suggests an attitude of celebrating the attachments which one finds oneself unavoidably to have, the familial ties, and so forth. But some relationships compete with others, and some relationships provide standpoints from which other relationships appear threatening or dangerous to oneself, one's integrity, or one's well-being. In such cases, simple formulas about the value of community provide no guidance. The problem is not simply to appreciate community per se but, rather, to reconcile the conflicting claims, demands, and identity-defining influences of the variety of communities of which one is a part.

It is worth recalling that liberalism has always condemned, in principle if not in practice, the norms of social hierarchy and political subordination based on inherited or ascribed status. Where liberals historically have applied this tenet at best only to the public realm of civic relationships, feminism seeks to extend it more radically to the "private" realm of family and other communities of place. Those norms and claims of local communities which sustain gender hierarchies have no intrinsic legitimacy from a feminist standpoint. A feminist interest in community must certainly aim for social institutions and relational structures which diminish and, finally, erase gender subordination.

Reflections such as these characterize the concerns of the modern self, the self who acknowleges no a priori loyalty to any feature of situation or role, and who claims the right to question the moral legitimacy of any contingent moral claim.[21] We can agree with the communitarians that it would be impossible for the self to question all her contingencies at once, yet at the same time, unlike the communitarians, still emphasize the critical importance of morally questioning various communal norms and circumstances.

A third problem with communitarian philosophy has to do with the sorts of communities evidently endorsed by communitarian theorists. Human beings participate in a variety of communities and social relationships, not only across time, but at any one time. However, when people think of "community," it is common for them to think of certain particular social networks, namely, those formed primarily out of family, neighborhood, school, and church.[22] MacIntyre and Sandel both emphasize

21. Compare Cornell, p. 323.
22. This point is made by Young, p. 12.

family specifically. MacIntyre cites neighborhood along with clan, tribe, city, and nation, while Sandel includes "nation or people, . . . bearers of this history, . . . sons and daughters of that revolution, . . . citizens of this republic."[23]

But where, one might ask, is the International Ladies Garment Workers' Union, the Teamsters, the Democratic Party, Alcoholics Anonymous, or the Committee in Solidarity with the People of El Salvador?

The substantive examples of community listed by MacIntyre and Sandel fall largely into two groups: one, governmental communities which constitute our civic and national identities in a public world of nation-states; and two, local communities centered around family and neighborhood. Although MacIntyre does mention professions and, rather archaically, "guilds,"[24] these references are anomolous in his work, which, for the most part, ignores such communities as trade unions, political action groups, associations of hobbyists, and so forth.

Some of the communities cited by MacIntyre and Sandel will resonate with the historical experiences of women, especially the inclusive communities of family and neighborhood. However, it should not be forgotten that governing communities have, until only recently, excluded the legitimate participation of women. It would seem to follow that they have accordingly not historically constituted the identities of women in profound ways. As "daughters" of the American revolution, looking back to the "fathers of our country," we find that we have inconveniently been deprived of the self-identifying heritage of our cultural mothers. In general, the contribution made to the identities of various groups of people by governing communities is quite uneven, given that they are communities to which many are subject but in which far fewer actively participate.

At any rate, there is an underlying commonality to most of the communities which MacIntyre and Sandel cite as constitutive of self-identity and definitive of our moral starting points. Sandel himself explicates this commonality when he writes that, for people "bound by a sense of community," the notion of community describes *"not a relationship they choose (as in a voluntary association) but an attachment they discover,* not merely an attribute but a constituent of their identity" (italics mine).[25] Not voluntary but "discovered" relationships and communities are what Sandel takes to define subjective identity for those who are bound by a "sense of community." It is the communities to which we are involuntarily bound to which Sandel accords metaphysical pride of place in the constitution of subjectivity. What are important are not simply the "associations" in which people "cooperate" but the "communities" in which people "participate," for these latter: "describe a form of life in which the members find themselves commonly situated 'to begin with,' their commonality

23. MacIntyre, p. 204; Sandel, p. 179.
24. MacIntyre, p. 204.
25. Sandel, p. 150.

consisting less in relationships they have entered than in attachments they have found."[26] Thus, the social relationships which one finds, the attachments which are discovered and not chosen, become the points of reference for self-definition by the communitarian subject.

For the child maturing to self-consciousness in her community of origin, typically the family-neighborhood-school-church complex, it seems uncontroversial that "the" community is found, not entered, discovered, not created. But this need not be true of an adult's communities of mature self-identification. Many of these adult communities are, for at least some of their members, communities of choice to a significant extent: labor unions, philanthropic associations, political coalitions, and, if one has ever moved or migrated, even the communities of neighborhood, church, city, or nation-state might have been chosen to an important extent. One need not have simply discovered oneself to be embedded in them in order that one's identity or the moral particulars of one's life be defined by them. Sandel is right to indicate the role of found communities in constituting the unreflective, "given" identity which the self discovers when *first* beginning to reflect on itself. But for mature self-identity, we should also recognize a legitimate role for communities of choice, supplementing, if not displacing, the communities and attachments which are merely found.

Moreover, the discovered identity constituted by one's original community of place might be fraught with ambivalences and ambiguities. Thus, poet Adrienne Rich writes about her experiences growing up with a Christian mother, a Jewish father who suppressed his ethnicity, and a family community which taught Adrienne Rich contempt for all that was identified with Jewishness. In 1946, while still a high school student, Rich saw, for the first time, a film about the Allied liberation of Nazi concentration camps. Writing about this experience in 1982, she brooded: "I feel belated rage that I was so impoverished by the family and social worlds I lived in, that I had to try to figure out by myself what this did indeed mean for me. That I had never been taught about resistance, only about passing. That I had no language for anti-Semitism itself."[27] As a student at Radcliffe in the late forties, Rich met "real" Jewish women who inducted her into the lore of Jewish background and customs, holidays and foods, names and noses. She plunged in with trepidation: "I felt I was testing a forbidden current, that there was danger in these revelations. I bought a reproduction of a Chagall portrait of a rabbi in striped prayer shawl and hung it on the wall of my room. I was admittedly young and trying to educate myself, but I was also doing something that *is* dangerous: I was flirting with

26. Ibid., pp. 151–52.
27. Adrienne Rich, "Split at the Root: An Essay on Jewish Identity," in her *Blood, Bread, and Poetry* (New York: Norton, 1986), p. 107; reprinted from Evelyn Torton Beck, ed., *Nice Jewish Girls: A Lesbian Anthology* (Trumansburg, N.Y.: Crossing Press, 1982), pp. 67–84.

identity."[28] And she was doing it apart from the family community from which her ambiguous ethnic identity was originally derived.

For Sandel, Rich's lifelong troubled reflections on her ethnic identity might seem compatible with his theory. In his view, the subject discovers the attachments which are constitutive of its subjectivity through reflection on a multitude of values and aims, differentiating what is self from what is not-self. He might say that Rich discriminated among the many loyalties and projects which defined who she was in her original community, that is, her family, and discerned that her Jewishness appeared "essential"[29] to who she was. But it is not obvious, without question begging, that her original community really defined her as essentially Jewish. Indeed, her family endeavored to suppress loyalties and attachments to all things Jewish. Thus, one of Rich's quests in life, so evidently not inspired by her community of origin alone, was to reexamine the identity found in that original context. The communitarian view that found communities and social attachments constitute self-identity does not, by itself, explicate the source of such a quest. It seems more illuminating to say that her identity became, in part, "chosen," that it had to do with social relationships and attachments which she sought out, rather than merely found, created as well as discovered.

Thus, the commitments and loyalties of our found communities, our communities of origin, may harbor ambiguities, ambivalences, contradictions, and oppressions which complicate as well as constitute identity and which have to be sorted out, critically scrutinized. And since the resources for such scrutiny may not be found in all "found" communities, our theories of community should recognize that resources and skills derived from communities which are not merely found or discovered may equally well contribute to the constitution of identity. The constitution of identity and moral particularity, for the modern self, may well require radically different communities from those so often invoked by communitarians.

The whole tenor of communitarian thinking would change once we opened up the conception of the social self to encompass chosen communities, especially those which lie beyond the typical original community of family-neighborhood-school-church. No longer would communitarian thought present a seemingly conservative complacency about the private and local communities of place which have so effectively circumscribed, in particular, the lives of most women.

In the second part of this article, I will explore more fully the role of communities and relationships of "choice," which point the way toward a notion of community more congenial to feminist aspirations.

---

28. Ibid., p. 108.
29. This term is used by Sandel, p. 180.

MODERN FRIENDSHIP, URBAN COMMUNITY, AND BEYOND

My goals are manifold: to retain the communitarian insights about the contribution of community and social relationship to self-identity, yet open up for critical reflection the moral particulars imparted by those communities, and identify the sorts of communities which will provide nonoppressive and enriched lives for women.

Toward this end, it will be helpful to consider models of human relationship and community which contrast with those cited by communitarians. I believe that friendship and urban community can offer us crucial insights into the social nature of the modern self. It is in moving forward from these relationships that we have the best chance of reconciling the communitarian conception of the social self with the longed-for communities of feminist aspiration.

Both modern friendship and the stereotypical urban community share an important feature which is either neglected or deliberately avoided in communitarian conceptions of human relationship. From a liberal, or Enlightenment, or modernist standpoint, this feature would be characterized as voluntariness: those relationships are based partly on choice.

Let us first consider friendship as it is understood in this culture. Friends are supposed to be people whom one chooses on one's own to share activities and intimacies. No particular people are assigned by custom or tradition to be a person's friends. From among the larger number of one's acquaintants, one moves toward closer and more friendlike relationships with some of them, motivated by one's own needs, values, and attractions. No consanguineous or legal connections establish or maintain ties of friendship. As this relationship is widely understood in our culture, its basis lies in voluntary choice.

In this context, "voluntary choice" refers to motivations arising out of one's own needs, desires, interests, values, and attractions, in contrast to motivations arising from what is socially assigned, ascribed, expected, or demanded. This means that friendship is more likely than many other relationships, such as those of family and neighborhood, to be grounded in and sustained by shared interests and values, mutual affection, and possibilities for generating mutual respect and esteem.

In general, friendship has had an obvious importance to feminist aspirations as the basis of the bond which is (ironically) called "sisterhood."[30] Friendship is more likely than many other close personal relationships to provide social support for people who are idiosyncratic, whose unconventional values and deviant life-styles make them victims of intolerance from family members and others who are unwillingly related to them. In this regard, friendship has socially disruptive possibilities, for out of

30. Martha Ackelsberg points out the ironic and misleading nature of this use of the term "sisterhood" in " 'Sisters' or 'Comrades'? The Politics of Friends and Families," in *Families, Politics, and Public Policy,* ed. Irene Diamond (New York: Longman, 1983), pp. 339–56.

the unconventional living which it helps to sustain there often arise influential forces for social change. Friendship among women has been the cement not only of the various historical waves of the feminist movement, but as well of numerous communities of women throughout history who defied the local conventions for their gender and lived lives of creative disorder.[31] In all these cases, women moved out of their given or found communities into new attachments with other women by their own choice, that is, motivated by their own needs, desires, attractions, and fears rather than, and often in opposition to, the expectations and ascribed roles of their found communities.

Like friendship, many urban relationships are also based more on choice than on socially ascribed roles, biological connections, or other nonvoluntary ties. Voluntary associations, such as political action groups, support groups, associations of co-hobbyists, and so on, are a common part of modern urban life, with its large population centers and the greater availability of critical masses of people with special interests or needs. But while friendship is almost universally extolled, urban communities and relationships have been theorized in wildly contradictory ways. Cities have sometimes been taken as "harbingers" of modern culture per se[32] and have been particularly associated with the major social trends of modern life, such as industrialization and bureaucratization.[33] The results of these trends are often thought to have been a fragmentation of "real" community and the widely lamented alienation of modern urban life: people seldom know their neighbors; population concentration generates massive psychic overload;[34] fear and mutual distrust, even outright hostility, generated by the dangers of urban life, may dominate most daily associations. Under such circumstances, meaningful relationships are often theorized to be rare, if at all possible.

But is this image a complete portrait of urban life? It is probably true, in urban areas, that communities of place are diminished in importance; neighborhood plays a far less significant role in constituting community than it does in nonurban areas.[35] But this does not mean that the social networks and communities of urban dwellers are inferior to those of nonurban residents.

Much evidence suggests that urban settings do not, as commonly stereotyped, promote only alienation, isolation, and psychic breakdown. The communities available to urban dwellers are different from those

31. Compare Janice Raymond, *A Passion for Friends* (Boston: Beacon, 1986), esp. chaps. 2 and 3.

32. Claude Fischer, *To Dwell among Friends* (Chicago: University of Chicago Press, 1982), p. 1.

33. Compare Richard Sennett, "An Introduction," in *Classic Essays on the Culture of Cities,* ed. Richard Sennett (New York: Appleton-Century-Crofts, 1969), pp. 3–22.

34. Compare Stanley Milgram, "The Experience of Living in Cities," *Science* 167 (1970): 1461–68.

35. Fischer, pp. 97–103.

available to nonurban dwellers, but not necessarily less gratifying or fulfilling.[36] Communities of place are relatively nonvoluntary; one's extended family of origin is given or ascribed, and the relationships found as one grows. Sociological research has shown that urban dwellers tend to form their social networks, their communities, out of people who are brought together for reasons other than geographical proximity. As sociologist Claude Fischer has stated it, in urban areas, "population concentration stimulates allegiances to subcultures based on more significant social traits" than common locality or neighborhood.[37] Communities of place, centered around the family-neighborhood-church-school web, are more likely, for urban dwellers, to be supplanted by other sorts of communities, resulting in what the sociologist Melvin Webber has called "community without propinquity."[38] But most important for our purposes, these are still often genuine communities, and not the cesspools of "Rum, Romanism, and Rebellion" sometimes depicted by anti-urbanists.

Literature reveals that women writers have been both repelled and inspired by cities. The city, as a concentrated center of male political and economic power, seems to exclude women altogether.[39] However, as literary critic Susan Merrill Squier points out, the city can provide women not only with jobs, education, and the cultural tools with which to escape imposed gender roles, familial demands, and domestic servitude, but can also bring women together, in work or in leisure, and lay the basis for bonds of sisterhood.[40] The quests of women who journey to cities leaving behind men, home, and family, are subversive, writes literary critic Blanche Gelfant, and may well be perceived by others "as assaults upon society."[41] Thus, cities open up for women possibilities of supplanting communities of place with relationships and communities of choice. These chosen communities can provide the resources for women to surmount the moral particularities of family and place which define and limit their moral starting points.

Social theorists have long decried the interpersonal estrangement of urban life, an observation which seems predominantly inspired by the public world of conflict between various subcultural groups. Urbanism does not create interpersonal estrangement within subcultures but, rather,

---

36. Ibid., pp. 193–232.

37. Ibid., p. 273.

38. Melvin Webber, "Order in Diversity: Community without Propinquity," in *Neighborhood, City and Metropolis,* ed. R. Gutman and D. Popenoe (New York: Random House, 1970), pp. 792–811.

39. Compare the essays in Catharine Stimpson et al., eds., *Women and the American City* (Chicago: University of Chicago Press, 1980, 1981); and the special issue on "Women in the City," *Urban Resources,* vol. 3, no. 2 (Winter 1986).

40. Introduction to Susan Merrill Squier, ed., *Women Writers and the City* (Knoxville: University of Tennessee Press, 1984), pp. 3–10.

41. Blanche Gelfant, "Sister to Faust: The City's 'Hungry' Woman as Heroine," in Squier, ed., p. 267.

tends to promote social involvement.[42] This is especially true for people with special backgrounds and interests, for people who are members of small minorities, and for ethnic groups. Fischer has found that social relationships in urban centers are more "culturally specialized: urbanites were relatively involved with associates in the social world they considered most important and relatively uninvolved with associates, if any, in other worlds."[43] As Fischer summarizes it, "Urbanism . . . fosters social involvement in the subculture(s) of *choice,* rather than the subculture(s) of circumstances."[44] This is doubtless reinforced by the recent more militant expression of group values and group demands for rights and respect on the parts of urban subcultural minorities.

We might describe urban relationships as being characteristically "modern" to signal their relatively greater voluntary basis. We find, in these relationships and the social networks formed of them, not a loss of community but an increase in importance of community of a different sort from that of family-neighborhood-church-school complexes. Yet these more voluntary communities may be as deeply constitutive of the identities and particulars of the individuals who participate in them as are the communities of place so warmly invoked by communitarians.

Perhaps it is more illuminating to say that communities of choice foster not so much the constitution of subjects but their reconstitution. They may be sought out as contexts in which people relocate the various constituents of their identities, as Adrienne Rich sought out the Jewish community in her college years. While people in a community of choice may not share a common history, their shared values or interests are likely to manifest backgrounds of similar experiences, as, for example, among the members of a lesbian community. The modern self may seek new communities whose norms and relationships stimulate and develop her identity and self-understanding more adequately than her unchosen community of origin, her original community of place.

In case it is chosen communities which help us to define ourselves, the project of self-definition would not be arising from communities in which we merely found or discovered our immersion. It is likely that chosen communities, lesbian communities, for example, attract us in the first place because they appeal to features of ourselves which, though perhaps merely found or discovered, were inadequately or ambivalently sustained by our unchosen families, neighborhoods, schools, or churches. Thus, unchosen communities are sometimes communities which we can, and should, leave, searching elsewhere for the resources to help us discern who we really are.

Our communities of origin do not necessarily constitute us as selves who agree or comply with the norms which unify those communities.

42. Fischer, pp. 247–48.
43. Ibid., p. 230.
44. Ibid.

Some of us are constituted as deviants and resisters by our communities of origin, and our defiance may well run to the foundational social norms which ground the most basic social roles and relationships upon which those communities rest. The feminist challenge to sex/gender arrangements is precisely of this foundational sort.

A community of choice might be a community of people who share a common oppression. This is particularly critical in those instances in which the shared oppression is not concentrated within certain communities of place, as it might be, for example, in the case of ethnic minorities, but, rather, is focused on people who are distributed throughout social and ethnic groupings and who do not themselves constitute a traditional community of place. Women are a prime example of such a distributed group. Women's communities are seldom the original, nonvoluntary, found communities of their members.

To be sure, nonvoluntary communities of place are not without value. Most lives contain mixtures of relationships and communities, some given/found/discovered and some chosen/created. Most people probably are, to some extent, ineradicably constituted by their communities of place, the community defined by some or all of their family, neighborhood, school, or church. It is noteworthy that dependent children, elderly persons, and all other individuals whose lives and well-being are at great risk, need the support of communities whose other members do not or cannot choose arbitrarily to leave. Recent philosophical investigation into communities and relationships not founded or sustained by choice has brought out the importance of these social networks for the constitution of social life.[45] But these insights should not obscure the additional need for communities of choice to counter oppressive and abusive relational structures in those nonvoluntary communities by providing models of alternative social relationships as well as standpoints for critical reflection on self and community.

Having attained a critically reflective stance toward one's communities of origin, one's community of place, toward family, neighborhood, church, school, and nation, one has probably at the same time already begun to question and distance oneself from aspects of one's "identity" in that community and, therefore, to have embarked on the path of personal redefinition. From such a perspective, the uncritically assumed communities of place invoked by the communitarians appear deeply problematic. We can concede the influence of those communities without having unreflectively to endorse it. We must develop communitarian thought beyond its complacent regard for the communities in which we once found ourselves toward (and beyond) an awareness of the crucial importance of dislocated communities, communities of choice.

---

45. Compare Baier; Held; and Pateman.

Talking about Needs: Interpretive Contests as Political Conflicts in Welfare-State Societies*

Nancy Fraser

Need is also a political instrument, meticulously prepared, calculated and used. [MICHEL FOUCAULT][1]

In late-capitalist, welfare-state societies, talk about people's needs is an important species of political discourse. We argue, in the United States, for example, about whether the government ought to provide for health and day-care needs, and indeed, about whether such needs exist. And we dispute whether existing social-welfare programs really do meet the needs they purport to satisfy or whether, instead, they misconstrue those needs. We also argue about what exactly various groups of people really do need and about who should have the last word in such matters. In all these cases, needs-talk functions as a medium for the making and contesting of political claims. It is an idiom in which political conflict is played out and through which inequalities are symbolically elaborated and challenged.

Talk about needs has not always been central to Western political culture; it has often been considered antithetical to politics and relegated to the margins of political life. However, in welfare-state societies, needs-talk has been institutionalized as a major vocabulary of political discourse.[2]

* Many of the ideas in this paper were first developed in my "Social Movements versus Disciplinary Bureaucracies," CHS Occasional Paper no. 8 (Minneapolis: University of Minnesota, Center for Humanistic Studies, 1987). I am grateful for helpful comments from Sandra Bartky, Paul Mattick, Frank Michelman, Martha Minow, Linda Nicholson, and Iris Young. The Mary Ingraham Bunting Institute of Radcliffe College provided crucial financial support and a utopian working situation.

1. Michel Foucault, *Discipline and Punish: The Birth of the Prison*, trans. Alan Sheridan (New York: Vintage, 1979), p. 26.

2. In this article, I shall use the terms 'welfare-state societies' and 'late-capitalist societies' interchangeably to refer to the industrialized countries of Western Europe and North America in the present period. Of course, the process of welfare-state formation begins at different times, proceeds at different rates, and takes different forms in these countries. Still, I assume that it is possible in principle to identify and characterize some features of these societies which transcend such differences. On the other hand, most of the examples

This essay originally appeared in *Ethics* 99, January 1989.

It coexists, albeit often uneasily, with talk about rights and interests at the very center of political life. Indeed, this peculiar juxtaposition of a discourse about needs with discourses about rights and interests is one of the distinctive marks of late-capitalist political culture.

Why has needs-talk become so prominent in the political culture of welfare-state societies? What is the relation between this development and changes in late-capitalist social structure? What does the emergence of the needs idiom imply about shifts in the boundaries between "political," "economic," and "domestic" spheres of life? Does it betoken an extension of the political sphere or, rather, a colonization of that domain by newer modes of power and social control? What are the major varieties of needs-talk and how do they interact polemically with one another? What opportunities and/or obstacles does the needs idiom pose for movements interested in social transformation?

In what follows, I outline an approach for thinking about such questions rather than proposing definitive answers to them. What I have to say falls into four parts. In Section I, I suggest a break with standard theoretical approaches by shifting the focus of inquiry from needs to discourses about needs, from the distribution of need satisfactions to the "politics of need interpretation." I propose a model of social discourse designed to bring into relief the contested character of needs-talk in welfare-state societies. Then, in Section II, I relate this discourse model to social-structural considerations, especially to shifts in the boundaries between "political," "economic," and "domestic" or "personal" spheres of life in late-capitalist societies. Then, in Section III, I identify three major strands of needs-talk in contemporary political culture and I map some of the ways in which they compete for potential adherents. Finally, in Section IV, I apply the model to some concrete cases of contemporary needs politics in the United States.

I

Let me begin by explaining some of the peculiarities of the approach I am trying to develop. In my approach, the focus of inquiry is not needs but rather *discourses* about needs. The point is to shift our angle of vision on the politics of needs. Usually, the politics of needs is understood to concern the distribution of satisfactions. In my approach, by contrast, the focus is the *politics of need interpretation*.

The reason for focusing on discourses and interpretation is to bring into view the contextual and contested character of needs claims. As many theorists have noted, needs claims have a relational structure; implicitly or explicitly, they have the form '*A* needs *x* in order to *y*.' Now, this structure poses no problems when we are considering very general or "thin" needs such as food or shelter *simpliciter*. Thus, we can uncon-

invoked here are from the U.S. context, and it is possible that this skews the account. Further comparative work would be needed to determine the precise scope of applicability of the model presented here.

troversially say that homeless people, like everyone else in nontropical climates, need shelter in order to live. And most people will infer that governments, as guarantors of life and liberty, have a responsibility to provide for this need. However, as soon as we descend to a lesser level of generality, needs claims become far more controversial. What, more "thickly," do homeless people need in order to be sheltered from the cold? What specific forms of provision are implied once we acknowledge their very general, thin need? Do homeless people need forbearance to sleep undisturbed next to a hot air vent on a street corner? A space in a subway tunnel or a bus terminal? A bed in a temporary shelter? A permanent home? Suppose we say the latter. What kind of permanent housing do homeless people need? Rental units in high-rises in center city areas remote from good schools, discount shopping, and job opportunities? Single-family homes designed for single-earner, two-parent families? And what else do homeless people need in order to have permanent homes? Rent subsidies? Income supports? Jobs? Job training and education? Day care? Finally, what is needed, at the level of housing policy, in order to insure an adequate stock of affordable housing? Tax incentives to encourage private investment in low-income housing? Concentrated or scattered site public housing projects within a generally commodified housing environment? Rent control? Decommodification of urban housing?

We could continue proliferating such questions indefinitely. And we would, at the same time, be proliferating controversy. That is precisely the point about needs claims. These claims tend to be nested, connected to one another in ramified chains of "in-order-to" relations. Moreover, when these chains are unraveled in the course of political disputes, disagreements usually deepen rather than abate. Precisely how such chains are unraveled depends on what the interlocutors share in the way of background assumptions. Does it go without saying that policy designed to deal with homelessness must not challenge the basic ownership and investment structure of urban real estate? Or is that a point of rupture in the network of in-order-to relations, a point at which people's assumptions and commitments diverge?

It is this network of deeply contested in-order-to relations that I mean to call attention to when I propose to focus on the politics of need interpretation. I believe that thin theories of needs which do not descend into the murky depths of such networks are unable to shed much light on contemporary needs politics. Such theories assume that the politics of needs concerns only whether various predefined needs will or will not be provided for. As a result, they deflect attention from a number of important political questions.[3] First, they take the *interpretation* of people's

---

3. A recent example of the kind of theory I have in mind is David Braybrooke, *Meeting Needs* (Princeton, N.J.: Princeton University Press, 1987). Braybrooke claims that a thin concept of need "can make a substantial contribution to settling upon policies without having to descend into the melee" (p. 68). Thus, he does not take up any of the issues I am about to enumerate.

needs as simply given and unproblematic; they thus occlude the interpretive dimension of needs politics—the fact that not just satisfactions but *need interpretations* are politically contested. Second, they assume that it is unproblematic who interprets the needs in question and from what perspective and in the light of what interests; they thus occlude the fact that *who* gets to establish authoritative, thick definitions of people's needs is itself a political stake. Third, they take for granted that the socially authorized forms of public discourse available for interpreting people's needs are adequate and fair; they thus occlude the question whether these forms of public discourse are skewed in favor of the self-interpretations and interests of dominant social groups and, so, work to the disadvantage of subordinate or oppositional groups; they occlude, in other words, the fact that the means of public discourse themselves may be at issue in needs politics.[4] Fourth, such theories fail to focalize the social and institutional logic of processes of need interpretation; they thus occlude such important political questions as where in society, in what institutions, are authoritative need interpretations developed, and what sorts of social relations are in force among the interlocutors or co-interpreters?

In order to remedy these blindspots, I am trying to develop a more politically critical, discourse-oriented alternative. As I said, my approach shifts the focus of inquiry from needs to discourses about needs. Moreover, I take the politics of needs to comprise three analytically distinct but practically interrelated moments. The first is the struggle to establish or deny the political status of a given need, that is, the struggle to validate the need as a matter of legitimate political concern or to enclave it as a nonpolitical matter. The second is the struggle over the interpretation of the need, the struggle for the power to define it and, so, to determine what would satisfy it. The third moment is the struggle over the satisfaction of the need, that is, the struggle to secure or withhold provision.

Now, a focus on the politics of need interpretation requires a model of social discourse. The model I have developed foregrounds the multivalent and contested character of needs-talk, the fact that in welfare-state societies we encounter a plurality of competing ways of talking about people's needs. The model theorizes what I call "the sociocultural means of interpretation and communication." By sociocultural means of interpretation and communication (MIC), I mean the historically and culturally specific ensemble of discursive resources available to members of a given social collectivity in pressing claims against one another. Included among these resources are things like the following.

1. The officially recognized idioms in which one can press claims; for example, needs-talk, rights-talk, and interests-talk.

2. The vocabularies available for instantiating claims in these recognized idioms; thus, with respect to needs-talk, what are the vocabularies

4. For a fuller discussion of this issue, see Nancy Fraser, "Toward a Discourse Ethic of Solidarity," *Praxis International* 5 (1986): 425–29.

available for interpreting and communicating one's needs? For example, therapeutic vocabularies, administrative vocabularies, religious vocabularies, feminist vocabularies, and socialist vocabularies.

3. The paradigms of argumentation accepted as authoritative in adjudicating conflicting claims; thus, with respect to needs-talk, how are conflicts over the interpretation of needs resolved? By appeals to scientific experts, by brokered compromises, by voting according to majority rule, by privileging the interpretations of those whose needs are in question?

4. The narrative conventions available for constructing the individual and collective stories which are constitutive of people's social identities.

5. Modes of subjectification; the ways in which various discourses position the people to whom they are addressed as specific sorts of subjects endowed with specific sorts of capacities for action; for example, as "normal" or "deviant," as causally conditioned or freely self-determining, as victims or as potential activists, and as unique individuals or as members of social groups.[5]

Now, in welfare-state societies, there are a plurality of forms of association, roles, groups, institutions, and discourses. Thus, the means of interpretation and communication are not all of a piece. They do not constitute a coherent, monolithic web but rather a heterogeneous, polyglot field of diverse possibilities and alternatives.

In fact, in welfare-state societies, discourses about needs typically make at least implicit reference to alternative interpretations. Particular claims about needs are "internally dialogized"; implicitly or explicitly they evoke resonances of competing need interpretations. They therefore allude to a conflict of need interpretations.[6]

5. The expression 'mode of subjectification' is inspired by Foucault, although his term is 'mode of subjection' and his usage differs somewhat from mine. Compare Michel Foucault, "On the Genealogy of Ethics: An Overview of Work in Progress," in *The Foucault Reader*, ed. Paul Rabinow (New York: Pantheon, 1984), pp. 340–73. For another account of this idea of the sociocultural means of interpretation and communication, see Fraser, "Toward a Discourse Ethic of Solidarity."

6. The expression 'internally dialogized' comes from Mikhail Bakhtin. By invoking it here, I mean to suggest that the Bakhtinian notion of a "dialogic heteroglossia" (or a cross-referential, multivoiced field of significations) is more apt as a description of the MIC in complex societies than is the more monolithic Lacanian idea of The Symbolic or the Saussurean idea of a seamless code. However, in claiming that the Bakhtinian conceptions of heteroglossia and dialogization are especially apt with respect to complex, differentiated societies, including late-capitalist, welfare-state societies, I am intentionally breaking with Bakhtin's own view. He assumed, on the contrary, that these conceptions found their most robust expression in the "carnivalesque" culture of late medieval Europe and that the subsequent history of Western societies brought a flattening out of language and a restriction of dialogic heteroglossia to the specialized, esoteric domain of "the literary." This seems patently false—especially when we recognize that the dialogic, polemical character of speech is related to the availability in a culture of a plurality of competing discourses and of subject-positions from which to articulate them. Thus, conceptually, one would expect what, I take it, is in fact the case: that speech in complex, differentiated societies would be especially suitable for analysis in terms of these Bakhtinian categories. For the Bakhtinian conceptions of heteroglossia and internal dialogization, see "Discourse in the Novel," in

On the other hand, welfare-state societies are not simply pluralist. Rather, they are stratified, differentiated into social groups with unequal status, power, and access to resources, and traversed by pervasive axes of inequality along lines of class, gender, race, ethnicity, and age. The MIC in these societies are also stratified, that is, organized in ways which are congruent with societal patterns of dominance and subordination.

It follows that we must distinguish those elements of the MIC which are hegemonic, authorized, and officially sanctioned, on the one hand, from those which are nonhegemonic, disqualified, and discounted, on the other hand. Some ways of talking about needs are institutionalized in the central discursive arenas of late-capitalist societies: parliaments, academies, courts, and mass circulation media. Other ways of talking about needs are enclaved as subcultural sociolects and are normally excluded from the central discursive arenas.[7] For example, moralistic and scientific discourses about the needs of people with AIDS, and of people at risk with respect to AIDS, are represented on government commissions; in contrast, gay and lesbian rights activists' interpretations of those needs are excluded.

From this perspective, needs-talk appears as a site of struggle where groups with unequal discursive (and nondiscursive) resources compete to establish as hegemonic their respective interpretations of legitimate social needs. Dominant groups articulate need interpretations intended to exclude, defuse, and/or co-opt counterinterpretations. Subordinate or oppositional groups, on the other hand, articulate need interpretations intended to challenge, displace, and/or modify dominant ones. In both cases, the interpretations are acts and interventions.[8]

II

Now I should like to try to situate the discourse model I have just sketched with respect to some social-structural features of late-capitalist societies. Here, I seek to relate the rise of politicized needs-talk to shifts in the

---

The Dialogic Imagination: Four Essays by M. M. Bakhtin, trans. Caryl Emerson and Michael Holquist (Austin: University of Texas Press, 1981), pp. 259–422. For a helpful secondary account, see Dominick LaCapra, "Bakhtin, Marxism and the Carnivalesque," in his *Rethinking Intellectual History* (Ithaca, N.Y.: Cornell University Press, 1983), pp. 294–324. For a critique of the Romantic, antimodernist bias in both Bakhtin and LaCapra, see Nancy Fraser, "On the Political and the Symbolic: Against the Metaphysics of Textuality," *Enclitic* 9 (1987): 100–114.

7. If the previous point was Bakhtinian, this one could be considered Bourdieuian. There is probably no contemporary social theorist who has worked more fruitfully than Bourdieu at understanding cultural contestation in relation to societal inequality. See Pierre Bourdieu, *Outline of a Theory of Practice,* trans. Richard Nice (Cambridge: Cambridge University Press, 1977), and also *Distinction: A Social Critique of the Judgment of Pure Taste* (Cambridge, Mass.: Harvard University Press, 1979).

8. Here the model aims to marry Bakhtin with Bourdieu. For the use of (what looks to me like) a similar theoretical perspective in a different context, see T. J. Clarke, "Beliefs and Purposes in David's *Death of Marat,*" seminar 2 (typescript).

boundaries separating "political," "economic," and "domestic" dimensions of life. However, unlike many social theorists, I shall treat the terms 'political,' 'economic,' and 'domestic' as cultural classifications and ideological labels rather than as designations of structures, spheres, or things.[9]

Let me begin by noting that the terms 'politics' and 'political' are highly contested, and they have a number of different senses.[10] In the present context, the two most important senses are the following. First, there is the institutional sense in which a matter is deemed "political" if it is handled directly in the institutions of the official governmental system, including parliaments, administrative apparatuses, and the like. In this sense, what is "political"—call it "official-political"—contrasts with what is handled in institutions like the "family" and the "economy," which are defined as being outside the official-political system, even though they are in actuality underpinned and regulated by it. Second, there is the discourse sense in which something is "political" if it is contested across a range of different discursive arenas and among a range of different publics. In this sense, what is "political"—call it 'discursive-political' or 'politic*ized*'—contrasts both with what is not contested in public at all and also with what is contested only by and within relatively specialized, enclaved, and/or segmented publics.[11] These two senses are not unrelated. In democratic theory, if not always in practice, a matter does not usually become subject to legitimate state intervention until it has been debated across a wide range of discourse publics.

9. I owe this formulation to Paul Mattick. For a thoughtful discussion of the advantages of this sort of approach, see his "On *Feminism as Critique*" (typescript).

10. Included among the senses I shall not discuss are (1) the pejorative colloquial sense according to which a decision is "political" when personal jockeying for power overrides germane substantive considerations; and (2) the radical political-theoretical sense according to which all interactions traversed by relations of power and inequality are 'political.'

11. Let me spell out some of the presuppositions and implications of the discourse sense of 'politics.' This sense stipulates that a matter is 'political' if it is contested across a range of different discursive arenas and among a range of different discourse publics. Thus, it depends on the idea of discursive publicity. However, in this conception, publicity is not understood in a simple unitary way as the undifferentiated opposite of discursive privacy. Rather, publicity is understood differentiatedly, on the assumption that it is possible to identify a plurality of distinct discourse publics and to theorize the relations among them. Clearly, publics can be distinguished along a number of different axes, e.g., by ideology (the readership of *The Nation* versus the readership of *The Public Interest*), by stratification principles like gender (the viewers of "Cagney and Lacey" versus the viewers of "Monday Night Football") and class (the readership of the *New York Times* versus that of the *New York Post*), by profession (the membership of the American Economic Association versus that of the American Bar Association), by central mobilizing issue (the Nuclear Freeze movement versus the 'Pro-Life' movement). Publics can also be distinguished in terms of relative power. Some are large, authoritative, and able to set the terms of debate for many of the rest. Others, by contrast, are small, self-enclosed, and enclaved, unable to make much of a mark beyond their own borders. Publics of the former sort are often able to take the lead in the formation of hegemonic blocs: concatenations of different publics which together construct "the common sense" of the day. As a result, such leading publics usually have a heavy hand in defining what is "political" in the discourse sense. They can

There do not seem to be any a priori constraints dictating that some matters simply are intrinsically political and others simply are intrinsically not. As a matter of fact, these boundaries are drawn differently from culture to culture and from historical period to historical period. For example, health and reproduction were cast as political matters in late nineteenth-century France in a context of nationalist and racist concern for "the declining birth rate." Throughout much of the twentieth century in the United States, in contrast, health and reproduction have been considered to be outside the domain of politics.[12]

On the other hand, it would be misleading to suggest that, for any society in any period, the boundary between what is political and what is not is simply fixed or given. On the contrary, this boundary may itself be an object of conflict. For example, struggles over Poor Law "reform" in nineteenth-century England were also conflicts about the scope of the political. And as I shall argue shortly, one of the primary stakes of social conflict in late-capitalist societies is precisely where the limits of the political will be drawn.

Now, how should we conceptualize the politicization of needs in late-capitalist societies? Clearly, this involves processes whereby some matters break out of zones of discursive privacy and out of specialized or enclaved publics so as to become foci of generalized contestation. When this happens, previously taken for granted interpretations of these matters are called into question, and heretofore reified chains of in-order-to relations become subject to dispute.

What are the zones of privacy and the specialized publics which previously enveloped newly politicized needs in late-capitalist societies? What are the institutions in which these needs were enclaved and de-politicized, where their interpretations were reified by being embedded in taken for granted networks of in-order-to relations?

In male-dominated, capitalist societies, what is "political" is normally defined contrastively over against what is "economic" and "domestic" or "personal." Thus, we can identify two principal sets of institutions here which depoliticize social discourses. They are, first, domestic institutions, especially the normative domestic form, namely, the modern, restricted, male-headed, nuclear family; and, second, official-economic capitalist system institutions, especially paid workplaces, markets, credit mechanisms,

---

politicize an issue simply by entertaining contestation concerning it, since such contestation will be transmitted as a matter of course to and through other allied and opposing publics. Smaller, counterhegemonic publics, by contrast, generally lack the power to politicize issues in this way. When they succeed in fomenting widespread contestation over what was previously "nonpolitical," it is usually by far slower and more laborious means.

12. For France, see Karen Offen, "Minotaur or Mother? The Gendering of the State in Early Third Republic France" (typescript). For the United States, see Susan Reverby, "The Body and the Body Politic: Towards a History of Women and Health Care" (typescript); and Linda Gordon, *Woman's Body, Woman's Right* (New York: Viking, 1976).

and "private" enterprises and corporations.[13] Domestic institutions depoliticize certain matters by personalizing and/or familializing them; they cast these as private-domestic or personal-familial matters in contradistinction to public, political matters. Official-economic capitalist system institutions, on the other hand, depoliticize certain matters by economizing them; the issues in question here are cast as impersonal market imperatives or as "private" ownership prerogatives or as technical problems for managers and planners, all in contradistinction to political matters. In both cases, the result is a foreshortening of chains of in-order-to relations for interpreting people's needs; interpretive chains are truncated and prevented from spilling across the boundaries separating the "domestic" and the "economic" from the "political."

Clearly, domestic and official-economic system institutions differ in many important respects. However, in *these* respects they are exactly on a par with one another: both enclave certain matters into specialized discursive arenas; both thereby shield such matters from generalized contestation and from widely disseminated conflicts of interpretation; and, as a result, both entrench as authoritative certain specific interpretations of needs by embedding them in certain specific, but largely unquestioned, chains of in-order-to relations.

Moreover, since both domestic and official-economic system institutions support relations of dominance and subordination, the specific interpretations they naturalize usually tend, on the whole, to advantage dominant groups and individuals and to disadvantage their subordinates. If wife-battering, for example, is enclaved as a "personal" or "domestic" matter within male-headed, restricted families, and if public discourse about this phenomenon is canalized into specialized publics associated with, say, family law, social work, and the sociology and psychology of "deviance," then this serves to reproduce gender dominance and subordination. Similarly, if questions of workplace democracy are enclaved as "economic" or "managerial" problems in profit-oriented, hierarchically managed paid workplaces, and if discourse about these questions is shunted into specialized publics associated with, say, "industrial relations" sociology, labor law, and "management science," then this serves to perpetuate class (and usually also gender and race) dominance and subordination.

Moreover, members of subordinated groups commonly internalize need interpretations that work to their own disadvantage. They are subject to pressures to scale back their aspirations and adapt their beliefs so that they can participate with reduced "cognitive and affective dissonance" in culturally sanctioned institutions and practices. However, sometimes

---

13. Throughout this paper, I refer to paid workplaces, markets, credit systems, etc. as "*official*-economic system institutions" so as to avoid the androcentric implication that domestic institutions are not also "economic." For a discussion of this issue, see Nancy Fraser, "What's Critical about Critical Theory? The Case of Habermas and Gender," *New German Critique* 35 (1985): 97–131.

culturally dominant need interpretations are superimposed upon latent or embryonic oppositional interpretations. This is most likely where there persist, however fragmentedly, subculturally transmitted traditions of resistance, as in some sections of the U.S. labor movement and in the collective historical memory of many African-Americans. Under special circumstances, which are hard to specify theoretically, processes of depoliticization are disrupted. Then, dominant classifications of needs as "economic" or "domestic," as opposed to "political," come to lose their "self-evidence" and alternative, oppositional, and *politicized* interpretations emerge in their stead.[14]

In any case, family and official economy are the principal depoliticizing enclaves which needs must exceed in order to become "political" in the discourse sense in male-dominated, capitalist societies. Thus, the emergence of needs-talk as a political idiom in these societies is the other side of the increased permeability of domestic and official-economic institutions, that is, their growing inability fully to depoliticize certain matters. The politicized needs at issue in late-capitalist societies, then, are "leaky" or "runaway" needs: they are needs which have broken out of the discursive enclaves constructed in and around domestic and official-economic institutions.

Runaway needs are a species of excess with respect to the normative modern domestic and economic institutions. Initially at least, they bear the stamp of those institutions, remaining embedded in conventional chains of in-order-to relations. For example, many runaway needs are colored by the assumption that the "domestic" is supposed to be separated from the "economic" in male-dominated, capitalist societies. Thus, throughout most of U.S. history, child care has been cast as a "domestic" rather than an "economic" need; it has been interpreted as the need of children for the full-time care of their mothers rather than as the need of workers for time away from their children; and its satisfaction has been construed along the lines of "mothers' pensions" rather than of day care.[15] Here, the assumption of "separate spheres" truncates possible

14. The difficulty in specifying theoretically the conditions under which processes of depoliticization are disrupted stems from the difficulty of relating what are usually, and doubtless misleadingly, considered "economic" and "cultural" "factors." Thus, rational choice models seem to me to err in overweighting "economic" at the expense of "cultural" determinants, as in the (not always accurate) prediction that culturally dominant but ultimately disadvantageous need interpretations lose their hold when economic prosperity heralds reduced inequality and promotes "rising expectations." See Jon Elster, "Sour Grapes," in *Utilitarianism and Beyond,* ed. Amartya Sen and Bernard Williams (Cambridge: Cambridge University Press, 1982). An alternative model developed by Jane Jenson emphasizes the cultural-ideological lens through which "economic" effects are filtered. Jenson relates "crises in the mode of regulation" to shifts in cultural "paradigms" that cast into relief previously present but nonemphasized elements of people's social identities. See her "Re-Writing History: Lessons for Feminist Theory" (typescript).

15. See Sonya Michel, "American Women and the Discourse of the Democratic Family in World War II," in *Behind the Lines: Gender and the Two World Wars,* ed. Margaret Higonnet, Jane Jenson, and Sonya Michel (New Haven, Conn.: Yale University Press, 1987), and

chains of in-order-to relations which would yield alternative interpretations of social needs.

Now, where do runaway needs run to when they break out of domestic or official-economic enclaves? I propose that runaway needs enter a historically specific and relatively new societal arena. Following Hannah Arendt, I call this arena the "social" in order to mark its noncoincidence with the family, official economy, and the state.[16] As the site where runaway needs "run to," the "social" cuts across these traditional divisions. It is a site of contested discourse about runaway needs, an arena of conflict among rival interpretations of needs embedded in rival chains of in-order-to relations.[17]

As I conceive it, the social is a switch point for the meeting of heterogeneous contestants associated with a wide range of different discourse publics. These contestants range from proponents of politicization to defenders of (re)depoliticization, from loosely organized social movements to members of specialized, expert publics in and around the social state. Moreover, they vary greatly in relative power. Some are associated with leading publics capable of setting the terms of political debate; others, by contrast, are linked to enclaved publics and must oscillate between marginalization and co-optation.

The social is also the site where successfully politicized runaway needs get translated into claims for government provision. Here, rival need interpretations get translated into rival programmatic conceptions, rival alliances are forged around rival policy proposals, and unequally endowed groups compete to shape the formal policy agenda. For example, in the United States today, various interest groups, movements, professional associations, and parties are scrambling for formulations around which

---

"Children's Interests/Mothers' Rights: A History of Public Child Care in the United States" (typescript). For an account of the current U.S. social-welfare system as a two-track, gendered system based on the assumption of separate economic and domestic spheres, see Nancy Fraser, "Women, Welfare and the Politics of Need Interpretation," *Hypatia: A Journal of Feminist Philosophy* 2 (1987): 103–21.

16. See Hannah Arendt, *The Human Condition* (Chicago: University of Chicago Press, 1958), esp. chap. 11, pp. 22–78. However, it should be noted that my view of the "social" differs significantly from Arendt's. Whereas she sees the social as a one-dimensional space wholly under the sway of administration and instrumental reason, I see it as multivalent and contested. Thus, my view incorporates some features of the Gramscian conception of "civil society."

17. It is significant that, in some times and places, the idea of the "social" has been elaborated explicitly as an alternative to the "political." For example, in nineteenth-century England, "the social" was understood as the sphere in which (middle-class) women's supposed distinctive domestic virtues could be diffused for the sake of the larger collective good without suffering the "degradation" of participation in the competitive world of "politics." Thus, "social" work, figured as "municipal motherhood," was heralded as an alternative to suffrage. See E. M. D. Riley, *"Am I That Name?" Feminism and the Category of 'Women' in History* (London: Macmillan, in press). Similarly, the invention of sociology required the conceptualization of an order of "social" interaction distinct from "politics." See Jacques Donzelot, *The Policing of Families* (New York: Pantheon, 1979).

to build alliances sufficiently powerful to dictate the shape of impending welfare "reform."

Eventually, if and when such contests are (at least temporarily) resolved, runaway needs may become objects of state intervention. Then, they become targets and levers for various strategies of crisis management. And they also become the raison d'être for the proliferation of the various agencies constituting the social state.[18] These agencies are engaged in regulating and/or funding and/or providing for the satisfaction of social needs. In so doing, they are in the business of interpreting, as well as of satisfying, the needs in question. For example, the U.S. social-welfare system is currently divided into two, gender-linked and unequal subsystems: an implicitly "masculine" social insurance subsystem tied to "primary" labor force participation and geared to (white male) "breadwinners"; and an implicitly "feminine" relief subsystem tied to household income and geared to homemaker-mothers and their "defective" (i.e., female-headed) families. With the underlying (but counterfactual) assumption of "separate spheres," the two subsystems differ markedly in the degree of autonomy, rights, and presumption of desert they accord beneficiaries, as well as in their funding base, mode of administration, and character and level of benefits.[19] Thus, the various agencies constituting the social-welfare system provide more than material aid. They also provide clients, and the public at large, with a tacit but powerful interpretive map of normative, dif-ferentially valued gender roles and gendered needs. Therefore, the dif-ferent branches of the social state, too, are players in the politics of need interpretation.[20]

To summarize: in late-capitalist societies, runaway needs which have broken out of domestic or official-economic enclaves enter that hybrid discursive space that Arendt aptly dubbed the "social." They may then become foci of state intervention geared to crisis management. These needs are thus markers of major social-structural shifts in the boundaries separating what are classified as "political," "economic," and "domestic" or "personal" spheres of life.

III

There are two analytically distinct but practically articulated directions from which needs get politicized in welfare-state societies: roughly "from

18. Of course, the social state is not a unitary entity but a multiform, differentiated complex of agencies and apparatuses. In the United States, the social state comprises the welter of agencies that make up especially the Departments of Labor and of Health and Human Services—or what currently remains of them.

19. For an analysis of the gendered structure of the U.S. social-welfare system, see Fraser, "Women, Welfare and the Politics of Need Interpretation." Also, Barbara Nelson, "Women's Poverty and Women's Citizenship: Some Political Consequences of Economic Marginality," *Signs: Journal of Women in Culture and Society* 10 (1984): 209–31; and Diana Pearce, "Women, Work and Welfare: The Feminization of Poverty," in *Working Women and Families,* ed. Karen Wolk Feinstein (Beverly Hills, Calif.: Sage, 1979).

20. For an analysis of U.S. social-welfare agencies as purveyors and enforcers of need interpretations, see Fraser, "Women, Welfare and the Politics of Need Interpretation."

below" and "from above." In the first case, the initiative resides in what I call "oppositional" needs-talk; and the process involves the crystallization of new social identities on the part of subordinated persons and groups. In the second case, the initiative resides in what I call "expert" needs discourses, and the process involves "social problem-solving," institution-building, and professional class formation. Oppositional discourses and expert discourses represent two of the three major strands of needs-talk I discuss in this section, the other being the more reactive "reprivatization" discourses. In general, it is the polemical interaction of these three strands of needs-talk that structures the politics of needs in late-capitalist societies.[21]

Let us look first at the politicization of runaway needs via oppositional discourses. Here, needs become politicized when, for example, women, workers, and/or peoples of color come to contest the subordinate identities and roles, the traditional, reified, and disadvantageous need interpretations previously assigned to and/or embraced by them. By insisting on speaking publicly of heretofore depoliticized needs, by claiming for these needs the status of legitimate political issues, such persons and groups do several things simultaneously. First, they contest the established boundaries separating "politics" from "economics" and "domestics." Second, they offer alternative interpretations of their needs embedded in alternative chains of in-order-to relations. Third, they create new discourse publics from which they try to disseminate their interpretations of their needs throughout a wide range of different discourse publics. Finally, they challenge, modify, and/or displace hegemonic elements of the means of interpretation and communication; they invent new forms of discourse for interpreting their needs.

In oppositional discourses, needs-talk is a moment in the self-constitution of new collective agents or social movements. For example, in the current wave of feminist ferment, groups of women have politicized and reinterpreted various needs, have instituted new vocabularies and forms of address, and, so, have become "women" in a different, though not uncontested or univocal sense. By speaking publicly the heretofore unspeakable, by coining terms like 'sexism,' 'sexual harassment,' 'marital, date, and acquaintance rape,' 'labor force sex-segregation,' 'the double shift,' 'wife-battery,' and so forth, feminist women have become "women" in the sense of a discursively self-constituted political collectivity, albeit a very heterogeneous and fractured one.[22]

21. This picture is at odds with the one implicit in the writings of Foucault. From my perspective, Foucault focuses too single-mindedly on expert, institution-building discourses at the expense of oppositional and reprivatization discourses. Thus, he misses the dimension of contestation among competing discourses and the fact that the outcome is a result of such contestation. For all his theoretical talk about power without a subject, then, Foucault's practice as a social historian is surprisingly traditional in that de facto it treats expert institution builders as the only historical subjects.

22. The point could be reformulated more skeptically as follows: feminists have shaped discourses embodying a claim to speak for "women." In fact, this question of "speaking for 'women' " is currently a burning issue within the feminist movement. For an interesting

Of course, the politicization of needs in oppositional discourses does not go uncontested. One type of resistance involves defense of the established boundaries separating "political," "economic," and "domestic" spheres by means of "reprivatization" discourses. In these discourses, speakers oppose state provision for runaway needs and they seek to privatize or segment needs discourses that threaten to spill across a wide range of discourse publics.[23] Thus, reprivatizers may insist, for example, that domestic battery is not a legitimate subject of political discourse but a familial or religious matter. Or, to take a different example, that a factory closing is not a political question but an unimpeachable prerogative of "private" ownership or an unassailable imperative of an impersonal market mechanism. In both cases, the speakers are contesting the breakout of runaway needs and trying to (re)depoliticize them.

Interestingly, reprivatization discourses blend the old and the new. On the one hand, they seem merely to render explicit need interpretations which could earlier go without saying. But, on the other hand, by the very act of articulating such interpretations, they simultaneously modify them. Because reprivatization discourses respond to competing, oppositional interpretations, they are internally dialogized, incorporating references to the alternatives they resist, even while rejecting them. For example, although "pro-family" discourses of the social New Right are explicitly antifeminist, some of them incorporate in a depoliticized form feminist inspired motifs implying women's right to sexual pleasure and to emotional support from their husbands.[24]

In defending the established social division of discourses, reprivatization discourses deny the claims of oppositional movements for the legitimate political status of runaway needs. However, in so doing, they tend further to politicize those needs in the sense of increasing their cathectedness as foci of contestation. Moreover, in some cases, reprivatization discourses, too, become vehicles for mobilizing social movements and for reshaping social identities. Doubtless the most stunning example is Thatcherism in Britain where a set of reprivatization discourses articulated in the accents of authoritarian populism has refashioned the subjectivities

---

take on it, see Riley, *"Am I That Name?"* For a thoughtful discussion of the general problem of the constitution and representation (in both senses) of social groups as sociological classes and as collective agents, see Pierre Bourdieu, "The Social Space and the Genesis of Groups," *Social Science Information* 24 (1985): 195–220.

23. 'Reprivatization' has become the standard social-theoretical term for initiatives aimed at dismantling or cutting back social-welfare services, selling off nationalized assets, and/or deregulating "private" enterprise. My own usage combines this standard institutional, antistatist sense with the discursive sense of depoliticization.

24. See the chapter on "Fundamentalist Sex: Hitting below the Bible Belt," in Barbara Ehrenreich, Elizabeth Hess, and Gloria Jacobs, *Re-making Love: The Feminization of Sex* (New York: Anchor, 1987). For a fascinating account of "postfeminist" women incorporating feminist motifs into born-again Christianity, see Judith Stacey, "Sexism by a Subtler Name? Postindustrial Conditions and Postfeminist Consciousness in the Silicon Valley," *Socialist Review*, no. 96 (1987), pp. 7–28.

of a wide range of disaffected constituencies and united them in a powerful coalition.[25]

Together, oppositional discourses and reprivatization discourses codefine one axis of needs-struggle in late-capitalist societies. But there is also a second, rather different line of conflict. Here, the focal issue is no longer politicization versus depoliticization but rather the interpreted content of contested needs once their political status has been successfully secured. And the principal contestants are oppositional social movements and organized interests like businesses which seek to influence public policy.

For example, today in the United States, day care is gaining increasing legitimacy as a political issue. As a result, we are seeing the proliferation of competing interpretations and programmatic conceptions. In one view, day care would serve poor children's needs for "enrichment" and/or moral supervision. In a second, it would serve the middle-class taxpayer's need to get Aid to Families with Dependent Children (AFDC) recipients off the welfare rolls. A third interpretation would shape day care as a measure for increasing the productivity and competitiveness of American business, while yet a fourth would treat it as part of a package of policies aimed at redistributing income and resources to women. Each of these interpretations carries a distinct programmatic orientation with respect to funding, institutional siting and control, service design, and eligibility. As they collide, we see a struggle to shape the hegemonic understanding of day care which may eventually make its way onto the formal political agenda. Clearly, not just feminist groups, but also business interests, trade unions, children's rights advocates, and educators are contestants in this struggle. And they bring to it vast differentials in power.[26]

The struggle for hegemonic need interpretations usually points toward the future involvement of the state. Thus, it anticipates yet a third axis of needs-struggle in late-capitalist societies. Here, the focal issues concern politics versus administration, and the principal contestants are oppositional social movements and the expert publics and agencies in the orbit of the social state.

Recall that the "social" is a site where needs which have become politicized in the discourse sense become candidates for state-organized provision. Consequently, these needs become the object of yet another group of discourses: the complex of "expert" "public policy" discourses based in various "private," "semi-public," and state institutions.

25. See Stuart Hall, "Moving Right," *Socialist Review,* no. 55 (January–February 1981), pp. 113–37. For an account of New Right reprivatization discourses in the United States, see Barbara Ehrenreich, "The New Right Attack on Social Welfare," in Fred Block, Richard A. Cloward, Barbara Ehrenreich, and Frances Fox Piven, *The Mean Season: The Attack on the Welfare State* (New York: Pantheon, 1987), pp. 161–95.

26. I am indebted to Teresa Ghilarducci for this point (personal communication, February 1988).

Expert needs discourses are the vehicles for translating sufficiently politicized runaway needs into objects of potential state intervention. And they are closely connected with institutions of knowledge production and utilization.[27] They include qualitative and especially quantitative social-scientific discourses generated in universities and "think-tanks"; legal discourses generated in judicial institutions and their satellite schools, journals, and professional associations; administrative discourses circulated in various preexisting agencies of the social state; and therapeutic discourses circulated in public and private medical and social service agencies.

As the term suggests, "expert" discourses tend to be restricted to specialized publics. Thus, they are associated with professional class formation, institution-building, and social "problem-solving." But in some cases, such as law and psychotherapy, expert vocabularies and rhetorics are disseminated to a wider spectrum of educated laypersons, some of whom are participants in social movements. Moreover, social movements sometimes manage to co-opt or create critical, oppositional segments of expert discourse publics. For all these reasons, expert discourse publics sometimes acquire a certain porousness. And, expert discourses become the *bridge* discourses linking loosely organized social movements with the social state.

Because of this bridge role, the rhetoric of expert needs discourses tends to be administrative. These discourses consist in a series of rewriting operations, that is, procedures for translating politicized needs into administerable needs. Typically, the politicized need is redefined as the correlate of a bureaucratically administerable satisfaction—a "social service." It is specified in terms of an ostensibly general state of affairs which could, in principle, befall anyone—for example, unemployment, disability, or death or desertion of a spouse.[28] As a result, the need is decontextualized and recontextualized: on the one hand, it is represented in abstraction from its class, race, and gender specificity and from whatever oppositional meanings it may have acquired in the course of its politicization; on the other hand, it is cast in terms which tacitly presuppose such entrenched, specific background institutions as ("primary" versus "secondary") wage labor, privatized child rearing, and their gender-based separation.

As a result of these expert redefinitions, the people whose needs are in question are repositioned. They become individual "cases" rather than

27. In *Discipline and Punish*, Foucault provides a useful account of some elements of the knowledge production apparatuses which contribute to administrative redefinitions of politicized needs. However, Foucault overlooks the role of social movements in politicizing needs and the conflicts of interpretation which arise between such movements and the social state. His account suggests, incorrectly, that policy discourses emanate unidirectionally from specialized, governmental or quasi-governmental institutions; thus it misses the contestatory interplay among hegemonic and nonhegemonic, institutionally bound and institutionally unbound, interpretations.

28. Compare the discussion of the administrative logic of need definition in Jürgen Habermas, *Theorie des kommunikativen Handelns*, vol. 2, *Zur Kritik der funktionalistischen Vernunft* (Frankfurt am Main: Suhrkamp, 1981), pp. 522–47.

members of social groups or participants in political movements. In addition, they are rendered passive, positioned as potential recipients of predefined services rather than as agents involved in interpreting their needs and shaping their life conditions.

By virtue of this administrative rhetoric, expert needs discourses, too, tend to be depoliticizing. They construe persons simultaneously as rational utility-maximizers and as causally conditioned, predictable, and manipulable objects, thereby screening out those dimensions of agency which involve the construction and deconstruction of social meanings.

Moreover, when expert needs discourses are institutionalized in state apparatuses, they tend to become normalizing, aimed at "reforming" or more often stigmatizing "deviancy."[29] This sometimes becomes explicit when services incorporate a therapeutic dimension designed to close the gap between clients' recalcitrant self-interpretations and the interpretations embedded in administrative policy.[30] Now the rational utility-maximizer-cum-causally-conditioned-object becomes, in addition, a deep self to be unraveled therapeutically.[31]

To summarize: when social movements succeed in politicizing previously depoliticized needs, they enter the terrain of the social where two other kinds of struggle await them. First, they have to contest powerful organized interests bent on shaping hegemonic need interpretations to their own ends. Second, they encounter expert needs discourses in and around the social state. These encounters define two additional axes of needs-struggle in late-capitalist societies. They are highly complex struggles, since social movements typically seek state provision of their runaway needs even while they tend to oppose administrative and therapeutic need interpretations. Thus, these axes, too, involve conflicts among rival interpretations of social needs and among rival constructions of social identity.

IV

Now I would like to try to apply the model I have been developing to some concrete cases of conflicts of need interpretation. The first example is designed to identify a tendency in welfare-state societies whereby the politics of need interpretation devolves into the management of need satisfactions. The second example, by contrast, charts the countertendency

29. See Foucault, *Discipline and Punish,* for an account of the normalizing dimensions of social science and of institutionalized social services.

30. Habermas discusses the therapeutic dimension of welfare-state social services, pp. 522–47.

31. In *Discipline and Punish,* Foucault discusses the tendency of social-scientifically informed administrative procedures to posit a deep self. In *The History of Sexuality,* vol. 1, *An Introduction,* trans. Robert Harley (New York: Pantheon, 1976), he discusses the positing of a deep self by therapeutic psychiatric discourses.

which runs from administration to resistance and potentially back to politics.[32]

First, consider the example of the politics of needs surrounding wife-battering. Until about fifteen years ago, the term 'wife-battering' did not exist. When spoken of publicly at all, this phenomenon was called 'wife-beating' and was often treated comically, as in "Have you stopped beating your wife?" Linguistically, it was classed with the disciplining of children and servants as a "domestic," as opposed to a "political," matter. Then, feminist activists renamed the practice with a term drawn from criminal law and created a new kind of public discourse. They claimed that battery was not a personal, domestic problem but a systemic, political one; its etiology was not to be traced to individual women's or men's emotional problems but, rather, to the ways these refracted pervasive social relations of male dominance and female subordination.

Thus, feminist activists contested established discursive boundaries and politicized a heretofore depoliticized phenomenon. In addition, they reinterpreted the experience of battery and they posited a set of associated needs. Here, they situated battered women's needs in a long chain of in-order-to relations which spilled across conventional separations of "spheres"; they claimed that, in order to be free from dependence on batterers, battered women needed not just temporary shelter but also jobs paying a "family wage," day care, and affordable permanent housing. Further, feminists created new discourse publics, new spaces and institutions in which such oppositional need interpretations could be developed and from which they could be spread to wider publics. Finally, feminists modified elements of the authorized means of interpretation and communication; they coined new terms of description and analysis and devised new ways of addressing female subjects. In their discourse, battered women were not addressed as individualized victims but as potential feminist activists, members of a politically constituted collectivity.

This discursive intervention was accompanied by feminist efforts to provide for some of the needs they had politicized and reinterpreted. Activists organized battered women's shelters—places of refuge and of consciousness-raising. The organization of these shelters was nonhierarchical; there were no clear lines between staff and users. Many of the counselors and organizers had themselves been battered; and a high percentage of the women who used the shelters went on to counsel other battered women and to become movement activists. Concomitantly, these women came to adopt new self-descriptions. Whereas most had originally blamed themselves and defended their batterers, many came to reject that interpretation in favor of a politicized view which offered them new

32. For the sake of simplicity, I shall restrict the examples treated to cases of contestation between two forces only, where one of the contestants is an agency of the social state. Thus, I shall not consider examples of three-sided contestation, nor shall I consider examples of two-sided contestation between competing social movements.

models of agency. In addition, these women modified their affiliations and social identifications. Whereas many had originally felt deeply identified with their batterers, they later came to affiliate with other women.

This organizing eventually had an impact on wider discursive publics. By the late 1970s, feminists had largely succeeded in establishing domestic violence against women as a legitimate political issue. They managed in some cases to change attitudes and policies of police and the courts, and they won for this issue a place on the informal political agenda. Now the needs of battered women were sufficiently politicized to become candidates for publicly organized satisfaction. Finally, in several munici-palities and localities, movement shelters began receiving local government funding.

From the feminist perspective, this represented a significant victory, but it was not without cost. Municipal funding brought with it a variety of new administrative constraints ranging from accounting procedures to regulation, accreditation, and professionalization requirements. As a consequence, publicly funded shelters underwent a transformation. In-creasingly, they came to be staffed by professional social workers, many of whom had not themselves experienced battery. Thus, a division between professional and client supplanted the more fluid continuum of relations which characterized the earlier shelters. Moreover, many social work staff had been trained to frame problems in a quasi-psychiatric perspective. This perspective structures the practices of many publicly funded shelters even despite the intentions of individual staff, many of whom are politically committed feminists. Consequently, the practices of such shelters have become more individualizing and less politicized. Battered women tend now to be positioned as clients. They are increasingly psychiatrized; they are addressed as victims with deep, complicated selves. They are only rarely addressed as potential feminist activists. Increasingly, the language-game of therapy has supplanted that of consciousness-raising. And the neutral scientific language of "spouse abuse" has supplanted more political talk of "male violence against women."[33] Finally, the needs of battered women have been substantially reinterpreted. The very far-reaching earlier claims for the social and economic prerequisites of independence have tended to give way to a narrower focus on the individual woman's problems of "low self-esteem."

The battered women's shelter case exemplifies one tendency of needs politics in late-capitalist societies: the tendency for the politics of need interpretation to devolve into the administration of need satisfaction. However, there is also a countertendency which runs from administration to client resistance and potentially back to politics. I would like now to document this countertendency by drawing on sociologist Prudence Rains's

33. For an account of the history of battered women's shelters, see Susan Schechter, *Women and Male Violence: The Visions and Struggles of the Battered Women's Movement* (Boston: South End Press, 1982).

comparative study of the "moral careers" of black and white pregnant teenagers in the late 1960s.[34]

Rains contrasts the ways the two groups of young women related to therapeutic constructions of their experience in two different institutional settings. One was a group of young middle-class white women in an expensive, private, residential facility; the other was a group of poor young black women in a nonresidential, municipal program. Both groups were provided with therapeutic services in addition to prenatal care and schooling. Both were required to attend individual and group counseling sessions with psychiatric social workers in which they were addressed as deep, complicated selves. Both were encouraged to regard their pregnancies as unconsciously motivated, meaningful acts expressive of latent emotional problems. This meant that a girl was to interpret her pregnancy—and the sex which was its superficial cause—as a form of acting out, say, a refusal of parental authority or a demand for parental love. She was warned that, unless she came to understand and acknowledge these deep, hidden motives, she would probably not succeed in avoiding future pregnancies. If, on the other hand, she did achieve such an understanding, the result would be a new autobiographical narrative which would occult the girl's sexuality and evade the potentially explosive issue of consent versus coercion in the teenage heterosexual milieu.

Rains contrasts the relative ease with which most of the young white women came to internalize this psychiatric perspective with the resistance of the young black women. The latter group was put off by the social worker's stance of nondirectiveness and moral neutrality—her unwillingness to say what *she* thought—and they resented what they considered her intrusive, overly personal questions in a context, they noted, in which they were not permitted to ask her such questions in return. In some instances, they openly challenged the rules of the therapeutic language-game. In others, they resisted indirectly by humor, quasi-deliberately misunderstanding the social worker's vague, nondirective, yet "personal" questions. For example, one girl construed, "How did you become pregnant?" as a "stupid" question and replied, "Shouldn't you know?" Another deflected the constant therapeutic, "How did it feel?" by taking it as a request for a graphic phenomenology of sexual pleasure and responding with banter and innuendo. In short, these young women devised a varied repertoire of strategies for resisting expert, normalizing, therapeutic constructions of their life stories and capacities for agency. They refused pressures to rewrite themselves as deep, complicated selves, while availing themselves of the health services at the facility. Thus, they made use of those aspects of the agency's program which they considered appropriate to their self-interpreted needs and ignored or side stepped the others.

34. Prudence Mors Rains, *Becoming an Unwed Mother: A Sociological Account* (Chicago: Aldine Atherton, 1971). I am indebted to Kathryn Pyne Addelson for bringing Rains's work to my attention.

Rains's work documents the sort of client resistance that remains informal, ad hoc, and cultural. However, there are also more formally organized, explicitly political forms of resistance. Clients of social-welfare programs may join together *as clients* to challenge administrative interpretations of their needs. They may take hold of the passivizing, normalizing, and individualizing or familializing identity fashioned for them by expert discourses and transform it into an identity which provides a basis for collective political action. Frances Fox Piven and Richard A. Cloward have documented an example of this sort of move from administration to politics in their account of the process by which AFDC recipients organized the National Welfare Rights movement of the 1960s.[35] Notwithstanding the atomizing and depoliticizing dimensions of AFDC administration, these women were brought together in welfare waiting rooms. It was as a result of their participation as program clients, then, that they came to articulate common grievances and to act together. Thus, the same welfare practices which generated these grievances simultaneously generated the conditions for the possibility of collective organizing to combat them. As Piven put it, "the structure of the welfare state itself has helped to create new solidarities and generate the political issues that continue to cement and galvanize them."[36]

V

Let me conclude by flagging some issues which are central to this project but which I have not yet discussed in this essay. I have concentrated on social-theoretical issues at the expense of normative issues. But the latter are very important for a project, like mine, which aspires to be a critical social theory.

My analysis of needs-talk raises two very obvious and pressing normative issues. One is the question whether and how it is possible to distinguish better from worse interpretations of people's needs. The other is the question of the relationship between needs claims and rights. Although I cannot offer full answers to these questions here, I would like to indicate something about how I would approach them.

Pace the relativists, I would argue that we *can* distinguish better from worse interpretations of people's needs. To say that needs are culturally constructed and discursively interpreted is not to say that any need inter-

35. Frances Fox Piven and Richard A. Cloward, *Regulating the Poor: The Functions of Public Welfare* (New York: Vintage, 1971), pp. 285–340, and *Poor People's Movements* (New York: Vintage, 1979). Unfortunately, Piven and Cloward's account is gender-blind and, as a consequence, androcentric. For a feminist critique, see Linda Gordon, "What Does Welfare Regulate? A Review Essay on the Writings of Frances Fox Piven and Richard A. Cloward," (typescript). For a more gender-sensitive account of the history of the National Welfare Rights Organization (NWRO), see Guida West, *The National Welfare Rights Movement: The Social Protest of Poor Women* (New York: Praeger, 1981).

36. Frances Fox Piven, "Women and the State: Ideology, Power and the Welfare State," *Socialist Review*, no. 74 (1984), pp. 11–19.

pretation is as good as any other. On the contrary, it is to underline the importance of an account of interpretive justification.

In my view, there are at least two distinct kinds of considerations such an account would have to encompass and to balance. First, there are procedural considerations concerning the social processes by which various competing need interpretations are generated. For example, how exclusive or inclusive are various rival needs discourses? How hierarchical or egalitarian are the relations among the interlocutors? In general, procedural considerations dictate that, all other things being equal, the best need interpretations are those reached by means of communicative processes that most closely approximate ideals of democracy, equality, and fairness.[37]

In addition, consequentialist considerations are also relevant in justifying need interpretations. These considerations involve comparing alternative distributive outcomes of rival interpretations. For example, would widespread acceptance of some given interpretation of a social need disadvantage some groups of people vis-à-vis others? Does the interpretation conform to rather than challenge societal patterns of dominance and subordination? Are the rival chains of in-order-to relations to which competing need interpretations belong more or less respectful, as opposed to transgressive, of ideological boundaries that delimit "separate spheres" and thereby rationalize inequality? In general, consequentialist considerations dictate that, all other things being equal, the best need interpretations are those that do not disadvantage some groups of people vis-à-vis others.

In sum, justifying some interpretations of social needs as better than others involves balancing procedural and consequentialist considerations. More simply, it involves balancing democracy and equality.

What, then, of the relationship between needs and rights? Very briefly, I would argue in favor of the translatability of justified needs claims into social rights.[38] Like many radical critics of existing social-welfare programs, I am committed to opposing the forms of paternalism that arise when needs claims are divorced from rights claims. And unlike some communitarian, socialist, and feminist critics, I do not believe that rights-talk is inherently individualistic, bourgeois-liberal, and androcen-

37. In its first-order normative content, this formulation is Habermassian. However, I do not wish to follow Habermas in giving it a transcendental or quasi-transcendental metainterpretation. Thus, while Habermas purports to ground "communicative ethics" in the conditions of possibility of speech understood universalistically and ahistorically, I consider it a contingently evolved, historically specific possibility. See Jürgen Habermas, *The Theory of Communicative Action,* vol. 1, *Reason and the Rationalization of Society,* trans. Thomas McCarthy (Boston: Beacon, 1984), *Communication and the Evolution of Society,* trans. Thomas McCarthy (Boston: Beacon, 1979), and *Moralbewusstsein und kommunikatives Handeln* (Frankfurt: Suhrkamp, 1983).

38. I owe this formulation to Martha Minow (personal communication).

tric.[39] That is only the case where societies establish the *wrong* rights, for example, where the (putative) right to private property is permitted to trump other, social rights.

Moreover, to treat justified needs claims as the bases for new social rights is to begin to overcome obstacles to the effective exercise of some existing rights. It is true, as Marxists and others have claimed, that classical liberal rights to free expression, suffrage, and so forth are "merely formal." But this says more about the social context in which they are currently embedded than about their "intrinsic" character. For, in a context devoid of poverty, inequality, and oppression, formal liberal rights could be broadened and transformed into substantive rights, say, to collective self-determination.

Finally, I should stress that this work is motivated by the conviction that, for the time being, needs-talk is with us for better or worse. For the foreseeable future, political agents, including members of oppositional social movements, will have to operate on a terrain where needs-talk is the discursive coin of the realm. But, as I have tried to show, this idiom is neither inherently emancipatory nor inherently repressive. Rather, it is multivalent and contested. The larger aim of my project is to help clarify the prospects for democratic and egalitarian social change by sorting out the emancipatory from the repressive possibilities of needs-talk.

39. For an interesting discussion of the uses and abuses of rights discourse, see Elizabeth M. Schneider, "The Dialectic of Rights and Politics: Perspectives from the Women's Movement," *New York University Law Review* 61 (1986): 589–652. Also Martha Minow, "Interpreting Rights: An Essay for Robert Cover," *Yale Law Journal* 96 (1987): 1860–1915; and Patricia J. Williams, "Alchemical Notes: Reconstructed Ideals from Deconstructed Rights," *Harvard Civil Rights Civil Liberties Law Review* 22 (1987): 401–33.

Part III

Coercion versus Consent, Public versus Private, and Sexuality

Should Feminists Oppose Prostitution?*

Laurie Shrage

> Because sexuality is a social construction, individuals as individuals
> are not free to experience *eros* just as they choose. Yet just as the
> extraction and appropriation of surplus value by the capitalist rep-
> resents a choice available, if not to individuals, to society as a whole,
> so too sexuality and the forms taken by *eros* must be seen as at some
> level open to change. [NANCY HARTSOCK, *Money, Sex and Power*][1]

INTRODUCTION

Prostitution raises difficult issues for feminists. On the one hand, many
feminists want to abolish discriminatory criminal statutes that are mostly
used to harass and penalize prostitutes, and rarely to punish johns and
pimps—laws which, for the most part, render prostitutes more vulnerable
to exploitation by their male associates.[2] On the other hand, most feminists
find the prostitute's work morally and politically objectionable. In their
view, women who provide sexual services for a fee submit to sexual
domination by men, and suffer degradation by being treated as sexual
commodities.[3]

My concern, in this paper, is whether persons opposed to the social
subordination of women should seek to discourage commercial sex. My
goal is to marshal the moral arguments needed to sustain feminists'

* I am grateful to Sandra Bartky, Alison Jaggar, Elizabeth Segal, Richard Arneson,
and the anonymous reviewers for *Ethics* for their critical comments and suggestions. Also,
I am indebted to Daniel Segal for suggesting many anthropological and historical examples
relevant to my argument. In addition, I would like to thank the philosophy department
of the Claremont Graduate School for the opportunity to present an earlier draft of this
paper for discussion.

1. Nancy Hartsock, *Money, Sex and Power* (Boston: Northeastern University Press,
1985), p. 178.

2. See Rosemarie Tong, *Women, Sex, and the Law* (Totowa, N.J.: Rowman & Allanheld,
1984), pp. 37–64. See also Priscilla Alexander and Margo St. James, "Working on the
Issue," National Organization for Women (NOW) National Task Force on Prostitution
Report (San Francisco: NOW, 1982).

3. See Carole Pateman, "Defending Prostitution: Charges against Ericsson," *Ethics* 93
(1983): 561–65; and Kathleen Barry, *Female Sexual Slavery* (New York: Avon, 1979).

This essay originally appeared in *Ethics* 99, January 1989.

condemnation of the sex industry in our society. In reaching this goal, I reject accounts of commercial sex which posit cross-cultural and transhistorical causal mechanisms to explain the existence of prostitution or which assume that the activities we designate as "sex" have a universal meaning and purpose. By contrast, I analyze mercenary sex in terms of culturally specific beliefs and principles that organize its practice in contemporary American society. I try to show that the sex industry, like other institutions in our society, is structured by deeply ingrained attitudes and values which are oppressive to women. The point of my analysis is not to advocate an egalitarian reformation of commercial sex, nor to advocate its abolition through state regulation. Instead, I focus on another political alternative: that which must be done to subvert widely held beliefs that legitimate this institution in our society. Ultimately, I argue that nothing closely resembling prostitution, as we currently know it, will exist, once we have undermined these cultural convictions.

WHY PROSTITUTION IS PROBLEMATIC

A number of recent papers on prostitution begin with the familiar observation that prostitution is one of the oldest professions.[4] Such 'observations' take for granted that 'prostitution' refers to a single transhistorical, transcultural activity. By contrast, my discussion of prostitution is limited to an activity that occurs in modern Western societies—a practice which involves the purchase of sexual services from women by men. Moreover, I am not interested in exploring the nature and extension of our moral concept "to prostitute oneself"; rather, I want to examine a specific activity we regard as prostitution in order to understand its social and political significance.

In formulating my analysis, I recognize that the term 'prostitute' is ambiguous: it is used to designate both persons who supply sex on a commercial basis and persons who contribute their talents and efforts to base purposes for some reward. While these extensions may overlap, their relationship is not a logically necessary one but is contingent upon complex moral and social principles. In this paper, I use the term 'prostitute' as shorthand for 'provider of commercial sexual services,' and correspondingly, I use the term 'prostitution' interchangeably with 'commercial sex.' By employing these terms in this fashion, I hope to appear consistent with colloquial English, and not to be taking for granted that a person who provides commercial sexual services "prostitutes" her- or himself.

Many analyses of prostitution aim to resolve the following issue: what would induce a woman to prostitute herself—to participate in an

4. For example, see Gerda Lerner, "The Origin of Prostitution in Ancient Mesopotamia," *Signs: Journal of Women in Culture and Society* 11 (1986): 236–54; Lars Ericsson, "Charges against Prostitution: An Attempt at a Philosophical Assessment," *Ethics* 90 (1980): 335–66; and James Brundage, "Prostitution in the Medieval Canon Law," *Signs: Journal of Women in Culture and Society* 1 (1976): 825–45.

impersonal, commercial sexual transaction? These accounts seek the deeper psychological motives behind apparently voluntary acts of prostitution. Because our society regards female prostitution as a social, if not natural, aberration, such actions demand an explanation. Moreover, accepting fees for sex seems irrational and repugnant to many persons, even to the woman who does it, and so one wonders why she does it. My examination of prostitution does not focus on this question. While to do so may explain why a woman will choose prostitution from among various options, it does not explain how a woman's options have been constituted. In other words, although an answer to this question may help us understand why some women become sellers of sexual services rather than homemakers or engineers, it will not increase our understanding of why there is a demand for these services. Why, for example, can women not as easily achieve prosperity by selling child-care services? Finding out why there is a greater market for goods of one type than of another illuminates social forces and trends as much as, if not more than, finding out why individuals enter a particular market. Moreover, theorists who approach prostitution in this way do not assume that prostitution is "a problem about the women who are prostitutes, and our attitudes to them, [rather than] a problem about the men who demand to buy them."[5] This assumption, as Carole Pateman rightly points out, mars many other accounts.

However, I do not attempt to construct an account of the psychological, social, and economic forces that presumably cause men to demand commercial sex, or of the factors which cause a woman to market her sexual services. Instead, I first consider whether prostitution, in all cultural contexts, constitutes a degrading and undesirable form of sexuality. I argue that, although the commercial availability of sexuality is not in every existing or conceivable society oppressive to women, in our society this practice depends upon the general acceptance of principles which serve to marginalize women socially and politically. Because of the cultural context in which prostitution operates, it epitomizes and perpetuates pernicious patriarchal beliefs and values and, therefore, is both damaging to the women who sell sex and, as an organized social practice, to all women in our society.

HISTORICAL AND CROSS-CULTURAL PERSPECTIVES

In describing Babylonian temple prostitution, Gerda Lerner reports: "For people who regarded fertility as sacred and essential to their own survival, the caring for the gods included, in some cases, offering them sexual services. Thus, a separate class of temple prostitutes developed. What seems to have happened was that sexual activity for and in behalf of the god or goddesses was considered beneficial to the people and sacred."[6] Similarly, according to Emma Goldman, the Babylonians believed

5. Pateman, p. 563.
6. Lerner, p. 239.

that "the generative activity of human beings possessed a mysterious and sacred influence in promoting the fertility of Nature."[7] When the rationale for the impersonal provision of sex is conceived in terms of the promotion of nature's fecundity, the social meaning this activity has may differ substantially from the social significance it has in our own society.

In fifteenth-century France, as described by Jacques Rossiaud, commercial sex appears likewise to have had an import that contrasts with its role in contemporary America. According to Rossiaud:

> By the age of thirty, most prostitutes had a real chance of becoming reintegrated into society. . . . Since public opinion did not view them with disgust, and since they were on good terms with priests and men of the law, it was not too difficult for them to find a position as servant or wife. To many city people, public prostitution represented a partial atonement for past misconduct. Many bachelors had compassion and sympathy for prostitutes, and finally, the local charitable foundations of the municipal authorities felt a charitable impulse to give special help to these repentant Magdalens and to open their way to marriage by dowering them. Marriage was definitely the most frequent end to the career of communal prostitutes who had roots in the town where they have publicly offered their bodies.[8]

The fact that prostitutes were regarded by medieval French society as eligible for marriage, and were desired by men for wives, suggests that the cultural principles which sustained commercial exchanges of sex in this society were quite different than those which shape our own sex industry. Consequently, the phenomenon of prostitution requires a distinct political analysis and moral assessment vis-à-vis fifteenth-century France. This historically specific approach is justified, in part, because commercial sexual transactions may have different consequences for individuals in an alien society than for individuals similarly placed in our own. Indeed, it is questionable whether, in two quite different cultural settings, we should regard a particular outward behavior—the impersonal provision of sexual services for fees or their equivalent—as the same practice, that is, as prostitution.

Another cross-cultural example may help to make the last point clear. Anthropologists have studied a group in New Guinea, called the Etoro, who believe that young male children need to ingest male fluid or semen in order to develop properly into adult males, much like we believe that young infants need their mother's milk, or some equivalent, to be properly nurtured. Furthermore, just as our belief underlies our

7. Emma Goldman, "The Traffic in Women," in *Red Emma Speaks,* ed. Alix Kates Shulman (New York: Schocken, 1983), p. 180.

8. Jacques Rossiaud, "Prostitution, Youth, and Society in the Towns of Southeastern France in the Fifteenth Century," in *Deviants and the Abandoned in French Society: Selections from the Annales Economies, Sociétés, Civilisations,* ed. Robert Forster and Orest Ranum (Baltimore: Johns Hopkins University Press, 1978), p. 21.

practice of breast-feeding, the Etoro's belief underlies their practice of penis-feeding, where young male children fellate older males, often their relatives.[9] From the perspective of our society, the Etoro's practice involves behaviors which are highly stigmatized—incest, sex with children, and homosexuality. Yet, for an anthropologist who is attempting to interpret and translate these behaviors, to assume that the Etoro practice is best subsumed under the category of "sex," rather than, for example, "child rearing," would reflect ethnocentrism. Clearly, our choice of one translation scheme or the other will influence our attitude toward the Etoro practice. The point is that there is no practice, such as "sex," which can be morally evaluated apart from a cultural framework.

In general, historical and cross-cultural studies offer little reason to believe that the dominant forms of sexual practice in our society reflect psychological, biological, or moral absolutes that determine human sexual practice. Instead, such studies provide much evidence that, against a different backdrop of beliefs about the world, the activities we designate as "sex"—impersonal or otherwise—have an entirely different meaning and value. Yet, while we may choose not to condemn the "child-rearing" practices of the Etoro, we can nevertheless recognize that "penis-feeding" would be extremely damaging to children in our society. Similarly, though we can appreciate that making an occupation by the provision of sex may not have been oppressive to women in medieval France or ancient Babylon, we should nevertheless recognize that in our society it can be extremely damaging to women. What then are the features which, in our culture, render prostitution oppressive?

THE SOCIAL MEANING OF PROSTITUTION

Let me begin with a simple analogy. In our society there exists a taboo against eating cats and dogs. Now, suppose a member of our society wishes to engage in the unconventional behavior of ingesting cat or dog meat. In evaluating the moral and political character of this person's behavior, it is somewhat irrelevant whether eating cats and dogs "really" is or isn't healthy, or whether it "really" is or isn't different than eating cows, pigs, and chickens. What is relevant is that, by including cat and dog flesh in one's diet, a person may really make others upset and, therefore, do damage to them as well as to oneself. In short, how actions are widely perceived and interpreted by others, even if wrongly or seemingly irrationally, is crucial to determining their moral status because, though such interpretations may not hold up against some "objective reality," they are part of the "social reality" in which we live.

---

9. See Gilbert H. Herdt, ed., *Rituals of Manhood* (Berkeley and Los Angeles: University of California Press, 1982). Also see Harriet Whitehead, "The Varieties of Fertility Cultism in New Guinea: Part 1," *American Ethnologist* 13 (1986): 80–99. In comparing penis-feeding to breast-feeding rather than to oral sex, some anthropologists point out that both involve the use of a culturally erotic bodily part for parental nurturing.

I am not using this example to argue that unconventional behavior is wrong but, rather, to illustrate the relevance of cultural convention to how our outward behaviors are perceived. Indeed, what is wrong with prostitution is not that it violates deeply entrenched social conventions—ideals of feminine purity, and the noncommoditization of sex—but precisely that it epitomizes other cultural assumptions—beliefs which, reasonable or not, serve to legitimate women's social subordination. In other words, rather than subvert patriarchal ideology, the prostitute's actions, and the industry as a whole, serve to perpetuate this system of values. By contrast, lesbian sex, and egalitarian heterosexual economic and romantic relationships, do not. In short, female prostitution oppresses women, not because some women who participate in it "suffer in the eyes of society" but because its organized practice testifies to and perpetuates socially hegemonic beliefs which oppress all women in many domains of their lives.

What, then, are some of the beliefs and values which structure the social meaning of the prostitute's business in our culture—principles which are not necessarily consciously held by us but are implicit in our observable behavior and social practice? First, people in our society generally believe that human beings naturally possess, but socially repress, powerful, emotionally destabilizing sexual appetites. Second, we assume that men are naturally suited for dominant social roles. Third, we assume that contact with male genitals in virtually all contexts is damaging and polluting to women. Fourth, we assume that a person's sexual practice renders her or him a particular "kind" of person, for example, "a homosexual," "a bisexual," "a whore," "a virgin," "a pervert," and so on. I will briefly examine the nature of these four assumptions, and then discuss how they determine the social significance and impact of prostitution in our society. Such principles are inscribed in all of a culture's communicative acts and institutions, but my examples will only be drawn from a common body of disciplinary resources: the writings of philosophers and other intellectuals.

The universal possession of a potent sex drive.—In describing the nature of sexual attraction, Schopenhauer states:

> The sexual impulse in all its degrees and nuances plays not only on the stage and in novels, but also in the real world, where, next to the love of life, it shows itself the strongest and most powerful of motives, constantly lays claim to half the powers and thoughts of the younger portion of mankind, is the ultimate goal of almost all human effort, exerts an adverse influence on the most important events, interrupts the most serious occupations every hour, sometimes embarrasses for a while even the greatest minds, does not hesitate to intrude with its trash interfering with the negotiations of statesmen and the investigation of men of learning, knows how to slip its love letters and locks of hair even into ministerial portfolios and philosophical manuscripts, and no less devises daily the most entangled

and the worst actions, destroys the most valuable relationships, breaks the firmest bonds, demands the sacrifice sometimes of life or health, sometimes of wealth, rank, and happiness, nay robs those who are otherwise honest of all conscience, makes those who have hitherto been faithful, traitors; accordingly to the whole, appears as a malevolent demon that strives to pervert, confuse, and overthrow everything.[10]

Freud, of course, chose the name "libido" to refer to this powerful natural instinct, which he believed manifests itself as early as infancy.

The assumption of a potent "sex drive" is implicit in Lars Ericsson's relatively recent defense of prostitution: "We must liberate ourselves from those mental fossils which prevent us from looking upon sex and sexuality with the same naturalness as upon our cravings for food and drink. And, contrary to popular belief, we may have something to learn from prostitution in this respect, namely, that coition resembles nourishment in that if it cannot be obtained in any other way it can always be bought. And bought meals are not always the worst."[11] More explicitly, he argues that the "sex drive" provides a noneconomic, natural basis for explaining the demand for commercial sex.[12] Moreover, he claims that because of the irrational nature of this impulse, prostitution will exist until all persons are granted sexual access upon demand to all other persons.[13] In a society where individuals lack such access to others, but where women are the social equals of men, Ericsson predicts that "the degree of female frustration that exists today . . . will no longer be tolerated, rationalized, or sublimated, but channeled into a demand for, inter alia, mercenary sex."[14] Consequently, Ericsson favors an unregulated sex industry, which can respond spontaneously to these natural human wants. Although Pateman, in her response to Ericsson, does not see the capitalist commoditization of sexuality as physiologically determined, she nevertheless yields to the assumption that "sexual impulses are part of our natural constitution as humans."[15]

Schopenhauer, Freud, Ericsson, and Pateman all clearly articulate what anthropologists refer to as our "cultural common sense" regarding the nature of human sexuality. By contrast, consider a group of people in New Guinea, called the Dani, as described by Karl Heider: "Especially striking is their five year post-partum sexual abstinence, which is uniformly observed and is not a subject of great concern or stress. This low level of sexuality appears to be a purely cultural phenomenon, not caused by

10. Arthur Schopenhauer, "The Metaphysics of the Love of the Sexes," in *The Works of Schopenhauer*, ed. Will Durant (New York: Simon & Schuster, 1928), p. 333.

11. Ericsson, p. 355.

12. Ibid., p. 347.

13. Ibid., pp. 359–60.

14. Ibid., p. 360.

15. Pateman, p. 563.

any biological factors."[16] The moral of this anthropological tale is that our high level of sexuality is also "a purely cultural phenomenon," and not the inevitable result of human biology. Though the Dani's disinterest in sex need not lead us to regard our excessive concern as improper, it should lead us to view one of our cultural rationalizations for prostitution as just that—a cultural rationalization.

The "natural" dominance of men.—One readily apparent feature of the sex industry in our society is that it caters almost exclusively to a male clientele. Even the relatively small number of male prostitutes at work serve a predominantly male consumer group. Implicit in this particular division of labor, and also the predominant division of labor in other domains of our society, is the cultural principle that men are naturally disposed to dominate in their relations with others.

Ironically, this cultural conviction is implicit in some accounts of prostitution by feminist writers, especially in their attempts to explain the social and psychological causes of the problematic demand by men for impersonal, commercial sex. For example, Marxist feminists have argued that prostitution is the manifestation of the unequal class position of women vis-à-vis men: women who do not exchange their domestic and sexual services with the male ruling class for their subsistence are forced to market these services to multiple masters outside marriage.[17] The exploitation of female sexuality is a ruling-class privilege, an advantage which allows those socially identified as "men" to perpetuate their economic and cultural hegemony. In tying female prostitution to patriarchy and capitalism, Marxist accounts attempt to tie it to particular historical forces, rather than to biological or natural ones. However, without the assumption of men's biological superiority, Marxist feminist analyses cannot explain why women, at this particular moment under capitalism, have evolved as an economic under-class, that is, why capitalism gives rise to patriarchy. Why did women's role in production and reproduction not provide them a market advantage, a basis upon which they could subordinate men or assert their political equality?

Gayle Rubin has attempted to provide a purely social and historical analysis of female prostitution by applying some insights of structuralist anthropology.[18] She argues that economic prostitution originates from the unequal position of men and women within the mode of reproduction (the division of society into groups for the purpose of procreation and child rearing). In many human cultures, this system operates by what

16. Karl Heider, "Dani Sexuality: A Low Energy System," *Man* 11 (1976): 188–201.

17. See Friedrich Engels, *The Origin of the Family, Private Property and the State* (New York: Penguin, 1985); Goldman; Alison Jaggar, "Prostitution," in *The Philosophy of Sex*, ed. Alan Soble (Totowa, N.J.: Rowman & Littlefield, 1980), pp. 353–58.

18. Gayle Rubin, "The Traffic in Women: Notes on the 'Political Economy' of Sex," in *Toward an Anthropology of Women*, ed. Rayna Reiter (New York: Monthly Review Press, 1975).

Lévi-Strauss referred to as "the exchange of women": a practice whereby men exchange their own sisters and daughters for the sisters and daughters of other men. These exchanges express or affirm "a social link between the partners of the exchange . . . confer[ing] upon its participants a special relationship of trust, solidarity, and mutual aid."[19] However, since women are not partners to the exchange but, rather, the objects traded, they are denied the social rights and privileges created by these acts of giving. The commoditization of female sexuality is the form this original "traffic in women" takes in capitalist societies. In short, Rubin's account does not assume, but attempts to explain, the dominance of men in production, by appealing to the original dominance of men in reproduction. Yet this account does not explain why women are the objects of the original affinal exchange, rather than men or opposite sex pairs.[20]

In appealing to the principle that men naturally assume dominant roles in all social systems, feminists uncritically accept a basic premise of patriarchy. In my view such principles do not denote universal causal mechanisms but represent naturally arbitrary, culturally determined beliefs which serve to legitimate certain practices.

Sexual contact pollutes women.—To say that extensive sexual experience in a woman is not prized in our society is to be guilty of indirectness and understatement. Rather, a history of sexual activity is a negative mark that is used to differentiate kinds of women. Instead of being valued for their experience in sexual matters, women are valued for their "innocence."

That the act of sexual intercourse with a man is damaging to a woman is implicit in the vulgar language we use to describe this act. As Robert Baker has pointed out, a woman is "fucked," "screwed," "banged," "had," and so forth, and it is a man (a "prick") who does it to her.[21] The metaphors we use for the act of sexual intercourse are similarly revealing. Consider, for example, Andrea Dworkin's description of intercourse:

---

19. Ibid., p. 172.

20. In his attempt to describe the general principles of kinship organization implicit in different cultures, Lévi-Strauss admits it is conceivable that he has over-emphasized the patrilineal nature of these exchanges: "It may have been noted that we have assumed what might be called . . . a paternal perspective. That is, we have regarded the woman married by a member of the group as acquired, and the sister provided in exchange as lost. The situation might be altogether different in a system with matrilineal descent and matrilocal residence. . . . The essential thing is that every right acquired entails a concomitant obligation, and that every renunciation calls for a compensation. . . . Even supposing a very hypothetical marriage system in which the man and not the woman were exchanged . . . the total structure would remain unchanged" (Claude Lévi-Strauss, *The Elementary Structures of Kinship* [Boston: Beacon, 1969], p. 132). A culture in which men are gifts in a ritual of exchange is described in Michael Peletz, "The Exchange of Men in Nineteenth-Century Negeri Sembilan (Malaya)," *American Ethnologist* 14 (1987): 449–69.

21. Robert Baker, " 'Pricks' and 'Chicks': A Plea for 'Persons,' " in *Philosophy and Sex,* ed. R. Baker and F. Elliston (Buffalo, N.Y.: Prometheus, 1984), pp. 260–66. In this section, Baker provides both linguistic and nonlinguistic evidence that intercourse, in our cultural mythology, hurts women.

"The thrusting is persistent invasion. She is opened up, split down the center. She is occupied—physically, internally, in her privacy."[22] Dworkin invokes both images of physical assault and imperialist domination in her characterization of heterosexual copulation. Women are split, penetrated, entered, occupied, invaded, and colonized by men. Though aware of the nonliteralness of this language, Dworkin appears to think that these metaphors are motivated by natural, as opposed to arbitrary, cultural features of the world. According to Ann Garry, "Because in our culture we connect sex with harm that men do to women, and because we think of the female role in sex as that of harmed object, we can see that to treat a woman as a sex object is automatically to treat her as less than fully human."[23] As the public vehicles for "screwing," "penetration," "invasion," prostitutes are reduced to the status of animals or things— mere instruments for human ends.

The reification of sexual practice.—Another belief that determines the social significance of prostitution concerns the relationship between a person's social identity and her or his sexual behavior.[24] For example, we identify a person who has sexual relations with a person of the same gender as a "homosexual," and we regard a woman who has intercourse with multiple sexual partners as being of a particular type—for instance, a "loose woman," "slut," or "prostitute." As critics of our society, we may find these categories too narrow or the values they reflect objectionable. If so, we may refer to women who are sexually promiscuous, or who have sexual relations with other women, as "liberated women," and thereby show a rejection of double (and homophobic) standards of sexual morality. However, what such linguistic iconoclasm generally fails to challenge is that a person's sexual practice makes her a particular "kind" of person.

I will now consider how these cultural convictions and values structure the meaning of prostitution in our society. Our society's tolerance for commercially available sex, legal or not, implies general acceptance of principles which perpetuate women's social subordination. Moreover, by their participation in an industry which exploits the myths of female social inequality and sexual vulnerability, the actions of the prostitute and her clients imply that they accept a set of values and beliefs which

22. Andrea Dworkin, *Intercourse* (New York: Free Press, 1987), p. 122.

23. Ann Garry, "Pornography and Respect for Women," in Baker and Elliston, eds., p. 318.

24. In "Defending Prostitution," Pateman states: "The services of the prostitute are related in a more intimate manner to her body than those of other professionals. Sexual services, that is to say, sex and sexuality, are constitutive of the body in a way in which the counseling skills of the social worker are not. . . . Sexuality and the body are, further, integrally connected to conceptions of femininity and masculinity, and all these are constitutive of our individuality, our sense of self-identity" (p. 562). On my view, while our social identities are determined by our outward sexual practice, this is due to arbitrary, culturally determined conceptual mappings, rather than some universal relationship holding between persons and their bodies.

assign women to marginal social roles in all our cultural institutions, including marriage and waged employment. Just as an Uncle Tom exploits noxious beliefs about blacks for personal gain, and implies through his actions that blacks can benefit from a system of white supremacy, the prostitute and her clients imply that women can profit economically from patriarchy. Though we should not blame the workers in the sex industry for the social degradation they suffer, as theorists and critics of our society, we should question the existence of such businesses and the social principles implicit in our tolerance for them.

Because members of our society perceive persons in terms of their sexual orientation and practice, and because sexual contact in most set-tings—but especially outside the context of a "secure" heterosexual relationship—is thought to be harmful to women, the prostitute's work may have social implications that differ significantly from the work of persons in other professions. For instance, women who work or have worked in the sex industry may find their future social prospects severely limited. By contrast to medieval French society, they are not desired as wives or domestic servants in our own. And unlike other female sub-ordinates in our society, the prostitute is viewed as a defiled creature; nonetheless, we rationalize and tolerate prostitutional sex out of the perceived need to mollify men's sexual desires.

In sum, the woman who provides sex on a commercial basis and the man who patronizes her epitomize and reinforce the social principles I have identified: these include beliefs that attribute to humans potent, subjugating sex drives that men can satisfy without inflicting self-harm through impersonal sexual encounters. Moreover, the prostitute cannot alter the political implications of her work by simply supplying her own rationale for the provision of her services. For example, Margo St. James has tried to represent the prostitute as a skilled sexual therapist, who serves a legitimate social need.[25] According to St. James, while the com-mercial sex provider may be unconventional in her sexual behavior, her work may be performed with honesty and dignity. However, this defense is implausible since it ignores the possible adverse impact of her behavior on herself and others, and the fact that, by participating in prostitution, her behavior does little to subvert the cultural principles that make her work harmful. Ann Garry reaches a similar conclusion about pornography: "I may not think that sex is dirty and that I would be a harmed object; I may not know what your view is; but what bothers me is that this is the view embodied in our language and culture. . . . As long as sex is connected with harm done to women, it will be very difficult not to see

25. Margo St. James, Speech to the San Diego County National Organization for Women, La Jolla, California, February 27, 1982, and from private correspondence with St. James (1983). Margo St. James is the founder of COYOTE (Call Off Your Old Tired Ethics) and the editor of *Coyote Howls*. COYOTE is a civil rights organization which seeks to change the sex industry from within by gaining better working conditions for prostitutes.

pornography as degrading to women. . . . The fact that audience attitude is so important makes one wary of giving whole-hearted approval to any pornography seen today."[26] Although the prostitute may want the meaning of her actions assessed relative to her own idiosyncratic beliefs and values, the political and social meaning of her actions must be assessed in the political and social context in which they occur.

One can imagine a society in which individuals sought commercial sexual services from women in order to obtain high quality sexual experiences. In our society, people pay for medical advice, meals, education in many fields, and so on, in order to obtain information, services, or goods that are superior to or in some respect more valuable than those they can obtain noncommercially. A context in which the rationale for seeking a prostitute's services was to obtain sex from a professional—from a person who knows what she is doing—is probably not a context in which women are thought to be violated when they have sexual contact with men. In such a situation, those who supplied sex on a commercial basis would probably not be stigmatized but, instead, granted ordinary social privileges.[27] The fact that prostitutes have such low social status in our society indicates that the society in which we live is not congruent with this imaginary one; that is, the prostitute's services in our society are not generally sought as a gourmet item. In short, if commercial sex was sought as a professional service, then women who provided sex commercially would probably not be regarded as "prostituting" themselves—as devoting their bodies or talents to base purposes, contrary to their true interests.

SUBVERTING THE STATUS QUO

Let me reiterate that I am not arguing for social conformism. Rather, my point is that not all nonconformist acts equally challenge conventional morality. For example, if a person wants to subvert the belief that eating cats and dogs is bad, it is not enough to simply engage in eating them. Similarly, it is unlikely that persons will subvert prevalent attitudes toward gender and sexuality by engaging in prostitution.

Consider another example. Suppose that I value high quality child care and am willing to pay a person well to obtain it. Because of both racial and gender oppression, the persons most likely to be interested in and suitable for such work are bright Third World and minority First World women who cannot compete fairly for other well-paid work. Suppose,

---

26. Garry, pp. 318–23.

27. According to Bertrand Russell: "In Japan, apparently, the matter is quite otherwise. Prostitution is recognized and respected as a career, and is even adopted at the instance of parents. It is often a not uncommon method of earning a marriage dowry" (*Marriage and Morals* [1929; reprint, New York: Liveright, 1970], p. 151). Perhaps contemporary Japan is closer to our imaginary society, a society where heterosexual intercourse is not felt to be polluting to women.

then, I hire a person who happens to be a woman and a person of color to provide child care on the basis of the belief that such work requires a high level of intelligence and responsibility. Though the belief on which this act is based may be unconventional, my action of hiring a "sitter" from among the so-called lower classes of society is not politically liberating.[28]

What can a person who works in the sex industry do to subvert widely held attitudes toward her work? To subvert the beliefs which currently structure commercial sex in our society, the female prostitute would need to assume the role not of a sexual subordinate but of a sexual equal or superior. For instance, if she were to have the authority to determine what services the customer could get, under what conditions the customer could get them, and what they would cost, she would gain the status of a sexual professional. Should she further want to establish herself as a sexual therapist, she would need to represent herself as having some type of special technical knowledge for solving problems having to do with human sexuality. In other words, experience is not enough to establish one's credentials as a therapist or professional. However, if the industry were reformed so that all these conditions were met, what would distinguish the prostitute's work from that of a bona fide "sexual therapist"? If her knowledge was thought to be only quasilegitimate, her work might have the status of something like the work of a chiropractor, but this would certainly be quite different than the current social status of her work.[29] In sum, the political alternatives of reformation and abolition are not mutually exclusive: if prostitution were sufficiently transformed to make it completely nonoppressive to women, though commercial transactions involving sex might still exist, prostitution as we now know it would not.

If our tolerance for marriage fundamentally rested on the myth of female subordination, then the same arguments which apply to prostitution would apply to it. Many theorists, including Simone de Beauvoir and Friedrich Engels, have argued that marriage, like prostitution, involves female sexual subservience. For example, according to de Beauvoir: "For both the sexual act is a service; the one is hired for life by one man; the other has several clients who pay her by the piece. The one is protected by one male against all others; the other is defended by all against the exclusive tyranny of each."[30] In addition, Lars Ericsson contends that

28. This of course does not mean we should not hire such people for child care, for that would simply be to deny a good person a better job than he or she might otherwise obtain—a job which unlike the prostitute's job is not likely to hurt their prospects for other work or social positions. Nevertheless, one should not believe that one's act of giving a person of this social description such a job does anything to change the unfair structure of our society.

29. I am grateful to Richard Arneson for suggesting this analogy to me.

30. Simone de Beauvoir, *The Second Sex* (New York: Vintage, 1974), p. 619. According to Engels: "Marriage of convenience turns often enough into the crassest prostitution—

marriage, unlike prostitution, involves economic dependence for women: "While the housewife is totally dependent on her husband, at least economically, the call girl in that respect stands on her own two feet. If she has a pimp, it is she, not he, who is the breadwinner in the family."[31]

Since the majority of marriages in our society render the wife the domestic and sexual subordinate of her husband, marriage degrades the woman who accepts it (or perhaps only the woman who accepts marriage on unequal terms), and its institutionalization in its present form oppresses all women. However, because marriage can be founded on principles which do not involve the subordination of women, we can challenge oppressive aspects of this institution without radically altering it.[32] For example, while the desire to control the sinful urges of men to fornicate may, historically, have been part of the ideology of marriage, it does not seem to be a central component of our contemporary rationalization for this custom.[33] Marriage, at present in our society, is legitimated by other widely held values and beliefs, for example, the desirability of a long-term, emotionally and financially sustaining, parental partnership. However, I am unable to imagine nonpernicious principles which would legitimate the commercial provision of sex and which would not substantially alter or eliminate the industry as it now exists. Since commercial sex, unlike marriage, is not reformable, feminists should seek to undermine the beliefs and values which underlie our acceptance of it. Indeed, one way to do this is to outwardly oppose prostitution itself.

CONCLUSIONS

If my analysis is correct, then prostitution is not a social aberration or disorder but, rather, a consequence of well-established beliefs and values that form part of the foundation of all our social institutions and practices. Therefore, by striving to overcome discriminatory structures in all aspects of society—in the family, at work outside the home, and in our political institutions—feminists will succeed in challenging some of the cultural presuppositions which sustain prostitution. In other words, prostitution needs no unique remedy, legal or otherwise; it will be remedied as feminists make progress in altering patterns of belief and practice that oppress

---

sometimes of both partners, but far more commonly of the woman, who only differs from the ordinary courtesan in that she does not let out her body on piecework as a wage worker, but sells it once and for all into slavery" (p. 102).

31. Ericsson, p. 354.

32. Pateman argues: "The conjugal relation is not necessarily one of domination and subjection, and in this it differs from prostitution" (p. 563). On this I agree with her.

33. Russell informs us that "Christianity, and more particularly St. Paul, introduced an entirely novel view of marriage, that it existed not primarily for the procreation of children, but to prevent the sin of fornication. . . . I remember once being advised by a doctor to abandon the practice of smoking, and he said that I should find it easier if, whenever the desire came upon me, I proceeded to suck an acid drop. It is in this spirit that St. Paul recommends marriage" (pp. 44–46).

women in all aspects of their lives. Yet, while prostitution requires no special social cure, some important strategic and symbolic feminist goals may be served by selecting the sex industry for criticism at this time. In this respect, a consumer boycott of the industry is especially appropriate.

In examining prostitution, I have not tried to construct a theory which can explain the universal causes and moral character of prostitution. Such questions presuppose that there is a universal phenomenon to which the term refers and that commercial sex is always socially deviant and undesirable. Instead, I have considered the meaning of commercial sex in modern Western cultures. Although my arguments are consistent with the decriminalization of prostitution, I conclude from my investigation that feminists have legitimate reasons to politically oppose prostitution in our society. Since the principles which implicitly sustain and organize the sex industry are ones which underlie pernicious gender asymmetries in many domains of our social life, to tolerate a practice which epitomizes these principles is oppressive to women.

Defending Prostitution: Charges against Ericsson

Carole Pateman

Ericsson's contractarian defense of prostitution[1] extends the liberal ideals of individualism, equality of opportunity, and the free market to sexual life. The real problem with prostitution, Ericsson claims, is the hypocrisy, prejudice, and punitive attitudes that surround it. Once unblinkered, we can see that prostitution is merely one service occupation among others and that, with some reforms, a morally acceptable, or "sound," prostitution could exist. This defense has its appeal at a time when strict control of sexual conduct is again being strenuously advocated. However, Ericsson's argument fails to overcome the general weaknesses of abstract contractarianism, and his claim that he has rebutted the feminist charge against prostitution cannot be granted. The central feminist argument is that prostitution remains morally undesirable, no matter what reforms are made, because it is one of the most graphic examples of men's domination of women.

Ericsson's argument illustrates nicely how liberal contractarianism systematically excludes the patriarchal dimension of our society from philosophical scrutiny. He interprets feminists as arguing that prostitution is "undesirable on the ground that it constitutes an extreme instance of the inequality between the sexes" (p. 348), and he then interprets inequality to be a matter of the distribution of benefits and burdens. It thus appears that a remedy can be found for the withholding of a benefit (access to prostitutes) from women by extending equality of opportunity to buy and sell sexual services on the market to both sexes. Ericsson ignores the fact that men earn a good deal more than women, so the latter would still have a greater incentive to be sellers than buyers (or would be confined to the cheaper end of the market as buyers; Ericsson pays no attention to the different categories of prostitution). Moreover, Ericsson notes that three-quarters of the men who are in the market for prostitutes are married. Any change in attitudes would have to be sufficient to make it acceptable that wives could spend what they save from housekeeping

---

1. L. O. Ericsson, "Charges against Prostitution: An Attempt at a Philosophical Assessment," *Ethics* 90 (1980): 335–66. Page references to this paper are in parentheses in the text.

This essay originally appeared in *Ethics* 93, April 1983.

money, or spend part of their own earnings, on prostitutes. Second, Ericsson dismisses as meaningless the charge that prostitution unfairly burdens women because they are oppressed as prostitutes; properly understood, prostitution is an example of a free contract between individuals in the market in which services are exchanged for money. Ericsson's defense does not and cannot confront the feminist objection to prostitution. Feminists do not see prostitution as unacceptable because it distributes benefits and burdens unequally; rather, to use Ericsson's language of inequality, because prostitution is grounded in the inequality of domination and subjection. The problem of domination is both denied by and hidden behind Ericsson's assertion that prostitution is a free contract or an equal exchange.

The most striking feature of Ericsson's defense is that he makes no attempt to substantiate the key claim that prostitution *is* the sale of sexual services. His assertion relies on the conventional assumption that free wage labor stands at the opposite pole from slavery. The worker freely contracts to sell labor power or services for a specific period, whereas the person of the slave is sold for an unlimited time. Ericsson comments that if a prostitute "actually did sell herself, she would no longer be a prostitute but a sexual slave" (p. 341). More exactly, since she has the civil and juridical status of a free individual in the capitalist market, she would be in a form of subjection that fell short of slavery. Ericsson avoids discussing whether this is indeed the position of the prostitute because he ignores the problems involved in separating the sale of services through contract from the sale of the body and the self. In capitalist societies it appears as if labor power and services are bought and sold on the market, but "labor power" and "services" are abstractions. When workers sell labor power, or professionals sell services to clients (and Ericsson regards some prostitutes as "small scale private entrepreneurs"),[2] neither the labor power nor services can in reality be separated from the person offering them for sale. Unless the "owners" of these abstractions agree to, or are compelled to, use them in certain ways, which means that the "owners" act in a specified manner, there is nothing to be sold. The employer appears to buy labor power; what he actually obtains is the right of command over workers, the right to put their capacities, their bodies, to use as he determines.

Services and labor power are inseparably connected to the body and the body is, in turn, inseparably connected to the sense of self. Ericsson writes of the prostitute as a kind of social worker, but the services of the prostitute are related in a more intimate manner to her body than those of other professionals. Sexual services, that is to say, sex and sexuality, are constitutive of the body in a way in which the counseling skills of the

---

2. On workers as "petty entrepreneurs," their labor power or services, see R. P. Wolff, "A Critique and Reinterpretation of Marx's Labor Theory of Value," *Philosophy and Public Affairs* 10 (1981): 89–120, esp. 109–11.

social worker are not (a point illustrated in a backhanded way by the ubiquitous use by men of vulgar terms for female sexual organs to refer to women themselves). Sexuality and the body are, further, integrally connected to conceptions of femininity and masculinity, and all these are constitutive of our individuality, our sense of self-identity. When sex becomes a commodity in the capitalist market so, necessarily, do bodies and selves. The prostitute cannot sell sexual services alone; what she sells is her body. To supply services contracted for, professionals must act in certain ways, or use their bodies; to use the labor power he has bought the employer has command over the worker's capacities and body; to use the prostitute's "services," her purchaser must buy her body and use her body. In prostitution, because of the relation between the commodity being marketed and the body, it is the body that is up for sale.

Critics of marriage have often claimed that wives are no different from prostitutes. Women who marry also contract away their bodies but (in principle) for life rather than for minutes or hours like the prostitute. However, a form of marriage in which the husband gains legal right of sexual use of his wife's body is only one possible form. The conjugal relation is not necessarily one of domination and subjection, and in this it differs from prostitution. Ericsson's defense is about prostitution in capitalist societies; that is, the practice through which women's bodies become commodities in the market which can be bought (contracted for) for sexual use. The questions his defense raises are why there is a demand for this commodity, exactly what the commodity is, and why it is *men* who demand it.

Ericsson cannot admit that the first two questions arise. The third he treats as unproblematic. He stands firmly in the patriarchal tradition which discusses prostitution as a problem about the women who are prostitutes, and our attitudes to them, not a problem about the men who demand to buy them. For Ericsson it is merely a contingent fact that most prostitutes are women and customers men.[3] He claims that the demand for prostitution could never disappear because of some "ubiquitous and permanent imperfections" (p. 337) of human existence arising from the sexual urge. In other words, prostitution is a natural feature of human life. Certainly, sexual impulses are part of our natural constitution as humans, but the sale of "sexual services" as a commodity in the capitalist market cannot be reduced to an expression of our natural biology and physiology. To compare the fulfillment of sexual urges through prostitution to other natural necessities of human survival, to argue from the fact that we need food, so it should be available, to the claim that "our sexual desires are just as basic, natural, and compelling as our appetite for food, [so] this also holds for them" (p. 341), is, to say the least, disingenuous.

---

3. In cities like Sydney, male homosexual prostitutes are not uncommon. Following Ericsson, I discuss only heterosexual (genitally oriented) prostitution. It is not immediately clear that homosexual prostitution has the same social significance.

What counts as "food" varies widely, of course, in different cultures, but, at the most fundamental level of survival there is one obvious difference between sex and other human needs. Without a certain minimum of food, drink, and shelter, people die; but, to my knowledge, no one has yet died from want of sexual release. Moreover, sometimes food and drink are impossible to obtain no matter what people do, but every person has the means to find sexual release at hand.

To treat prostitution as a natural way of satisfying a basic human need, to state that "bought meals are not always the worst" (p. 355), neatly, if vulgarly, obscures the real, social character of contemporary sexual relations. Prostitution is not, as Ericsson claims, the same as "sex without love or mutual affection" (p. 341). The latter is morally acceptable *if* it is the result of mutual physical attraction that is freely expressed by both individuals. The difference between sex without love and prostitution is not the difference between cooking at home and buying food in restaurants; the difference is that between the reciprocal expression of desire and unilateral subjection to sexual acts with the consolation of payment: it is the difference for women between freedom and subjection.

To understand why men (not women) demand prostitutes, and what is demanded, prostitution has to be rescued from Ericsson's abstract contractarianism and placed in the social context of the structure of sexual relations between women and men. Since the revival of the organized feminist movement, moral and political philosophers have begun to turn their attention to sexual life, but their discussions are usually divided into a set of discrete compartments which take for granted that a clear distinction can be drawn between consensual and coercive sexual relationships. However, as an examination of consent and rape makes graphically clear,[4] throughout the whole of sexual life domination, subjection, and enforced submission are confused with consent, free association, and the reciprocal fulfillment of mutual desire. The assertion that prostitution is no more than an example of a free contract between equal individuals in the market is another illustration of the presentation of submission as freedom. Feminists have often argued that what is fundamentally at issue in relations between women and men is not sex but power. But, in the present circumstances of our sexual lives, it is not possible to separate power from sex. The expression of sexuality and what it means to be feminine and a woman, or masculine and a man, is developed within, and intricately bound up with, relations of domination and subordination.

Ericsson remarks that "the best prostitutional sex available is probably much better from the customer's point of view than average marital sex" (p. 340). It is far from obvious that it is either "quality" or the "need" for sex, in the commonsense view of "quality" and "sex," that explains why three-quarters of these customers are husbands. In the "permissive society" there are numerous ways in which men can find sex without

4. See my "Women and Consent," *Political Theory* 8 (1980): 149–68.

payment, in addition to the access that husbands have to wives. But, except in the case of the most brutal husbands, most spouses work out a modus vivendi about all aspects of their lives, including the wife's bodily integrity. Not all husbands exercise to the full their socially and legally recognized right—which is the right of a master. There is, however, another institution which enables all men to affirm themselves as masters. To be able to purchase a body in the market presupposes the existence of masters. Prostitution is the public recognition of men as sexual masters; it puts submission on sale as a commodity in the market.

The outline of an answer to the complex question of why men demand this commodity can be found in recent feminist interpretations of psychoanalytic theory. Feminist discussions of the differential development of gendered individuality suggest that the masculine sense of self is grounded in separateness, especially separation from those other (opposing) feminine selves which proclaim what masculinity is not.[5] Hegel showed theoretically in his famous dialectic of mastery and servitude that a self so conceived always attempts to gain recognition and maintain its subjective isolation through domination. When women and men are seen in their substantive individuality, and not as abstract makers of contracts, an explanation can be found for why it is *men* who demand to buy women's bodies in the market. The demand by men for prostitutes in patriarchal capitalist society is bound up with a historically and culturally distinctive form of masculine individuality. The structure of the relation between the sexes reaches into the unconscious early development of little boys and girls and out into the form of economic organization in which the capacities of individuals, and even women's bodies, become commodities to be alienated to the control and use of others.

The peculiarity of Ericsson's argument for equality of opportunity in "sound" prostitution should now be apparent. He assumes that the (sexual) selves of women and men are interchangeable. This may appear radical, but it is a purely abstract radicalism that reduces differentiated, gendered individuality to the seemingly natural, undifferentiated, and universal figure of the "individual"—which is an implicit generalization of the masculine self. The feminist exploration of gendered individuality provides the material, sociological grounding for that familiar, liberal abstraction, the possessive, atomistic self that appears as the bearer of rights and the maker of contracts in civil society. The logic of Ericsson's sexual contractarianism also leads to two unpalatable conclusions that he is unwilling to draw. The first is that all sexual relations should take the form of universal prostitution, the buying and selling of sexual services on the market. The equal right of access to sexual use of a body (or "sexual services") can be established more economically and advantageously

5. See, esp., J. Benjamin, "The Bonds of Love: Rational Violence and Erotic Domination," *Feminist Studies* 6 (1980): 175–96. Benjamin builds on N. Chodorow, *The Reproduction of Mothering: Psychoanalysis and the Sociology of Gender* (Berkeley: University of California Press, 1978).

for the individual through universal prostitution than through (the contract of) marriage. Second, it is unnecessary to confine the buying and selling of sexual services to adults. Ericsson is fainthearted in his contractarianism when he excludes children from the market. Strictly, the capacity to make a contract is all that is required; surely not a capacity confined to those who are statutorily adults.

Ericsson shows how complete is his misunderstanding of feminism and the feminist criticism of prostitution when he complains that "so many feminists seem unable to understand that contempt for harlotry involves contempt for the female sex" (p. 365). Neither contempt for women nor their ancient profession underlies feminist arguments; rather, they are sad and angry about what the demand for prostitution reveals of the general character of (private and public) relations between the sexes. The claim that what is really wrong with prostitution is hypocrisy and outdated attitudes to sex is the tribute that liberal permissiveness pays to political mystification.

Sexuality, Pornography, and Method: "Pleasure under Patriarchy"*

Catharine A. MacKinnon

> then she says (and this is what I live through over
>   and over)—she says: *I do not know if sex is an*
>   *illusion*
> *I do not know*
> *who I was when I did those things*
> *or who I said I was*
> *or whether I willed to feel*
> *what I had read about*
> *or who in fact was there with me*
> *or whether I knew, even then*
> *that there was doubt about these things*
>
> [ADRIENNE RICH, "Dialogue"]

I had always been fond of her in the most innocent, asexual way. It was as if her body was always entirely hidden behind her radiant mind, the modesty of her behavior, and her taste in dress. She had never offered me the slightest chink through which to view the glow of her nakedness. And now suddenly the butcher knife of fear had slit her open. She was as open to me as the carcass of a heifer slit down the middle and hanging on a hook. There we were . . . and suddenly I felt a violent desire to make love to her. Or to be more exact, a violent desire to rape her. [MILAN KUNDERA, *The Book of Laughter and Forgetting*]

She had thought of something, something about the body, about the passions which it was unfitting for her as a woman to say. Men,

* Prior versions of these views are published in J. Geer and W. O'Donohue, *Theories of Human Sexuality* (New York: Plenum Press, 1987) and as preface to J. Masson's *A Dark Science: Women, Sexuality, and Psychiatry in the Nineteenth Century* (New York: Farrar, Straus & Giroux, 1986). This article is a chapter from *Toward a Feminist Theory of the State*, to be published by Harvard University Press in 1989. The quotation in the title is from a note by Judith Friedlander in *Diary*, a preconference publication of the Barnard Conference on Sexuality, 1982, p. 25. Sources for the epigraphs are as follows: Adrienne Rich, "Dialogue," in *Poems: Selected and New, 1950–1974* (New York: Norton, 1975), p. 195. Milan Kundera, *The Book of Laughter and Forgetting* (New York: Knopf, 1980), p. 75; Virginia Woolf, "Professions for Women," in her *The Death of the Moth and Other Essays* (1942; reprint, New York: Harcourt, Brace, Jovanovich, 1974), pp. 240–41.

her reason told her, would be shocked. . . . Telling the truth about my own experiences as a body, I do not think I solved. I doubt that any woman has solved it yet. The obstacles against her are still immensely powerful—and yet they are very difficult to define. [VIRGINIA WOOLF, "Professions for Women"]

What is it about women's experience that produces a distinctive perspective on social reality? How is an angle of vision and an interpretive hermeneutics of social life created in the group women? What happens to women to give them a particular interest in social arrangements, something to have a consciousness *of*? How are the qualities we know as male and female socially created and enforced on an everyday level? Sexual objectification of women—first in the world, then in the head, first in visual appropriation, then in forced sex, finally in sexual murder—provides answers.[1]

Male dominance is sexual. Meaning: men in particular, if not men alone, sexualize hierarchy; gender is one. As much a sexual theory of gender as a gendered theory of sex, this is the theory of sexuality that has grown out of consciousness raising in the women's movement. Recent feminist work, both interpretive and empirical—on rape, battery, sexual harassment, sexual abuse of children, prostitution, and pornography—supports it (see Appendix). These practices, taken together, express and actualize the distinctive power of men over women in society; their effective permissibility confirms and extends it. If one believes women's accounts of sexual use and abuse by men;[2] if the pervasiveness of male sexual violence against women substantiated in these studies is not denied, minimized, or excepted as deviant[3] or episodic; if the fact that only 7.8 percent of women in the United States are not sexually assaulted or harassed in their lifetimes[4] is considered not ignorable or inconsequential;

1. See Jane Caputi, *The Age of Sex Crime* (Bowling Green, Ohio: Bowling Green State University Popular Press, 1987); Deborah Cameron and Elizabeth Frazer, *The Lust to Kill: A Feminist Investigation of Sexual Murder* (New York: New York University Press, 1987).

2. Freud's decision to disbelieve women's accounts of being sexually abused as children was apparently central in the construction of the theories of fantasy and possibly also of the unconscious. That is, his belief that the sexual abuse his patients told him about did not actually occur created the need for a theory like fantasy, like unconscious, to explain the reports (see Rush [Appendix]; J. Moussaieff Masson, *The Assault on Truth: Freud's Suppression of the Seduction Theory* [New York: Farrar, Straus & Giroux, 1983]). One can only speculate on the course of the modern psyche (not to mention modern history) had the women been believed.

3. E. Schur, *Labeling Women Deviant: Gender, Stigma and Social Control* (New York: Random House, 1983) (a superb review urging a "continuum" rather than a "deviance" approach to issues of sex inequality).

4. Diana Russell produced this figure at my request from the random sample data base of 930 San Francisco households discussed in her *The Secret Trauma: Incest in the Lives of Girls and Women*, pp. 20–37 [Appendix], and *Rape in Marriage*, pp. 27–41 [Appendix]. The figure includes all the forms of rape or other sexual abuse or harassment surveyed, noncontact as well as contact, from gang rape by strangers and marital rape to obscene phone calls, unwanted sexual advances on the street, unwelcome requests to pose for pornography, and subjection to peeping toms and sexual exhibitionists (flashers).

if the women to whom it happens are not considered expendable; if violation of women is understood as sexualized on some level—then sexuality itself can no longer be regarded as unimplicated. The meaning of practices of sexual violence cannot be categorized away as violence, not sex, either. The male sexual role, this work taken together suggests, centers on aggressive intrusion on those with less power. Such acts of dominance are experienced as sexually arousing, as sex itself.[5] They therefore are. The evidence on the sexual violation of women by men thus frames an inquiry into the place of sexuality in gender and of gender in sexuality.

A feminist theory of sexuality would locate sexuality within a theory of gender inequality, meaning the social hierarchy of men over women. To make a theory feminist, it is not enough that it be authored by a biological female. Nor that it describe female sexuality as different from (if equal to) male sexuality, or as if sexuality in women ineluctably exists in some realm beyond, beneath, above, behind—in any event, fundamentally untouched and unmoved by—an unequal social order. A theory of sexuality becomes feminist to the extent it treats sexuality as a social construct of male power: defined by men, forced on women, and constitutive in the meaning of gender. Such an approach centers feminism on the perspective of the subordination of women to men as it identifies sex—that is, the sexuality of dominance and submission—as crucial, as a fundamental, as on some level definitive, in that process. Feminist theory becomes a project of analyzing that situation in order to face it for what it is, in order to change it.

Focusing on gender inequality without a sexual account of its dynamics, as most work has, one could criticize the sexism of existing theories of sexuality and emerge knowing that men author scripts to their own advantage, women and men act them out; that men set conditions, women and men have their behavior conditioned; that men develop developmental categories through which men develop, and that women develop or not; that men are socially allowed selves hence identities with personalities into which sexuality is or is not well integrated, women being that which is or is not integrated, that through the alterity of which a self experiences itself as having an identity; that men have object relations, women are the objects of those relations, and so on. Following such critique, one could attempt to invert or correct the premises or applications of these theories to make them gender neutral, even if the reality to which they refer looks more like the theories—once their gender specificity is revealed—than it looks gender neutral. Or, one could attempt to enshrine a distinctive "women's reality" as if it really were permitted to exist as

5. S. D. Smithyman, "The Undetected Rapist" (Ph.D. diss., Claremont Graduate School, 1978); N. Groth, *Men Who Rape: The Psychology of the Offender* (New York: St. Martin's, 1982); D. Scully and J. Marolla, " 'Riding the Bull at Gilley's': Convicted Rapists Describe the Rewards of Rape," *Social Problems* 32 (1985): 251. (The manuscript version of this paper was subtitled "Convicted Rapists Describe the Pleasure of Raping.")

something more than one dimension of women's response to a condition of powerlessness. Such exercises would be revealing and instructive, even deconstructive, but to limit feminism to correcting sex bias by acting in theory as if male power did not exist in fact, including by valorizing in writing what women have had little choice but to be limited to becoming in life, is to limit feminist theory the way sexism limits women's lives: to a response to terms men set.

A distinctively feminist theory conceptualizes social reality, including sexual reality, on its own terms. The question is, What are they? If women have been substantially deprived not only of their own experience but of terms of their own in which to view it, then a feminist theory of sexuality that seeks to understand women's situation in order to change it, must first identify and criticize the construct "sexuality" as a construct that has circumscribed and defined experience as well as theory. This requires capturing it *in the world,* in its situated social meanings, as it is being constructed in life on a daily basis. It must be studied in its experienced empirical existence, not just in the texts of history (as Foucault), in the social psyche (as Lacan) or in language (as Derrida). Sexual meaning is not made only, or even primarily, by words and in texts. In feminist terms, the fact that male power has power means that the interests of male sexuality construct what sexuality as such means in life, including the standard way it is allowed and recognized to be felt and expressed and experienced, in a way that determines women's biographies, including sexual ones. Existing theories, until they grasp this, will not only misattribute what they call female sexuality to women as such, as if it is not imposed on women daily, they will participate in enforcing the hegemony of the social construct "desire," hence its product, "sexuality," hence its construct "woman," on the world.

The gender issue thus becomes the issue of what is taken to be "sexuality": what sex means and what is meant by sex, when, how, and with whom and with what consequences to whom. Such questions are almost never systematically confronted, even in discourses that purport feminist awareness. What sex is—how it comes to be attached and attributed to what it is, embodied and practiced as it is, contextualized in the ways it is, signifying and referring to what it does—is taken as a baseline, a given, except when explaining what happened when it is thought to have gone wrong. It is as if "erotic," for example, can be taken as having an understood referent, although it is never defined. Except to imply that it is universal yet individual, ultimately variable and plastic. Essentially indefinable but overwhelmingly positive. "Desire," the vicissitudes of which are endlessly extolled and philosophized in culture high and low, is not seen as fundamentally problematic or calling for explanation on the concrete, interpersonal operative level, unless (again) it is supposed to be there and is not. To list and analyze what seem to be the essential elements for male sexual arousal, what has to be there for the penis to work, seems faintly blasphemous, like a pornographer doing market research. Sex is supposed both too individual and too universally tran-scendant for that. To suggest that the sexual might be continuous with something other than sex itself—something like politics—is seldom done, is treated as detumescent, even by feminists. It is as if sexuality comes from the stork.

Sexuality, in feminist light, is not a discrete sphere of interaction or feeling or sensation or behavior in which preexisting social divisions may or may not be played out. It is a pervasive dimension throughout the whole of social life, a dimension along which gender pervasively occurs and through which gender is socially constituted; in this culture, it is a dimension along which other social divisions, like race and class, partly play themselves out. Dominance eroticized defines the imperatives of its masculinity, submission eroticized defines its femininity. So many distinctive features of women's status as second class—the restriction and constraint and contortion, the servility and the display, the self-mutilation and requisite presentation of self as a beautiful thing, the enforced passivity, the humiliation—are made into the content of sex for women. Being a thing for sexual use is fundamental to it. This identifies not just a sexuality that is shaped under conditions of gender inequality but this sexuality itself as the dynamic of the inequality of the sexes. It is to argue that the excitement at reduction of a person to a thing, to less than a hu-man being, as socially defined, is its fundamental motive force. It is to argue sexual difference as a function of sexual dominance. It is to argue a sexual theory of the distribution of social power by gender, in which this sexuality that is sexuality is substantially what makes the gender division be what it is, which is male dominant, wherever it is, which is nearly everywhere.

Across cultures, from this perspective, sexuality is whatever a given culture defines it as. The next questions concern its relation to gender asymmetry and to gender as a division of power. Male dominance appears to exist cross-culturally, if in locally particular forms. Is whatever defines women as "different" the same as whatever defines women as "inferior" the same as whatever defines women's "sexuality"? Is that which defines gender inequality as merely the sex difference also the content of the erotic, cross-culturally? In this view, the feminist theory of sexuality is its theory of politics, its distinctive contribution to social and political explanation. To explain gender inequality in terms of "sexual politics"[6] is to advance not only a political theory of the sexual that defines gender but also a sexual theory of the political to which gender is fundamental.

In this approach, male power takes the social form of what men as a gender want sexually, which centers on power itself, as socially defined. Masculinity is having it; femininity is not having it. Masculinity precedes male as femininity precedes female and male sexual desire defines both. Specifically, "woman" is defined by what male desire requires for arousal

6. K. Millett, *Sexual Politics* (New York: Doubleday, 1970).

and satisfaction and is socially tautologous with "female sexuality" and "the female sex." In the permissible ways a woman can be treated, the ways that are socially considered not violations but appropriate to her nature, one finds the particulars of male sexual interests and requirements. In the concomitant sexual paradigm, the ruling norms of sexual attraction and expression are fused with gender identity formation and affirmation, such that sexuality equals heterosexuality equals the sexuality of (male) dominance and (female) submission.

Post-Lacan, actually post-Foucault,[7] it has become customary to affirm that sexuality is socially constructed.[8] Seldom specified is what, socially, it is constructed of, far less who does the constructing or how, when, or where.[9] When capitalism is the favored social construct, sexuality is shaped and controlled and exploited and repressed by capitalism; not, capitalism creates sexuality as we know it. When sexuality is a construct of discourses of power, gender is never one of them; force is central to its deployment but only through repressing it, not through constituting it; speech is not concretely investigated for its participation in this construction process. "Constructed" seems to mean influenced by, directed, channeled, like a highway constructs traffic patterns. Not: Why cars? Who's driving? Where's everybody going? What makes mobility matter? Who can own a car? Are all these accidents not very accidental? Although there are partial exceptions (but disclaimers notwithstanding), the typical model of sexuality that is tacitly accepted remains deeply Freudian[10] and essentialist: sexuality is an innate primary natural prepolitical unconditioned[11] drive divided

7. J. Lacan, *Feminine Sexuality,* trans. J. Rose (New York: Norton, 1982); M. Foucault, *The History of Sexuality,* vol. 1, *An Introduction* (New York: Random House, 1980), and *Power/ Knowledge,* ed. C. Gordon (New York: Pantheon, 1980).

8. See generally (including materials reviewed in) R. Padgug, "Sexual Matters: On Conceptualizing Sexuality in History," *Radical History Review* 70 (1979): 9; M. Vicinus, "Sexuality and Power: A Review of Current Work in the History of Sexuality," *Feminist Studies* 8 (1982): 133–55; S. Ortner and H. Whitehead, *Sexual Meanings: The Cultural Construction of Gender and Sexuality* (Cambridge: Cambridge University Press, 1981); Red Collective, *The Politics of Sexuality in Capitalism* (London: Black Rose Press, 1978); J. Weeks, *Sex, Politics and Society: The Regulation of Sexuality since 1800* (New York: Longman, 1981); J. D'Emilio, *Sexual Politics, Sexual Communities: The Making of a Homosexual Minority in the United States, 1940–1970* (Chicago: University of Chicago Press, 1983); A. Snitow, C. Stansell, and S. Thompson, introduction to *Powers of Desire: The Politics of Sexuality,* ed. A. Snitow, C. Stansell, and S. Thompson (New York: Monthly Review Press, 1983); E. Dubois and L. Gordon, "Seeking Ecstasy on the Battlefield: Danger and Pleasure in Nineteenth-Century Feminist Social Thought," *Feminist Studies* 9 (1983): 7–25.

9. An example is Jeffrey Weeks, *Sexuality and Its Discontents* (London: Routledge & Kegan Paul, 1985).

10. Luce Irigaray's critique of Freud in *Speculum de l'autre femme* (Paris: Minuit, 1974) acutely shows how Freud constructs sexuality from the male point of view, with woman as deviation from the norm. But she, too, sees female sexuality not as constructed by male dominance but only repressed under it.

11. For those who think that such notions are atavisms left behind by modern behaviorists, see one entirely typical conceptualization of "sexual pleasure, a powerful unconditioned stimulus and reinforcer" in N. Malamuth and B. Spinner, "A Longitudinal Content Analysis

along the biological gender line, centering on heterosexual intercourse, that is, penile intromission, full actualization of which is repressed by civilization. Even if the sublimation aspect of this theory is rejected, or the reasons for the repression are seen to vary (for the survival of civilization or to maintain fascist control or to keep capitalism moving), sexual expression is implicitly seen as the expression of something that is to a significant extent presocial and is socially denied its full force. Sexuality remains precultural and universally invariant to some extent, social only in that it needs society to take what are always to some extent socially specific forms. The impetus itself is a hunger, an appetite founded on a biological need; what it is specifically hungry for and how it is satisfied is then open to endless cultural and individual variance, like cuisine, like cooking.

Allowed/not-allowed are this sexuality's basic ideological axes. The fact that sexuality is ideologically bounded is known. That there are its axes, central to the way its "drive" is driven, and that this is fundamental to the gender difference, is not.[12] Its basic normative assumption is that whatever is considered sexuality should be allowed to be "expressed." Whatever is called sex is attributed a normatively positive valence, an affirmative valuation. This ex cathedra assumption, affirmation of which appears indispensable to one's credibility on any subject that gets near the sexual, means that sex as such (whatever it is) is good—natural, healthy, positive, appropriate, pleasurable, wholesome, fine, one's own, and to be approved and expressed. This, sometimes characterized as "sex-positive" is, rather obviously, a value judgment.

Kinsey and his followers, for example, clearly thought (and think) the more sex the better. Accordingly, they trivialize even most of those cases of rape and child sexual abuse they discern as such, decry women's sexual refusal as sexual inhibition, and repeatedly interpret women's sexual disinclination as "restrictions" on men's natural sexual activity, which left alone would emulate (some) animals.[13] Followers of the neo-Freudian derepression imperative have similarly identified the frontier of sexual freedom with transgression of social restraints on access, with making the sexually disallowed allowed, especially male sexual access to anything. The struggle to have everything sexual allowed in a society we are told would collapse if it were, creates a sense of resistance to, and an

of Sexual Violence in the Best-Selling Erotic Magazines," *Journal of Sex Research* 16 (1980): 5. See also B. Ollman's discussion of Wilhelm Reich in *Social and Sexual Revolution* (Boston: South End Press, 1979), pp. 186–87.

12. The contributions and limitations of Foucault in such an analysis are discussed illuminatingly in Frigga Haug, ed., *Female Sexualization*, trans. Erica Carter (London: Verso, 1987), pp. 190–98.

13. A. Kinsey, W. Pomeroy, C. Martin, and P. Gebhard, *Sexual Behaviour in the Human Female* (Philadelphia: W. B. Saunders, 1953); A. Kinsey, W. Pomeroy, and C. Martin, *Sexual Behaviour in the Human Male* (Philadelphia: W. B. Saunders, 1948). See the critique of Kinsey in Dworkin, *Pornography* (see Appendix), pp. 179–98.

aura of danger around, violating the powerless. If we knew the boundaries were phony, existed only to eroticize the targeted transgressable, would penetrating them feel less sexy? Taboo and crime may serve to eroticize what would otherwise feel about as much like dominance as taking candy from a baby. Assimilating actual powerlessness to male prohibition, to male power, provides the appearance of resistance, which makes over-coming possible, while never undermining the reality of power, or its dignity, by giving the powerless actual power. The point is, allowed/not-allowed become the ideological axes along which sexuality is experienced when and because sex, hence gender, is about power.

One version of the derepression hypothesis that purports feminism is: civilization having been male-dominated, female sexuality has been repressed, not allowed. Sexuality as such still centers on what would otherwise be considered the reproductive act, on intercourse: penetration of the erect penis into the vagina (or appropriate substitute orifices) followed by thrusting to male ejaculation. If reproduction actually had anything to do with what sex was for, it would not happen every night (or even twice a week) for forty or fifty years, nor would prostitutes exist. "We had sex three times" typically means the man entered the woman three times and orgasmed three times. Female sexuality in this model refers to the presence of this theory's 'sexuality,' or the desire to be so treated, in biological females; 'female' is somewhere between an adjective and a noun, half possessive and half biological ascription. Sexual freedom means women being allowed to behave as freely as men to express this sexuality, to have it allowed, that is, to (hopefully) shamelessly and without social constraints initiate genital drive satisfaction through heterosexual intercourse.[14] Hence, the liberated woman. Hence, the sexual revolution.

The pervasiveness of such assumptions about sexuality throughout otherwise diverse methodological traditions is suggested by the following comment by a scholar of violence against women: "If women were to escape the culturally stereotyped role of disinterest in and resistance to sex and to take on an assertive role in expressing their own sexuality, rather than leaving it to the assertiveness of men, it would contribute to

---

14. Examples include: D. English, "The Politics of Porn: Can Feminists Walk the Line?" *Mother Jones* (1980), pp. 20–23, 43–44, 48–50; D. English, A. Hollibaugh, and G. Rubin, "Talking Sex: A Conversation on Sexuality and Feminism," *Socialist Review*, vol. 11 (1981); J. B. Elshtain, "The Victim Syndrome: A Troubling Turn in Feminism," *Progressive* (1982), pp. 40–47; Ellen Willis, "Feminism, Moralism, and Pornography," *Village Voice* (1979). This approach also tends to characterize the basic ideology of "Human Sexuality Courses" as analyzed by C. Vance in Snitow, Stansell, and Thompson, eds., pp. 371–84. The view of sex so promulgated is distilled in the following quotation and taught to doctors through *Materials from Courses on Human Sexuality*. After an alliterative list, perhaps intended to be humorous, headed "determinants of sexuality" (on which "power" does not appear, although every other word begins with "p") appears: "Persistent puritanical pressures promoting propriety, purity, and prudery are opposed by a powerful, primeval, procreative passion to plunge his pecker into her pussy" (College of Medicine and Dentistry of New Jersey, Rutgers Medical School, January 29–February 2, 1979, p. 39).

the reduction of rape. . . . First, and most obviously, voluntary sex would be available to more men, thus reducing the 'need' for rape. Second, and probably more important, it would help to reduce the confounding of sex and aggression."[15] In this view, somebody must be assertive for sex to happen. Voluntary sex—sexual equality—means equal sexual aggression. If women freely expressed "their own sexuality," more heterosexual intercourse would be initiated. Women's "resistance" to sex is an imposed cultural stereotype, not a form of political struggle. Rape is occasioned by women's resistance not by men's force; or, male force, hence rape, is created by women's resistance to sex. Men would rape less if they got more voluntarily compliant sex from women. Corollary: the force in rape is not sexual to men.

Underlying this quotation lurks the view, as common as it is tacit, that if women would just accept the contact men now have to rape to get—if women would stop resisting or (in one of the pornographers' favorite scenarios) become sexual aggressors—rape would wither away. On one level, this is a definitionally obvious truth. When a woman accepts what would be a rape if she did not accept it, what happens is sex. If women were to accept forced sex as sex, "voluntary sex would be available to more men." If such a view is not implicit in this text, it is a mystery how women equally aggressing against men sexually would eliminate, rather than double, the confounding of sex and aggression. Without such an assumption, only the confounding of sexual aggression with gender would be eliminated. If women don't resist male sexual aggression anymore, the confounding of sex with aggression would, indeed, be so epistemologically complete that it would be eliminated. No woman would ever be sexually violated because sexual violation would be sex. The situation might resemble that evoked by a society Sanday categorized as "rape-free" in part because the men assert there is no rape there: "Our women never resist."[16] Such pacification also occurs in "rape-prone" societies like the United States, where some force may be perceived as force but only above certain threshold standards.[17]

15. A third reason is also given: "To the extent that sexism in societal and family structure is responsible for the phenomena of 'compulsive masculinity' and structured antagonism between the sexes, the elimination of sexual inequality would reduce the number of 'power trip' and 'degradation ceremony' motivated rapes" (M. Straus, "Sexual Inequality, Cultural Norms, and Wife-beating," *Victimology: An International Journal* 1 [1976]: 54–76). Note that these structural factors seem to be considered nonsexual, in the sense that "power trip" and "degradation ceremony" motivated rapes are treated as not erotic to the perpetrators *because* of the elements of dominance and degradation, nor is "structured antagonism" seen as an erotic element of rape or sex (or family).

16. P. R. Sanday, "The Socio-cultural Context of Rape: A Cross-cultural Study," *Journal of Social Issues* 37 (1981): 16. See also M. Lewin, "Unwanted Intercourse: The Difficulty of Saying 'No,' " *Psychology of Women Quarterly* 9 (1985): 184–92.

17. See Catharine A. MacKinnon, *Toward a Feminist Theory of the State* (Cambridge, Mass.: Harvard University Press, 1989), chap. 9 for discussion.

While intending the opposite, some feminists have encouraged and participated in this type of analysis by conceiving rape as violence not sex.[18] While this approach gave needed emphasis to rape's previously effaced elements of power and dominance, it obscured its elements of sex. Aside from failing to answer the rather obvious question, if it's violence not sex why didn't he just hit her, this approach made it impossible to see that violence is sex when it is practiced as sex.[19] This is obvious once what sexuality is, is understood as a matter of what it means, of how it is interpreted. To say rape is violence not sex preserves the "sex is good" norm by simply distinguishing forced sex as "not sex," whether it means sex to the perpetrator or even, later, to the victim, who has difficulty experiencing sex without reexperiencing the rape. Whatever is sex, cannot be violent; whatever is violent, cannot be sex. This analytic wish-fulfillment makes it possible for rape to be opposed by those who would save sexuality from the rapists while leaving the sexual fundamentals of male dominance intact.

While much prior work on rape has analyzed it as a problem of inequality between the sexes but not as a problem of unequal sexuality on the basis of gender,[20] other contemporary explorations of sexuality that purport to be feminist lack comprehension either of gender as a form of social power or of the realities of sexual violence. For instance, the editors of *Powers of Desire* take sex "as a central form of expression, one that defines identity and is seen as a primary source of energy and pleasure."[21] This may be how it "is seen" but it is also how they, operatively, see it. As if women choose sexuality as definitive of identity. As if it is as much a form of women's "expression" as it is men's. As if violation and abuse are not equally central to sexuality as women live it.

The *Diary* of the Barnard conference on sexuality pervasively equates sexuality with 'pleasure.' "Perhaps the overall question we need to ask is: How do women . . . negotiate sexual pleasure?"[22] As if women under male supremacy have power to. As if "negotiation" is a form of freedom.

18. Brownmiller, *Against Our Will* (see Appendix), originated this approach, which has since become ubiquitous.

19. Annie McCombs helped me express this thought (letter to *off our backs* [1984], p. 34).

20. Brownmiller did analyze rape as something men do to women, hence as a problem of gender, even if her concept of gender is biologically based (see, e.g., her pp. 4, 6, and discussion in chap. 3). An exception is Clark and Lewis (see Appendix).

21. Snitow, Stansell, and Thompson (n. 8 above), p. 9.

22. C. Vance, "Concept Paper: Toward a Politics of Sexuality," in H. Alderfer, B. Jaker, and M. Nelson, eds., *Diary of a Conference on Sexuality*, record of the planning committee of the Conference, the Scholar and the Feminist IX: Toward a Politics of Sexuality, April 24, 1982, p. 27: to address "women's sexual pleasure, choice, and autonomy, acknowledging that sexuality is simultaneously a domain of restriction, repression and danger as well as a domain of exploration, pleasure and agency." Parts of the *Diary*, with the conference papers, were later published. C. Vance, ed., *Pleasure and Danger: Exploring Female Sexuality* (London: Routledge & Kegan Paul, 1984).

As if pleasure and how to get it, rather than dominance and how to end it, is the "overall" issue sexuality presents feminism. As if women do just need a good fuck. In these texts, taboos are treated as real restrictions—as things that really are not allowed—instead of as guises under which hierarchy is eroticized. The domain of the sexual is divided into "restriction, repression and danger" on the one hand and "exploration, pleasure and agency" on the other.[23] This division parallels the ideological forms through which dominance and submission are eroticized, variously socially coded as heterosexuality's male/female, lesbian culture's butch/femme, and sadomasochism's top/bottom.[24] Speaking in role terms, the one who pleasures in the illusion of freedom and security within the reality of danger is the "girl"; the one who pleasures in the reality of freedom and security within the illusion of danger is the "boy." That is, the *Diary* uncritically adopts as an analytical tool the central dynamic of the phenomenon it purports to be analyzing. Presumably, one is to have a sexual experience of the text.

The terms of these discourses preclude or evade crucial feminist questions. What do sexuality and gender inequality have to do with each other? How do dominance and submission become sexualized, or, why is hierarchy sexy? How does it get attached to male and female? Why does sexuality center on intercourse, the reproductive act by physical design? Is masculinity the enjoyment of violation, femininity the enjoyment of being violated? Is that the central meaning of intercourse? Why do "men love death"?[25] What is the etiology of heterosexuality in women? Is its pleasure women's stake in subordination?

Taken together and taken seriously, feminist inquiries into the realities of rape, battery, sexual harassment, incest, child sexual abuse, prostitution, and pornography answer these questions by suggesting a theory of the sexual mechanism. Its script, learning, conditioning, developmental logos, imprinting of the microdot, its deus ex machina, whatever sexual process term defines sexual arousal itself, is force, power's expression. Force is sex, not just sexualized; force is the desire dynamic, not just a response to the desired object when desire's expression is frustrated. Pressure, gender socialization, withholding benefits, extending indulgences, the how-to books, the sex therapy are the soft end; the fuck, the fist, the street, the chains, the poverty are the hard end. Hostility and contempt, or arousal of master to slave, together with awe and vulnerability, or arousal of slave to master—these are the emotions of this sexuality's excitement. "Sadomasochism is to sex what war is to civil life: the mag-

---

23. Vance, "Concept Paper," p. 38.

24. For examples, see A. Hollibaugh and C. Moraga, "What We're Rolling around in Bed with: Sexual Silences in Feminism," in Snitow, Stansell, and Thompson, eds., pp. 394–405, esp. 398; Samois, *Coming to Power* (Berkeley, Calif.: Samois, 1983).

25. A. Dworkin, "Why So-called Radical Men Love and Need Pornography," in Lederer, ed. (see Appendix), p. 48.

nificent experience," writes Susan Sontag.[26] "It is hostility—the desire, overt or hidden, to harm another person—that generates and enhances sexual excitement," writes Robert Stoller.[27] Harriet Jacobs, a slave, speaking of her systematic rape by her master, writes, "It seems less demeaning to give one's self, than to submit to compulsion."[28] Looking at the data, the force in sex and the sex in force is a matter of simple empirical description—unless one accepts that force in sex is not force anymore, it is just sex; or, if whenever a woman is forced it is what she really wants or it or she does not matter; or, unless prior aversion or sentimentality substitutes what one wants sex to be, or will condone or countenance as sex, for what is actually happening.

To be clear: what is sexual is what gives a man an erection. Whatever it takes to make a penis shudder and stiffen with the experience of its potency is what sexuality means culturally. Whatever else does, fear does, hostility does, hatred does, the helplessness of a child or a student or an infantilized or restrained or vulnerable woman does, revulsion does, death does. Hierarchy, a constant creation of person/thing, top/bottom, dominance/subordination relations, does. What is understood as violation, conventionally penetration and intercourse, defines the paradigmatic sexual encounter. The scenario of sexual abuse is: you do what I say. These textualities become sexuality. All this suggests that that which is called sexuality is the dynamic of control by which male dominance—in forms that range from intimate to institutional, from a look to a rape—eroticizes as man and woman, as identity and pleasure. It is also that which maintains and defines male supremacy as a political system. Male sexual desire is thereby simultaneously created and serviced, never satisfied once and for all, while male force is romanticized, even sacralized, potentiated, and naturalized, by being submerged into sex itself.

In contemporary philosophical terms, nothing is "indeterminate" in the post-structuralist sense here; it is all too determinate.[29] Nor does its reality provide just one perspective on a relativistic interpersonal world

26. S. Sontag, "Fascinating Fascism," in her *Under the Sign of Saturn* (New York: Farrar, Straus & Giroux, 1975), p. 103.

27. R. Stoller, *Sexual Excitement: Dynamics of Erotic Life* (New York: Pantheon, 1979), p. 6.

28. Harriet Jacobs, quoted by Rennie Simson, "The Afro-American Female: The Historical Context of the Construction of Sexual Identity," in Snitow, Stansell, and Thompson, eds., p. 231. Jacobs subsequently resisted by hiding in an attic cubbyhole "almost deprived of light and air, and with no space to move my limbs, for nearly seven years" to avoid him.

29. A similar rejection of indeterminacy can be found in Linda Alcoff, "Cultural Feminism versus Post-Structuralism: The Identity Crisis in Feminist Theory," *Signs: Journal of Women in Culture and Society* 13 (1988): 419–20. The article otherwise misdiagnoses the division in feminism as that between so-called cultural feminists and post-structuralism, when the division is between those who take sexual misogyny seriously as a mainspring to gender hierarchy and those who wish, liberal-fashion, to affirm "differences" without seeing that sameness/difference is a dichotomy of exactly the sort post-structuralism purports to deconstruct.

that could mean anything or its opposite.[30] The reality of pervasive sexual abuse and its erotization does not shift relative to perspective, although whether or not one will see it or accord it significance may. Interpretation varies relative to place in sexual abuse, certainly; but the fact that women are sexually abused as women, in a social matrix of sexualized subordination does not go away because it is often ignored or authoritatively disbelieved or interpreted out of existence. Indeed, some ideological supports for its persistence rely precisely upon techniques of social indeterminancy: no language but the obscene to describe the unspeakable; denial by the powerful casting doubt on the facticity of the injuries; actually driving its victims insane. Indeterminacy is a neo-Cartesian mind game that undermines the actual social meaning of words by raising acontextualized interpretive possibilities that have no real social meaning or real possibility of any, dissolving the ability to criticize actual meanings without making space for new ones. The feminist point is simple. Men are women's material conditions. If it happens to women, it happens.

Women often find ways to resist male supremacy and to expand their spheres of action. But they are never free of it. Women also embrace the standards of women's place in this regime as "our own" to varying degrees and in varying voices—as affirmation of identity and right to pleasure, in order to be loved and approved and paid, in order just to make it through another day. This, not inert passivity, is the meaning of being a victim.[31] The term is not moral: who is to blame or to be pitied or condemned or held responsible. It is not prescriptive: what we should do next. It is not strategic: how to construe the situation so it can be changed. It is not emotional: what one feels better thinking. It is descriptive: who does what to whom and gets away with it?

Thus the question Freud never asked is the question that defines sexuality in a feminist perspective: What do men want? Pornography provides an answer. Pornography permits men to have whatever they want sexually. It is their "truth about sex."[32] It connects the centrality of visual objectification to both male sexual arousal and male models of knowledge and verification, connecting objectivity with objectification. It shows how men see the world, how in seeing it they access and possess it, and how this is an act of dominance over it. It shows what men want and gives it to them. From the testimony of the pornography, what men want is: women bound, women battered, women tortured, women hu-

30. See Sandra Harding, "Introduction: Is There a Feminist Methodology?" in *Feminism and Methodology*, ed. Sandra Harding (Bloomington: Indiana University Press, 1987).

31. One of the most compelling accounts of active victim behavior is provided in *Give Sorrow Words: Maryse Holder's Letters from Mexico* (New York: Grove Press, 1979). Holder wrote a woman friend of her daily frantic, and always failing pursuit of men, sex, beauty, and feeling good about herself. "Fuck fucking, will *feel* self-respect" (p. 89). She was murdered soon after by an unknown assailant.

32. This phrase comes from M. Foucault, "The West and the Truth of Sex," *Sub-stance* (1978), p. 20. The ironic meaning given to it here is mine.

miliated, women degraded and defiled, women killed. Or, to be fair to
the soft core, women sexually accessible, have-able, there for them, wanting
to be taken and used, with perhaps just a little light bondage. Each
violation of women—rape, battery, prostitution, child sexual abuse, sexual
harassment—is made sexuality, made sexy, fun, and liberating of women's
true nature in the pornography. Each specifically victimized and vulnerable
group of women, each tabooed target group—black women, Asian women,
Latin women, Jewish women, pregnant women, disabled women, retarded
women, poor women, old women, fat women, women in women's jobs,
prostitutes, little girls—distinguishes pornographic genres and subthemes,
classified according to diverse customers' favorite degradation. Women
are made into and coupled with anything considered lower than human:
animals, objects, children, and (yes) other women. Anything women have
claimed as their own—motherhood, athletics, traditional men's jobs, les-
bianism, feminism—is made specifically sexy, dangerous, provocative,
punished, made men's in pornography.

Pornography is a means through which sexuality is socially constructed,
a site of construction, a domain of exercise. It constructs women as things
for sexual use and constructs its consumers to desperately want women
to desperately want possession and cruelty and dehumanization. Inequality
itself, subjection itself, hierarchy itself, objectification itself, with self-
determination ecstatically relinquished, is the apparent content of women's
sexual desire and desirability. "The major theme of pornography as a
genre," writes Andrea Dworkin, "is male power."[33] Women are in pornography to be violated and taken, men to violate and take them, either
on screen or by camera or pen, on behalf of the viewer. Not that sexuality
in life or in media never expresses love and affection; only that love and
affection are not what is sexualized in this society's actual sexual paradigm,
as pornography testifies to it. Violation of the powerless, intrusion on
women, is. The milder forms, possession and use, the mildest of which
is visual objectification, are. The sexuality of observation, visual intrusion
and access, of entertainment, makes sex largely a spectator sport for its
participants.

If pornography has not become sex to and from the male point of
view, it is hard to explain why the pornography industry makes a known
ten billion dollars a year selling it as sex mostly to men; why it is used
to teach sex to child prostitutes, recalcitrant wives and girlfriends and
daughters, and to medical students, and to sex offenders; why it is nearly
universally classified as a subdivision of "erotic literature"; why it is protected
and defended as if it were sex itself.[34] And why a prominent sexologist

33. Dworkin, *Pornography* (see Appendix), p. 24.
34. J. Cook, "The X-rated Economy," *Forbes* (1978), p. 18; Langelan (see Appendix),
p. 5; *Public Hearings on Ordinances to Add Pornography as Discrimination against Women,*
Minneapolis, Minnesota: December 12 and 13, 1983 (hereafter cited as *Public Hearings*);
F. Schauer, "Response: Pornography and the First Amendment," *University of Pittsburgh
Law Review* 40 (1979): 616.

fears that enforcing the views of feminists against pornography in society would make men "erotically inert wimps."[35] No pornography, no male sexuality.

A feminist critique of sexuality in this sense is advanced in Andrea Dworkin's *Pornography: Men Possessing Women*. Building on her earlier identification of gender inequality as a system of social meaning,[36] an ideology lacking basis in anything other than the social reality its power constructs and maintains, she argues that sexuality is a construct of that power, given meaning by, through, and in pornography. In this perspective, pornography is not harmless fantasy or a corrupt and confused misrepresentation of otherwise natural healthy sex, nor is it fundamentally a distortion, reflection, projection, expression, representation, fantasy, or symbol of it.[37] Through pornography, among other practices, gender inequality becomes both sexual and socially real. Pornography "reveals that male pleasure is inextricably tied to victimizing, hurting, exploiting."[38] "Dominance in the male system is pleasure."[39] Rape is "the defining paradigm of sexuality,"[40] to avoid which boys choose manhood and homophobia.[41]

Women, who are not given a choice, are objectified, or, rather, "the object is allowed to desire, if she desires to be an object."[42] Psychology sets the proper bounds of this objectification by terming its improper excesses "fetishism,"[43] distinguishing the uses from the abuses of women. Dworkin shows how the process and content of women's definition as women, an underclass, are the process and content of their sexualization as objects for male sexual use. The mechanism is (again) force, imbued

35. John Money, professor of Medical Psychology and Pediatrics, Johns Hopkins Medical Institutions, letter to Clive M. Davis, April 18, 1984. The same view is expressed by Al Goldstein, editor of *Screw*, a pornographic newspaper, concerning anti-pornography feminists, termed "nattering nabobs of sexual negativism": "We must repeat to ourselves like a mantra: sex is good; nakedness is a joy; an erection is beautiful. . . . Don't let the bastards get you limp" ("Dear Playboy," *Playboy* [1985], p. 12).

36. A. Dworkin, "The Root Cause," in *Our Blood: Prophesies and Discourses on Sexual Politics* (New York: Harper & Row, 1976), pp. 96–111.

37. See MacKinnon, *Toward a Feminist Theory of the State* (n. 17 above), chap. 12 for further discussion.

38. Dworkin, *Pornography* (Appendix), p. 69.

39. Ibid., p. 136.

40. Ibid., p. 69. "In practice, fucking is an act of possession—simultaneously an act of ownership, taking, force; it is conquering; it expresses in intimacy power over and against, body to body, person to thing. 'The sex act' means penile intromission followed by penile thrusting, or fucking. The woman is acted on, the man acts and through action expresses sexual power, the power of masculinity. Fucking requires that the male act on one who has less power and this valuation is so deep, so completely implicit in the act, that the one who is fucked is stigmatized as feminine during the act even when not anatomically female. In the male system, sex is the penis, the penis is sexual power, its use in fucking is manhood" (p. 23).

41. Ibid., chap. 2, "Men and Boys."

42. Ibid., p. 109.

43. Ibid., pp. 113–28.

with meaning because it is the means to death[44] and death is the ultimate sexual act, the ultimate making of a person into a thing.

Why, one wonders at this point, is intercourse "sex" at all? In pornography, conventional intercourse is one act among many; penetration is crucial but can be done with anything; penis is crucial but not necessarily in the vagina. Actual pregnancy is a minor subgeneric theme, about as important in pornography as reproduction is in rape. Thematically, intercourse is incidental in pornography, especially when compared with force, which is primary. From pornography one learns that forcible violation of women is the essence of sex. Whatever is that and does that is sex. Everything else is secondary. Perhaps the reproductive act is considered sexual because it is considered an act of forcible violation and defilement of the female distinctively as such, not because it 'is' sex a priori.

To be sexually objectified means having a social meaning imposed on your being that defines you as to be sexually used, according to your desired uses, and then using you that way. Doing this is sex in the male system. Pornography is a sexual practice of this because it exists in a social system in which sex in life is no less mediated than it is in representation. There is no irreducible essence, no "just sex." If sex is a social construct of sexism, men have sex with their image of a woman. Pornography creates an accessible sexual object, the possession and consumption of which is male sexuality, to be possessed and consumed as which is female sexuality. This is not because pornography depicts objectified sex but because it creates the experience of a sexuality which is itself objectified. The appearance of choice or consent, with their attribution to inherent nature, are crucial in concealing the reality of force. Love of violation, variously termed female masochism and consent,[45] comes to

44. Ibid., p. 174.

45. Freud believed that the female nature was inherently masochistic (S. Freud, "The Psychology of Women," in his *New Introductory Lectures on Psychoanalysis* [London: Hogarth Press, 1933], chap. 23). Helene Deutsch, Marie Bonaparte, Sandor Rado, Adolf Grunberger, Melanie Klein, Helle Thorning, George Battaille, Theodore Reik, Jean-Paul Sartre, and Simone de Beauvoir all described some version of female masochism in their work, each with a different theoretical account for virtually identical observations. H. Deutsch, "The Significance of Masochism in the Mental Life of Women," *International Journal of Psychoanalysis* 11 (1930): 48–60; *Psychology of Women* (New York: Grune & Stratton, 1944), vol. 1. Several are summarized by Janine Chasseguet-Smirgel, ed., in her introduction to *Female Sexuality: New Psychoanalytic Views* (London: Virago, 1981); Theodore Reik, *Masochism in Sex and Society* (New York: Grove Press, 1962), p. 217; Helle Thorning, "The Mother-Daughter Relationship and Sexual Ambivalence," *Heresies* 12 (1979): 3–6; Georges Bataille, *Death and Sensuality* (New York: Walker & Co., 1962); Jean-Paul Sartre, *Being and Nothingness: An Essay on Phenomenological Ontology*, trans. Hazel E. Barnes (New York: Philosophical Library, 1956), pt. 3, chap. 3, "Concrete Relations with Others," pp. 361–430. Betsy Belote states, "Masochistic and hysterical behavior is so similar to the concept of 'femininity' that the three are not clearly distinguishable" ("Masochistic Syndrome, Hysterical Personality, and the Illusion of the Healthy Woman," in *Female Psychology: The Emerging Self*, ed. Sue Cox [Chicago: Science Research Associates, 1976], p. 347). I was directed to these sources by Sandra Lee Bartky's valuable examination, "Feminine Masochism and the Politics of

define female sexuality, legitimizing this political system by concealing the force on which it is based.

In this system, a victim, usually female, always feminized, is "never forced, only actualized."[46] Women whose attributes particularly fixate men—such as women with large breasts—are seen as full of sexual desire. Women men want, want men. Women fake vaginal orgasms, the only 'mature' sexuality, because men demand that they enjoy vaginal penetration.[47] Raped women are seen as asking for it: if a man wanted her, she must have wanted him. Men force women to become sexual objects, "that thing which causes erection, then hold themselves helpless and powerless when aroused by her."[48] Men who sexually harass, say women sexually harass them. They mean they are aroused by women who turn them down. This elaborate projective system of demand characteristics—taken to pinnacles like fantasizing a clitoris in women's throats[49] so that men can enjoy forced fellatio in real life assured that women do too—is surely a delusional and projective structure deserving of serious psychological study. Instead, it is women who resist it that are studied, seen as in need of explanation and adjustment, stigmatized as inhibited and repressed and asexual. The assumption that, in matters sexual, women really want what men want from women makes male force against women in sex invisible. It makes rape sex. Women's sexual "reluctance, dislike, and frigidity," women's puritanism and prudery in the face of this sex, is the "silent rebellion of women against the force of the penis . . . an ineffective rebellion, but a rebellion nonetheless."[50]

Nor is homosexuality without stake in this gendered sexual system. Putting to one side the obviously gendered content of expressly adopted roles, clothing, and sexual mimicry, to the extent the gender of a sexual object is crucial to arousal, the structure of social power that stands behind and defines gender is hardly irrelevant, even if it is rearranged. Some have argued that lesbian sexuality—meaning here simply women having sex with women not men—solves the problem of gender by

---

Personal Transformation," *Women's Studies International Forum* 7 (1984): 327–28. Andrea Dworkin writes: "I believe that freedom for women must begin in the repudiation of our own masochism. . . . I believe that ridding ourselves of our own deeply entrenched masochism, which takes so many tortured forms, is the first priority; it is the first deadly blow that we can strike against systematized male dominance" (*Our Blood* [n. 36 above], p. 111).

46. Dworkin, *Pornography* (Appendix), p. 146.

47. A. Koedt, "The Myth of the Vaginal Orgasm," *Notes from the Second Year: Women's Liberation*, vol. 2 (1970); Ti-Grace Atkinson, *Amazon Odyssey* (New York: Link Books, 1974); Phelps (see Appendix).

48. Dworkin, *Pornography* (Appendix), p. 22.

49. This is the plot of *Deep Throat*, the pornographic film Linda "Lovelace" was forced to make. It is reportedly the largest grossing film in the history of the world. That this plot is apparently so widely enjoyed suggests that something extant in the male psyche is appealed to by it.

50. Dworkin, "The Root Cause," p. 56.

eliminating men from women's voluntary sexual encounters.[51] Yet women's sexuality remains constructed under conditions of male supremacy; women remain socially defined as women in relation to men; the definition of women as men's inferiors remains sexual even if not heterosexual, whether men are present at the time or not. To the extent gay men choose men because they are men, the meaning of masculinity is affirmed as well as undermined. It may also be that sexuality is so gender marked that it carries dominance and submission with it, no matter the gender of its participants.

Each structural requirement of this sexuality as revealed in pornography is professed in recent defenses of sadomasochism, described by proponents as that sexuality in which "the basic dynamic . . . is the power dichotomy."[52] Exposing the prohibitory underpinnings on which this violation model of the sexual depends, one advocate says, "We select the most frightening, disgusting or unacceptable activities and transmute them into pleasure." The relational dynamics of sadomasochism do not even negate the paradigm of male dominance, but conform precisely to it: the ecstasy in domination ("I like to hear someone ask for mercy or protection"); the enjoyment of inflicting psychological as well as physical torture ("I want to see the confusion, the anger, the turn-on, the helplessness"); the expression of belief in the inferior's superiority belied by the absolute contempt ("the bottom must be my superior . . . playing a bottom who did not demand my respect and admiration would be like eating rotten fruit"); the degradation and consumption of women through sex ("she feeds me the energy I need to dominate and abuse her"); the health and personal growth rationale ("it's a healing process"); the anti-puritan radical therapy justification ("I was taught to dread sex. . . . It is shocking and profoundly satisfying to commit this piece of rebellion, to take pleasure exactly as I want it, to exact it like tribute"); the bipolar doublethink in which the top enjoys "sexual service" while the "will to please is the bottom's source of pleasure." And the same bottom line of all top-down sex: "I want to be in control." The statements are from a female sadist. The good news is, it's not biological.

As pornography connects sexuality with gender in social reality, the feminist critique of pornography connects feminist work on violence against women with its inquiry into women's consciousness and gender roles. It is not only that women are the principal targets of rape, which by conservative definition happens to almost half of all women at least once in their lives. It is not only that over a third of all women are sexually molested by older trusted male family members or friends or authority figures as an early, perhaps initiatory, interpersonal sexual

51. A prominent if dated example is Jill Johnston, *Lesbian Nation* (New York: Simon & Schuster, 1974).
52. This and the rest of the quotations in this paragraph are from P. Califia, "A Secret Side of Lesbian Sexuality," *Advocate* (December 27, 1979), pp. 19–21, 27–28.

encounter. It is not only that at least the same percentage as adult women are battered in homes by male intimates. It is not only that about a fifth of American women have been or are known to be prostitutes, and most cannot get out of it. It is not only that 85 percent of working women will be sexually harassed on the job, many physically, at some point in their working lives.[53] All this documents the extent and terrain of abuse and the effectively unrestrained and systematic sexual aggression of one-half of the population against the other half. It suggests that it is basically allowed.

It does not by itself show that availability for this treatment defines the identity attributed to that other half of the population; or, that such treatment, all this torment and debasement, is socially considered not only rightful but enjoyable, and is in fact enjoyed by the dominant half; or, that the ability to engage in such behaviors defines the identity of that half. And not only of that half. Now consider the content of gender roles. All the social requirements for male sexual arousal and satisfaction are identical to the gender definition of "female." All the essentials of the male gender role are also the qualities sexualized as 'male' in male dominant sexuality. If gender is a social construct, and sexuality is a social construct, and the question is, of what is each constructed, the fact that their contents are identical—not to mention that the word 'sex' refers to both—might be more than a coincidence.

As to gender, what is sexual about pornography is what is unequal about social life. To say that pornography sexualizes gender and genders sexuality means that it provides a concrete social process through which gender and sexuality become functions of each other. Gender and sexuality, in this view, become two different shapes taken by the single social equation of male with dominance and female with submission. Being this as identity, acting it as role, inhabiting and presenting it as self, is the domain of gender. Enjoying it as the erotic, centering upon when it elicits genital arousal, is the domain of sexuality. Inequality is what is sexualized through pornography; it is what is sexual about it. The more unequal, the more sexual. The violence against women in pornography is an expression of gender hierarchy, the extremity of the hierarchy expressed and created through the extremity of the abuse, producing the extremity of the male sexual response. Pornography's multiple variations on and departures from the male dominant/female submissive sexual/gender theme are not exceptions to these gender regularities. They affirm them. The capacity of gender reversals (dominatrixes) and inversions (homosexuality) to stimulate sexual excitement is derived precisely from their mimicry or parody or negation or reversal of the standard arrangement. This affirms rather than undermines or qualifies the standard sexual arrangement as

---

53. The statistics in this paragraph are drawn from the sources referenced in the Appendix, as categorized by topic. Kathleen Barry (see Appendix) defines "female sexual slavery" as a condition of prostitution that one cannot get out of.

the standard sexual arrangement, the definition of sex, the standard from which all else is defined, that in which sexuality as such inheres.

Such formal data as exist on the relationship between pornography and male sexual arousal tend to substantiate this connection between gender hierarchy and male sexuality. 'Normal' men viewing pornography over time in laboratory settings become more aroused to scenes of rape than to scenes of explicit but not expressly violent sex, even if (especially if?) the woman is shown as hating it.[54] As sustained exposure perceptually inures subjects to the violent component in expressly violent sexual material, its sexual arousal value remains or increases. "On the first day, when they see women being raped and aggressed against, it bothers them. By day five, it does not bother them at all, in fact, they enjoy it."[55] Sexual material that is seen as nonviolent, by contrast, is less arousing to begin with, becomes even less arousing over time,[56] after which exposure to sexual violence is sexually arousing.[57] Viewing sexual material containing express aggression against women makes normal men more willing to aggress against women.[58] It also makes them see a woman rape victim

54. E. Donnerstein, testimony, *Public Hearings* (see n. 34 above), pp. 35–36. The relationship between consenting and nonconsenting depictions and sexual arousal among men with varying self-reported propensities to rape are examined in the following studies: N. Malamuth, "Rape Fantasies as a Function of Exposure to Violent-Sexual Stimuli," *Archives of Sexual Behavior* 6 (1977): 33–47; N. Malamuth and J. Check, "Penile Tumescence and Perceptual Responses to Rape as a Function of Victim's Perceived Reactions," *Journal of Applied Social Psychology* 10 (1980): 528–47; N. Malamuth, M. Heim, and S. Feshbach, "The Sexual Responsiveness of College Students to Rape Depictions: Inhibitory and Dis-inhibitory Effects," *Journal of Personality and Social Psychology* 38 (1980): 399–408; N. Malamuth and J. Check, "Sexual Arousal to Rape and Consenting Depictions: The Importance of the Woman's Arousal," *Journal of Abnormal Psychology* 39 (1980): 763–66; N. Malamuth, "Rape Proclivity among Males," *Journal of Social Issues* 37 (1981): 138–57; E. Donnerstein and L. Berkowitz, "Victim Reactions in Aggressive Erotic Films as a Factor in Violence against Women," *Journal of Personality and Social Psychology* 41 (1981): 710–24; J. Check and T. Guloien, "Reported Proclivity for Coercive Sex Following Repeated Exposure to Sexually Violent Pornography, Nonviolent Dehumanizing Pornography, and Erotica," in *Pornography: Recent Research, Interpretations, and Policy Considerations*, ed. D. Zillman and J. Bryant (Hillsdale, N.J.: Erlbaum, in press).

55. Donnerstein, testimony, *Public Hearings*, p. 36.

56. The soporific effects of explicit sex depicted without express violence are apparent in the *Report of the President's Commission on Obscenity and Pornography* (Washington, D.C.: Government Printing Office, 1971).

57. Donnerstein, testimony, *Public Hearings*, p. 36.

58. Donnerstein and Berkowitz (see n. 54 above); E. Donnerstein, "Pornography: Its Effect on Violence against Women," in Malamuth and Donnerstein, eds. (Appendix). This conclusion is the cumulative result of years of experimental research showing that "if you can measure sexual arousal to sexual images and measure people's attitudes about rape you can predict aggressive behavior with women" (Donnerstein, testimony, *Public Hearings*, p. 29). Some of the more prominent supporting experimental work, in addition to citations previously referenced here, include E. Donnerstein and J. Hallam, "The Facilitating Effects of Erotica on Aggression toward Females," *Journal of Personality and Social Psychology* 36 (1978): 1270–77; R. G. Green, D. Stonner, and G. L. Shope, "The Facilitation of Aggression by Aggression: Evidence against the Catharsis Hypothesis," *Journal of Personality and Social*

as less human, more object-like, less worthy, less injured, and more to blame for the rape. Sexually explicit material that is not seen as expressly violent but presents women as hysterically responsive to male sexual demands, in which women are verbally abused, dominated and degraded, and treated as sexual things, makes men twice as likely to report willingness to sexually aggress against women than they were before exposure. So-called nonviolent materials like these make men see women as less than human, as good only for sex, as objects, as worthless and blameworthy when raped, and as really wanting to be raped and as unequal to men.[59] As to material showing violence only, it might be expected that rapists would be sexually aroused to scenes of violence against women, and they are.[60] But many normal male subjects, too, when seeing a woman being aggressed against by a man, perceive the interaction to be sexual even if no sex is shown.[61]

Male sexuality is apparently activated by violence against women and expresses itself in violence against women to a significant extent. If violence is seen as occupying the most fully achieved end of a dehumanization continuum on which objectification occupies the least express

---

Psychology 31 (1975): 721–26; D. Zillman, J. Hoyt, and K. Day, "Strength and Duration of the Effects of Aggressive, Violent, and Erotic Communications on Subsequent Aggressive Behavior," *Communications Research* 1 (1974): 286–306; B. Sapolsky and D. Zillman, "The Effect of Soft-core and Hard-core Erotica on Provoked and Unprovoked Hostile Behavior," *Journal of Sex Research* 17 (1981): 319–43; D. L. Mosher, "Pornographic Films, Male Verbal Aggression against Women, and Guilt," in *Technical Report of the Commission on Obscenity and Pornography* (Washington, D.C.: Government Printing Office, 1971), vol. 8. See also E. Summers and J. Check, "An Empirical Investigation of the Role of Pornography in the Verbal and Physical Abuse of Women," *Violence and Victims* 2 (1987): 189–209; and P. Harmon, "The Role of Pornography in Women Abuse" (Ph.D. diss., York University, 1987). These experiments establish that the relationship between expressly violent sexual material and subsequent aggression against women is causal, not correlational.

59. Key research is summarized and reported in Check and Galoien (see n. 54 above); see also D. Zillman, "Effects of Repeated Exposure to Nonviolent Pornography," presented to U.S. Attorney General's Commission on Pornography, Houston, Texas (June 1986). Donnerstein's most recent experiments, as reported in *Public Hearings* and his book edited with Malamuth (see Appendix), clarify, culminate, and extend years of experimental research by many. See, e.g., D. Mosher, "Sex Callousness toward Women," in *Technical Report of the Commission on Obscenity and Pornography*, vol. 8; N. Malamuth and J. Check, "The Effects of Mass Media Exposure on Acceptance of Violence against Women: A Field Experiment," *Journal of Research in Personality* 15 (1981): 436–46. The studies are tending to confirm women's reports and feminist analyses of the consequences of exposure to pornography on attitudes and behaviors toward women. See J. Check and N. Malamuth (Appendix).

60. G. G. Abel, D. H. Barlow, E. Blanchard, and D. Guild, "The Components of Rapists' Sexual Arousal," *Archives of General Psychiatry* 34 (1977): 395–403; G. G. Abel, J. V. Becker, and L. J. Skinner, "Aggressive Behavior and Sex," *Psychiatric Clinics of North America* 3 (1980): 133–55; G. G. Abel, E. B. Blanchard, J. V. Becker, and A. Djenderedjian, "Differentiating Sexual Aggressiveness with Penile Measures," *Criminal Justice and Behavior* 2 (1978): 315–32.

61. Donnerstein, testimony, *Public Hearings*, p. 31.

end, one question that is raised is whether some form of hierarchy—the dynamic of the continuum—is currently essential for male sexuality to experience itself. If so, and gender is understood to be a hierarchy, perhaps the sexes are unequal so that men can be sexually aroused. To put it another way, perhaps gender must be maintained as a social hierarchy so that men will be able to get erections; or, part of the male interest in keeping women down lies in the fact that it gets men up. Maybe feminists are considered castrating because equality is not sexy.

Recent inquiries into rape support such suspicions. Men often rape women, it turns out, because they want to and enjoy it. The act, including the dominance, is sexually arousing, sexually affirming, and supportive of the perpetrator's masculinity. Many unreported rapists report an increase in self-esteem as a result of the rape.[62] Indications are that reported rapists perceive that getting caught accounts for most of the unpleasant effects of raping.[63] About a third of all men say they would rape a woman if they knew they wouldn't get caught.[64] That the low conviction rate[65] may give them confidence is supported by the prevalence rate.[66] Some convicted rapists see rape as an "exciting" form of interpersonal sex, a recreational activity or "adventure," or as a means of revenge or punishment on all women or some subgroup of women or an individual woman. Even some of those who did the act out of bad feelings make it clear that raping made them feel better. "Men rape because it is rewarding to do so."[67] If rapists experience rape as sex, does that mean there can be nothing wrong with it?

Once an act is labeled rape—indeed, this is much of the social function served by labeling acts rape—there is an epistemological problem

62. Smithyman (n. 5 above).

63. Scully and Marolla (n. 5 above).

64. In addition to previous citations to Malamuth, "Rape Proclivity among Males" (see n. 54 above); and Malamuth and Check, "Sexual Arousal to Rape and Consenting Depictions" (see n. 54 above); see T. Tieger, "Self-Reported Likelihood of Raping and the Social Perception of Rape," *Journal of Research in Personality* 15 (1981): 147–58; and N. Malamuth, S. Haber, and S. Feshbach, "Testing Hypotheses Regarding Rape: Exposure to Sexual Violence, Sex Differences, and the 'Normality' of Rape," *Journal of Research in Personality* 14 (1980): 121–37.

65. M. Burt and R. Albin, "Rape Myths, Rape Definitions and Probability of Conviction," *Journal of Applied Social Psychology*, vol. 11 (1981); G. D. LaFree, "The Effect of Sexual Stratification by Race on Official Reactions to Rape," *American Sociological Review* 4–5 (1984): 842–54, esp. 850; J. Galvin and K. Polk, "Attribution in Case Processing: Is Rape Unique?" *Journal of Research in Crime and Delinquency* 20 (1983): 126–54. The latter work seems not to understand that rape can be institutionally treated in a way that is sex-specific even if comparable statistics are generated by crimes against the other sex. Further, this study assumes that 53 percent of rapes are reported, when the real figure is closer to 10 percent (Russell, *Sexual Exploitation* [see Appendix]).

66. Russell, "The Prevalence and Incidence of Forcible Rape and Attempted Rape of Females" (see Appendix), pp. 1–4.

67. Scully and Marolla, p. 2.

with seeing it as sex.[68] Rape becomes something a rapist does, as if he is a separate species. But no personality disorder distinguishes most rapists from normal men.[69] Psychopaths do rape, but only about 5 percent of all known rapists are diagnosed psychopathic.[70] In spite of the number of victims, the normalcy of rapists, and the fact that most women are raped by men that they know (making it most unlikely that a few lunatics know around half of all women in the United States), rape remains considered psychopathological and therefore not about sexuality.

Add this to rape's pervasiveness and permissibility, together with the belief that it is both rare and impermissible. Combine this with the similarity between the patterns, rhythms, roles, and emotions, not to mention acts, which make up rape (and battery) on the one hand and intercourse on the other. All this makes it difficult to sustain the customary distinctions between pathology and normalcy, parophilia and nomophilia, violence and sex, in this area. Some researchers have previously noticed the centrality of force to the excitement value of pornography but have tended to put it down to perversion. Robert Stoller, for example, observes that pornography today depends upon hostility, voyeurism, and sado-masochism and calls perversion the erotic form of hatred.[71] If the perverse is seen as not the other side of a bright normal/abnormal line but as an undiluted expression of a norm which permeates many ordinary inter-actions, hatred—that is, misogyny—becomes a dimension of sexual excitement itself.

Compare victims' reports of rape with women's reports of sex. They look a lot alike.[72] Compare victims' reports of rape with what pornography says is sex. They look a lot alike.[73] In this light, the major distinction

68. Sometimes this is a grudging realism: "Once there is a conviction, the matter cannot be trivial even though the act may have been" (P. Gebhard, J. Gagnon, W. Pomeroy, and C. Christenson, *Sex Offenders: An Analysis of Types* [New York: Harper & Row, 1965], p. 178). It is telling that if an act that has been adjudicated rape is still argued to be sex, that is thought to exonerate the rape rather than indict the sex.

69. R. Rada, *Clinical Aspects of Rape* (New York: Grune & Stratton, 1978); C. Kirkpatrick and E. Kanin, "Male Sex Aggression on a University Campus," *American Sociological Review* 22 (1957): 52–58; see also Malamuth, Haber, and Feshbach.

70. Abel, Becker, and Skinner (n. 60 above), pp. 133–51.

71. Robert Stoller, *Perversion: The Erotic Form of Hatred* (New York: Pantheon, 1975), p. 87.

72. Compare, e.g., Hite (see Appendix) with Russell, *The Politics of Rape* (see Appendix).

73. This is truly obvious from looking at the pornography. A fair amount of pornography actually calls the acts it celebrates "rape." Too, "In depictions of sexual behavior [in por-nography] there is typically evidence of a difference of power between the participants" (L. Baron and M. A. Straus, "Conceptual and Ethical Problems in Research on Pornography" [paper presented at the annual meeting of the Society for the Study of Social Problems, 1983], p. 6). Given that this characterizes the reality, consider the content attributed to "sex itself" in the following methodologically liberal quotations on the subject: "Only if one thinks of *sex itself* as a degrading act can one believe that all pornography degrades and harms women" (P. Califia, "Among Us, against Us—the New Puritans," *Advocate* [April 17, 1980], p. 14 [emphasis added]). Given the realization that violence against women *is*

between intercourse (normal) and rape (abnormal) is that the normal happens so often that one cannot get anyone to see anything wrong with it. Which also means that anything sexual that happens often and one cannot get anyone to consider wrong is intercourse not rape, no matter what was done. The distinctions that purport to divide this territory look more like the ideological supports for normalizing the usual male use and abuse of women as "sexuality" through authoritatively pretending that whatever is exposed of it is deviant. This may have something to do with the conviction rate in rape cases (making all those unconvicted men into normal men, and all those acts into sex). It may have something to do with the fact that most convicted rapists, and many observers, find rape convictions incomprehensible.[74] And the fact that marital rape is considered by many to be a contradiction in terms. ("But if you can't rape your wife, who can you rape?")[75] And the fact that so many rape victims have trouble with sex afterward.[76]

What effect does the pervasive reality of sexual abuse of women by men have on what are deemed the more ordinary forms of sexual interaction? How do these material experiences create interest and point of view? Consider women. Recall that over a third of all girls experience sex, perhaps are sexually initiated, under conditions that even this society recognizes are forced or at least unequal.[77] Perhaps they learn this process of sexualized dominance as sex. Top-down relations feel sexual. Is sexuality throughout life then ever not on some level a reenactment of, a response to, that backdrop? Rape, adding more women to the list, can produce similar resonance. Sexually abused women—most women—seem to become either sexually disinclined or compulsively promiscuous or both in series, trying to avoid the painful events, and/or repeating them over

---

sexual, consider the content of the "sexual" in the following criticism: "The only form in which a politics opposed to violence against women is being expressed is anti-sexual" (English, Hollibaugh, and Rubin [n. 14 above], p. 51). And "the feminist anti-pornography movement has become deeply erotophobic and anti-sexual" (A. Hollibaugh, "The Erotophobic Voice of Women," *New York Native* [1983], p. 34).

74. J. Wolfe and V. Baker, "Characteristics of Imprisoned Rapists and Circumstances of the Rape," in *Rape and Sexual Assault*, ed. C. G. Warner (Germantown, Md.: Aspen Systems Co., 1980).

75. This statement was widely attributed to California State Senator Bob Wilson; see Joanne Schulman, "The Material Rape Exemption in the Criminal Law," *Clearinghouse Review*, vol. 14 [1980]) on the Rideout marital rape case. He has equally widely denied that the comment was seriously intended. I consider it by now apocryphal as well as stunningly revelatory, whether or not humorously intended, on the topic of the indistinguishability of rape from intercourse from the male point of view.

76. Carolyn Craven, "No More Victims: Carolyn Craven Talks about Rape, and What Women and Men Can Do to Stop It," ed. Alison Wells (Berkeley, Calif., 1978, mimeographed) p. 2.; Russell, *The Politics of Rape* (see Appendix), pp. 84–85, 105, 114, 135, 147, 185, 196, and 205; P. Bart, "Rape Doesn't End with a Kiss," *Viva* 11 (1975): 39–41 and 100–101; J. Becker, L. Skinner, G. Abel, R. Axelrod, and J. Cichon, "Sexual Problems of Sexual Assault Survivors," *Women and Health* 9 (1984): 5–20.

77. See sources on incest and child sexual abuse, Appendix.

and over almost addictively, in an attempt to reacquire a sense of control or to make them come out right. Too, women widely experience sexuality as a means to male approval; male approval translates into nearly all social goods. Violation can be sustained, even sought out, to this end. Sex can, then, be a means of trying to feel alive by redoing what has made one feel dead, of expressing a denigrated self-image seeking its own reflection in self-action in order to feel fulfilled, or of keeping up one's stock with the powerful.

Many women who have been sexually abused (like many survivors of concentration camps and ritual torture) report having distanced themselves as a conscious strategy for coping with the abuse. With women, this dissociation often becomes a part of their sexuality per se and of their experience of the world, especially their experience of men. Women widely report this sensation during sex. Not feeling pain, including during sex, may have a similar etiology. As one pornography model put it,

> O: I had quite a bit of difficulty as a child. I was suicidal for a time, because I never felt attached to my body. I just felt completely detached from my body; I felt like a completely separate entity from it. I still see my body as a tool, something to be used.
> DR: Give me an example of how today you sense not being attached to your body.
> O: I don't feel pain.
> DR: What do you mean, literally?
> O: I really don't feel pain. . . .
> DR: When there is no camera and you are having sexual relations, are you still on camera?
> O: Yes. I'm on camera 24 hours a day. . . .
> DR: Who are you?
> O: Who? Olympia Dancing-Doll: The Sweet with the Super-Supreme.
> DR: What the hell is that?
> O: That's the title of my act. . . .
> DR: [Pointing to her.] This is a body. Is it your body?
> O: Yes.
> DR: Are you your body?
> O: No. I'm not my body, but it is my body.[78]

Women often begin alienating themselves from their body's self-preserving reactions under conditions under which they cannot stop the pain from being inflicted, and then find the deadening process difficult to reverse. Some then seek out escalating pain to feel sexual or to feel alive or to feel anything at all. One particularly devastating and confusing consequence of sexual abuse for women's sexuality—and a crisis for consciousness—occurs when one's body experiences abuse as pleasurable. Feeling loved and aroused and comforted during incest, or orgasm during rape, are examples. Because body is widely regarded as access to un-

---

78. Olympia, a woman who poses for soft-core pornography, interviewed by Robert Stoller, "Centerfold: An Essay on Excitement," *Archives of General Psychiatry* (1979).

mediated truth in this culture, women feel betrayed by their bodies and seek mental justifications (Freudian derepression theory provides an excellent one) for why their body's reactions are their own true reactions, and their values and consciousness (which interprets the event as a violation) is socially imposed. That is, they come to believe they really wanted the rape or the incest and interpret violation as their own sexuality.[79]

Interpreting women's responses to pornography, in which there is often a difference between so-called objective indices of arousal, like vaginal secretions, and self-reported arousal, raises similar issues. Repression is the typical explanation.[80] It seems at least as likely that women disidentify with their bodies' conditioned responses. Not to be overly behavioral, but does anyone think Pavlov's dogs were really hungry every time they salivated at the sound of the bell? If it is possible that hunger is inferred from salivation, perhaps humans experience[81] sexual arousal from pornographic cues and, since sexuality is social, that *is* sexual arousal. Identifying that as a conditioned response to a set of social cues, conditioned to what is for political reasons, is not the same as considering the response proof of sexual truth simply because it physically happens. Further, research shows that sexual fetishism can be experimentally induced readily in 'normal' subjects.[82] If this can be done with sexual responses that the society does not condone out front, why is it so unthinkable that the same process might occur with those sexual responses it does?

If the existing social model and reality of sexuality centers on male force, and if that sex is socially learned and ideologically considered positive and is rewarded, what is surprising is that not all women eroticize dominance, not all love pornography, and many resent rape. As Valerie Heller has said of her experience with incest and use in pornography, both as a child and as an adult, "I believed I existed only after I was turned on, like a light switch by another person. When I needed to be nurtured I thought I wanted to be used. . . . Marks and bruises and being used was the way I measured my self worth. You must remember that I was taught that because men were fucking my body and using it for their needs it meant I was loved."[83] Given the pervasiveness of such experiences,

79. It is interesting that, in spite of everything, many women who once thought of their abuse as self-actualizing come to rethink it as a violation, while very few who have ever thought of their abuse as a violation come to rethink it as self-actualizing.

80. See G. Schmidt and V. Sigusch, "Psychosexual Stimulation by Film and Slides: A Further Report on Sex Differences," *Journal of Sex Research* 6 (1970): 268–83; G. Schmidt, "Male-Female Differences in Sexual Arousal and Behavior during and after Exposure to Sexually Explicit Stimuli," *Archives of Sexual Behavior* 4 (1975): 353–65; D. Mosher, "Psychological Reactions to Pornographic Films," in *Technical Reports of the Commission on Obscenity and Pornography* (n. 58 above), 8:286–312.

81. Using the term "experience" as a verb like this seems to be the way one currently negotiates the subjective/objective split in Western epistemology.

82. S. Rachman and R. Hodgson, "Experimentally Induced 'Sexual Fetishism': Replication and Development," *Psychological Record* 18 (1968): 25–27; S. Rachman, "Sexual Fetishism: An Experimental Analogue," *Psychological Record* 16 (1966): 293–96.

83. March for Women's Dignity, New York City, May 1984.

the truly interesting question becomes why and how sexuality in women is ever other than masochistic.

All women live in sexual objectification like fish live in water. Given the statistical realities, all women live all the time under the shadow of the threat of sexual abuse. The question is, what can life as a woman mean, what can sex mean to targeted survivors in a rape culture? Given the statistical realities, much of women's sexual lives will occur under post-traumatic stress. Being surrounded by pornography—which is not only socially ubiquitous but often directly used as part of sex[84]—makes this a relatively constant condition. Women cope with objectification through trying to meet the male standard, and measure their self-worth by the degree to which they succeed. Women seem to cope with sexual abuse principally through denial or fear. On the denial side, immense energy goes into defending sexuality as just fine and getting better all the time, and into trying to make sexuality feel all right, like it is supposed to feel. Women who are compromised, cajoled, pressured, tricked, black-mailed, or outright forced into sex (or pornography) often respond to the unspeakable humiliation, coupled with the sense of having lost some irreplaceable integrity, by claiming that sexuality as their own. Faced with no alternatives, the strategy to acquire self-respect and pride is: I chose it.

Consider the conditions under which this is done. This is a culture in which women are socially expected—and themselves necessarily expect and want—to be able to distinguish the socially, epistemologically, in-distinguishable. Rape and intercourse are not authoritatively separated by any difference between the physical acts or amount of force involved but only legally, by a standard that revolves around the man's interpretation of the encounter. Thus, although raped women, that is, most women, are supposed to be able to feel every day and every night that they have some meaningful determining part in having their sex life—their life, period—not be a series of rapes, the most they provide is the raw data for the man to see as he sees it. And he has been seeing pornography. Similarly, "consent" is supposed the crucial line between rape and in-tercourse, but the legal standard for it is so passive, so acquiescent, that a woman can be dead and have consented under it. The mind fuck of all of this makes the complicitous collapse into "I chose it" feel like a strategy for sanity. It certainly makes a woman at one with the world.

On the fear side, if a woman has ever been beaten in a relationship, even if "only once," what does that do to her everyday interactions, or her sexual interactions, with that man? With other men? Does her body ever really forget that behind his restraint he can do that any time she pushes an issue, or for no reason at all? Does her vigilance ever really relax? If she tried to do something about it, as many women do, and

---

84. *Public Hearings* (n. 34 above); M. Atwood, *Bodily Harm* (Toronto: McClelland & Stewart, 1983), pp. 207–12.

nothing was done, as it usually isn't, does she ever forget that that is what can be done to her at any time and nothing will be done about it? Does she smile at men less—or more? If she writes at all, does she imitate men less—or more? If a woman has been raped, ever, does a penis ever enter her without some body memory, if not a flashback then the effort of keeping it back; or does she hurry up or keep trying, feeling something gaining on her, trying to make it come out right? If a woman has ever been raped, does she ever fully regain the feeling of physical integrity, of self-respect, of having what she wants count somewhere, of being able to make herself clear to those who have not gone through what she has gone through, of living in a fair society, of equality?

Given the effects of learning sexuality through force or pressure or imposition; given the constant roulette of sexual violence; given the daily sexualization of every aspect of a woman's presence—for a woman to be sexualized means constant humiliation or threat of it, being both invisible as human being and always center stage as sex object, low pay, and being a target for assault or being assaulted. Given that this is the situation of all women, that one never knows for sure that one is not next on the list of victims until the moment one dies (and then, who knows?), it does not seem exaggerated to say that women are sexual, meaning that women exist, in a context of terror. Yet most professionals in the area of sexuality persist in studying the inexplicabilities of what is termed female sexuality acontextually, outside the context of gender inequality and its sexual violence, navel-gazing only slightly further down.[85]

The general theory of sexuality emerging from this feminist critique does not consider sexuality to be an inborn force inherent in individuals, nor cultural in the Freudian sense, in which sexuality exists always in a cultural context but in universally invariant stages and psychic representations. It appears instead to be culturally specific, even if so far largely invariant because male supremacy is largely universal, if always in specific forms. It does not vary by class, although class is one hierarchy it sexualizes. Sexuality becomes, in this view, social and relational, constructing and constructed of power. Infants, although sensory, cannot be said to possess sexuality in this sense because they have not had the experiences (and do not speak the language) that give it social meaning. Since sexuality is its social meaning, infant erections, for example, are clearly sexual in the sense that this society centers its sexuality on them, but to relate to a child as though his erections mean what adult erections have been

85. This is also true of Foucault, *The History of Sexuality* (n. 7 above), vol. 1. Foucault understands that sexuality must be discussed with method, power, class, and the law. Gender, however, eludes him. So he cannot distinguish between the silence about sexuality that Victorianism has made into a noisy discourse and the silence that has *been* women's sexuality under conditions of subordination by and to men. Although he purports to grasp sexuality, including desire itself, as social, he does not see the content of its determination as a sexist social order that eroticizes potency as male and victimization as female. Women are simply beneath significant notice.

conditioned to mean is a form of child abuse. Such erections have the meaning they acquire in social life only to observing adults.

When Freud changed his mind[86] and declared that women were not telling the truth about what had happened to them when they said they were abused as children, he attributed their accounts to "fantasy." This was regarded as a theoretical breakthrough. Under the aegis of Freud, it is often said that victims of sexual abuse imagine it, that it is fantasy, not real, and their sexuality caused it. The feminist theory of sexuality suggests that it is the doctors who, because of their sexuality, as constructed, imagine that sexual abuse is a fantasy when it is real—real both in the sense that the sex happened and in the sense that it was abuse. Pornography is also routinely defended as "fantasy," meaning not real. It is real: the sex that makes it is real and is often abuse, and the sex that it makes is sex and is often abuse. Both the psychoanalytic and the pornographic "fantasy" worlds are what men imagine women imagine and desire because they are what men, raised on pornography, imagine and desire about women. Thus is psychoanalysis used to legitimize pornography, calling it fantasy, and pornography used to legitimize psychoanalysis, to show what women really want. Psychoanalysis and pornography, seen as epistemic sites in the same ontology, are mirrors of each other, male supremacist sexuality looking at itself looking at itself.

Perhaps the Freudian process of theory-building occurred like this: men heard accounts of child abuse, felt aroused by the account, and attributed their arousal to the child who is now a woman. Perhaps men respond sexually when women give an account of sexual violation because sexual words constitute sexual reality, in the same way that men respond to pornography, which is (among other things) an account of the sexual violation of a woman. Seen in this way, much therapy as well as court testimony in sexual abuse cases are live oral pornography. Classical psychoanalysis attributes the connection between the experience of abuse (hers) and the experience of arousal (his) to the fantasy of the girl child. When he does it, he likes it, so when she did it, she must have liked it, or she must have thought it happened because she as much enjoys thinking about it happening to her as he enjoys thinking about it happening to her. Thus it cannot be abusive to her. Because he wants to do it, she must want it done.

Feminism also doubts the mechanism of repression in the sense that unconscious urges are considered repressed by social restrictions. Male sexuality is expressed and expressed and expressed, with a righteousness driven by the notion that something is trying to keep it from expressing itself. Too, there is a lot of doubt both about biology and about drives. Women are less repressed than oppressed, so-called women's sexuality largely a construct of male sexuality searching for someplace to happen, repression providing the reason for women's inhibition, meaning their

86. Masson (n. 2 above).

unwillingness to make themselves available on demand. In this view, one function of the Freudian theory of repression (a function furthered rather than qualified by neo-Freudian adaptations) is ideologically to support the freeing of male sexual aggression while delegitimizing women's refusal to respond.

There may be a feminist unconscious, but it is not the Freudian one. Perhaps equality lives there. Its laws, rather than a priori, objective, or universal, might as well be a response to the historical regularities of sexual subordination, which under bourgeois ideological conditions require that the truth of male dominance be concealed in order to preserve the belief that women are sexually self-acting: that women want it. The feminist psychic universe certainly recognizes that people do not always know what they want, have hidden desires and inaccessible needs, lack awareness of motivation, have contorted and opaque interactions, and have an interest in obscuring what is really going on. But this does not essentially conceal that what women really want is more sex. It is true, as Freudians have persuasively observed, that many things are sexual that do not present themselves as such. But in ways Freud never dreamed.

At risk of further complicating the issues, perhaps it would help to think of women's sexuality as women's like black culture is blacks'—it is, and it is not. The parallel cannot be precise because, due to segregation, black culture developed under more autonomous conditions than women, intimately integrated with men by force, have had. Still, both can be experienced as a source of strength, joy, expression and as an affirmative badge of pride.[87] Both remain nonetheless stigmatic in the sense of a brand, a restriction, a definition as less. This is not because of any intrinsic content or value but because the social reality is that their shape, qualities, texture, imperative, and very existence are a response to powerlessness. They exist as they do because of lack of choice. They are created out of social conditions of oppression and exclusion. They may be part of a strategy for survival or even of change—but, as is, they are not the whole world, and it is the whole world that one is entitled to. This is why interpreting female sexuality as an expression of women's agency and autonomy is always denigrating and bizarre and reductive, as if sexism does not exist, just as it would be to interpret black culture as if racism did not exist. As if black culture just arose freely and spontaneously on the plantations and in the ghettos of North America, adding diversity to American pluralism.

---

87. On sexuality, see, e.g., A. Lorde, *Uses of the Erotic: The Erotic as Power* (Brooklyn, N.Y.: Out and Out Books, 1978); and Haunani-Kay Trask, *Eros and Power: The Promise of Feminist Theory* (Philadelphia: University of Pennsylvania Press, 1986); both attempt such a reconstitution. The work of Trask suffers from an underlying essentialism in which the realities of sexual abuse are not examined or seen as constituting women's sexuality as such. Thus, a return to mother and body can be urged as social bases for reclaiming a feminist eros.

So long as sexual inequality remains unequal and sexual, attempts to value sexuality as women's, possessive as if women possess it, will remain part of limiting women to it, to what women are now defined as being. Outside of truly rare and contrapuntal glimpses (which almost everyone thinks they live almost their entire sex life within), to seek an equal sexuality, to seek sexual equality, without political transformation is to seek equality under conditions of inequality. Rejecting this, and rejecting the glorification of settling for the best inequality has to offer or has stimulated the resourceful to invent, are what Ti-Grace Atkinson meant to reject when she said, "I do not know any feminist worthy of that name who, if forced to choose between freedom and sex, would choose sex. She'd choose freedom every time."[88]

APPENDIX

A few basic citations from the massive body of work on which this article draws are:

On rape: D. Russell and N. Howell, "The Prevalence of Rape in the United States Revisited," *Signs: Journal of Women in Culture and Society* 8 (1983): 668–95; D. Russell, *Rape in Marriage* (New York: Macmillan, 1982); L. Clark and D. Lewis, *Rape: The Price of Coercive Sexuality* (Toronto: Canadian Women's Press, 1977); D. Russell, *The Politics of Rape* (New York: Stein & Day, 1975); A. Medea and K. Thompson, *Against Rape* (New York: Farrar, Straus & Giroux, 1974); S. Brownmiller, *Against Our Will: Men, Women and Rape* (New York: Simon & Schuster, 1975); I. Frieze, "Investigating the Causes and Consequences of Marital Rape," *Signs: Journal of Women in Culture and Society* 8 (1983): 532–53; N. Gager and C. Schurr, *Sexual Assault: Confronting Rape in America* (New York: Grosset & Dunlap, 1976); G. LaFree, "Male Power and Female Victimization: Towards a Theory of Interracial Rape," *American Journal of Sociology* 88 (1982): 311–28; M. Burt, "Cultural Myths and Supports for Rape," *Journal of Personality and Social Psychology* 38 (1980): 217–30; Kalamu ya Salaam, *Our Women Keep Our Skies from Falling* (New Orleans: Nkombo, 1980); J. Check and N. Malamuth, "An Empirical Assessment of Some Feminist Hypotheses about Rape," *International Journal of Women's Studies* 8 (1985): 414–23.

On battery: D. Martin, *Battered Wives* (San Francisco: Glide Productions, 1976); S. Steinmetz, *The Cycle of Violence: Assertive, Aggressive, and Abusive Family Interaction* (New York: Praeger, 1977); R. E. Dobash and R. Dobash, *Violence against Wives* (New York: Free Press, 1979); R. Langley and R. Levy, *Wife Beating: The Silent Crises* (New York: E. P. Dutton, 1977); E. Stark, A. Flitcraft, and W. Frazier, "Medicine and Patriarchal Violence: The Social Construction of a 'Private' Event," *International Journal of Health Services* 9 (1979): 461–93; L. Walker, *The Battered Woman* (New York: Harper & Row, 1979).

On sexual harassment: Merit Systems Protection Board, *Sexual Harassment in the Federal Workplace: Is It a Problem?* (Washington, D.C.: Government Printing Office, 1981); C. A. MacKinnon, *Sexual Harassment of Working Women* (New Haven, Conn.: Yale University Press, 1979); D. Benson and G. Thomson, "Sexual Har-

---

88. Ti-Grace Atkinson, "Why I'm against S/M Liberation," in *Against Sadomasochism: A Radical Feminist Analysis*, ed. R. Linden, D. Pagano, D. Russell, and S. Star (East Palo Alto, Calif.: Frog in the Well, 1982), p. 91.

assment on a University Campus: The Confluence of Authority Relations, Sexual Interest and Gender Stratification," *Social Problems* 28 (1981): 263–51; P. Crocker and A. Simon, "Sexual Harassment in Education," *Capital University Law Review* 10 (1981): 541–84.

On incest and child sexual abuse: D. Finkelhor, *Sexually Victimized Children* (New York: Free Press, 1979); J. Herman, *Father-Daughter Incest* (Cambridge, Mass.: Harvard University Press, 1981); D. Finkelhor, *Child Sexual Abuse: Theory and Research* (New York: Free Press, 1984); A. Jaffe, L. Dynneson, and R. TenBensel, "Sexual Abuse: An Epidemiological Study," *American Journal of Diseases of Children* 129 (1975): 689–92; K. Brady, *Father's Days: A True Story of Incest* (New York: Seaview Books, 1979); L. Armstrong, *Kiss Daddy Goodnight* (New York: Hawthorn Press, 1978); S. Butler, *Conspiracy of Silence: The Trauma of Incest* (San Francisco: New Glide Publications, 1978); A Burgess, N. Groth, L. Homstrom, and S. Sgroi, *Sexual Assault of Children and Adolescents* (Lexington, Mass.: Lexington Books, 1978); F. Rush, *The Best-kept Secret: Sexual Abuse of Children* (Englewood Cliffs, N.J.: Prentice-Hall, 1980); D. Russell, "The Prevalence and Seriousness of Incestuous Abuse: Stepfathers v. Biological Fathers," *Child Abuse and Neglect: The International Journal* 8 (1984): 15–22, "The Incidence and Prevalence of Intrafamilial and Extrafamilial Sexual Abuse of Female Children," *Child Abuse and Neglect: The International Journal* 7 (1983): 133–46, and *The Secret Trauma: Incest in the Lives of Women and Girls* (New York: Basic Books, 1986).

On prostitution: K. Barry, *Female Sexual Slavery* (Englewood Cliffs, N.J.: Prentice-Hall, 1979); J. James and J. Meyerding, "Early Sexual Experience as a Factor in Prostitution," *Archives of Sexual Behavior* 7 (1977): 31–42; United Nations Economic and Social Council, Commission on Human Rights, Sub-Commission on Prevention of Discrimination and Protection of Minorities, Working Group on Slavery, *Suppression of the Traffic in Persons and of the Exploitation of the Prostitution of Others* E/ Cn.4/AC.2/5 (New York: United Nations, June 16, 1976); J. James, *The Politics of Prostitution* (Social Research Association, 1975); K. Millett et al., *The Prostitution Papers* (New York: Avon Books, 1973).

On pornography: L. Lederer, ed., *Take Back the Night: Women on Pornography* (New York: William Morrow, 1980); A. Dworkin, *Pornography: Men Possessing Women* (New York: Perigee, 1981); L. Lovelace and M. McGrady, *Ordeal* (New York: Berkeley Books, 1980); P. Bogdanovich, *The Killing of the Unicorn: Dorothy Stratten, 1960–1980* (New York: William Morrow, 1984); M. Langelan, "The Political Economy of Pornography," *Aegis: Magazine on Ending Violence against Women* 32 (1981): 5–7; D. Leidholdt, "Pornography Meets Fascism," *WIN*, March 15, 1983, 18–22; E. Donnerstein, "Erotica and Human Aggression," in *Aggression: Theoretical and Empirical Reviews*, ed. R. Green and E. Donnerstein (New York: Academic Press, 1983), and "Pornography: Its Effects on Violence against Women," in *Pornography and Sexual Aggression*, ed. N. Malamuth and E. Donnerstein (New York: Academic Press: 1985); Geraldine Finn, "Against Sexual Imagery, Alternative or Otherwise," Symosium on Images of Sexuality in Art and Media, Ottawa, Canada (March 13–16, 1985); Diana E. H. Russell, "Pornography and Rape: A Causal Model," *Political Psychology* 9 (1988): 41–73; *Report of the Attorney General's Commission on Pornography* (Washington, D.C.: Government Printing Office, 1986).

See generally: D. Russell, *Sexual Exploitation* (New York: Russell Sage, 1984); D. Russell and N. Van de Ven, *Crimes against Women: Proceedings of the International Tribunal* (Les Femmes, 1976); E. Morgan, *The Erotization of Male Dominance/Female Submission* (Pittsburgh: Know, Inc., 1975); A. Rich, "Compulsory Heterosexuality and Lesbian Existence," *Signs: Journal of Women in Culture and Society* 5 (1980): 631–60; J. Long Laws and P. Schwartz, *Sexual Scripts: The Social Construction of Female Sexuality* (Hinsdale, Ill.: Dryden Press, 1976); L. Phelps, "Female Sexual Alienation," in *Women: A Feminist Perspective,* ed. J. Freeman (Palo Alto, Calif.: Mayfield, 1979); S. Hite, *The Hite Report: A Nationwide Survey of Female Sexuality* (New York: Macmillan, 1976); Andrea Dworkin, *Intercourse* (New York: Free Press, 1987). Recent comparative work provides confirmation and contrasts: Pat Caplan, ed., *The Cultural Construction of Sexuality* (New York: Tavistock, 1987); Marjorie Shostak, *Nisa: The Life and Words of a !Kung Woman* (New York: Vintage Books, 1983).

Part IV

Trust and Responsibility

Responsibility and Reproach

Cheshire Calhoun

> Feminist consciousness is often afflicted with category confusion—
> an inability to know how to classify things. [SANDRA LEE BARTKY][1]

Feminist thinking about moral responsibility for oppressive and sexist behavior illustrates just this kind of confusion. When wrongdoing takes the form of social oppression, the relationship between individuals and their actions shifts in ways that render uncertain our judgments about moral responsibility and, with those, our judgments about the blameworthiness of individuals and our entitlement to reproach them. Part of the uncertainty about how to assign moral responsibility derives from the atypical character of the wrongdoing that feminists critique. Unlike ordinary cases of individual wrongdoing, oppressive wrongdoing often occurs at the level of *social practice,* where social acceptance of a practice impedes the individual's awareness of wrongdoing. Thus questions about moral responsibility become very difficult questions about how to weigh the social determinants producing moral ignorance against the individual's competence to engage in moral reasoning. The social scale at which oppression occurs complicates thinking about moral responsibility in other ways as well. If we assume, as we often do, that only morally flawed individuals could act oppressively, then we will have to conclude that the number of morally flawed individuals is more vast than we had dreamed and includes individuals whom we would otherwise rank high on scales of moral virtue and goodwill. The oddity of this conclusion forces serious questions about the possibility of morally unflawed individuals committing serious wrongdoing. Finally, when wrongdoing occurs at a social level— that is, at a level that places whole social groups at risk, and where wrongdoing stands a much greater chance of being perpetuated by its very normalcy—our moral and personal stake in intervening in the pattern is much higher. The question of blame becomes not just a question about blameworthiness, but more important a question about our entitlement to use moral reproach as a tool for effecting social change. Does the justified use of moral reproach require, as it does in ordinary cases, being

1. Sandra Lee Bartky, "Toward a Phenomenology of Feminist Consciousness," in *Feminism and Philosophy,* ed. Mary Vetterling-Braggin, Frederick A. Elliston, and Jane English (Totowa, N.J.: Littlefield, Adams & Co., 1981), p. 29.

This essay originally appeared in *Ethics* 99, January 1989.

justified in assigning moral responsibility and blameworthiness? In what follows, I want to explore the differences between ordinary cases of wrongdoing and oppression as a way of clarifying why questions about moral responsibility for oppressive behavior are so difficult to resolve. In the course of that exploration, I will argue, first, that the central difference lies in the normality versus the abnormality of the context in which wrongdoing occurs; second, that oppressive behavior need not proceed from some morally culpable flaw; and third, that in what I will be calling "abnormal moral contexts," our entitlement to use moral reproach is independent of the blameworthiness of individuals.

I. LOCATING CONFUSION ABOUT MORAL RESPONSIBILITY

For women who have had even the slightest exposure to feminist thinking, confusion over moral responsibility arises at an immediate, personal level in the form of contradictory reactive attitudes. Condemnatory attitudes—anger, indignation, contempt—war with exculpating attitudes—forgiveness, tolerance, pity. Confused emotions and confusion over what one ought to feel stem from a kind of double vision. On the one hand, feminist consciousness "is a consciousness of *victimization*. To apprehend oneself as victim is to be aware of an alien and hostile force which is responsible for the blatantly unjust treatment of women and for a stifling and oppressive system of sex roles; it is to be aware, too, that this victimization, in no way earned or deserved, is an *offense*."[2] The level and extent of offense seem to call for reactive attitudes predicated on moral responsibility. Yet at the same time, feminist consciousness is a consciousness of inhabiting a new reality, of seeing what one did not, could not, see before and what others still do not, cannot, see. The social invisibility of offense seems to call, by contrast, for more tolerant reactive attitudes, ones predicated on excuse.

In feminist literature, the language of oppression iterates the same tension between responsibility and excuse. The sheer volume of oppressive, exploitive, sexist, and power-abusing practices documented by feminists seems to call for a suitably large number of culpable agents. Indeed, talk about "oppression," "exploitation," "sexism," and "power relations" implicitly points toward oppressors, exploiters, sexists, and abusers of power, that is, to the responsible villains. Yet the "villains" are mostly ordinary men, with ordinary characters, living out ordinary lives as husbands, scientists, ad men, construction workers, and so forth. Pimps, porn magnates, rapists, and self-proclaimed chauvinists are exceptional figures in women's oppression. Without the ordinary man's participation in routine social practices—in marriage, in the workplace, in daily conversation—oppression would not take the universal form it does. But the disanalogy between pimps and husbands may make us hesitate to name both 'op-

2. Ibid., pp. 26–27.

pressors.' The ordinary man may act oppressively, but is he an oppressor? How do we locate individual responsibility when oppression occurs at the level of social practice?

There are no quick and easy answers. On critical reflection, neither holding individuals responsible for their participation in oppressive social practices nor excusing them seems an appropriate response. Why this is so will be developed in Parts II and III; but it will help to begin by turning a critical eye on some of the arguments for responsibility and for excuse.

Ruth Bleier blames scientists for some actions done in the course of ordinary science. She says,

> However unreflective the process may be, scientists, such as those [who "document" women's deficiency in visuo-spatial skills] are able to stop just short of making the kinds of assertions that their own and others' data cannot defensibly support yet they can remain secure in the knowledge that their readers will supply the relevant cultural meaning to their text; for example, that women *are* innately inferior in the visuo-spatial and (therefore) the mathematical skills, and that no amount of education or social change can abolish this biological gap. It is disingenuous for scientists to pretend ignorance of their readers' beliefs and expectations and unethical to disclaim responsibility for the effects of their work and for presumed mis-interpretations of their "pure" texts. Scientists are responsible, since they themselves build ambiguities and misinterpretations into the writing itself.[3]

In blaming scientists, Bleier uses the language of agency—"disin-genuous," "pretending ignorance," "building ambiguities and misinter-pretations in"; but the disclaimer "however unreflective the process may be" undermines her charge, especially since Bleier notes that the practice of science requires not reflecting on normative implications. If "doing normal science" means not engaging in moral reflection, why castigate individual scientists for *pretending* ignorance or for *building* misinterpre-tations into their literature? Only if they were doing science abnormally, that is, in a morally reflective way, would they be in a position to feign ignorance or to deliberately cultivate misinterpretation.

In a somewhat different vein, Mary Daly argues vehemently in *Gyn/Ecology* for universal male responsibility, pointing out that a refusal to "name the enemy" and speak in the active voice covers up the fact that it is men, rather than abstract forces, who oppress women and benefit from it. She says, "Despite all the evidence that women are attacked as projections of The Enemy, the accusers ask sardonically: 'Do you really think that *men* are the enemy?' This deception/reversal is so deep that

3. Ruth Bleier, "Lab Coat: Robe of Innocence or Klansman's Sheet?" in *Feminist Studies/Critical Studies*, ed. Teresa de Lauretis (Bloomington: Indiana University Press, 1986), p. 62.

women—even feminists—are intimidated into Self-deception, becoming the only Self-described oppressed who are unable to name their oppressor, referring instead to vague 'forces,' 'roles,' 'stereotypes,' 'constraints,' 'attitudes,' 'influences.' This list could go on. The point is that no agent is named—only abstractions."[4] Naming only abstract forces as "agents" veils the fact that *individuals* play out roles, impose constraints, hold attitudes, and thus *cause* harm.

Causing harm, however, is not the same as being responsible for harm.[5] Ordinarily, evidence of strong conditioning excuses, and Daly acknowledges just that conditioning. Oppressive social practices, she remarks, "are acted out over and over again in performances that draw the participants into emotional complicity. Such re-enactment trains both victims and victimizers to perform uncritically their preordained roles."[6] If this is so, why does she refuse to excuse men? Daly's resistance to accepting excuses may derive from a belief that the logic of the language of moral responsibility changes when the moral picture includes participation in immoral social practices and the power to legitimize those practices. This is a possibility worth pursuing, because however wrong blaming individuals for publicly unacknowledged faults in a social practice may seem, *not* blaming them seems equally wrong.

In "The Man of Professional Widsom," Kathryn Pyne Addelson argues that prestige structures in science enable some researchers to exercise cognitive authority over the direction scientific theorizing takes.[7] That authority can be misused to deprive competitive work of serious attention, to cut off resources for competitive work, and ultimately to irrationally bias the development of science.[8] Of specifically feminist concern is the use of cognitive authority to stunt female scientists' careers or to perpetuate male bias in scientific theories. In illustrating prestige structures, Addelson describes how Robert Yerkes used his cognitive authority to promote the career and theories of Clarence Ray Carpenter. But she says, "it would be a mistake to describe Yerkes as showing favoritism and bias. . . . Researchers are also the judges of which competing theories it makes sense to pursue or to encourage others in pursuing. If this seems to result in bias, the way to correct it is *not by blaming individual researchers for showing favoritism* because they depart from some mythical set of abstract canons [namely the canon that rational criticism requires competing theories]."[9] Yerkes's and similar cognitive authorities' *ignorance* of prestige

4. Mary Daly, *Gyn/Ecology: The Metaethics of Radical Feminism* (Boston: Beacon, 1978), p. 29.

5. Here, I am not speaking for Daly but simply voicing a common distinction in moral theory. I suspect that Daly reconstructs the notion of responsibility. There is some suggestion that she uses causing harm and benefiting from it as a sufficient condition for responsibility.

6. Daly, p. 109.

7. Kathryn Pyne Addelson, "The Man of Professional Wisdom," in *Discovering Reality*, ed. Sandra Harding and Merrill B. Hintikka (Boston: D. Reidel, 1983), pp. 165–86.

8. Ibid., p. 178.

9. Ibid., pp. 178–79.

structures and of the importance of promoting competition excuse their abuses of cognitive authority. Thus she suggests that "the way to avoid harmful uses of cognitive authority, is to broaden rational criticism in science *by requiring* that both philosophers of science and scientists understand how prestige and power are factors in the way cognitive authority is exercized."[10] Moreover, "*we* should institutionalize this sort of criticism [namely, feminist criticism] and make it an explicit part of 'scientific method.' We should also try using the notion of cognitive authority and expanding the range of the criteria of scientific rationality and criticism so that it includes social arrangements within the scientific professions."[11] Addelson's shift into the passive voice ("should be required") and an anonymous "we" help her avoid confronting the questions, "Required by whom?" and "Which 'we' bears responsibility for making what amount to substantive changes in the practices of science and scientific criticism?" Taking seriously Addelson's claim that only those with cognitive authority can effectively *require* new directions, it would seem that *they* are responsible for critiquing and changing scientific practice. Outsiders (like Addelson) can only hope that their critiques are heard, taken seriously, and promoted. (Feminists in general bear the status of outsiders—outsiders to the scientific, academic, and everyday social communities, where their critiques are not simply nonlegitimated but are actively delegitimated. They, too, can only hope that their critiques are heard, taken seriously, and promoted by insiders.)

The problem, then, with excusing is this: If the excuse for wrongdoing is the normalcy and social legitimacy of one's actions, this same excuse can be repeated for ongoing resistance to seeing that there is anything wrong with what one is doing. If, for instance, Bleier's scientist ought to be excused for his lack of moral reflection because he is just doing science normally, he ought similarly to be excused for not accepting gender bias as a good reason for rejecting his theory, since here again he would just be doing science normally. From his point of view, rationality requires giving greater weight to beliefs held by a consensus of rational knowers, in this case scientists; and it is not his fault if the community of rational knowers happens to have reached consensus on the wrong beliefs (e.g., the belief that a theory's normative implications are irrelevant to its scientific merits). The problem with this perspective is that unless individuals accept moral responsibility for the practices in which they participate and for the social justifications of those practices, individuals will lack a motive to listen to outsiders' moral critiques.

II. NORMAL VERSUS ABNORMAL MORAL CONTEXTS

In the above examples, the ordinary man acting oppressively, the scientist employing a morally unreflective writing style, and the prestigious scientist misusing his cognitive authority all suffer from a moral ignorance shared

---

10. Ibid., p. 179, my italics.
11. Ibid., p. 182, my italics.

by their compatriots and sustained by the normalcy of their wrongdoing. The culpability of their wrongdoing thus turns on the culpability of their moral ignorance. Ought they to have known better?

Susan Wolf suggests that the freedom necessary for responsibility is a freedom to be determined by the Good. This requires "that the world cooperate in such a way that our most fundamental selves have the opportunity to develop into the selves they ought to be."[12] In particular, it requires that the world enable us to become knowledgeable about the Good. But the world fails to cooperate in the above cases. Unlike the pimp who violates public moral standards, these individuals are *misguided* by public standards of morally permissible action. Moreover, the esoteric, often publicly inaccessible, and socially delegitimated nature of feminist moral criticism works against their acquiring, or taking seriously, moral doubts about those public standards. Thus it would seem that, because the world does not cooperate, their ignorance is not culpable.

But this is too simple. These individuals possess (we may assume) the full array of moral competencies that can be expected in any normal, adult agent. As average moral citizens, it would seem that they are responsible for applying accepted moral canons (e.g., against exploiting others) to cases not covered, or incorrectly covered, in the social stock of moral knowledge. Moreover, their ignorance is not simply due to an uncooperative world. Their participation in oppressive social practices helps sustain the social acceptance of those practices.

In order to move forward, we need to examine more closely how the moral ignorance in these cases and the "abnormal" moral context in which it occurs differ from more familiar forms of moral ignorance in "normal" moral contexts. The moral ignorance at issue here clearly differs from that typically appealed to in excusing wrongdoing. First, it occurs at a social rather than individual level; and second, it occurs in individuals with generally good moral reasoning skills. Exploring these differences matters because our intuitions about moral responsibility and warranted reproach typically presuppose a normal moral context. When this presupposition breaks down, we may find ourselves forced to give different answers to questions about responsibility and reproach.

Moral ignorance in normal moral contexts.—In normal moral contexts, the rightness or wrongness of different courses of action is "transparent" to individuals, where "transparent" does not mean self-evident, but simply that participants in normal moral contexts share a common moral language, agree for the most part on moral rules, and use similar methods of moral reasoning. We expect people to be familiar with moral language—to know, for example, that 'promise,' 'respect,' 'polluting,' and 'drunkenness' are typically used in and signal moral contexts as 'mechanism,' 'operating,' and 'sleepiness' do not. We also expect people to know what sorts of

---

12. Susan Wolf, "Asymmetrical Freedom," in *Moral Responsibility,* ed. John Martin Fischer (Ithaca, N.Y.: Cornell University Press, 1986), p. 234.

things count as promises, signs of respect, and so forth, as well as the moral rules and principles that go along with moral language. The sharing of moral knowledge allows us to assume that most rational, reflective people could come to correct judgments about which courses of action would be right, wrong, or controversial; and this is what I meant by the "transparency" of normal moral contexts.

In such moral contexts, the idea that moral agents are self-legislators makes sense. Put differently, moral individualism—a reliance on the individual's ability to judge correctly—is a luxury affordable in a morally homogeneous society where individual choices are likely to concur, thus contributing to an *institution* of morality.[13]

The shared nature of moral knowledge and the self-legislating ability of moral agents in normal moral contexts determine the form moral ignorance can take. First, it will be an ignorance of what the moral community in general knows. Thus in normal contexts, moral ignorance is necessarily exceptional. This is why claims of moral ignorance make such poor excuses. It would, for example, take a very special story for "I didn't know that polluting public waterways is wrong" or "I didn't know that dumping thousands of gallons of toxic waste in public waterways is polluting" to be an acceptable excuse. To count as an excuse, one would have to show that ignorance originated in some atypical defect in moral education or moral development beyond the individual's control.

That moral ignorance is an ignorance of what others know means that it is difficult to become ignorant in the first place, and even more difficult to sustain that ignorance. Susan Wolf gives this example of ignorance's etiology:

> We imagined a case . . . of a man who embezzled some money, fully aware of what he was doing. He was neither coerced nor overcome by an irresistible impulse, and he was in complete possession of normal adult faculties of reason and observation. Yet it seems he ought not to be blamed for committing his crime, for, from his point of view, one cannot reasonably expect him to see anything wrong with his action. We may suppose that in his childhood he was given no love—he was beaten by his father, neglected by his mother. And that the people to whom he was exposed when he was growing up gave him examples only of evil and selfishness. From his point of view, it is natural to conclude that respecting other people's property would be foolish. For presumably no one had ever respected his. And it is natural for him to feel that he should treat other people as adversaries.[14]

---

13. Self-legislation has sometimes been presented (e.g., by Kant) as purely a function of rationality. One of my assumptions throughout this article is that philosophical moral theories need to take into account the sociological aspects of moral knowledge and action. Thus I understand self-legislation to be a function of a particular kind of moral society.

14. Wolf, p. 233.

The embezzler's exceptional ignorance is obvious: "Whereas our childhoods fell within a range of normal decency, his was severely deprived."[15] Because moral ignorance will be hard to come by in societies where moral knowledge is shared and constantly confirmed in daily interactions without some gross defect in the individual's moral education and development, morally ignorant people will also likely suffer from a general inability to take the moral point of view and will be poor candidates for moral agents.

A final point about moral ignorance. Not excusing moral ignorance matters to morality in the same way that not excusing legal ignorance matters to a legal system. Moral and legal rules place people under an obligation to conform to those rules. But there is little point in having either system of obligations if people can easily avoid the sanctions against nonconformity by pleading ignorance. In normal contexts, moral rules have a point because moral ignorance so rarely excuses.

Moral ignorance in abnormal moral contexts.—Abnormal moral contexts arise at the frontiers of moral knowledge when a subgroup of society (for instance, bioethicists or business ethicists) makes advances in moral knowledge faster than they can be disseminated to and assimilated by the general public and subgroups at special moral risk (e.g., physicians and corporate executives). As a result, the rightness or wrongness of some courses of action (for instance, routine involuntary sterilization of the mentally retarded) are, for a time, transparent only to the knowledge-acquiring subgroup but "opaque" to outsiders. Because moral knowledge is not shared, the presumption that all agents are equally capable of self-legislation breaks down. In order to normalize the moral context, channels for moral communication may be institutionalized. Following the rise of medical ethics, for instance, hospitals instituted ethics committees, health care schools added ethics coursework, and there were changes in laws governing health care practice.

Moral ignorance in abnormal contexts obviously differs from that in normal contexts. It is, first, an ignorance of what only a limited group of others know. Moral ignorance is the norm. Second, because it is an ignorance of advances in an existing base of moral knowledge, being morally ignorant in abnormal contexts is perfectly compatible with taking the moral point of view and being self-legislating in other spheres of one's moral life. One need be neither morally defective (like Wolf's embezzler) nor morally corrupt to be at risk of wrongdoing in abnormal contexts.

Most feminist moral critique occurs in an abnormal moral context, since those critiques have made only limited inroads on popular consciousness. Public consensus on the wrongness of discriminatory hiring, sexual harassment, and marital rape makes the moral context in which these oppressive acts occur a normal one. But feminists also critique a wide range of actions and practices that would not, in popular con-

---

15. Ibid., p. 234.

sciousness, be considered wrong (male bias in psychological and other theories, the design of female fashions, the use of 'he' neutrally, heterosexual marriage, and so on). Here the context of these actions shifts to an abnormal one.

Because of idiosyncracies not shared by other new areas of applied ethics, feminist criticism creates an abnormal moral context that is particularly resistant to normalization. Most obvious, feminists lack the sort of institutionalized channels of communication between insiders and outsiders that bioethicists and business ethicists have. Women's studies programs and feminist publications and professional organizations institutionalize communication *within* the feminist community. More significant, feminist moral criticism diverges from both traditional moral language and styles of moral reasoning. Other areas of applied ethics reshape moral language by straightforwardly playing off existing moral language—"corporate responsibility," "patient rights," "involuntary sterilization," and so forth. Feminists, of course, do this too. Such neologisms as 'sexual harassment' and 'date rape' facilitate both our seeing moral issues where we had not previously and our drawing connections between these and already acknowledged moral issues (e.g., between rape by strangers and date rape).[16] But feminists also reshape moral language in less readily accessible ways—"marginalize," "the Other," "silencing," "rapist society," "marriage as prostitution." Understanding the meaning, extension, and legitimacy of this kind of moral language requires a much deeper familiarity with feminist criticism than the first sort of neologisms do. Thus the language of feminist moral criticism may obstruct its dissemination and assimilation. Feminists reshape moral reasoning in similarly radical ways. Other areas of applied ethics extend existing consequentialist and rights-based theories to new areas of moral interest. Although feminists do this too, they also reconstruct moral reasoning by, for instance, stressing systematic harm—that is, by assessing harm *contextualized* in an interlocking system of harmful practices. Consequentialists may sometimes assess how actions contribute to other desirable or undesirable practices, but they certainly have not started by assuming that individual actions cannot be morally assessed without first understanding the system of practices of which individual actions are a part.[17] In addition, through the work of

16. Jean Grimshaw makes and develops these points in *Philosophy and Feminist Thinking* (Minneapolis: University of Minnesota Press, 1986), pp. 87–89.

17. Much feminist moral criticism concerns systematic disrespect or oppression of women. While individual action types may in themselves be harmful to women (e.g., discriminatory hiring and promotion policies, rape, sexual harassment), they are additionally harmful to the extent that they fit into a system of harmful actions. Indeed, the actual harmfulness of some forms of behavior becomes visible only when contextualized in a system of offenses. Failure to imagine offenses in systemic context results in the perception of women as overreacting. It results in a failure to understand, e.g., that the object of women's anger is not being called "honey," but being called "honey" *as part of a system of disrespectful linguistic practices.* Some neologisms, e.g., 'rapist society' refer to such systems of harms.

Carol Gilligan and others, some feminists are beginning to develop an alternative moral theory, the ethics of care, which is neither clearly consequentialist nor rights-based, and which emphasizes the moral importance of personal, noncontractual relationships, compassion and sympathy, sustaining connection, and highly contextualized moral reasoning.[18] When moral knowledge advances by overhauling, not just extension, becoming morally knowledgeable requires moral reeducation and not just supplementary coursework. Thus there are especially strong reasons in this abnormal context for having diminished expectations of the level of moral knowledge about oppression attainable by individuals outside the feminist community.

III. RESPONSIBILITY

Let us return now to the question of moral responsibility, addressing it with sensitivity to both the analogies and the disanalogies between Wolf's embezzler, who suffers from moral ignorance in a normal moral context, and the individuals in our earlier examples, who suffer moral ignorance in an abnormal moral context.

We might tell an excusing story for the ordinary man analogous to the embezzler's excuse. Imagine, for example, a man who always refers to women as 'girls' or 'ladies.' He, too, is uncoerced into doing so and is in complete possession of normal adult reasoning faculties. Yet it seems he ought not to be blamed for linguistically infantilizing or patronizing women, for, from his point of view, one cannot reasonably expect him to see anything wrong with his actions. We may suppose that in his childhood, his father and mother referred to women as 'girls' or 'ladies.' He may also have come to understand that the former is flattering because it suggests youth and the latter simply polite. We may suppose that the people to whom he was exposed when he was growing up gave him examples only of this linguistic use and this understanding of its significance. From his point of view, it is natural to conclude that 'girl' is flattering rather than infantilizing and that 'lady' is polite rather than patronizing.

What makes this excuse more problematic than the embezzler's? First, the embezzler is not just ignorant of property rights. More fundamentally, he lacks the capacity to take the moral point of view, a capacity that might enable him to rise above childhood conditioning and to reassess his father's, mother's, and others' actions. By contrast, the ordinary man, Bleier's unreflective scientist, and Addelson's prestigious scientist *are* capable of taking the moral point of view and reassessing the morality of what "everyone else" does. They thus lack the embezzler's

18. See, for instance, Carol Gilligan, *In a Different Voice* (Cambridge, Mass: Harvard University Press, 1982); Annette C. Baier, "Hume, the Women's Moral Theorist," and Virginia Held, "Feminism in Moral Theory," in *Women and Moral Theory,* ed. Eva Feder Kittay and Diana T. Meyers (Totowa, N.J.: Rowman & Littlefield, 1987).

strong excuse for moral ignorance, since "he ought to have known better" applies, however weakly, to them as it does not to the embezzler.

This disanalogy will not bear much weight. While the ordinary man, the unreflective scientist, and the prestigious scientist are capable of taking the moral point of view and are equipped with many of the tools necessary for moral reasoning, there are limits to the powers of moral self-critique. The husband who refuses to pay child support could know his error even before this became a media issue. He knows about promises, parental obligations, and fair play; and it takes no heroic effort to apply these to the child support case. But feminist moral criticism also constructs new moral categories, new modes of moral reasoning, and new priorities among old principles. Where self-criticism depends on having acquired new tools for moral reasoning, it hardly seems reasonable to blame those who have not acquired these things for failing to be sufficiently reflective. (This was Addelson's point.) Here one must resist the temptation to suppose that anyone who has not been severely deprived, in the way Wolf's embezzler was, but who nevertheless acts wrongly must suffer some culpable vice of intellect or character. This reassuring supposition (reassuring because it places moral rectitude fully within the power of individual will) ignores the social dimension of moral knowledge, specifically, the possibility in abnormal moral contexts of sharp disparities in the social distribution of moral knowledge.

One might still object that there may be less exonerating reasons for these individuals' failure to reassess the practices in which they participate. Self-interest can motivate the suppression of moral reflection. Business executives, for example, may suppress moral reflection about their business practices because they tacitly recognize that ethics and profit maximization rarely coincide. And people can certainly take advantage of abnormal contexts, pretending or cultivating ignorance when prudent to do so. One of the points stressed by feminists is that men's benefiting from oppressive social practices provides them with a *motive* for resisting critical reflection and for exercising self-deception about their own motives and about the consequences for women of their actions. This possibility of *motivated* ignorance makes excuses suspect.

How strong is this objection? Self-deception is a matter of being motivated *not to* examine one's actions or reasoning too carefully lest something unpleasant turn up. Suppose a man who uses "he" neutrally says, when challenged, "What's wrong with that? After all, it's proper English." Is he deceiving himself that there is no moral issue here or that its being proper English is a good reason? If he has had no exposure to feminist moral criticism and hears almost everyone around him using "proper English," he will have no motive *to* examine his grammar or his reasons for using it. But this is very different from being motivated *not to* examine his grammar. Lacking a motive to be morally reflective is not self-deception. And a motive to be morally reflective is exactly what people will lack when moral ignorance is the norm.

While the embezzler and the ordinary man "acquire" their ignorance in very different contexts, in neither case does the charge that "he ought to have known better" stick. At most we have learned to be more cautious about excusing in abnormal contexts, asking such questions as, "Could he, with a reasonable amount of extra effort, have come to the conclusion that his actions were wrong? Was his moral ignorance motivated and self-deceiving?"

IV. THE SANCTIONING FORCE OF EXCUSING

I have argued that the individuals in Part I's examples are not morally responsible for participating in accepted but unacceptable social practices, since their wrongdoing occurs in an abnormal moral context where items of moral knowledge that are crucial for assessing those practices are not socially available to them, and hence their moral ignorance is not culpable. Yet our interest in questions of moral responsibility is more than an intellectual one, satisfiable by achieving correct *judgments* about responsibility. We also take a practical interest in determining how we ought to *respond* to wrongdoers. I said at the beginning that in abnormal moral contexts our entitlement to respond with moral reproach is independent of the blameworthiness of individuals. I turn now to that argument.

Imagine an analogue to Wolf's embezzler who embezzles in an abnormal moral context. He lives in a society where employees routinely embezzle money whenever they think they can get away with it (an extreme version of employees' habit, in our own society, of appropriating office supplies). His father, mother, and the people to whom he was exposed had embezzled varying amounts, and employers had come to expect this. Indeed, because embezzling is so commonplace, people find it hard to view embezzling as theft. From his point of view, it is natural for him to feel that embezzling is not wrong, or at worst, only a minor infraction.

While we may believe that his ignorance is excusable, the consequences of our acting on that belief differ substantially from the consequences of excusing Wolf's original embezzler. Because Wolf's embezzler appeals to extremely unusual causes for his ignorance, we can afford to take pity on him. In the second case, the embezzler appeals to causal factors that also cause widespread ignorance of the wrongness of embezzling. Here, acting on our belief in his excusability has the effect of sanctioning embezzling and of committing ourselves to putting up with routinely having our money embezzled. To see why this is so, we need to look at what we *do* when we excuse individuals both in face-to-face encounters with wrongdoers and in moral theorizing about excusable wrongdoing.

Suppose a student calls his female professor 'Mrs. _____,' although he knows of her doctorate and uses 'Dr.' for his male professors. If she excuses him for doing so because he could not have known how insulting this is, showing that she excuses him means letting the insult pass. Pointing out that using 'Mrs.' rather than 'Dr.' is insulting, even if done with a smile, would show that she blames, rather than excuses him. This is because, in normal contexts, which he will assume this is, people usually *are* responsible for their deeds. Thus "Using 'Mrs.,' not 'Dr.,' is insulting" says something not only about the action but about the doer's responsibility for it. It is partly because "letting it pass" is what we do when we excuse that an excusing response in abnormal moral contexts has a sanctioning force. Drawing on experimental evidence, Sabini and Silver argue that "in cases where an individual sees others doing what she would not do but doesn't voice her objections, moral drift occurs. The failure to establish publicly the wrongness of a particular action gives it an implicit legitimacy; even those who would be disposed to find it wrong have a difficulty sustaining that view when others, presumably as competent on moral matters as they, give evidence by their actions of finding it acceptable."[19] In normal moral contexts, excusing responses to morally controversial actions are ambiguous. Not pointing out wrongdoing may show either that we excuse or that we sanction. In abnormal contexts, where wrong actions are socially accepted, not pointing out wrongdoing is not even ambiguous. It will automatically be interpreted as sanctioning.

One might object that it *is* possible to make clear that one excuses while simultaneously offering moral correction. Parents do this all the time: "I know you didn't know any better and I'm not blaming you. Just remember in the future that you shouldn't . . ." While this works in parent-child interactions (or similar cases where the interacters acknowledge their unequal moral status), it does not work in most adult-adult interactions, particularly not in abnormal moral contexts. First, in parent-child cases, the presumably more knowledgeable adult is, for that reason, entitled to make corrections. In adult-adult cases, excusing a presumably knowledgeable adult for *moral* ignorance and providing moral correction are likely to be viewed by the recipient either as insulting, because it impugns his status as a normal adult, or arrogant, because it claims privileged moral authority.[20] Feminists are, of course, claiming privileged moral authority because of the abnormal moral context. But from nonfeminists' point of view, the context is normal and they need neither excuses nor remedial education.

Second, mentioning the *reason* for excusing wrongdoing in abnormal contexts, namely, because everyone else also (mistakenly) believes that the behavior is acceptable may well backfire into sanctioning. This is because when appeals to what everyone else does/thinks work meaningfully as justifications, they cannot be used as excuses. Consider the use of 'he' neutrally. Grammar textbooks spell out rules of proper English, including

19. John Sabini and Maury Silver, *Moralities of Everyday Life* (Oxford: Oxford University Press, 1982), p. 83.

20. See Sabini and Silver, "Moral Reproach," in *Moralities of Everyday Life*. They discuss the way that not having standing inhibits individuals' willingness to offer moral reproach and, by implication, others' willingness to accept reproach.

using 'he' neutrally. Teachers correct and/or punish students for not following the rules. Daily conversation reconfirms the propriety of using 'he' neutrally. The normalcy and social acceptability of this usage provides both the causal explanation and the justifying reason for participating in this linguistic practice. Social determinants *cause* people to use 'he' neutrally by providing the *reason* for doing so, namely, its propriety. Social conditioning that instilled only an automatic reflex to use 'he' neutrally and not the belief that this is proper English would be failed social conditioning. When the propriety of a practice is socially accepted, citing as an excusing condition the social determinants that created a belief in the practice's propriety thus has a sanctioning rather than an excusing force. Imagine telling Bleier's scientist that we excuse him for being morally unreflective because "everyone else" in science writes in a morally unreflective way. What will his response be? "That's not an excuse, that's my reason!" In short, citing the social determinants behind participation in a practice can have excusing force only after that practice has been delegitimated. A feminist can excuse Bleier's scientist, citing social determinants, *to another feminist.* She cannot so excuse Bleier's scientist to his face or to another scientist, since the "excuse" will appear to justify the behavior.

Citing the excusing conditions also sanctions by making the practice appear unalterable. Recall my earlier qualms about excusing the misuse of cognitive authority. Yerkes's excuse was that he could not have known that there was anything wrong with his use of cognitive authority, because the scientific community's acceptance of this use impeded his moral reflection. While true in part, this excuse misrepresents the relationship between social practice and individual action by implying a one-way causal determination: social practice shapes individual thought and action. In fact, causal determination proceeds dialectically. Social practices can be sustained only through the concerted thought and action of individual practitioners. Thus, an excusing response to individuals who participate in harmful social practices sanctions those social practices by obscuring the individual's role in sustaining and, potentially, disrupting them.

How ought people to think of their relation to social practices? Would encouraging a sense of responsibility for one's participation in social practices facilitate moral and social progress better than encouraging an awareness of one's excusability? Does moral theorizing construct the wrong sorts of self-images by focusing (as I have done) on excusing conditions? To answer these questions, let us return briefly to the society where embezzling is a social practice. Suppose, as moral theorists, we wish to criticize this practice while excusing individual embezzlers. How would we carry this off? We would need to explain what makes embezzling wrong: it results in company owners suffering undeservedly and it violates owners' rights to property. But in order to make clear that we do not hold embezzlers responsible, we would have to frame this discussion carefully. We might explicitly state that individuals are not blameworthy.

Alternatively or in addition, we might draw attention to the social forces producing embezzling, to the social practice of embezzling, to the social roles embezzling employee and passively suffering employer, and to the ideologies that mistakenly legitimate embezzling. Showing that we excuse would *preclude* describing embezzlers in such morally reproachful language as "greedy" and "depraved" and as "rights violators."

Drawing attention to excusing conditions and refraining from reproaching embezzlers will, I think, have the net effect of sanctioning the practice of embezzling *even when* the reasons for embezzling's wrongness have been fully articulated. This is because such theorizing constructs self-images that are antithetical both to conveying the obligatoriness of respecting property rights and to motivating right action. To see this, keep in mind the natural history of moral discoveries. In the beginning, when the moral context is abnormal, an understanding of embezzling's wrongness and of how social forces produce embezzlers will be confined to those in the know: moral theorists and those who read them. Later, the fact that there are moral doubts being raised about embezzling will filter down into popular consciousness without those doubts yet being absorbed into popular consciousness. People may then know that embezzling is thought wrong by some without themselves feeling or thinking that embezzling is wrong. Finally, the wrongness of embezzling may be absorbed into popular consciousness, normalizing the moral context. When the moral context is abnormal, how will the person who refrains from embezzling, because he is in the know, as well as the embezzler, who merely knows that some people think it wrong, regard themselves? And how are we (in the know) likely to think about them?

If theorizing about embezzling presents it as a social ill about which there is widespread moral ignorance, the nonembezzler will likely see himself as a man of refined moral sensibilities, a morally enlightened man. Because he refrains from doing what "everyone else" does, he may see himself as someone to be admired and as deserving employers' gratitude for respecting their rights. Because he *is* exceptionally enlightened, we may concur. Here is the first danger: in drawing attention to widespread but excusable moral ignorance, we construct a conceptual scenario in which the nonembezzler can see his not embezzling as heroic, supererogatory, and hence deserving gratitude. Simultaneously, this scenario impedes his seeing that not embezzling is simply what he *ought not to do*—he is neither heroic nor deserving of gratitude.

These consequences are far from hypothetical. Sensitive to the social determinants of oppression, women often feel grateful when husbands volunteer to babysit or when administrators show minimal support for their feminist research interests. The driving force behind such misplaced feelings of gratitude is the logic of moral language. "X is obligatory" means, "Unless there are exceptional excusing conditions you are blameworthy and reproachable for not doing X." And "X is supererogatory" means, "You are not blameworthy and reproachable for failing to do X and deserve special praise for doing X." Unfortunately this logic breaks down in abnormal contexts where individuals are routinely rather than exceptionally exempted from blameworthiness, and hence reproach, for failing to do the obligatory. No wonder, then, that women have trouble sustaining their sense of what is owed them and find themselves feeling grateful when given their due. The logic of moral language dooms any attempt to sustain or convey the obligatoriness of X while simultaneously excusing most failures to do X. Thus, in abnormal contexts, we face a choice: either we can convey the obligatoriness of X via moral reproach or we can excuse, by withholding reproach, those who deserve to be excused; but not both.

Now for the embezzler. How are we likely to see him and how will he see himself? If we believe that social forces have conspired to make him both an embezzler and also dim to the moral wrongness of what he does, we will likely see him as a product of his times or just an old-fashioned guy. If we are company owners, we might say, "I don't let his little pilferings get to me. He's such a nice old man. He just doesn't understand." (Just as women say, "I don't let his little sexist remarks get to me. He's such a nice old man. . . .") If the embezzler is the least enlightened—he realizes that others condemn embezzling but can't himself see what the fuss is all about—he may present himself to us as a product of his times or as an old-fashioned guy, saying, "I'm sorry if my embezzling bothers you, but I was brought up to take as take can," or "I guess I'm just old-fashioned. I just don't feel right not dipping in the till now and then." (Women are all too familiar with this old-fashioned man.) Here is the second danger: in drawing attention to the social determinants of moral ignorance, we construct a conceptual scenario in which we see the embezzler and he sees himself as incapable of self-legislation. We thus refrain from doing the one thing that might awaken him from his deterministic slumbers: reproach him. Once again, we seem to face a choice: either we can convey individuals' self-legislative capacity to rise above social conditioning by reproaching failures to do so, or we can excuse, by withholding reproach, those who deserve to be excused; but not both.

The point here is that theorizing is not just descriptive but also reality constructing. In the process of *describing* the social forces producing and excusing dimness to certain kinds of wrongdoing, we are also "making up" persons: the enlightened man and the one who is dim-to-wrongdoing-as-a-result-of-social-determinants, that is, the old fashioned man.[21] We are making particular identities publicly available for self-conscious wearing and labeling. Some identities, though, are best kept out of the common market. The enlightened and the old-fashioned man are two. Both images

---

21. "Making up people" is borrowed from Ian Hacking's article of the same title in *Reconstructing Individualism: Autonomy, Individuality, and the Self in Western Thought*, ed. Thomas C. Heller, Morton Sosna, and David E. Wellbery (Stanford, Calif.: Stanford University Press, 1986). The idea of making up people comes primarily from social constructionists such as Erving Goffman, Peter L. Berger, and Thomas Luckmann.

encourage wearers and labelers to focus on the obstacles to self-legislation and the heroic effort it would take to learn a different way of thinking and acting. What is the alternative? Recall the first disanalogy I mentioned between Wolf's and my embezzler. My embezzler and the old-fashioned man, unlike Wolf's embezzler, are capable of taking the moral point of view and of learning a new moral language and new moral reasoning skills. They are, in short, capable of rising above their social conditioning. Moreover, even though this might take heroic effort, refraining from participating in oppressive practices is obligatory, not an elective, supererogatory act. Given this, we would be better off making up a different set of identities, ones that draw attention both to self-legislative capacities and to the moral obligatoriness of not participating in oppressive social practices. The identities "rights violator" and "oppressor" do the former, while "not deserving gratitude" does the latter.

To summarize the moral of these stories: social vulnerability to moral reproach is necessary to (1) publicizing moral standards, (2) conveying the obligatory force of moral commands, and (3) sustaining our sense of ourselves as self-legislators. In abnormal moral contexts, excusing excusable ignorance by withholding moral reproach inhibits the publicizing and adopting of new moral standards. Thus, in abnormal contexts, it may be reasonable to reproach moral failings even when individuals are not blameworthy.

V. JUSTIFICATION VERSUS POINT

Feminist confusion about moral responsibility is not the confusion of muddled thinking but grows out of very real conflicts, in abnormal contexts, between being justified in assigning responsibility or excusing and there being a point to doing so. Justifications appeal to things like rationality, ability to take the moral point of view, having moral knowledge and moral reasoning skills, having free will (at least in the sense of not being overwhelmed by causal determinants), and so on. But after we justify assignments of responsibility or excusability, we can still ask, "What's the point?" Why do we find it worthwhile to worry about moral responsibility? Assigning responsibility licenses reproachful or approving responses: anger, admiration, chastisement, praise, seeking out, and snubbing. Moral reproach reminds or perhaps teaches us what actions are morally unacceptable. So the first point is educational. The second point is motivational. Moral reproach motivates us to change the way we act. The third is conceptual. Reproachful labels—for example, "oppressor," "exploiter," "sexist"—confirm our identities as moral agents. By contrast, an excusing response has a limited point at best: to recognize those who cannot reasonably be further educated, or motivated, or made more alive to their agency.[22]

22. This distinction between justification and point is not new. Determinists and utilitarians have frequently observed that even if there is no *justification* for assigning moral responsibility, there may nevertheless be a *point* to doing so, or at least to acting as if people

I have argued that, in normal contexts, decisions about responsibility can be both justified and have a point. Where "everyone" knows what treatments of women are wrong, most people will be responsible for their mistreatments of women, and thus women will be licensed to reproach mistreatments in ways that promote conformity to correct moral standards. I have also argued that, in abnormal contexts, decisions about responsibility can*not* be both justified and have a point. Where moral ignorance is the norm, an excusing response to moral ignorance precludes the social growth of moral knowledge.

Should women never be tolerant? Should we call the ordinary man an oppressor? Should we reproach Bleier's and Addelson's scientists? Does point always override justification in abnormal contexts? I do not know. But a commitment to moral improvement seems to require sometimes going for the point.

---

were responsible. Blaming, praising, punishing, and rewarding cause people to conform to moral and legal standards; and that is a worthwhile goal. My own view differs substantially from this one, since my claim, that reproaching those who are not blameworthy is warranted by the "benefits" of doing so, is strictly limited to abnormal moral contexts.

The Duty to Relieve Suffering*

Susan James

Suffering is an ineradicable part of human life and can sometimes be a precious condition of knowledge. But it is also, in many of its forms, an unmitigated misery, and we have only to imagine ourselves the victims of severe cold, hunger, or thirst to believe that suffering of this kind should be eradicated. Nevertheless, many millions are sick or starving, and the more affluent members of the world's population are far from doing everything in their power to help them. Perhaps this neglect will look as outrageous to our descendants as slavery now seems to us and the justifications offered for it as self-serving and contradictory as the moral beliefs of plantation owners.[1] Meanwhile, our capacity to feel justified in ignoring illness and starvation already provokes a widespread sense of uneasiness which is well expressed by Philippa Foot when she muses that "there is surely something wrong with us" in allowing this state of affairs to continue.[2] Surely there *is* something wrong with us; but the "something" is complex and hard to identify. In this paper I will discuss and criticize some recent attempts to pin it down, in the hope of seeing how we might come to think differently and more compassionately about our responsibility to relieve human suffering.

The belief that we are not bound to sacrifice our interests to reduce harm such as starvation is embedded in a prevailing theory of individual rights. The sense in which this view is dominant in Western societies does not, of course, require that everyone should hold it, for there is no moral standpoint that we all share. This position's prominence consists, rather, in the fact that it is widely adhered to and also underpins many of our major social institutions. Thus, although there are individuals who dissent from it—as utilitarians do, for example—their competing beliefs are not incorporated to the same extent in the organization of society and are therefore of less consequence. Conceptions of individual rights, like mor-

* I would like to thank John Dunn, Joel Kupperman, Scott Lehmann, Amartya Sen, Jerome Shaffer, Quentin Skinner, and John Troyer, all of whom made extremely helpful comments on an earlier draft of this paper.

1. I owe this analogy to Joel Kupperman.

2. Philippa Foot, "The Problem of Abortion and the Doctrine of Double Effect," in *Moral Problems*, ed. James Rachels, 2d ed. (New York: Harper & Row, 1975), pp. 59–70, p. 66.

This essay originally appeared in *Ethics* 93, October 1982.

al theories in general, vary from place to place and person to person; but in general rights are seen as founded on contracts, and this view is frequently thought to imply that individuals can dispose of their property as they wish, regardless of the needs of people to whom they have no contractual obligations. If they use their resources selfishly they may perhaps be condemned as "morally indecent," but as long as they are within their rights they cannot be punished.[3]

The arguments I discuss in Section II set out to show that this theory is inadequate. The first, proposed by Peter Singer, claims that we habitually underestimate the force of a utilitarian imperative to minimize suffering. The second—a more complex argument developed by John Harris— maintains that we treat our negative duty to prevent harm more lightly than our positive duty not to cause it, in a fashion that is inconsistent with the widespread belief that we are generally morally responsible for harm we have caused. Although these are important attempts to remedy a commonly recognized fault in our prevailing morality, I will suggest that neither is convincing as it stands and that their failure stems from a misunderstanding of the character of moral theories. Only when this character is grasped and appreciated will it be possible to modify specific theories in ways which do not appear merely arbitrary. In the final section of the paper I will try to take this lesson to heart and will offer a modest proposal as to how we might argue that our obligation to relieve suffering is greater than we currently realize.

I. OUR DUTY TO RELIEVE SUFFERING: THE CURRENT DEBATE

In a well-known article entitled "Famine, Affluence and Morality," Peter Singer deduces the conclusion that we have a duty to relieve suffering from three premises, two of them theoretical, the last empirical.[4] The first—that suffering is evil—is hardly open to dispute, but it is followed by the more controversial claim that people must relieve suffering whenever they are in a position to do so. Faced with this assumption, we are bound to ask how much suffering people are obliged to relieve, and Singer replies that they must at least give away their resources up to the point where they would sacrifice something of moral importance if they were to give more. For example, if I know that I can help to reduce hunger in Bangladesh by sending money to a famine relief organization, I am obliged to give as much as I can spare without damaging my own health, my children's education, or whatever else is considered morally important. Finally, Singer takes it for granted that we could in fact prevent a great

3. This view is crudely expressed by Robert Nozick in *Anarchy, State, and Utopia* (New York: Basic Books, 1974), but it can also be found in numerous other recent works. See, e.g., Judith Jarvis Thomson, "A Defense of Abortion," *Philosophy and Public Affairs* 1 (1971): 47–66; and Charles Fried, *Right and Wrong* (Cambridge, Mass.: Harvard University Press, 1978).

4. Peter Singer, "Famine, Affluence and Morality," *Philosophy and Public Affairs* 1 (1972): 229–43.

deal of harm without making morally serious sacrifices and thus concludes that we are obliged to relieve suffering by the most effective means
at our disposal.

In spite of its engaging simplicity, the persuasiveness of this argument is jeopardized by the peremptoriness of Singer's defense of its second
premise; many people just do not agree that we should give up our morally unimportant pursuits and pleasures for the sake of relieving harm, and
the claim therefore needs strenuous support. In an attempt to make it
acceptable, Singer offers an example designed to show that our intuitions
do in fact coincide with this contentious principle when we meet harm
face to face: coming upon a small child drowning in a shallow pond, most
people would unhesitatingly feel that they ought to rescue it, even though
this would mean muddying their clothes. He then suggests that there is no
morally relevant difference between this and more remote cases of harm,
so that our obligation to relieve suffering is wider than we generally
admit.

Singer thus suggests that the apparently eccentric view that we have
an overriding duty to allay harm is actually in line with a commonplace
intuition. But as it stands, his example provides such a scanty demonstra-
tion of this idea that, without further elaboration, the argument amounts
to little more than a challenge to deny the centrality of our duty to relieve
suffering. Other philosophers, however, have used the same strategy in
more developed forms to show that this duty is implied by other of our
moral beliefs, so that if we are to be consistent we must act in accord
with it.

An elegant and provocative example of this approach is offered by
John Harris, who bases his argument on the claim that causal responsibility for an event or state of affairs is a condition of moral responsibility
for it.[5] Harris does not defend this view, which he regards as uncontentious, and he simply assumes that once we have shown an action to be the
cause of another's suffering, we have reason to hold the actor morally
responsible, as long as there are no special grounds for excusing him. His
strategy is then to demonstrate that, while we enforce this criterion quite
strictly in dealing with commissions, we are far more lax in our attitude to
omissions, even though there is no relevant difference between the two
types of case. And he concludes that if we made ourselves morally responsible for the harm caused both by our actions and by our failures to act we
would find our responsibilities—and perhaps our liability for blame—
extended beyond recognition. "In whatever sense we are morally responsible for our positive actions, in the same sense we are morally responsible
for our negative actions. And the corollary of this is, of course, that whatever considerations mitigate our responsibility for positive acts, considerations of equal force are needed to mitigate our responsibility for negative
acts with the same consequences."[6]

5. John Harris, "The Marxist Conception of Violence," *Philosophy and Public Affairs* 3 (1974): 192–220.

6. Ibid., p. 211.

This argument may seem to be threatened from the start by the suggestion that we can be responsible for states of affairs we have not caused. For example, a mother may be held responsible for the consequences of her children's games, but no one would say that she had broken the windows, stolen the neighbor's prize nectarines, or started the fire in the basement. Situations of this sort are notoriously unclear, and we may feel inclined to say that the woman to whom moral responsibility is attributed must in some way be causally responsible as well; for how otherwise could it be right to hold her morally responsible? (In this vein, it might be claimed that she is causally responsible for her children's unruliness, if not for their particular misdeeds.) Although there may be cases which are not susceptible to this sort of interpretation, so that causal responsibility may not invariably be a condition of moral responsibility, our tendency to appeal to it provides support for Harris's premise. We usually only praise and blame people for the things they have done; and it is therefore reasonable to assume that people are not generally morally responsible for harm unless they have brought it about.

This criterion can be applied relatively easily to harm which is the result of our actions. But Harris is concerned with the more elusive category of harm which results from our failure to act—the suffering we fail to prevent—and he divides this into two broad classes. First, and probably best understood, is the suffering which comes about when things unexpectedly go wrong; for example, we might hear with shock that an old woman had died of cold during a spell of particularly bitter weather and want to know how this tragedy could have occurred. In searching for an explanation we look among the antecedents of the event for some factor which "made the difference" between what would normally have happened and what actually took place. Then, as Hart and Honoré point out, we designate this the cause.[7] Thus if we were to discover that a welfare officer who usually called on the old lady twice a week had gone on strike without making any provision for the people dependent on her, we would pick out this failure to visit as the cause of the woman's death because it made the difference between this week and other weeks of cold weather which she had survived. Hart and Honoré go on to observe that the distinction between abnormal and normal factors on which the identification of causes depends is itself relative to a context:

> What is taken as normal for the purposes of the distinction between causes and mere conditions is very often an artifact of human habit, custom and convention. This is because men have discovered that nature is not only sometimes harmful if we intervene, but is also sometimes harmful unless we intervene, and have developed customary techniques, procedures and routines to counteract such harm. These have become a second "nature" and so a second "norm." The effect of drought is regularly neutralised by government precautions in preserving water or food; disease is regularly neutralised by inoc-

7. H. L. A. Hart and A. M. Honoré, *Causation in the Law* (Oxford: Oxford University Press, 1959), p. 33.

ulation; rain by the use of umbrellas. When such man-made normal conditions are established, deviation from them will be regarded as exceptional, and so rank as the cause of them.[8]

They therefore conclude that, in explaining omissions of this sort, the selection of causes is relative to a more general set of expectations, including our knowledge of causal laws.

This analysis illuminates a large number of cases where the suffering which results from an omission is unexpected. However, Harris draws attention to a contrasting type of situation, where suffering is expected but is none the less disastrous for that.

> When we are seeking a causal explanation of the disasters that over-take human beings, we are often not seeking to explain why a disaster occurred on this occasion when normally it would not have occurred, but why it occurred on this occasion when it need not have done. Human life is often such a chapter of disasters that what we want explained is why these disasters happened when they could have been prevented. In these cases the question that interests us, and the question that must interest anyone who wants to explain why human beings so often needlessly come to grief is not: What made the difference?, but, What might have made the difference?[9]

The question "What made the difference?" may be inappropriate in two ways. First, there may be kinds of suffering which no one has any special responsibility to prevent. Second, there are disasters for which someone is responsible, but which are nevertheless not prevented. The fact that the world is still riddled with suffering is largely due to the unreliable character of the agents who are supposed to prevent harm, and their incompetence is often habitual and well known. The government of a poor country, for example, may be expected to prevent its citizens from starving; but if its resources always fall short of its needs, we cannot give a causal explanation of a particular famine by pointing out that government aid was inadequate, since that does not distinguish normal from abnormal functioning.

In such a case, no one would deny that groups and individuals who are not expected to intervene may nevertheless be able to help. But the fact that they may be capable of relieving suffering is generally regarded as logically independent of the attribution of causal responsibility for the suffering itself. The core of Harris's argument consists in a challenge to this distinction; for, as he puts it, "When we are looking for what might have made the difference between harm's occurring and its not occurring, anything that could have been done to prevent the harm in question is a likely candidate for causal status."[10] This view is encapsulated in a definition of our causal responsibility for negative actions which is designed to

8. Ibid., p. 35.
9. Harris, pp. 206–7.
10. Harris, p. 207.

apply both to harms which no one has a special duty to prevent and to harms which are not successfully prevented by the agents responsible for them. It is also intended to be symmetrical with the corresponding definition for positive actions.

A's failure to do X caused Y where
>   1) A could have done X.
>   2) X would have prevented Y.
>   3) Y involves harm to human beings.

This definition has the consequence that we are causally responsible for all the harm we fail to prevent, and to accept it would thus be to commit ourselves to a far more strenuous morality than the one we currently live by. Harris certainly intends this conclusion; but while it is clear that our causal responsibilities would increase if his argument were accepted, the scope of our potential moral responsibilities is still opaque, since it depends on the range of excuses which are held to exempt us from praise or blame. This in turn depends on the interpretation of the condition "A could have done X," and I will have more to say about this in Section II. For the moment it is enough to point out that if "A could have done X" is read in the manner suggested by Singer, as "A could have done X without sacrificing anything of moral importance," our responsibilities will be far less than if it is read as, for example, "It would have been physically possible for A to do X."

II. THE SHORTCOMINGS OF THE CURRENT ARGUMENTS

In another context, Harris himself points out that his argument is open to two kinds of refutation: "The obvious ways to criticise the negative responsibility thesis are either to attack the causal linkage between inaction and consequence, and to claim that this is somehow more tenuous than that between action and consequence, or to 'discredit' it by insisting on the basic moral relevance of the distinction between action and inaction."[11] In this section I will argue that Harris's thesis is in fact vulnerable to the first of these lines of criticism, and I will claim that his definition of negative causation fails to do the work he demands of it. I will first suggest that the relation he posits between causal and moral responsibility is viciously circular and will then show that his definition of negative responsibility is not symmetrical with that of positive responsibility. These failings undermine the connection between causal and moral responsibility on which his argument depends and put his conclusion in serious doubt.

Harris's definition of negative causation can most easily be understood by means of an example, and I will take a case of harm for which no one has any special responsibility. Imagine that a hundred people die in Bali when a normally quiescent volcano erupts during the night, engulf-

11. John Harris, "Williams on Negative Responsibility and Integrity," *Philosophical Quarterly* 24 (1974): 267–73, p. 265.

ing their village in gas and lava. The victims, we suppose, had no warning of the disaster; but in the early hours of the previous morning an old man in a neighboring village had seen the crater glowing in the dark and realized that the volcano was active, although he had said nothing about it. According to Harris he is causally responsible for the hundred deaths, because if he had raised the alarm (which he could have done) the villagers could have left their homes before they were suffocated by fumes. His omission was among the things that caused them to die.

The oddity of this view arises, I think, from the fact that Harris does not distinguish sufficiently carefully between the prevention and the explanation of human harm. To be sure, our attempts to explain and control the world both rely on a knowledge of causal connections; but the questions "Why did X happen?" and "What would stop X happening?" are nevertheless provoked by very different interests—so much so that the causal factors we pick out in trying to explain a particular event may be quite different from those we identify in seeking to prevent it. (An unexpected volcanic eruption, for example, may explain the deaths of a hundred Balinese villagers, but we cannot in general prevent deaths by preventing eruptions.)

In Harris's account of negative causation an interest in the prevention of harm is emphasized at the expense of much concern with explanation. Since he is concerned with control, and since we control the world by acting on it, his definition is bound to pick out actions and failures to act as the causes of suffering. This naturally concentrates the attention on a certain sort of causal factor and draws it away from others, although the causal influence of nonhuman events and states of affairs is not denied. It is open to Harris to argue that a complex set of factors—including, perhaps, the eruption of the volcano, the direction of the wind, and the old man's failure to raise the alarm—caused the hundred deaths. But we may well wonder why this negative action should be counted as a causal factor at all. For it seems merely arbitrary to build into the definition the requirement that negative actions should be identified as the causes of human suffering.

In their discussion of the suffering which results from unexpected omissions on the part of agents who have some special responsibility for relieving it, Hart and Honoré claim that our identification of causes is relative to a more general set of beliefs and interests. We can now see that the same is true of Harris's analysis of causes of suffering which cannot be explained in this manner. For the belief which prompts him to insist that negative actions are among those causes is precisely the belief that relieving human harm is of paramount importance. If suffering is caused by uncontrollable natural forces, there may not be much we can do about it. But if it is caused by our own omissions, we may be in a position to put a stop to it, and we may also be morally required to do so.

There is a strong case to be made for the claim that causal analysis is always relative to our interests, and it might be thought that, in appealing to a moral belief to elucidate the notion of causal responsibility, Harris is only doing what all theorists are bound to do. But before resting content with this conclusion it is important to look again at the structure of his argument. As we saw in Section I, it is based on the premise that we are generally only morally obliged to relieve harm if we have caused it. However, it is now clear that Harris's analysis of negative causation is only defensible if it is already assumed that we have this obligation. It therefore becomes important to ask whether this circle is vicious and undermines the conclusion that we are morally responsible for harm we fail to prevent.

A helpful analysis of circularity has recently been offered by Dummett, who makes a pertinent distinction between explanatory and suasive arguments.[12] When an argument is constructed to explain something, the conclusion may be given in advance and the premises accepted simply because they provide a plausible explanation of the truth of the conclusion. Suasive arguments, in contrast, seek to develop the consequences of a set of premises and to show that, since the premises are true, the conclusion must be granted. In the first sort of case circularity is not always objectionable, but in the second the polemical intention of the argument makes it more damaging. Since Harris's argument is clearly of the latter kind, and since it appeals to the very obligation it sets out to defend, the circle within which it moves is too small for comfort and undermines its ability to persuade us of the truth of its conclusion.

This disability becomes more evident when one considers the causal overdetermination which Harris's definition of negative causation implies—and of which he is well aware. In his view, a large number of people can be causally responsible for the suffering of a particular individual at a particular time. For example, ten thousand wealthy Americans may read a notice in the *New Yorker* describing the plight of a young Laotian girl who is homeless and starving and informing them that ten dollars, sent to a specific address, would feed and clothe her for a year. It is safe to assume that most of these readers could send off a check without putting any undue strain on their resources, and according to Harris anyone who fails to do so (and instead turns the page to study the advertisements for Tiffany's and Courvoisier) is causally responsible for the child's suffering. At least, they are responsible unless someone else donates the ten dollars; for we can then assume that aid will eventually reach the child, and there will be no suffering to be responsible for. But since we do not know what other readers of the *New Yorker* will do, we cannot tell in advance how much harm we will cause—if any—by failing to respond to this appeal and others like it.

If each of us were to assume responsibility for all the suffering we could relieve and which, as far as we knew, no one else had relieved, we would acquire an enormous burden of responsibility and guilt. And yet the burden would be unnecessarily heavy, since it would make large num-

12. M. A. E. Dummett, "The Justification of Deduction," *Proceedings of the British Academy* 59 (1973): 201–32, p. 207.

bers of people responsible for harm which any one of them could have alleviated. When Harris's definition is interpreted in this way, our inability to tell in advance what events our omissions will cause makes us unable to determine the scope of our responsibilities; and apart from being unsettling, this reveals an unsatisfactory vagueness in his argument. We usually only hold people responsible for harm they have caused when they were in a position to predict and assess the outcome of their action. But in cases like that of the Laotian child it is not possible to make such a prediction; for although I know that the child will suffer unless someone helps, I do not know that, unless I help, the suffering will be endured.

Perhaps Harris will reply that it is a mistake to concentrate on the suffering of individuals. We do not know whether anyone will send ten dollars to relieve the hunger of the Laotian child, but we do know that millions of people are starving and that the world's aid will not be enough to feed them all. Unless we do what we can to help, we will be causally responsible for some of their suffering. Such an answer successfully avoids the extreme overdetermination we have just discussed, but it also gives rise to two further difficulties. First, it implies that the only way to avoid causal responsibility for harm is to ensure that the condition "*A* could have done *X*" is false, and we then need to know what falsifies it. Second, it makes agents causally responsible for some harm (as much as they could have relieved), but not for particular cases of harm such as the Laotian girl's hunger. If they have no excuse for their behavior, these agents also bear moral responsibility and are presumably culpable for their failure to prevent suffering. However, while we can blame people for causing this or that instance of harm, it is hard to see how we can blame them for causing some harm or other, and a more precise way of identifying causes and effects will surely be needed.

Before Harris's definition of negative causation can be applied, the condition "*A* could have done *X*" must therefore be elaborated: the exact nature of *X* must be specified, and the force of the conditional "could have done" must be spelled out. But in addition to being incomplete, this criterion of moral responsibility plays a role in the definition which presents a serious threat to Harris's general argument. As we saw earlier, he aims to provide an account of negative causation symmetrical with that of positive causation and to show that they yield equally strong moral obligations. But we must now consider whether the two accounts really are symmetrical in the way he maintains.

The fact that the features of the definition of negative causation which have just proved puzzling do not seem to trouble its positive counterpart might at first seem to be due to an asymmetry between positive and negative acts. As the example of the Laotian child shows, there are far more omissions which can be cited in explaining a single event than commissions. If this were the only difference, Harris would have no need to worry, but I will suggest that the two definitions are also marked by a deeper dissimilarity. The presence of the criterion "*A* could have done *X*" in the definition of negative causation makes it asymmetrical with the corresponding definition of positive causation, and this in turn alters the relation between causal and moral responsibility on which Harris's argument is founded.

The omissions we have been considering have two salient characteristics: each is sufficient to bring about harm if other relevant factors are assumed to be constant, and in every case a number of agents are in a position to avert or to cause the harm by their actions. An analogous commission would therefore share both these traits, except that the harm would arise from a positive action rather than a negative one. Imagine, for example, a jury which has to conform to certain rules. To secure a conviction, all the members must vote the defendant guilty, but each jury member has a power of veto and has only to abstain from voting for the defendant to be released. Suppose we also happen to know that a particular conviction would be harmful because an innocent person would be sentenced to a painful death. We thus have a case where the commissions of the jury members (their votes) will cause suffering, while the omission of any one of them (an abstention) will avert it. Then, if the jury votes the defendant guilty, each vote is a causal factor contributing to a harmful outcome. But if one member abstains, that abstention is counted as the cause of the defendant's release.

The causal role played by the jury members' votes, when they do vote to convict the defendant, is unaffected by the fact that they have a power of veto. This becomes clear when we imagine the same case judged by a different jury which has no such power and can only vote for or against conviction. As before, they decide that the defendant is guilty, and as before their votes are causal factors which contribute to the death of an innocent person. In analyzing a series of events which includes the casting of votes, and in arriving at a judgment of causal responsibility, we take account of our knowledge of causal laws and of the conventions of *the* law, but we do not need to consider the range of alternatives open to the jury members. When we try to establish moral responsibility, however, this becomes a central consideration; for in certain circumstances the jury members will be excused from moral responsibility on the grounds that they had no choice, or could not have done otherwise.

This account of the factors relevant to establishing causal responsibility for events applies to commissions which result in harm, and it also applies to the class of omissions discussed by Hart and Honoré. (For example, if two trains crash when a signalman fails to change the points, we may cite his omission as the cause of the disaster. The fact that he had just had a severe stroke may excuse him from moral responsibility on the grounds that he could not have done what was expected of him, but it does not affect the claim that his omission caused the crash.) However, this analysis cannot apply to Harris's account of negative actions, for in his view my failure to perform an action is only a cause of a harmful outcome if I could have done the action. The question of whether I could have acted differently is therefore raised in order to establish whether I am causally responsible, and the problem of what we are to understand by the condition "*A* could have done *X*" is logically prior to the attribution of causal responsibility. But this contrasts sharply with the other cases we considered, where causal responsibility was established without asking what else an agent could have done.

The repercussions of this asymmetry are both serious and instructive. Harris's original strategy was to make use of an uncontentious connection between causal and moral responsibility to show that in ordinary circumstances we are morally responsible for any harm we cause. But his definition of negative causation treats what is usually a criterion of moral responsibility as a condition of causal responsibility, thus blurring the distinction between the two categories and undercutting the structure of his own arguments.

In an attempt to overcome this problem, one might ask whether Harris really needs the condition "*A* could have done *X*" as part of his definition. But I think it is clear that he does. If he were to abandon it he would be forced to allow not only that the millionaire who fails to give ten dollars to relieve the hunger of the Laotian child is causally responsible for her suffering, but also that the pauper, who has no dollars to give, plays the same causal role. And this seems only to make matters worse. However, one might also wonder whether the condition could be interpreted in a way that does not muddy the distinction between causal and moral responsibility. When we identify causes and effects we rely on a general knowledge of causal laws to tell us what is and is not possible—or, to put it another way, what could and could not happen. For example, the fact that people cannot turn grains of sand into grains of wheat prevents us from citing the failure of the president of Morocco to turn sand into wheat as a cause of famine in the Sahara. Here the move from "*A*'s cannot do *X*" to "This *A* cannot do *X*" is exemplary. But claims about what agents can do are less straightforward, and the general claim that people can relieve hunger by sending money to famine relief organizations does not imply that any particular person is capable of performing this action. If Harris's condition "*A* could have done *X*" were just a general affirmation that *X* is the sort of thing people can do, it would be possible to identify the causes of negative actions without taking the alternatives open to particular agents into account, and the usual distinction between causal and moral responsibility could then be maintained. But the philosophical cost of such an interpretation is prohibitive, for unless we know something about the capacities of specific agents, we will be unable to say whether they are causally responsible for particular cases of harm. We need to know what they could have done, rather than what people in general can do, and for this we must know whether they could have acted differently.

By introducing what is usually a criterion for moral responsibility into his definition of causal responsibility and then relying on a supposedly clear relation between the two, Harris creates another tight circle; and, as I have suggested, he thereby undercuts his own argument. Unless we are prepared to reconsider our concepts of causal and moral responsibility, we will be unable to accept his definition of negative causation and will not be be able to justify the claim that we have a duty to prevent harm on the grounds that our neglect has caused it. In some ways this is, of course, a disappointing conclusion, but it is perhaps not surprising that such an attempt should fail. Since moral theories are theories, and their terms are bound together by links of varying strength, it is often impossible to transform moral attitudes to a social practice such as our treatment of the hungry without transforming a great deal else as well. There are times when it can be shown that a concept has a broader application than people are generally willing to admit, without making great alterations in the theory surrounding it, and this is what Harris has tried to do. In this case, however, our concepts are too inflexible for his desires and will not stretch to the point where our obligation to prevent harm is as stringent as our duty not to bring it about.

III. A DIFFERENT APPROACH TO OUR DUTY
TO RELIEVE SUFFERING

Neither Singer nor Harris offers an adequate defense of the view that the extent of our obligation to avert harm is greater than we generally acknowledge. But one may nevertheless be sympathetic to their conclusion and share their wish to support it. Before searching for an argument to vindicate their position, it is helpful to try to understand at a general level why the accounts we have so far discussed are unsuccessful; for once we have identified the obstacles in our path, we will be in a better position to overcome them. Why, then, do Singer and Harris fail to persuade us that our duties to prevent and alleviate suffering are as extensive as they believe?

The answer, I think, is that they share a mistaken conception of the character of substantive moral argument. Faced with the sheer quantity of suffering in the world, it is tempting to believe that the plight of the sick and hungry will only be relieved when society and morality are transformed and to take refuge in a utopian philosophy. But if we wish to grapple with the problem, we must make use of the tools we possess to construct persuasive arguments for social change, and among the most powerful of these implements is our existing morality. In different ways, both Singer and Harris neglect this injunction, for they both ground the conclusion that we are obliged to relieve harm on premises which are at odds with the moral beliefs dominant in our society. The effect of their arguments is thus merely to point out that if our moral beliefs were not what they are, we would be in a better position to recognize more extensive moral obligations than we do. As we saw, Singer deliberately bases his argument on a quasi-utilitarian premise, and if our beliefs and institutions were predominantly utilitarian in character it would no doubt have considerable force. But since Singer's argument takes no account of the theory of rights which, for better or worse, plays a central part in modern Western societies, it does not answer to our everyday experience and morality. Harris, by contrast, tries to make use of our existing beliefs about the relation of moral and causal responsibility; but in his attempt to modify them, he produces a definition of negative responsibility which falls altogether outside our ordinary understanding of the term. In both cases the consequence is the same: the claim that we are obliged to relieve suffering is founded on a theory which appears merely arbitrary and thus lacks any immediate persuasive power.

A convincing argument will therefore have to be parasitic on the beliefs we already hold; and to argue in a constructive spirit for a more extensive duty to relieve harm, we will be well advised to begin by asking what well-entrenched aspects of our current morality lend themselves to this task. I will suggest that we can use two lines of existing argument in support of the view that our obligations in this area are far greater than those which our practice reflects.

One potentially fruitful approach is the idea of a theory of natural obligation, in which the demands people can legitimately make of one another are regarded as functions of their "natural" relations. Though fiercely resisted in some political and philosophical circles, such a theory already has a role in our moral life, since neither the duties of parents to their children, for example, nor all the relations between governments are contractual in character. Thus there may be cases where one country sends aid to another on the grounds that the rich have a natural obligation to help those who are less well-off, rather than in exchange for silence, loyalty, or the right to sell Coca-Cola. And although these arrangements have an equivocal status in places where the law bases most duties on contracts, some legal systems recognize and enforce natural obligations, at least on a limited scale. In French law, for instance, as in many other systems based on the Roman civil code, it is an offense to fail to help people who have come to harm, even if they are complete strangers, and one is only excused from this duty if one would endanger one's own life or health by giving aid.[13]

While the notion of a natural duty to relieve suffering is not altogether unfamiliar, it is true that we lack a thorough analysis of it. In order to build it into a persuasive theory we would need to know much more about the origins, extent, and character of such duties, as well as their relations with other connected concepts. Until we have such an account, appeals to natural obligation unfortunately raise as many problems as they solve, and they consequently lack the power to defend the claim that we are obliged to relieve suffering.

There is, however, a second way of approaching the question. As we have seen, Harris and Hart and Honoré discuss two kinds of case in which we already hold people morally responsible for harm. On the one hand,

13. See Aleksander W. Rudzinski, "The Duty to Rescue: A Comparative Analysis," in *The Good Samaritan and the Law*, ed. James M. Ratcliffe (Garden City, N.Y.: Doubleday & Co., 1975), pp. 91–134. For citations from the French criminal code, see ibid., pp. 130–31.

Harris points out that, where commissions are concerned, causal responsibility is a condition of moral responsibility; thus, unless an agent can show that he has some excuse, he will be blamed for causing harm by his positive actions. Hart and Honoré, on the other hand, define a class of cases where we hold agents culpable for harm which is the result of their omissions. If both these sets of criteria for moral responsibility are strictly adhered to in practice, we ought to find that agents are invariably blamed for causing suffering in either of these ways, and we would then be able to conclude that social behavior and moral theory are in line with one another. But it might turn out that agents who cause suffering sometimes escape moral responsibility and the punishment it implies, and such a discrepancy between theory and practice would require explanation. Furthermore, a widespread acceptance of the moral beliefs on which Harris and Hart and Honoré base their arguments would reveal an inconsistency in common mores and would enable us to argue that harm of these kinds is illegitimate in the sense that people have an obligation to relieve and prevent it.

It is possible, therefore, that existing arguments for our obligation to prevent suffering may be capable of doing much more work than is currently demanded of them, and if we were to apply them strictly we might find that they condemned many kinds of harm which are tolerated at present. I will suggest that a policy which imposed them rigorously could in fact reduce suffering to a considerable extent.

The theory of responsibility we use to assess praise and blame deals primarily with the actions of private individuals and aims to specify the types of circumstances in which people are morally responsible for harm they have caused and those in which they are excused. Much of this theory is clear and unproblematic; for example, it is generally agreed that if an action is done in self-defense, the agent's responsibility for it is reduced. But private individuals are not the only agents who perform actions, and when the theory is applied to groups and to individuals acting in public capacities it loses some of its clarity and rigor. A striking example of this arises in connection with the principle that, unless one of a standard range of excuses can be appealed to, causal responsibility implies moral responsibility. This precept is widely applied to the actions of individuals, and they are consequently regarded as culpable for harm they have brought about. But it is common knowledge that corporate agents frequently go unpunished in similar circumstances. As one example among many, consider the policy adopted by the Occupational Safety and Health Administration (OSHA)—a part of the Labor Department—toward the use of organophosphate pesticides. These chemicals are known to be extremely dangerous to humans, but ever since the banning of DDT in 1972 they have been widely used by farmers growing fruit and vegetables, despite the considerable risk to which this exposes their employees.[14] In 1970 the Environmental Protection Agency recorded 5,729 cases of severe poi-

14. David Zwerdling, "The New Pesticide Threat," *Food for People Not for Profit*, ed. Catherine Lerza and Michael Jacobson (New York: Random House, 1975), pp. 93–98.

soning among "pesticide formulators, air plane loaders and spreaders, and field workers, who suffered from dizziness, sweating, headaches, cramps, loss of appetite, pus-filled sores, bloody urine, muscle spasms in the oesophagus, bleeding from the mouth, nose and eyes, and respiratory arrest." And an official of the Federal Department of Agriculture estimated that there are 80,000 poisonings and 800 deaths from such pesticides each year. This state of affairs has not gone unnoticed, and some attempts have been made to ban the use of organophosphate sprays.

> In May 1973, OSHA yielded to a court suit by the Migrant Legal Action Project and issued temporary emergency regulations which would protect the farm workers from the organophosphate onslaught of the current growing season. The regulations, which prohibit a grower from sending workers into pesticide-sprayed fields until a certain number of days are up, were far weaker than the California State regulations—but not weak enough for the growers, who besieged OSHA and farm bloc senators with protest letters and petitions.

> On June 15th, OSHA suddenly suspended the emergency regulations, and, on June 29th, issued new ones falling more in line with the re-entry times the growers said they would accept. The standards exempt twelve organophosphates from any control at all—including Ethion, which is so toxic that sixteen farm workers fell ill when they entered a field sprayed two weeks earlier, according to the California Public Health Department. The new regulations slash re-entry times dramatically for the nine other pesticides.[15]

Faced with stricter rules, a number of growers pressed for a policy known to cause harm, the OSHA approved it, and some workers evidently fell ill, or even died, as a result. However, it might be argued that the farmers really had no choice but to lobby for the legalization of these pesticides. Perhaps they knew that, unless they were able to use organophosphate sprays, their levels of production and profit would fall sharply, endangering the livelihoods of themselves and their employees, so that the price of a few sick workers just had to be paid. Our attitude to this excuse will depend on our view of the market as a whole. If we picture it as a merciless force which constrains firms to maximize their profits by all the means at their disposal, then we will agree that policies of maximization are never chosen freely. But while it is clear that the market puts constraints on even the largest multinational corporations, we know that this general picture is false. Businesses have to make decisions about how much profit to make and how to make it, and in doing so they assess and choose between various alternatives. So although it may be hard for a farmer to accommodate to the effects of a decision to abide by a regulation restricting the use of pesticides, such a choice can be made, as was the fruit growers' actual choice to insist on a change in the rules. If this is right, the growers' action was among a number of factors which caused harm for

15. Ibid., p. 97.

which they are morally responsible. And yet they have not been charged or punished. The same sort of responsibility falls on the OSHA, though this organization seems to be doubly guilty. Because it not only repealed its own regulations and thus exposed the workers to harm, but also failed in its duty to protect them, harm resulted from both its omissions and its commissions, and it is condemned on both counts.

The story of the use of organophosphate pesticides is deeply shocking, but of course it is by no means unique. And the fact that such cases abound suggests that we can use existing moral beliefs to defend a considerable reduction in the amount of suffering we are prepared to tolerate. Before discussing the limits of this view, it is worth considering two relatively minor objections. First, it might be claimed that the causal networks containing the actions of groups such as governments, corporations, or fruit growers are so enormously complicated that we cannot hope to discern particular causal connections within them, let alone decide how to allocate moral responsibility for specific cases of suffering. This charge of complexity is certainly justified, but I cannot see that it is a criticism. Any account of the causes of human harm is bound to be labyrinthine, and there seems little reason to think that an account couched in terms of institutional groups will be more impenetrable than one which traces relations between individuals. However, it might also be objected that, by focusing on social groups as the causal agents of harm, we destroy the rhetorical force of the connection between causal and moral responsibility. Much of the strength of an argument like Harris's stems from the fact that it attributes responsibility for harm to individuals and puts the onus on them to do something about it. But since the claim that a group is morally responsible for a state of affairs does not entail that every member— or even any member—has an obligation to change it, the consciences of institutions are less easily pricked, and the shift from an individual to a social level of argument is accompanied by a loss of persuasive power. Again, this argument does not seem unduly damaging. First, the suggestion that we should be more strict about holding agents morally responsible for harm they have caused applies just as well to individuals as to groups. But more important, a concern with the responsibilities of groups might be regarded as a merit, rather than a defect, of an argument which aims to reveal the extent of our obligations to relieve and prevent harm, for much of the harm which afflicts people is both caused by groups and of a kind which can most readily be relieved by them. Single individuals often cannot do a great deal to prevent famine and disease, and they are relatively powerless to wreak these ills on others. But governments, hospitals, and corporations can obviously make great changes in the world. Thus what we need are detailed causal analyses which would demonstrate exactly how the actions of various agents combine to cause harm and suffering, and to go with this we need an extensive theory of corporate responsibility which would enable us to attribute praise and blame to groups and their members.

A further feature of our theory of responsibility which we apply less rigorously to groups than to individuals is the contentious notion of the *mens rea*. If we accept its supremacy as a criterion of responsibility and only hold agents responsible for harm they intended to bring about, our responsibilities will obviously be lighter than if we take the stronger line that agents are responsible for harm which they cause and should have foreseen, even if they may have caused it unintentionally. The proper relation between these alternatives is far from clear, even in cases concerning private individuals.[16] But the existence of charges such as negligence indicates that the law frequently does require people to consider whether a particular course of action is likely to have harmful effects and to avoid it if this seems probable. For example, take the case of Mrs. Hyam, who set fire to the house of a woman whom her lover was proposing to marry. In the fire two children were killed, and Mrs. Hyam was convicted of murder, even though she claimed she had only intended to give her rival a good fright. Here the court ruled that she ought to have foreseen the possibly disastrous consequences of her action and was guilty of failing to do so.[17]

That the actions of groups are not always subject to this stricture is evident from the case of the OSHA, since the harm which resulted from its pesticide policy was certainly foreseen. But there is a further respect in which the use of foresight rather than intention as the criterion of moral responsibility can reduce human suffering, and this arises from the fact that we are sometimes able to foresee the relatively remote consequences of our actions. To take a different example, some South African gold-mining companies are known to expose their workers to such terrible conditions that many of them are killed and injured each year, even though less dangerous mining techniques exist. The stockholders of such companies play a causal role in perpetuating this state of affairs, since without their money the companies could not go on, and these stockholders are also able to foresee that by using their resources in this way they will contribute to the suffering of the miners. At the moment we do not generally hold agents morally responsible for harm which results from the actions of companies in which they have invested. But if we were to regard it as incumbent on people to reflect on the consequences of their actions and to avoid such harm as they foresaw, thousands of lives would be changed. Many agents would be forced to act differently, and much suffering would be averted.[18]

The starting point of this article was the claim that our obligation to prevent harm is greater than we usually admit. I have argued that, if we are genuinely anxious to persuade people of this conclusion, it is a mis-

16. As an example of this uncertainty, see *D.P.P.* v. *Smith*, A.C. 290 (1961), and the controversy it aroused: e.g., H. L. A. Hart's letter to the *Times* (London) (November 12, 1960).

17. *Hyam* v. *D.P.P.*, 2 W.L.R. 607 (1974).

18. On this point, see also Onora Nell, "Lifeboat Earth," *Philosophy and Public Affairs* 4 (1975): 273–92.

take to appeal to an unfamiliar moral theory as Singer and Harris do, since a more efficacious approach lies in taking our existing beliefs seriously. As I have suggested, some of the best entrenched of these in fact provide us with a means of arguing that we have a duty to avert many kinds of suffering which are currently tolerated. It is true that the precise extent of these kinds of suffering remains to be discovered, for at present we do not have a good enough grasp of the causal relations between actions to identify them all. But it seems likely that the causal networks would be sufficiently far-reaching and complex to affect the lives of many of us. Even in our present state of knowledge, however, it is clear that this approach would not imply, for example, that governments ought to relieve harm which is causally unrelated to their own actions or those of their citizens. So if the proposal of the last section seems somewhat limited, I can only agree. But its limits are the limits of the moral theory which prevails, and a more humane society will need a new morality.

Trust and Antitrust*

Annette Baier

TRUST AND ITS VARIETIES

> "*Whatever* matters to human beings, trust is the atmosphere in which it thrives." [SISSELA BOK][1]

Whether or not everything which matters to us is the sort of thing that can thrive or languish (I may care most about my stamp collection) or even whether all the possibly thriving things we care about need trust in order to thrive (does my rubber tree?), there surely is something basically right about Bok's claim. Given that I cannot myself guard my stamp collection at all times, nor take my rubber tree with me on my travels, the custody of these things that matter to me must often be transferred to others, presumably to others I trust. Without trust, what matters to me would be unsafe, unless like the Stoic I attach myself only to what can thrive, or be safe from harm, *however* others act. The starry heavens above and the moral law within had better be about the only things that matter to me, if there is no one I can trust in any way. Even my own Stoic virtue will surely thrive better if it evokes some trust from others, inspires some trustworthiness in them, or is approved and imitated by them.

To Bok's statement, however, we should add another, that not all the things that thrive when there is trust between people, and which matter, are things that should be encouraged to thrive. Exploitation and

---

* I owe the second half of my title to the salutary reaction of Alexander Nehamas to an earlier and more sanguine version of this paper, read at Chapel Hill Colloquium in October 1984. I also owe many important points which I have tried to incorporate in this revised version to John Cooper, who commented helpfully on the paper on that occasion, to numerous constructive critics at later presentations of versions of it at CUNY Graduate Center, Brooklyn College, Columbia University, the University of Pennsylvania, and to readers for this journal. I received such a flood of helpful and enthusiastic advice that it became clear that, although few philosophers have written directly on this topic, very many have been thinking about it. It is only by ruthlessly putting finis to my potentially endless revisions and researches into hitherto unfamiliar legal, sociological, psychological, and economic literature that any paper emerged from my responses to these gratifying and generous responses.

1. Sissela Bok, *Lying* (New York: Pantheon Books, 1978), p. 31n. Bok is one of the few philosophers to have addressed the ethics of trust fairly directly. The title of the chapter from which this quotation comes is "Truthfulness, Deceit and Trust."

This essay originally appeared in *Ethics* 96, January 1986.

conspiracy, as much as justice and fellowship, thrive better in an atmosphere of trust. There are immoral as well as moral trust relationships, and trust-busting can be a morally proper goal. If we are to tell when morality requires the preservation of trust, when it requires the destruction of trust, we obviously need to distinguish different forms of trust, and to look for some morally relevant features they may possess. In this paper I make a start on this large task.

It is a start, not a continuation, because there has been a strange silence on the topic in the tradition of moral philosophy with which I am familiar. Psychologists and sociologists have discussed it, lawyers have worked out the requirements of equity on legal trusts, political philosophers have discussed trust in governments, and there has been some discussion of trust when philosophers address the assurance problem in Prisoner's Dilemma contexts. But we, or at least I, search in vain for any general account of the morality of trust relationships. The question, Whom should I trust in what way, and why? has not been the central question in moral philosophy as we know it. Yet if I am right in claiming that morality, as anything more than a law within, itself requires trust in order to thrive, and that immorality too thrives on some forms of trust, it seems pretty obvious that we ought, as moral philosophers, to look into the question of what forms of trust are needed for the thriving of the version of morality we endorse, and into the morality of that and other forms of trust. A minimal condition of adequacy for any version of the true morality, if truth has anything to do with reality, is that it not have to condemn the conditions needed for its own thriving. Yet we will be in no position to apply that test to the trust in which morality thrives until we have worked out, at least in a provisional way, how to judge trust relationships from a moral point of view.

Moral philosophers have always been interested in cooperation bet-ween people, and so it is surprising that they have not said more than they have about trust. It seems fairly obvious that any form of cooperative activity, including the division of labor, requires the cooperators to trust one another to do their bit, or at the very least to trust the overseer with his whip to do his bit, where coercion is relied on. One would expect contractarians to investigate the forms of trust and distrust parties to a contract exhibit. Utilitarians too should be concerned with the contribution to the general happiness of various climates of trust, so be concerned to understand the nature, roots, and varieties of trust. One might also have expected those with a moral theory of the virtues to have looked at trustworthiness, or at willingness to give trust. But when we turn to the great moral philosophers, in our tradition, what we find can scarcely be said to be even a sketch of a moral theory of trust. At most we get a few hints of directions in which we might go.

Plato in the *Republic* presumably expects the majority of citizens to trust the philosopher kings to rule wisely and expects that elite to trust their underlings not to poison their wine, nor set fire to their libraries, but neither proper trust nor proper trustworthiness are among the virtues he dwells on as necessary in the cooperating parties in his good society. His version of justice and of the "friendship" supposed to exist between ruler and ruled seems to *imply* such virtues of trust, but he does not himself draw out the implications. In the *Laws* he mentions distrust as an evil produced by association with seafaring traders, but it is only a mention.[2] The same sort of claim can also be made about Aristotle—his virtuous person, like Plato's, must place his trust in that hypothetical wise person who will teach him just how much anger and pride and fear to feel with what reasons, when, and toward which objects. Such a wise man presumably also knows just how much trust in whom, on what matters, and how much trustworthiness, should be cultivated, as well as who should show trust toward whom, but such crucial wisdom and such central virtues are not discussed by Aristotle, as far as I am aware. (He does, in the *Politics,* condemn tyrants for sowing seeds of distrust, and his discussion of friendship might be cited as one place where he implicitly recognizes the importance of trust; could someone one distrusted be a second self to one? But that is implicit only, and in any case would cover only trust between friends.) Nor do later moral philosophers do much better on this count.[3]

There are some forms of trust to which the great philosophers *have* given explicit attention. Saint Thomas Aquinas, and other Christian moralists, have extolled the virtue of faith and, more relevantly, of hope, and so have said something about trust in God. And in the modern period some of the great moral and political philosophers, in particular John Locke, looked at trust in governments and officials, and some have shown what might be called an obsessive trust in contracts and contractors, even if not, after Hobbes's good example here, an equal obsession with the grounds for such trust. It is selective attention then, rather than total inattention, which is the philosophical phenomenon on which I wish to remark, tentatively to explain, and try to terminate or at least to interrupt.

Trust, the phenomenon we are so familiar with that we scarcely notice its presence and its variety, is shown by us and responded to by

---

2. Plato, *Laws* 4.705a. I owe this reference to John Cooper, who found my charge that Plato and Aristotle had neglected the topic of trust ungenerous, given how much they fairly clearly took for granted about its value and importance. (But taking for granted is a form of neglect.)

3. Besides Bok and Locke, whom I refer to, those who have said something about it include N. Hartmann, *Ethik* (Berlin: W. de Gruyter, 1962), pp. 468 ff.; Virginia Held, *Rights and Goods* (New York and London: Free Press, 1984), esp. chap. 5, "The Grounds for Social Trust"; D. O. Thomas, "The Duty to Trust," *Aristotelian Society Proceedings* (1970), pp. 89–101. It is invoked in passing by Aurel Kolnai in "Forgiveness," in *Ethics, Value and Reality,* ed. Bernard Williams and David Wiggins (Indianapolis: Macmillan Co., 1978): "Trust in the world, unless it is vitiated by hairbrained optimism and dangerous irresponsibility, may be looked upon not to be sure as the very starting point and very basis but perhaps as the epitome and culmination of morality" (p. 223); and by John R. S. Wilson in "In One Another's Power," *Ethics* 88 (1978): 303.

us not only with intimates but with strangers, and even with declared enemies. We trust our enemies not to fire at us when we lay down our arms and put out a white flag. In Britain burglars and police used to trust each other not to carry deadly weapons. We often trust total strangers, such as those from whom we ask directions in foreign cities, to direct rather than misdirect us, or to tell us so if they do not know what we want to know; and we think we should do the same for those who ask the same help from us. Of course we are often disappointed, rebuffed, let down, or betrayed when we exhibit such trust in others, and we are often exploited when we show the wanted trustworthiness. We do in fact, wisely or stupidly, virtuously or viciously, show trust in a great variety of forms, and manifest a great variety of versions of trustworthiness, both with intimates and with strangers. We trust those we encounter in lonely library stacks to be searching for books, not victims. We sometimes let ourselves fall asleep on trains or planes, trusting neighboring strangers not to take advantage of our defenselessness. We put our bodily safety into the hands of pilots, drivers, doctors, with scarcely any sense of reck-lessness. We used not to suspect that the food we buy might be deliberately poisoned, and we used to trust our children to day-care centers.

We may still have no choice but to buy food and to leave our children in day-care centers, but now we do it with suspicion and anxiety. Trust is always an invitation not only to confidence tricksters but also to terrorists, who discern its most easily destroyed and socially vital forms. Criminals, not moral philosophers, have been the experts at discerning different forms of trust. Most of us notice a given form of trust most easily after its sudden demise or severe injury. We inhabit a climate of trust as we inhabit an atmosphere and notice it as we notice air, only when it becomes scarce or polluted.

We may have no choice but to continue to rely on the local shop for food, even after some of the food on its shelves has been found to have been poisoned with intent. We can still rely where we no longer trust. What is the difference between trusting others and merely relying on them? It seems to be reliance on their good will toward one, as distinct from their dependable habits, or only on their dependably exhibited fear, anger, or other motives compatible with ill will toward one, or on motives not directed on one at all. We may rely on our fellows' fear of the newly appointed security guards in shops to deter them from injecting poison into the food on the shelves, once we have ceased to trust them. We may rely on the shopkeeper's concern for his profits to motivate him to take effective precautions against poisoners and also trust him to *want* his customers not to be harmed by his products, at least as long as this want can be satisfied without frustrating his wish to increase his profits. Trust is often mixed with other species of reliance on persons. Trust which is reliance on another's good will, perhaps minimal good will, contrasts with the forms of reliance on others' reactions and attitudes which are shown by the comedian, the advertiser, the blackmailer, the kidnapper-extortioner, and the terrorist, who all depend on particular attitudes and reactions of others for the success of their actions. We all depend on one anothers' psychology in countless ways, but this is not yet to trust them. The trusting can be betrayed, or at least let down, and not just disappointed. Kant's neighbors who counted on his regular habits as a clock for their own less automatically regular ones might be disappointed with him if he slept in one day, but not let down by him, let alone had their trust betrayed. When I trust another, I depend on her good will toward me. I need not either acknowledge this reliance nor believe that she has either invited or acknowledged such trust since there is such a thing as unconscious trust, as unwanted trust, as forced receipt of trust, and as trust which the trusted is unaware of. (Plausible conditions for proper trust will be that it survives consciousness, by both parties, and that the trusted has had some opportunity to signify acceptance or rejection, to warn the trusting if their trust is unacceptable.)

Where one depends on another's good will, one is necessarily vulnerable to the limits of that good will. One leaves others an opportunity to harm one when one trusts, and also shows one's confidence that they will not take it. Reasonable trust will require good grounds for such confidence in another's good will, or at least the absence of good grounds for expecting their ill will or indifference. Trust then, on this first approximation, is accepted vulnerability to another's possible but not expected ill will (or lack of good will) toward one.

What we now need to do, to get any sense of the variety of forms of trust, is to look both at varieties of vulnerability and at varieties of grounds for not expecting others to take advantage of it. One way to do the former, which I shall take, is to look at the variety of sorts of goods or things one values or cares about, which can be left or put within the striking power of others, and the variety of ways we can let or leave others "close" enough to what we value to be able to harm it. Then we can look at various reasons we might have for wanting or accepting such closeness of those with power to harm us, and for confidence that they will not use this power. In this way we can hope to explicate the vague terms "good will" and "ill will." If it be asked why the initial emphasis is put on the trusting's vulnerability, on the risks rather than the benefits of trust, part of the answer has already been given—namely, that we come to realize what trust involves retrospectively and posthumously, once our vulnerability is brought home to us by actual wounds. The other part of the answer is that even when one does become aware of trust and intentionally continues a particular case of it, one need not intend to achieve any particular benefit from it—one need not trust a person in order to receive some gain, even when in fact one does gain. Trusting, as an intentional mental phenomenon, need not be purposive. But intentional trusting does require awareness of one's confidence that the trusted will not harm one, although they could harm one. It is not a Hobbesian obsession with strike force which dictates the form of analysis

I have sketched but, rather, the natural order of consciousness and self-consciousness of trust, which progresses from initially unself-conscious trust to awareness of risk along with confidence that it is a good risk, on to some realization of why we are taking this particular risk, and eventually to some evaluation of what we may generally gain and what we may lose from the willingness to take such risks. The ultimate point of what we are doing when we trust may be the last thing we come to realize.

The next thing to attend to is why we typically do leave things that we value close enough to others for them to harm them. The answer, simply, is that we need their help in creating, and then in not merely guarding but looking after the things we most value, so we have no choice but to allow some others to be in a position to harm them. The one in the best position to harm something is its creator or its nurse-cum-caretaker. Since the things we typically do value include such things as we cannot singlehandedly either create or sustain (our own life, health, reputation, our offspring and their well-being, as well as intrinsically shared goods such as conversation, its written equivalent, theater and other forms of play, chamber music, market exchange, political life, and so on) we must allow many other people to get into positions where they can, if they choose, injure what we care about, since those are the same positions that they must be in in order to help us take care of what we care about. The simple Socratic truth that no person is self-sufficient gets elaborated, once we add the equally Socratic truth that the human soul's activity is *caring* for things into the richer truth that no one is able by herself to look after everything she wants to have looked after, nor even alone to look after her own "private" goods, such as health and bodily safety. If we try to distinguish different forms of trust by the different valued goods we confidently allow another to have some control over, we are following Locke in analyzing trusting on the model of *en-trusting*. Thus, there will be an answer not just to the question, Whom do you trust? but to the question, *What* do you trust to them?—what good is it that they are in a position to take from you, or to injure? Accepting such an analysis, taking trust to be a three-place predicate (A trusts B with valued thing C) will involve some distortion and regimentation of some cases, where we may have to strain to discern any definite candidate for C, but I think it will prove more of a help than a hindrance.

One way in which trusted persons can fail to act as they were trusted to is by taking on the care of more than they were entrusted with—the babysitter who decides that the nursery would be improved if painted purple and sets to work to transform it, will have acted, as a babysitter, in an untrustworthy way, however great his good will. When we are trusted, we are relied upon to realize *what* it is for whose care we have some discretionary responsibility, and normal people can pick up the cues that indicate the limits of what is entrusted. For example, if I confide my troubles to a friend, I trust her to listen, more or less sympathetically, and to preserve confidentiality, but usually not, or not without consulting me, to take steps to remove the source of my worry. That could be interfering impertinence, not trustworthiness as a confidante. She will, nevertheless, within the restricted scope of what is trusted to her (knowledge of my affairs, not their management) have some discretion both as to how to receive the confidence and, unless I swear her to absolute secrecy, as to when to share it. The relativization of trust to particular things cared about by the truster goes along with the discretion the trusted usually has in judging just what should be done to "look after" the particular good entrusted to her care. This discretionary power will of course be limited by the limits of what is entrusted and usually by some other constraints.

It is plausible to construe all cases of being trusted not merely as cases of being trusted by someone with access to what matters to the truster, but as some control over that, expected to be used to take care of it, and involving some discretionary powers in so doing?[4] Can we further elaborate the analysis of a relationship of trust as one where A has entrusted B with some of the care of C and where B has some discretionary powers in caring for C? Admittedly there are many cases of trust where "caring for C" seems much more than A expects of B even when there is no problem in finding a fairly restricted value for C. Suppose I look quickly around me before proceeding into the dark street or library stacks where my business takes me, judge the few people I discern there to be nondangerous, and so go ahead. We can say that my bodily safety, and perhaps my pocketbook, are the goods I am allowing these people to be in a position to threaten. I trust them, it seems, merely to leave me alone. But this is not quite right, for should a piece of falling masonry or toppling books threaten to fall on my head, and one of these persons leap into action and shove me out of this danger, I would regard that as rather more than less than I had trusted these strangers to do— a case for gratitude, not for an assault charge, despite the sudden, un-ceremonious, possibly painful or even injurious nature of my close en-counter with my rescuer. So *what* do I trust strangers in such circumstances to do? Certainly not anything whatever as long as it is done with good will, nor even anything whatever for my bodily safety and security of property as long as it is done with good will. Suppose someone I have judged nondangerous as I proceed into the stacks should seize me from behind, frightening but not harming me, and claim with apparent sincerity that she did it for my own good, so that I would learn a lesson and be

4. A reader for this journal suggested that, when one trusts one's child to mail an important letter for one at the mailbox on the corner, no discretionary powers are given, although one is trusting him with the safe, speedy transfer of the letter to the box. But life is full of surprises—in Washington on Inauguration day mailboxes were sealed closed as a security precaution, and in some parts of Manhattan mailboxes are regularly sealed after dark. One trusts the child to do the sensible thing if such an unforeseen problem should arise—to bring the letter back, not leave it on the ledge of the sealed mailbox or go too far afield to find another.

more cautious in the future. I would not respond with gratitude but demand what business my long-term security of life was of hers, that she felt free to subject me to such unpleasant educational measures. In terms of my analysis, what I trusted her with was my peace and safety here and now, with "looking after" that, not with my long-term safety. We need some fairly positive and discretion-allowing term, such as "look after" or "show concern for," to let in the range of behavior which would not disappoint the library user's trust in fellow users. We also need some specification of what good was in question to see why the intrusive, presumptuous, and paternalistic moves disappoint rather than meet the trust one has in such circumstances. "Look after" and "take care of" will have to be given a very weak sense in some cases of trust; it will be better to do this than to try to construe cases where more positive care is expected of the trusted as cases of trusting them to leave alone, or merely safeguard, some valued thing. Trusting strangers to leave us alone should be construed as trusting them with the "care" of our valued autonomy. When one trusts one's child to one's separated spouse, it is all aspects of the child's good as a developing person which are entrusted to the other parent's care. Trusting him or her with our children can hardly be construed as trusting them not to "interfere" with the child's satisfactory development. The most important things we entrust to others are things which take more than noninterference in order to thrive.

The more extensive the discretionary powers of the trusted, the less clear-cut will be the answer to the question of when trust is disappointed. The truster, who always needs good judgment to know whom to trust and how much discretion to give, will also have some scope for discretion in judging what should count as failing to meet trust, either through incompetence, negligence, or ill will. In any case of a questionable exercise of discretion there will be room both for forgiveness of unfortunate outcomes and for tact in treatment of the question of whether there is anything to forgive. One thing that can destroy a trust relationship fairly quickly is the combination of a rigoristic unforgiving attitude on the part of the truster and a touchy sensitivity to any criticism on the part of the trusted. If a trust relationship is to continue, some tact and willingness to forgive on the part of the truster and some willingness on the part of the trusted both to be forgiven and to forgive unfair criticisms, seem essential.[5] The need for this will be greater the more discretion the trusted has.

5. This point I take from the fascinating sociological analysis of trust given by Niklas Luhmann (*Trust and Power* [Chichester, N.Y., 1979]) which I discovered while revising this paper. In many ways my analysis agrees with his, inasfar as I understand the implications of his account of it as "reduction of complexity," in particular of complex future contingencies. He makes much of the difference between absence of trust and distrust, and distinguishes trust from what it presupposes, a mere "familiarity," or taking for granted. I have blurred these distinctions. He treats personal trust as a risky investment and looks at mechanisms for initiating and maintaining trust. Tact is said to play an important role in both. It enables

If part of what the truster entrusts to the trusted are discretionary powers, then the truster risks abuse of those and the successful disguise of such abuse. The special vulnerability which trust involves is vulnerability to not yet noticed harm, or to disguised ill will. What one forgives or tactfully averts one's eyes from may be not well-meant but ill-judged or incompetent attempts to care for what is entrusted but, rather, ill-meant and cleverly disguised abuses of discretionary power. To understand the moral risks of trust, it is important to see the special sort of vulnerability it introduces. Yet the discretionary element which introduces this special danger is essential to that which trust at its best makes possible. To elaborate Hume: "'Tis impossible to separate the chance of good from the risk of ill."[6]

It is fairly easy, once we look, to see how this special vulnerability is involved in many ordinary forms of trust. We trust the mailman to deliver and not tamper with the mail, and to some extent we trust his discretion in interpreting what "tampering" covers. Normally we do not expect him to read our mail but to deliver it unread, even when the message is open, on a postcard. But on occasion it may be proper, or at least not wrong, for him to read it. I have had friendly mailmen (in Greek villages and in small Austrian towns) who tell me what my mail announces as they hand it over: "Your relatives have recovered and can travel now, and are soon arriving!" Such interest in one's affairs is not part of the normal idea of the role of mailman and could provide opportunity for blackmail, but in virtue of that very interest they could give much more knowledgeable and intelligent service—in the above case by knowing our plans they knew when and where we had moved and delivered to the new address without instructions. What do we trust our mailmen to do or not to do? To use their discretion in getting our mail to us, to take enough interest in us and in the nature of our mail, (compatibly with their total responsibility) to make intelligent decisions about what to do with it when such decisions have to be made. Similarly with our surgeons and plumbers—*just* what they should do to put right what is wrong is something we must leave to them. Should they act incompetently, negligently, or deliberately against our interests, they may conceal these features of their activities from us by pretense that whatever happened occurred as a result of an honest and well-meaning exercise of the discretion

---

trust-offering overtures to be rejected without hostility ensuing, and it enables those who make false moves in their attempts to maintain trust to recover their position without too much loss of face. "A social climate . . . institutionalizes tact and knows enough escape routes for self presentation in difficult situations" (p. 84). It is important, I think, to see that tact is a virtue which needs to be added to delicacy of discrimination in recognizing *what* one is trusted with, good judgment as to whom to trust with what, and a willingness to admit and forgive fault, as all functional virtues needed in those who would sustain trust.

6. See David Hume, *Treatise*, ed. L. A. Selby-Bigge and P. H. Nidditch (Oxford: Clarendon Press, 1978), p. 497.

given to them. This way they may retain our trust and so have opportunity to harm us yet further. In trusting them, we trust them to use their discretionary powers competently and nonmaliciously, and the latter includes not misleading us about how they have used them.

Trust, on the analysis I have proposed, is letting other persons (natural or artificial, such as firms, nations, etc.) take care of something the truster cares about, where such "caring for" involves some exercise of discretionary powers. But not all the variables involved in trust are yet in view. One which the entrusting model obscures rather than highlights is the degree of explicitness. To entrust is intentionally and usually formally to hand over the care of something to someone, but trusting is rarely begun by making up one's mind to trust, and often it has no definite initiation of any sort but grows up slowly and imperceptibly. What I have tried to take from the notion of entrusting is not its voluntarist and formalist character but rather the possible specificity and restrictedness of *what* is entrusted, along with the discretion the trustee has in looking after that thing. Trust can come with no beginnings, with gradual as well as sudden beginnings, and with various degrees of self-consciousness, voluntariness, and expressness. My earlier discussion of the delicacy and tact needed by the truster in judging the performance of the trusted applied only to cases where the truster not merely realizes that she trusts but has some conscious control over the continuation of the trust relationship. The discussion of abuses of discretionary power applied only to cases where the trusted realizes that she is trusted and trusted with discretionary powers. But trust relationships need not be so express, and some important forms of them cannot be verbally acknowledged by the persons involved. Trust between infant and parent is such a case, and it is one which also reminds us of another crucial variable in trust relations to which so far I have only indirectly alluded. This is the relative power of the truster and the trusted, and the relative costs to each of a breakdown of their trust relationship. In emphasizing the toleration of vulnerability by the truster I have made attitudes to relative power and powerlessness the essence of trust and distrust; I have not yet looked at the varieties of trust we discern when we vary the power of the truster in relation to the power of the trusted, both while the trust endures and in its absence. Trust alters power positions, and both the position one is in without a given form of trust and the position one has within a relation of trust need to be considered before one can judge whether that form of trust is sensible and morally decent. Infant trust reminds us not just of inarticulate and uncritical or blind trust, but of trust by those who are maximally vulnerable, whether or not they give trust.

TRUST AND RELATIVE POWER

I have been apparently preoccupied up till now with dimensions of trust which show up most clearly in trust between articulate adults, in a position to judge one another's performance, and having some control over their degree of vulnerability to others. This approach typifies a myopia which, once noticed, explains the "regrettably sparse" attempts to understand trust as a phenomenon of moral importance.[7] For the more we ignore dependency relations between those grossly unequal in power and ignore what cannot be spelled out in an explicit acknowledgment, the more readily will we assume that everything that needs to be understood about trust and trustworthiness can be grasped by looking at the morality of contract. For it takes an adult to be able to make a contract, and it takes something like Hegel's civil society of near equals to find a use for contracts. But one has to strain the contractarian model very considerably to see infant-parent relations as essentially contractual, both because of the nonexpressness of the infant's attitude and because of the infant's utter powerlessness. It takes inattention to cooperation between unequals, and between those without a common language, to keep one a contented contractarian. To do more, I must both show how infant trust, and other variations along the relative power dimension, can be covered and also indicate just where trust in contracts fits into the picture we then get.

Infant trust is like one form of non-contract-based trust to which some attention has been given in our philosophical tradition, namely, trust in God. Trust in God is total, in that whatever one cares about, it will not thrive if God wills that it not thrive. A young child too is totally dependent on the good will of the parent, totally incapable of looking after anything he cares about without parental help or against parental will. Such total dependence does not, in itself, necessarily elicit trust—some theists curse God, display futile distrust or despair rather than trust. Infants too can make suspicious, futile, self-protective moves against the powerful adults in their world or retreat into autism. But surviving infants will usually have shown some trust, enough to accept offered nourishment, enough not to attempt to prevent such close approach. The ultra-Hobbist child who fears or rejects the mother's breast, as if fearing poison from that source, can be taken as displaying innate distrust, and such newborns must be the exception in a surviving species. Hobbes tells us that, in the state of nature, "seeing the infant is in the power of the Mother, and is therefore obliged to obey her, so she may either nourish or expose it; if she nourish it, it oweth its life to the Mother and is therefore obliged to obey her rather than any other" (*Leviathan*, chap. 20). Even he, born a twin to fear, is apparently willing to take mother's

7. Luhmann, p. 8, n. 1. It is interesting to note that, unlike Luhmann and myself, Bernard Barber begins his sociological treatment of trust in *The Logic and Limits of Trust* (New Brunswick, N.J.: Rutgers University Press, 1983) not by remarking on the neglect of the topic but rather, by saying, "Today nearly everyone seems to be talking about 'trust' " (p. 1). He lists "moral philosophers" along with "presidential candidates, political columnists, pollsters, social critics and the man in the street" as among those talking so much about it but cites only two moral philosophers, Bok and Rawls (who by his own account is *not* always talking about it). Between Luhmann's work on trust, first published in Germany in 1973, and Barber's, sociologists had ten years to get the talk about trust going, but it has scarcely spread yet to most of the moral philosophers I have encountered.

milk on trust. Some degree of innate, if selective, trust seems a necessary element in any surviving creature whose first nourishment (if it is not exposed) comes from another, and this innate but fragile trust could serve as the explanation both of the possibility of other forms of trust and of their fragility.

Infant trust that normally does not need to be won but is there unless and until it is destroyed is important for an understanding of the possibility of trust. Trust is much easier to maintain than it is to get started and is never hard to destroy. Unless some form of it were innate, and unless that form could pave the way for new forms, it would appear a miracle that trust ever occurs. The postponement of the onset of distrust is a lot more explicable than hypothetical Hobbesian conversions from total distrust to limited trust. The persistent human adult tendency to profess trust in a creator-God can also be seen as an infantile residue of this crucial innate readiness of infants to initially impute goodwill to the powerful persons on whom they depend. So we should perhaps welcome, or at least tolerate, religious trust, if we value any form of trust. Nevertheless the theological literature on trust in God is of very limited help to us if we want to understand trust in human persons, even that trust in parents of which it can be seen as a nostalgic fantasy-memory. For the child soon learns that the parent is not, like God, invulnerable, nor even, like some versions of God, subject to offense or insult but not injury. Infant trust, although extreme in the discrepancy of power between the truster and the trusted, is to some extent a matter of mutual trust and mutual if unequal vulnerability. The parents' enormous power to harm the child and disappoint the child's trust is the power of ones also vulnerable to the child's at first insignificant but ever-increasing power, including power as one trusted by the parent. So not very much can be milked from the theological literature on the virtues of trust, faith, and hope in God and returned to the human context, even to the case of infant and parent. Indeed we might cite the theological contamination of the concept of trust as part of the explanation for the general avoidance of the topic in modern moral philosophy. If trust is seen as a variant of the suspect virtue of faith in the competence of the powers that be, then readiness to trust will be seen not just as a virtue of the weak but itself as a moral weakness, better replaced by vigilance and self-assertion, by self-reliance or by cautious, minimal, and carefully monitored trust. The psychology of adolescents, not infants, then gets glorified as the moral ideal. Such a reaction against a religious version of the ethics of trust is as healthy, understandable, and, it is hoped, as passing a phenomenon as is adolescent self-assertive individualism in the life of a normal person.

The goods which a trustworthy parent takes care of for as long as the child is unable to take care of them alone, or continues to welcome the parent's help in caring for them, are such things as nutrition, shelter, clothing, health, education, privacy, and loving attachment to others. Why, once the child becomes at all self-conscious about trusting parents to look after such goods for her, should she have confidence that parents are dependable custodians of such goods? Presumably because many of them are also goods to the parent, through their being goods to the child, especially if the parent loves the child. They will be common goods, so that for the trusted to harm them would be self-harm as well as harm to the child. The best reason for confidence in another's good care of what one cares about is that it is a common good, and the best reason for thinking that one's own good is also a common good is being loved. This may not, usually will not, ensure agreement on what best should be done to take care of that good, but it rules out suspicion of ill will. However, even when a child does not feel as loved by a parent as she would like, or as she thinks her siblings or friends are, she may still have complete confidence that at least many of the goods she cares about can be entrusted to her parents' care. She can have plenty of evidence that, for reasons such as pride, desire to perpetuate their name, or whatever, they do care as she herself does about her health, her success, and her ties with them. She can have good reason to be confident of the continued trustworthiness of her parents in many regards, from what she knows of their own concerns.

As the child approaches adulthood, and as the parents draw nearer to the likely dependency of old age, the trust may approximate much more closely to mutual trust and mutual vulnerability between equals, and they may then make explicit or even formal agreements about what is to be done in return for what. But no such contractual or quasi-contractual agreement can convert the young child's trust and the parent's trustworthiness retrospectively into part of a contractual mutual exchange. At most it can transform what was a continuing relation of mutual trust into a contractual obligation to render some sort of service to one's parents. The previous parental care could become a moral *reason* for making a contract with parents, but not what one received as 'consideration' in such a contract. At best that could be a virtual 'consideration,' perhaps symbolized by the parents' formal cancelling of any until then outstanding 'debt' of gratitude, in return for the rights the contract gives them. But normally whatever grateful return one makes to another is not made in exchange for a 'receipt' which is proof against any outstanding 'debt.' Only those determined to see every proper moral transaction as an exchange will construe every gift as made in exchange for an IOU, and every return gift as made in exchange for a receipt. Only such trade fetishists will have any reason to try to construe the appropriate adult response to earlier parental care as part of a virtual contract, or as proper content for an actual contract. As Hume says, contract should not replace "the more generous and noble intercourse of friendship and good offices," which he construes as a matter of spontaneous service responded to by "return in the same manner."[8] We can resist this reduction of the more

8. Hume, p. 521.

noble responses of gratitude to the fulfilling of contractual obligations if we focus our moral attention on other sorts of trust than trust in contracts. Looking at infant trust helps one do that. Not only has the child no concept of virtual contract when she trusts, but the parent's duty to the child seems in no way dependent on the expectation that the child will make a later return. The child or the parent may die before the reversal of dependency arrives. Furthermore, parent's knowledge either that the child, or that he himself, or both, will die within say ten years, in itself (and disability apart) makes no difference to the parent's responsibility while he lives, as that is usually understood. Parental and filial responsibility does not rest on deals, actual or virtual, between parent and child.

TRUST AND VOLUNTARY ABILITIES

The child trusts as long as she is encouraged to trust and until the trust is unmistakably betrayed. It takes childhood innocence to be able to trust simply because of encouragement to trust. "Trust me!" is for most of us an invitation which we cannot accept at will—either we do already trust the one who says it, in which case it serves at best as reassurance,[9] or it is properly responded to with, "Why should and how can I, until I have cause to?"[10] The child, of course, cannot trust at will any more than experienced adults can—encouragement is a condition of not lapsing into distrust, rather than of a move from distrust to trust. One constraint on an account of trust which postulates infant trust as its essential seed is that it not make essential to trusting the use of concepts or abilities which a child cannot be reasonably believed to possess. Acts of will of any sort are not plausibly attributed to infants; it would be unreasonable to suppose that they can do at will what adults cannot, namely, obey the instruction to trust, whether it comes from others or is a self-instruction.

To suppose that infants emerge from the womb already equipped with some ur-confidence in what supports them, so that no choice is needed to continue with that attitude, until something happens to shake or destroy such confidence, is plausible enough. My account of trust has been designed to allow for unconscious trust, for conscious but unchosen trust, as well as for conscious trust the truster has chosen to endorse and cultivate. Whereas it strains the concept of agreement to speak of un-conscious agreements and unchosen agreements, and overstrains the

9. My thoughts about the role of the words "Trust me!" are influenced by an unpublished paper on promising by T. M. Scanlon. Indeed Scanlon's talk on this topic to the University of Pittsburgh philosophy department in April 1984 was what, along with Hume's few remarks about it, started me thinking about trust in and out of voluntary exchanges.

10. Luhmann says, "It is not possible to demand the trust of others; trust can only be offered and accepted" (p. 43). I am here claiming something stronger, namely, that one cannot offer it or accept it by an act of will; that one cannot demand it of oneself or others until some trust-securing social artifice invents something like promise that *can* be offered and accepted at will.

concept of contract to speak of unconscious or unchosen contracts, there is no strain whatever in the concept of automatic and unconscious trust, and of unchosen but mutual trust. Trust between infant and parent, at its best, exhibits such primitive and basic trust. Once it is present, the story of how trust becomes self-conscious, controlled, monitored, critical, pretended, and eventually either cautious and distrustful of itself, or discriminatory and reflexive, so that we come to trust ourselves as trusters, is relatively easy to tell. What will need explanation will be the ceasings to trust, the transfers of trust, the restriction or enlargements in the fields of what is trusted, when, and to whom, rather than any abrupt switches from distrust to trust. Even if such occurrences do ever occur (when one suddenly falls in love or lust with a stranger or former enemy, or has a religious conversion), they take more than the mere invitation "Trust me."

In his famous account of what a promise (and a contract) involves, Hume strongly implies that it is an artificially contrived and secured case of mutual trust. The penalty to which a promisor subjects himself in promising, he says, is that of "never being trusted again in case of failure."[11] The problem which the artifice of promise solves is a generally disadvantageous "want of mutual confidence and security."[12] It is plausible to construe the offer whose acceptance counts as acceptance of a contract or a promise as at least implicitly including an invitation to trust. Part of what makes promises the special thing they are, and the philosophically intriguing thing they are, is that we *can* at will accept *this* sort of invitation to trust, whereas in general we cannot trust at will. Promises are puzzling because they seem to have the power, by verbal magic, to initiate real voluntary short-term trusting. They not merely create obligations apparently at the will of the obligated, but they create trust at the will of the truster. They present a very fascinating case of trust and trustworthiness, but one which, because of those very intriguing features, is ill suited to the role of paradigm. Yet in as far as modern moral philosophers have attended at all to the morality of trust, it is trust in parties to an agreement that they have concentrated on, and it is into this very special and artificial mold that they have tried to force other cases of trust, when they notice them at all.

Trust of any particular form is made more likely, in adults, if there is a climate of trust of that sort. Awareness of what is customary, as well as past experience of one's own, affects one's ability to trust. We take it for granted that people will perform their role-related duties and trust any individual worker to look after whatever her job requires her to. The very existence of that job, as a standard occupation, creates a climate of some trust in those with that job. Social artifices such as property, which allocate rights and duties as a standard job does, more generally also

11. Hume, p. 522.
12. Ibid., p. 521.

create a climate of trust, a presumption of a sort of trustworthiness. On the Humean account of promises and contracts which I find more or less correct,[13] their establishment as a customary procedure also reverses a presumption concerning trustworthiness, but only in limited conditions. Among these is a special voluntary act by the promisor, giving it to be understood that what he offers is a promise, and another voluntary act by the promisee, acceptance of that promise. Promises are "a bond or security,"[14] and "the sanction of the interested commerce of mankind."[15] To understand them is to see what sort of sanction is involved, what sort of security they provide, and the social preconditions of each. Then one understands how the presumption about the trustworthiness of self-interested strangers can be reversed, and how the ability to trust them (for a limited time, on a limited matter) can become a voluntary ability. To adapt Hume's words, "Hence I learn to count on a service from another, although he bears me no real kindness."[16] Promises are a most ingenious social invention, and trust in those who have given us promises is a complex and sophisticated moral achievement. Once the social conditions are right for it, once the requisite climate of trust in promisors is there, it is easy to take it for a simpler matter than it is and to ignore its background conditions. They include not merely the variable social conventions and punitive customs Hume emphasizes, but the prior existence of less artificial and less voluntary forms of trust, such as trust in friends and family, and enough trust in fellows to engage with them in agreed exchanges of a more or less simultaneous nature, exchanges such as barter or handshakes, which do not require one to rely on strangers over a period of time, as exchange of promises typically does.

Those who take advantage of this sophisticated social device will be, mainly, adults who are not intimate with one another, and who see one another more or less as equal in power to secure the enforcement of the rules of the contracting game (to extract damages for broken contracts, to set in motion the accepted penalty for fraudulent promises, and so on). As Nietzsche emphasized, the right to make promises and the power to have one's promises accepted are not possessed by everyone in relation to everyone else. Not only can the right be forfeited, but it is all along an elite right, possessed only by those with a certain social status. Slaves, young children, the ill, and the mentally incompetent do not fully possess it. For those who do possess it, whose offer or acceptance of a promise has moral force, the extent to which use of it regulates their relations with others varies with their other social powers. Women whose property, work, and sexual services became their husbands' on marriage did not

13. I have discussed and defended Hume's account in "Promises, Promises, Promises," in my *Postures of the Mind: Essays on Mind and Morals* (Minneapolis: University of Minnesota Press, 1985).

14. Hume, p. 541.

15. Ibid., p. 522.

16. Ibid., p. 521.

have much left to promise, and what was left could usually be taken from them without their consent and without the formality of exchange of promises. Their right to promise anything of significance was contracted into the right to make one vow of fixed and non-negotiable content, the marriage vow, and even that was often made under duress. The important relationships and trust relationships which structured women's lives for most of the known history of our species, relations to spouse, children, fellow workers, were not entered into by free choice, or by freely giving or receiving promises. They were, typically, relationships of which the more important were ones of intimacy, relationships to superiors or inferiors in power, relationships not in any strong sense freely chosen nor to chosen others. Like the infant, they found themselves faced with others to trust or distrust, found themselves trusted or not trusted by these given others. Their freely given and seriously taken promises were restricted in their content to trivialities. Contract is a device for traders, entrepreneurs, and capitalists, not for children, servants, indentured wives, and slaves. They were the traded, not the traders, and any participation they had in the promising game was mere play. It is appropriate, then, that Nietzsche, the moral philosopher who glorifies promise more even than contemporary contractarians, was also the one who advised his fellow male exchangers or givers of promises thus, "He must conceive of woman as a possession, as a property that can be locked, as something predestined for service and achieving her perfection in that."[17] Nietzsche faces squarely what Hume half faced, and what most moral philosophers have avoided facing, that the liberal morality which takes voluntary agreement as the paradigm source of moral obligation must either exclude the women they expect to continue in their traditional role from the class of moral subjects, or admit internal contradiction in their moral beliefs. Nor does the contradiction vanish once women have equal legal rights with men, as long as they are still expected to take responsibility for any child they conceive voluntarily or nonvoluntarily, either to abort or to bear and either care for or arrange for others to care for. Since a liberal morality both *must* let this responsibility rest with women, and yet cannot conceive of it as self-assumed, then the centrality of voluntary agreement to the liberal and contractarian morality must be challenged once women are treated as full moral fellows. Voluntary agreement, and trust in others to keep their agreements, must be moved from the center to the moral periphery, once servants, ex-slaves, and women are taken seriously as moral subjects and agents.

THE MALE FIXATION ON CONTRACT

The great moral theorists in our tradition not only are all men, they are mostly men who had minimal adult dealings with (and so were then

---

17. Nietzsche, *Beyond Good and Evil*, pt. 7, §238, trans. Walter Kaufmann, *Basic Writings of Nietzsche* (New York, 1968), p. 357.

minimally influenced by) women. With a few significant exceptions (Hume, Hegel, J. S. Mill, Sidgwick, maybe Bradley) they are a collection of gays, clerics, misogynists, and puritan bachelors. It should not surprise us, then, that particularly in the modern period they managed to relegate to the mental background the web of trust tying most moral agents to one another, and to focus their philosophical attention so single-mindedly on cool, distanced relations between more or less free and equal adult strangers, say, the members of an all male club, with membership rules and rules for dealing with rule breakers and where the form of cooperation was restricted to ensuring that each member could read his *Times* in peace and have no one step on his gouty toes. Explicitly assumed or recognized obligations toward others with the same obligations and the same power to see justice done to rule breakers then are seen as the moral norm.

Relations between equals and nonintimates will *be* the moral norm for adult males whose dealings with others are mainly business or restrained social dealings with similarly placed males. But for lovers, husbands, fathers, the ill, the very young, and the elderly, other relationships with their moral potential and perils will loom larger. For Hume, who had several strong-willed and manipulative women to cooperate or contend with in his adult life, for Mill, who had Harriet Taylor on his hands, for Hegel, whose domestic life was of normal complication, the rights and duties of equals to equals in a civil society which recognized only a male electorate could only be *part* of the moral story. They could not ignore the virtues and vices of family relationships, male-female relationships, master-slave, and employer-employee relationships as easily as could Hobbes, Butler, Bentham, or Kant. Nor could they as easily adopt the usual compensatory strategies of the moral philosophers who confine their attention to the rights and duties of free and equal adults to one another—the strategy of claiming, if pressed, that these rights are the *core* of all moral relationships and maybe also claiming that any other relationships, engendering additional or different rights and duties, come about only by an exercise of one of the core rights, the right to promise. Philosophers who remember what it was like to be a dependent child, or know what it is like to be a parent, or to have a dependent parent, an old or handicapped relative, friend, or neighbor will find it implausible to treat such relations as simply cases of comembership in a kingdom of ends, in the given temporary conditions of one-sided dependence.

To the extent that these claims are correct (and I am aware that they need more defense than I have given them here)[18] it becomes fairly easy to see one likely explanation of the neglect in Western moral philosophy of the full range of sorts of trust. Both before the rise of a society which needed contract as a commercial device, and after it, women were counted

18. I defend them a little more in "What Do Women Want in a Moral Theory?" *Nous* 19 (March 1985): 53–64.

on to serve their men, to raise their children to fill the roles they were expected to fill and not deceive their men about the paternity of these children. What men counted on one another for, in work and war, presupposed this background domestic trust, trust in women not merely not to poison their men (Nietzsche derides them for learning less than they might have in the kitchen), but to turn out sons who could trust and be trusted in traditional men's roles and daughters who would reduplicate their own capacities for trust and trustworthiness. Since the women's role did not include the writing of moral treatises, any thoughts they had about trust, based on their experience of it, did not get into our tradition (or did Diotima teach Socrates something about trust as well as love?). And the more powerful men, including those who did write the moral treatises, were in the morally awkward position of being, collectively, oppressors of women, exploiters of women's capacity for trustworthiness in unequal, nonvoluntary, and non-contract-based relationships. Understandably, they did not focus their attention on forms of trust and demands for trustworthiness which it takes a Nietzsche to recognize without shame. Humankind can bear only so much reality.

The recent research of Carol Gilligan has shown us how intelligent and reflective twentieth-century women see morality, and how different their picture of it is from that of men, particularly the men who eagerly assent to the claims of currently orthodox contractarian-Kantian moral theories.[19] Women cannot now, any more than they could when oppressed, ignore that part of morality and those forms of trust which cannot easily be forced into the liberal and particularly the contractarian mold. Men may but women cannot see morality as essentially a matter of keeping to the minimal moral traffic rules, designed to restrict close encounters between autonomous persons to self-chosen ones. Such a conception presupposes both an equality of power and a natural separateness from others, which is alien to women's experience of life and morality. For those most of whose daily dealings are with the less powerful or the more powerful, a moral code designed for those equal in power will be at best nonfunctional, at worst an offensive pretense of equality as a substitute for its actuality. But equality is not even a desirable ideal in all relationships—children not only are not but should not be equal in power to adults, and we need a morality to guide us in our dealings with those who either cannot or should not achieve equality of power (animals, the ill, the dying, children while still young) with those with whom they have unavoidable and often intimate relationships.

Modern moral philosophy has concentrated on the morality of fairly cool relationships between those who are deemed to be roughly equal in power to determine the rules and to instigate sanctions against rule breakers. It is not surprising, then, that the main form of trust that any

19. Carol Gilligan, *In a Different Voice* (Cambridge, Mass.: Harvard University Press, 1982).

attention has been given to is trust in governments, and in parties to voluntary agreements to do what they have agreed to do. As much as possible is absorbed into the latter category, so that we suppose that paying for what one takes from a shop, doing what one is employed to do, returning what one has borrowed, supporting one's spouse, are all cases of being faithful to binding voluntary agreements, to contracts of some sort. (For Hume, none of these would count as duties arising from contract or promise.) Yet if I think of the trust I show, say, in the plumber who comes from the municipal drainage authority when I report that my drains are clogged, it is not plausibly seen as trust that he will fulfill his contractual obligations to me or to his employer. When I trust him to do whatever is necessary and safe to clear my drains, I take his expertise and his lack of ill will for granted. Should he plant explosives to satisfy some unsuspected private or social grudge against me, what I might try to sue him for (if I escaped alive) would not be damages for breach of contract. His wrong, if wrong it were, is not breach of contract, and the trust he would have disappointed would not have been that particular form of trust.

Contract enables us to make explicit just what we count on another person to do, in return for what, and should they not do just that, what damages can be extracted from them. The beauty of promise and contract is its explicitness.[20] But we can only make explicit provisions for such contingencies as we imagine arising. Until I become a victim of a terrorist plumber I am unlikely, even if I should insist on a contract before giving plumbers access to my drains, to extract a solemn agreement that they not blow me up. Nor am I likely to specify the alternative means they *may* use to clear my drains, since if I knew enough to compile such a list I would myself have to be a competent plumber. Any such detailed instructions must come from their plumbing superiors; I know nothing or little about it when I confidently welcome the plumber into the bowels of my basement. I trust him to do a nonsubversive plumbing job, as he counts on me to do a nonsubversive teaching job, should he send his son to my course in the history of ethics. Neither of us relies on a contract with the other, and neither of us need know of any contract (or much about its contents) the other may have with a third coordinating party.

It does not, then, seem at all plausible, once we think about actual moral relations in all their sad or splendid variety, to model all of them

20. Norbert Hornstein has drawn my attention to an unpublished paper by economist Peter Murrell, "Commitment and Cooperation: A Theory of Contract Applied to Franchising." Murrell emphasizes the nonstandard nature of franchise contracts, in that they typically are vague about what is expected of the franchisee. The consequent infrequency of contract termination by the franchisor is linked by him to the long duration of the contracts and to the advantage, to the more powerful proprietor of the trademark, of keeping the trust of the less powerful scattered franchisees and maintaining quality control by means other than punitive contract terminations. This, I persuade myself, is a case where the exception proves the rule, where the nonstandardness of such inexplicit and trusting contracts points up to the explicitness and minimal trustingness of standard contracts.

on one rather special one, the relation between promisor to promisee. We count on all sorts of people for all sorts of vital things, without any contracts, explicit or implicit, with them or with any third coordinating party. For these cases of trust in people to do their job conscientiously and not to take the opportunity to do us harm once we put things we value into their hands are different from trust in people to keep their promises in part because of the very indefiniteness of what we are counting on them to do or not to do. The subtlety and point of promising is to declare precisely *what* we count on another to do, and as the case of Shylock and Bassanio shows, that very definiteness is a limitation as well as a functional excellence of an explicit agreement.

Another functional excellence of contracts, which is closely connected with the expressness that makes breach easily established and damages or penalty decidable with a show of reasonable justice, is the *security* they offer the trusting party. They make it possible not merely for us to trust at will but to trust with minimal vulnerability. They are a device for trusting others enough for mutually profitable future-involving exchanges, without taking the risks trusters usually do take. They are designed for cooperation between mutually suspicious risk-averse strangers, and the vulnerability they involve is at the other extreme from that incurred by trusting infants. Contracts distribute and redistribute risk so as to minimize it for both parties, but trusting those more powerful persons who purport to love one increases one's risks while increasing the good one can hope to secure. Trust in fellow contracters is a limit case of trust, in which fewer risks are taken, for the sake of lesser goods.

Promises do, nevertheless, involve some real trust in the other party's good will and proper use of discretionary powers. Hume said that "to perform promises is requisite to beget trust and confidence in the common offices of life."[21] But performing promises is not the only performance requisite for that. Shylock did not welsh on an agreement, but he was nevertheless not a trustworthy party to an agreement. For to insist on the letter of an agreement, ignoring the vague but generally understood unwritten background conditions and exceptions, is to fail to show that discretion and goodwill which a trustworthy person has. To be someone to be trusted with a promise, as well as to be trusted as a promisor, one must be able to use discretion not as to when the promise has been kept but, rather, as to when to insist that the promise be kept, or to instigate penalty for breach of promise, when to keep and when not to keep one's promise. I would feel morally let down if someone who had promised to help me move house arrived announcing, "I had to leave my mother, suddenly taken ill, to look after herself in order to be here, but I couldn't break my promise to you." From such persons I would accept no further promises, since they would have shown themselves untrustworthy in the always crucial respect of judgment and willingness to use their discretionary

21. Hume, p. 544.

powers. Promises *are* morally interesting, and one's performance as party to a promise is a good indicator of one's moral character, but not for the reasons contractarians suppose.

The domination of contemporary moral philosophy by the so-called Prisoner's Dilemma problem displays most clearly this obsession with moral relations between minimally trusting, minimally trustworthy adults who are equally powerful. Just as the only trust Hobbist man shows is trust in promises, provided there is assurance of punishment for promise breakers, so is this the only sort of trust nontheological modern moral philosophers have given much attention at all to, as if once we have weaned ourselves from the degenerate form of absolute and unreciprocated trust in God, all our capacity for trust is to be channelled into the equally degenerate form of formal voluntary and reciprocated trust restricted to equals. But we collectively cannot bring off such a limitation of trust to minimal and secured trust, and we can deceive ourselves that we do only if we avert our philosophical gaze from the ordinary forms of trust I have been pointing to. It was not really that, after Hobbes, people *did* barricade their bodies as well as their possessions against all others before daring to sleep. Some continued to doze off on stagecoaches, to go abroad unarmed, to give credit in business deals, to count on others turning up on time for appointments, to trust parents, children, friends, and lovers not to rob or assault them when welcomed into intimacy with them. And the usual array of vicious forms of such trust, trustworthiness, and demands for them, continued to flourish. Slaves continued to be trusted to cook for slaveowners; women, with or without marriage vows, continued to be trusted with the property of their men, trusted not to deceive them about the paternity of their children, and trusted to bring up their sons as patriarchs, their daughters as suitable wives or mistresses for patriarchs. Life went on, but the moral philosophers, or at least those we regard as the great ones, chose to attend only to a few of the moral relations normal life exhibited. Once Filmer was disposed of, they concentrated primarily *not* on any of the relations between those of unequal power—parent to child, husband to wife, adult to aged parent, slaveowner to slave, official to citizen, employer to employee—but on relations between roughly equal parties or between people in those respects in which they could be seen as equals.

Such relationships of mutual respect are, of course, of great moral importance. Hobbes, Locke, Rousseau, Hume, Kant, Sidgwick, Rawls, all have helped us to see more clearly how we stand in relation to anonymous others, like ourselves in need, in power, and in capacity. One need not minimize the importance of such work in moral philosophy in order to question its completeness. But a complete moral philosophy would tell us how and why we should act and feel toward others in relationships of shifting and varying power asymmetry and shifting and varying intimacy. It seems to me that we philosophers have left that task largely to priests and revolutionaries, the self-proclaimed experts on the proper attitude of the powerless to the powerful. But these relationships of inequality—some of them, such as parent-child, of unavoidable inequality—make up much of our lives, and they, as much as our relations to our equals, determine the state of moral health or corruption in which we are content to live. I think it is high time we look at the morality and immorality of relations between the powerful and the less powerful, especially at those in which there is trust between them.

A MORAL TEST FOR TRUST

The few discussions of trust that I have found in the literature of moral philosophy assume that trust is a good and that disappointing known trust is always prima facie wrong, meeting it always prima facie right. But what is a trust-tied community without justice but a group of mutual blackmailers and exploiters? When the trust relationship itself is corrupt and perpetuates brutality, tyranny, or injustice, trusting may be silly self-exposure, and disappointing and betraying trust, including encouraged trust, may be not merely morally permissible but morally praiseworthy. Women, proletarians, and ex-slaves cannot ignore the virtues of watchful distrust, and of judicious untrustworthiness. Only if we had reason to believe that most familiar types of trust relationship were morally sound would breaking trust be any more prima facie wrong than breaking silence. I now turn to the question of when a given form of trust is morally decent, so properly preserved by trustfulness and trustworthiness, and when it fails in moral decency. What I say about this will be sketchy and oversimplified. I shall take as the form of trust to test for moral decency the trust which one spouse has in the other, in particular as concerns their children's care.

Earlier in discussing infant trust I said that the child has reason to trust the parents when both child and parents care about the same good—the child's happiness, although the child may not see eye to eye with those trusted parents about how that is best taken care of. When one parent, say the old-style father, entrusts the main care of his young child's needs to the old-style mother, there, too, there can be agreement on the good they both want cared for but disagreement about how best it is cared for. The lord and master who entrusts such care to his good wife, the mother, and so gives her discretionary power in making moment-by-moment decisions about what is to be done, will have done so sensibly if these disagreements are not major ones, or if he has reason to think that she knows better than he does about such matters. He should defer to her judgment, as the child is encouraged to do to the parents', and as I do to my plumber's. He sensibly trusts if he has reason to think that the discretionary powers given, even when used in ways he does not fully understand or approve of, are still used to care for the goods he wants cared for. He would be foolish to trust if he had evidence that she had other ends in view in her treatment of the child, or had a radically different version of what, say, the child's healthy development and proper relation to his father consisted in. Once he suspects that she, the trusted nurse of his sons and daughters, is deliberately rearing the daughters to be patriarch-toppling Amazons, the sons to be subverters of the father's values, he will sensibly withdraw his trust and dispatch his children to suitably chosen female relatives or boarding schools. What would properly undermine his trust would be beliefs he came to hold about the formerly trusted person's motives and purposes in her care of what was entrusted to her. The disturbing and trust-undermining suspicion is not necessarily that she doesn't care about the children's good, or cares only about her own—it is the suspicion that what she cares about conflicts with rather than harmonizes with what he cares about and that she is willing to sacrifice his concerns to what she sees as the children's and her own. Trusting is rational, then, in the absence of any reason to suspect in the trusted strong and operative motives which conflict with the demands of trustworthiness as the truster sees them.

But trusting can continue to be rational, even when there are such unwelcome suspicions, as long as the truster is confident that in the conflict of motives within the trusted the subversive motives will lose to the conformist motives. Should the wife face economic hardship and loss of her children if she fails to meet the husband's trust, or incurs too much of his suspicion, then she will sensibly continue as the dutiful wife, until her power position alters—sensibly, that is, given what she cares about. The husband in a position to be sure that the costs to the wife of discovered untrustworthiness are a sufficient deterrent will sensibly continue in trusting her while increasing his vigilance. Nor is he relying only on her fear, since, by hypothesis, her motives are conflicting and so she is not without some good will and some sympathy for his goals. Should he conclude that *only* fear of sanctions keeps her at her wifely duties, then the situation will have deteriorated from trust to mere reliance on his threat advantage. In such a case he will, if he has any sense, shrink the scope of her discretionary powers to virtually zero, since it is under cover of those that she could not merely thwart his purposes for his children but work to change the power relations in her own favor. As long as he gives her any discretion in looking after what is entrusted to her, he must trust her, and not rely solely on her fear of threatened penalties for disappointing his expectations.

The trusted wife (who usually, of course, also trusts her husband with many things that matter to her) is sensible to try to keep his trust, as long as she judges that the goods which would be endangered should she fail to meet his trust matter more to her than those she could best look after only by breaking or abusing trust. The goods for the sake of whose thriving she sensibly remains trustworthy might include the loving relation between them, their mutual trust for its own sake, as well as their agreed version of their children's good; or it might be some vestiges of these plus her own economic support or even physical safety, which are vulnerable to his punitive rage should she be found guilty of breach of trust. She will sensibly continue to meet trust, even when the goods with whose case she is trusted are no longer clearly common goods, as long as she cares a lot about anything his punitive wrath can and is likely to harm.

Sensible trust could persist, then, in conditions where truster and trusted suspect each other of willingness to harm the other if they could get away with it, the one by breach of trust, the other by vengeful response to that. The stability of the relationship will depend on the trusted's skill in cover-up activities, or on the truster's evident threat advantage, or a combination of these. Should the untrustworthy trusted person not merely have skill in concealment of her breaches of trust but skill in directing them toward increasing her own power and increasing her ability to evade or protect herself against the truster's attempted vengeance, then that will destabilize the relation, as also would frequent recourse by the truster to punitive measures against the trusted.

Where the truster relies on his threat advantage to keep the trust relation going, or where the trusted relies on concealment, something is morally rotten in the trust relationship. The truster who in part relies on his whip or his control of the purse is sensible but not necessarily within his moral rights in continuing to expect trustworthiness; and the trusted who sensibly relies on concealment to escape the penalty for untrustworthiness, may or may not be within her moral rights. I tentatively propose a test for the moral decency of a trust relationship, namely, that its continuation need not rely on successful threats held over the trusted, or on her successful cover-up of breaches of trust. We could develop and generalize this test into a version of an expressibility test, if we note that knowledge of what the other party is relying on for the continuance of the trust relationship would, in the above cases of concealment and of threat advantage, itself destabilize the relation. Knowledge of the other's reliance on concealment does so fairly automatically, and knowledge of the other's partial reliance on one's fear of his revenge would tend, in a person of normal pride and self-assertiveness, to prompt her to look for ways of exploiting her discretionary powers so as to minimize her vulnerability to that threat. More generally, to the extent that what the truster relies on for the continuance of the trust relation is something which, once realized by the truster, is likely to lead to (increased) abuse of trust, and eventually to destabilization and destruction of that relation, the trust is morally corrupt. Should the wife come to realize that the husband relies on her fear of his revenge, or on her stupidity in not realizing her exploitation, or on her servile devotion to him, to keep her more or less trustworthy, that knowledge should be enough to begin to cure these weaknesses and to motivate untrustworthiness. Similarly, should the truster come to realize that the trusted relies on her skill at covering up or on her ability to charm him into forgiveness for breaches of trust, that is, relies on *his* blindness or gullibility, that realization will help cure that blindness and gullibility. A trust relationship is morally bad to the extent that either party relies on qualities in the other which would be weakened by the knowledge that the other relies on them. Where each relies on the other's love, or concern for some common good, or professional pride in competent discharge of responsibility, knowledge of what the other is relying on in one need not undermine but will more likely strengthen those relied-on features. They survive exposure as what others rely on in one, in a way that some forms of stupidity, fear, blindness, ignorance, and gullibility normally do not. There are other mental states whose sensitivity to exposure as relied on by others seems more variable: good nature, detachment, inattention, generosity, forgivingness, sexual bondage to the other party to the trust may not be weakened by knowledge that others count on their presence in one to sustain some wanted relationship, especially if they are found equally in both parties. But the knowledge that others are counting on one's nonreciprocated generosity or good nature or forgiveness can have the power of the negative, can destroy trust.

I assume that in some forms of trust the healthy and desired state will be mere self-maintenance, while in others it will be change and growth. Alteration of the trust relationship need not take the form of destruction of the old form and its replacement by a new form, but of continuous growth, of slight shifts in scope of discretionary powers, additions or alterations in scope of goods entrusted, and so on. Of course some excitement-addicted persons may cultivate a form of trust in part for the opportunity it provides for dramatic disruption. Trust is the atmosphere necessary for exhilarating disruptions of trust, and satisfyingly spectacular transfers of trust, as well as for other goods we value. For persons with such tastes, immoral forms of trust may be preferable to what, according to my test, are moral forms of trust.

It should be noted that my proposed test of the moral decency of trust is quite noncommittal as to what cases of reliance on another's psychology will be acceptable to the other. I have assumed that most people in most trust situations will not be content to have others rely on their fear, their ignorance, and their spinelessness. In some cases, however, such as trusting police to play their role effectively, and trusting one's fellows to refrain from open crime, some element of fear must play a role, and it is its absence not its presence which would destabilize trust in such contexts. In others, such as trust in national intelligence and security officers to look after national security, some ignorance in the trusting is proper, and awareness that such persons may be relying on one's not knowing what they know will not destabilize any trust one has in them to do what they are entrusted to do. What will be offensive forms of reliance on one's psychological state will vary from context to context, depending on the nature of the goods entrusted and on other relationships between the trusting and the trusted. Variations in individual psychology will also make a difference. Some are much more tolerant than others of having their good nature or preoccupation taken advantage of—not merely in that they take longer to recognize that they are victims of this, but they are less stirred to anger or resentment by the awareness that they are being deceived, blackmailed, or exploited in a given trust relation. I have used the phrase "tend to destroy" in the test for moral decency in the assumption that there is a normal psychology to be discerned and that it does include a strong enough element of Platonic *thumos*. Should that be false, then all sorts of horrendous forms of trust may pass my test. I do not, in any case, claim that it is the only test, merely an appropriate one. It is a test which amounts to a check on the will and good will of the truster and trusted, a look to see how good their will to one another is, knowing what they do about each other's psychology.

It may be objected that the expressibility test I have proposed amounts to a reversion, on my part, to the contractarian attitude which I have deplored.[22] Have I not finally admitted that we must treat trust relationships as hypothetical contracts, with all the terms fully spelled out in order to determine their moral status? The short answer is that contractualists do not have a monopoly on expressibility tests. In any case, I have applied it at a place no contractualist would, and *not* applied it where he does. Where he assumes self-interest as a motive and makes explicit what goods or services each self-interested party is to receive from the other, I have left it open what motives the trusting and trusted have for maintaining the relation, requiring only that these motives, insofar as they rely on responses from the other, survive the other's knowledge of that reliance, and I have not required that relied-on services be made explicit. What the contractualist makes explicit is a voluntary mutual commitment, and what services each is committed to provide. I have claimed that such explicitness is not only rare in trust relationships, but that many of them must begin inexplicitly and nonvoluntarily and would not do the moral and social work they do if they covered only what contract does—services that could be pretty exactly spelled out. My moral test does not require that these nonexplicit elements in trust should be made explicit but, rather, that something else survive being made explicit, one's reliance on facts about others' psychological states relevant to their willingness to continue serving or being served, states such as love, fear, ignorance, sense of powerlessness, good nature, inattention, which one can use for one's secret purposes. It is not part of contracts or social contracts to specify what assumptions each party needs to make about the other in respect of such psychological factors. Perhaps constraints regarding duress and fraud can be linked with the general offensiveness of having others rely on one's ignorance, fear, or sense of powerlessness, especially when these are contrived by the one who relies on them; but contracts themselves do not make express what it is in the state of mind of the other that each party relies on to get what he wants from the deal. What I have proposed as a general moral test of trust is indeed a generalization of one aspect

---

22. Objections of this sort were raised by a reader for this journal.

of the contractarian morality, namely, of the assumptions implicit in the restrictions of valid contracts to those not involving fraud or duress. Whereas contracts make explicit the services (or service equivalent) exchanged, trust, when made express, amounts to a sort of exchange of responses to the motives and state of mind of the other, responses, in the form of confident reliance. Contractualists and other exchange fetishists can see this as a spiritual exchange, if it pleases them to do so, but it is not voluntary in the way contracts are, nor does it presuppose any equality of need or of power in the parties to this "exchange." The relation of my account of the morality of trust to standard contractarian morality seems to me as close as it should be, and at roughly the right places, if, as I have claimed, trust in fellow contracters is a limit case of trust.

Nevertheless, there are two aspects of my test which worry me, which may indicate it is not sufficiently liberated from contractarian prejudices. One difficulty is that it ignores the *network* of trust, and treats only two-party trust relationships. This is unrealistic, since any person's attitude to another in a given trust relationship is constrained by all the other trust and distrust relationships in which she is involved. Although I have alluded to such society-wide phenomena as climates of trust affecting the possibilities for individual trust relationships, my test is not well designed for application to the whole network but has to be applied piecemeal. That is a defect, showing the same individualist limitations which I find in contractarianism. The second thing that worries me is that the test seems barely applicable to brief trusting encounters, such as those with fellow library frequenters. As the contractarian takes as his moral paradigm a relationship which has some but not a very complex temporal depth, assimilating simultaneous exchange to the delayed delivery which makes a contract useful, and treats lifelong mutual trust as iterated mutual delayed deliveries, so I have shown a bias toward the medium-length trust relationship, thereby failing to say or imply anything very helpful either about brief encounters or about cross-generational trust. Probably these two faults are connected. If one got a test for the whole network of trust, with all the dependencies between the intimate and the more impersonal forms properly noted, and had the right temporal dimensions in that, then both the morality of brief trusting encounters and the morality of trust between generations who do not encounter each other would fall into place.

Since I have thus oversimplified the problem of morally evaluating trust relationships by confining my attention to relationships one by one, my account of trusting as acceptance of having as it were entrusted and my consequent expansion of trusting from a two-place into a three-place predicate will seem forced and wrong. For there are some people whom one would not trust with anything, and that is not because one has considered each good one might entrust to that one and rejected that possibility. We want then to say that unless we first trust them we will not trust them *with anything*. I think that there is some truth in this, which my account has not captured. For some kinds of enemy (perhaps class enemies?) one will not trust even with one's bodily safety as one raises a white flag, but one will find it 'safer' to fight to the death. With some sorts of enemies, a contract may be too intimate a relation. If the network of relationships is systematically unjust or systematically coercive, then it may be that one's status within that network will make it unwise of one to entrust anything to those persons whose interests, given their status, are systematically opposed to one's own. In most such corrupt systems there will be limited opportunity for such beleaguered persons to "rescue" their goods from the power of their enemies—they usually will have no choice but to leave them exposed and so to act as if they trusted, although they feel proper distrust. In such conditions it may take fortitude to display distrust and heroism to disappoint the trust of the powerful. Courageous (if unwise) untrustworthiness and stoic withdrawal of trust may then be morally laudable. But since it usually will take such heroic disruptions of inherited trust relationships for persons to distance themselves from those the system makes their enemies, my test will at least be usable to justify such disruptions. In an earlier version of this paper I said that the ghost of plain trust and plain distrust haunted my account of goods-relativized or 'fancy' trust. I think that I now see that ghost for what it is and see why it ought to continue to haunt. Still, such total oppositions of interest are rare, and one satisfactory thing about my account is that it enables us to see how we can salvage some respects in which we may trust even those whose interests are to some extent opposed to our own.

Meanwhile, my account of what it is to trust, and my partial account of when it is immoral to expect or meet trust, will have to be treated as merely a beginning (or, for some, a resumption, since there doubtless are other attempts at this topic which have escaped my notice). Trust, I have claimed, is reliance on others' competence and willingness to look after, rather than harm, things one cares about which are entrusted to their care. The moral test of such trust relationships which I have proposed is that they be able to survive awareness by each party to the relationshipof *what* the other relies on in the first to ensure their continued trustworthiness or trustingness. This test elevates to a special place one formof trust, namely, trusting others with knowledge of what it is about them which enables one to trust them as one does, or expect them to be trustworthy. The test could be restated this way: trust is morally decent only if, in addition to whatever else is entrusted, knowledge of each party's reasons for confident reliance on the other to continue the relationship could in principle also be entrusted—since such mutual knowledge would be itself a good, not a threat to other goods. To the extent that mutual reliance can be accompanied by mutual knowledge of the conditions for that reliance, trust is above suspicion, and trustworthiness a nonsuspect virtue. "Rara temporum felicitas . . . quae sentias dicere licet."[23]

This paper has an antiphonal title and a final counterpoint may not be out of order. Although I think this test is an appropriate moral test, it is another matter to decide whether and when it should be applied to actual cases of trust. Clearly in some cases, such as infant trust and parental trustworthiness, which could in principle pass it, it cannot actually be applied by both parties to the relationship. That need not unduly worry us. But in other cases it may well be that the attempt to apply it will ensure its failing the test. Trust is a fragile plant, which may not endure inspection of its roots, even when they were, before the inspection, quite healthy. So, although some forms of trust would survive a suddenly achieved mutual awareness of them, they may not survive the gradual and possibly painful process by which such awareness actually comes about. It may then be the better part of wisdom, even when we have an acceptable test for trust, not to use it except where some distrust already exists, better to take nonsuspect trust on trust. Luhmann says that "it is a characteristic mark of civilizing trust that it incorporates an element of reflexivity."[24] But to trust one's trust and one's distrust enough to refrain from applying moral tests until prompted by some distrust is to take a very risky bet on the justice, if not the "civilization," of the system of trust one inhabits. We may have to trade off civilization for justice, unless we can trust not only our trust but, even more vitally, our distrust.

---

23. Hume placed on the title page of his *A Treatise of Human Nature* these words of Tacitus: "Rara Temporum felicitas, ubi sentire, quae velis, and quae sentias, dicere licet."
24. Luhmann, p. 69.

CONTRIBUTORS

ANNETTE BAIER is a professor of philosophy at the University of Pittsburgh. She has previously taught at Carnegie-Mellon University, the University of Sydney, the University of Aukland, and the University of Aberdeen. She studied at the University of Otago and Oxford University. She has published many articles in the philosophy of mind, ethics, and the history of philosophy, some of which are collected in her book, *Postures of Mind* (Minneapolis: University of Minnesota Press, 1985.) She is working on a book about David Hume and hopes to write more about trust.

CHESHIRE CALHOUN is associate professor of philosophy at the College of Charleston, Charleston, South Carolina. She is coeditor, with Robert C. Solomon, of *What Is an Emotion?* and has written on the emotions and feminist issues in moral theory.

OWEN FLANAGAN is Class of 1919 Professor of Philosophy at Wellesley College. His publications include *The Science of Mind* (1984), "Admirable Immorality and Admirable Imperfection" (Journal of Philosophy [1986]), and "Quinean Ethics" (*Ethics* 93 [1982]: 56–74). He is coeditor with Amelie O. Rorty of *Identity, Character, and Morality: Essays in Moral Psychology* (Cambridge, Mass.: MIT Press, 1990) and author of *Varieties of Moral Personality: Ethics and Psychological Realism* (Cambridge, Mass.: Harvard University Press, 1991).

NANCY FRASER teaches philosophy, women's studies, and comparative literature and theory at Northwestern University. She is the author of *Unruly Practices: Power, Discourse, and Gender in Contemporary Social Theory* (University of Minnesota and Polity Presses, 1989), which contains an expanded version of her essays in this anthology.

MARILYN FRIEDMAN teaches philosophy at Purdue University and writes in the areas of ethics, feminist theory, and social philosophy. She will soon finish a book entitled, *What Are Friends For? Essays on Feminism, Personal Relationships, and Moral Theory*.

JOHN HARDWIG teaches in the philosophy department and the college of medicine at East Tennessee State University. His articles on related themes include: "In Search of an Ethics of Personal Relationships" in *Person to Person*, ed. G. Graham and H. LaFollette (1988) and "What about the Family?" (*Hastings Center Report* [March 1990]). He is currently working on the epistemology and ethics of expertise.

VIRGINIA HELD is a professor of philosophy at the City University of New York Graduate School and Hunter College. She has also taught at Yale, Dartmouth, the University of California, Los Angeles, and Hamilton

College. Her most recent books are *Rights and Goods, Justifying Social Action,* and the edited collection *Property, Profits and Economic Justice.* She has published several essays in feminist philosophy.

NANCY HOLMSTROM is associate professor of philosophy at Rutgers University-Newark. She has published in the areas of metaphysics, Marxist theory, and feminism. She is a member of the editorial board of *Against the Current.*

SUSAN JAMES is lecturer in the philosophy faculty at Cambridge University and Fellow of Girton College. She is the author of *The Content of Social Explaination* (Cambridge: Cambridge University Press).

KATHRYN JACKSON teaches philosophy at Montclair State College. She has written on topics in moral theory and feminism, and is currently working on a book, *The Possibility of Justice: Gender and Liberal Political Theory.*

CATHARINE A. MACKINNON is a lawyer, teacher, and writer. She has written *Sexual Harrassment of Working Women* (1979) *Feminism Unmodified* (1987), *Toward a Feminist Theory of the State* and, with feminist author Andrea Dworkin, ordinances recognizing pornography as a sex equality violation. She is currently professor of law at the University of Michigan Law School.

SUSAN MOLLER OKIN is professor of politics at Brandeis University and the author of *Women in Western Political Thought* and *Justice, Gender, and the Family.* She has written on ethical issues in international relations, and her current work is on public policy issues of particular concern to women.

CAROLE PATEMAN is professor of political science at the University of California, Los Angeles, and a member of the editorial boards of *Ethics, Political Studies,* and *British Journal of Political Science.* She is first vice president of the International Political Science Association 1988–91. Her most recent publications are *The Sexual Contract* and *The Disorder of Women: Democracy, Feminism, and Political Theory.*

LAURIE SHRAGE is assistant professor of philosophy at California State Polytechnic University, Pomona. She has published on comparable worth, feminist film aesthetics, and formal semantics. She is currently working on a book entitled *The Ethics and Ethnography of Commercial Sex,* which focuses on international and interracial prostitution, and the principles of feminist regulation.

CASS R. SUNSTEIN is Karl N. Llewellyn Professor of Jurisprudence in the Law School and Department of Political Science at the University of

Chicago. He is coauthor of *Constitutional Law* (1986) and author of *After the Rights Revolution: Reconceiving the Regulatory State* (Harvard University Press, 1990). He has written on regulatory and environmental policy, administrative law, and constitutional law.

IRIS M. YOUNG is associate professor of public and international affairs at the University of Pittsburgh. She has published numerous articles on political philosophy and feminist theory. She is author of *Justice and the Politics of Difference* (Princeton University Press, 1990) and *Stretching Out: Essays in Feminist Social Theory and Female Body Experience* (Bloomington: Indiana University Press, 1990).

INDEX

Abstract individualism, 143–46

Addelson, Kathryn Pyne, 246–47, 252–53, 260

Adler, Jonathan, 38, 41

Affirmative action programs, 138–39

Anscombe, G. E. M., 23, 37

Anthropology from a Pragmatic Point of View (Kant), 19

Aquinas, Saint Thomas, 281

Arendt, Hannah, 100, 107, 110, 169, 170

Aristotle, 37, 42, 78, 281

Atkinson, Ti-Grace, 237

Baier, Annette, 1, 11, 42, 45–46, 279–308

Baker, Robert, 193

Barber, Benjamin, 123–25

Bartky, Sandra Lee, 243

Baumrind, Diana, 48

de Beauvoir, Simone, 100–101, 107, 110, 197

Beitz, Charles, 24–25

Benhabib, Seyla, 33–34

Bentham, Jeremy, 296

"Birth and Death" (Held), 4

Birth and death, 87–113
  and the aspect of awareness, 92–94
  and the aspect of choice, 89–92
  feminists and birth as "natural," 97–102, 110–12
  imaginative representation and, 94–96
  male attitudes toward "nature," 87–92, 97
  Marxist views on, 105–7
  in postpatriarchal society, 112–13
  and public/private spheres, 102–5
  women's consciousness of, 107–10
  See also Family, the

Bleier, Ruth, 245, 247, 252, 256, 260

Blum, Lawrence, 20, 38, 51

Bok, Sissela, 279

Bradley, Francis, 296

Butler, Joseph, 296

Calhoun, Cheshire, 11, 243–260

Carpenter, Clarence Ray, 246–47

Chodorow, Nancy, 44, 147

Cloward, Richard A., 179

Communitarian theories, 1–11, 143–58
  and consent, 1, 7–8
  feminist critique of, 147–53
  the social self and, 144–47
  See also Contractarian theories

Comparable worth policies, 139

Contractarian theories, 1–11, 120
  the "ethic of justice" and, 2
  and individualism, 1, 120
  as "male fixation," 295–301
  and prostitution, 201–6
  and rational choice theory, 3–4
  and trust, 288–301
  See also Communitarian theories

Daly, Mary, 245–46

Defending prostitution, 10, 201–6
  as a natural feature of human life, 203–4
  as sale of sexual services, 201–3
  and the subordination of women, 204–6
  See also Prostitution; Feminists and prostitution

Derepression theory, 213–15, 232, 235–36

Derrida, Jacques, 210

Different voice, 2–5, 32–33, 38–51

Dinnerstein, Dorothy, 147

The Doctrine of Virtue, pt. 2: *Metaphysic of Morals* (Kant), 18–19

Dummett, M. A. E., 268

Duty to relieve suffering, 11, 261–78
  convincing argument for, 273–78
  current positions on, 262–66
  inadequacy of current positions, 266–73

Dworkin, Andrea, 193–94, 220–22

Engels, Friedrich, 69, 70, 105, 197

Equality, 5–7
  group representation and, 6–7, 130–34
  universality of, 6–7
  See also Polity and group difference